Forever, Joanne

A Story of Love, Loss, and Leaps of Faith

LINDA L. SKIBSKI

Visit our website at
www.StillwaterPress.com
for more information.

First Stillwater River Publications Edition

Library of Congress Control Number: 2021900776

ISBN: 978-1-952521-78-2

1 2 3 4 5 6 7 8 9 10
Written by Linda L. Skibski
Published by Stillwater River Publications,
Pawtucket, RI, USA.

Publisher's Cataloging-In-Publication Data
(Prepared by The Donohue Group, Inc.)

Names: Skibski, Linda L., author.
Title: Forever, Joanne : a story of love, loss and leaps of faith / Linda L. Skibski.
Description: First Stillwater River Publications edition. |
Pawtucket, RI, USA : Stillwater River Publications, [2021]
Identifiers: ISBN 9781952521782
Subjects: LCSH: Skibski, Linda L.--Marriage. | DiBello, Joanne--Health. |
Lesbians--Rhode Island--Biography. | Lesbian couples--Rhode Island. |
Ovaries--Cancer--Patients--Family relationships. | Wives--Death--Psychological
aspects. | Spirits. | LCGFT: Autobiographies. | Biographies.
Classification: LCC HQ75.3 .S55 2021 |
DDC 301.41570922--dc23

The views and opinions expressed
in this book are solely those of the author
and do not necessarily reflect the views
and opinions of the publisher.

NOTE TO READER

In order to protect individuals' privacy, many names in this book have been changed with only the best of intentions. My apologies to those who would have preferred I had used their real names. In addition, a few names of businesses and institutions have also been altered for the same privacy protections.

To the best of my ability, I have attempted to recount events and interactions as my memory allows. Hopefully, my recollections and perceptions will suffice. Many thanks, dear reader, for your understanding.

To my Joanne,
who never gave up

And to all women with ovarian cancer,
who do the same.

"How we spend our days...
is how we spend our lives"
—Annie Dillard
The Writing Life

"If there ever comes a day
where we can't be together,
keep me in your heart.

I'll stay there forever."
—Winnie the Pooh

Contents

Foreword

I am humbled and honored to be writing the foreword for my dear friend, Joanne, and the book, *Forever, Joanne*.

Joanne and I were close friends for over thirty-five years before she passed. We lived on the same street and often sat on my front porch with a cup of tea, or in her backyard overlooking her beautiful garden. We supported one another through life's challenges and opportunities. She lives in my heart every day and forever.

Joanne was my "angel" and God's instrument when I needed wisdom or direction. When I struggled with something, she was my go-to person. God often spoke through her and, consequently, my life changed. She was very strong in her faith, never doubting the love of God and where she was going. She said, "I'm not afraid to die. I'm in God's hands and I'm okay." I admired her fierce determination to live and enjoy every minute of life. Nothing stopped her from living life to the fullest until her last days.

Forever, Joanne is a powerful love story of two souls that became ONE. This is not just a book about cancer, but a book about enduring love and faith between two hearts who were committed to each other, no matter what. With deep honesty, the author shares the rollercoaster ride of cancer and all it entailed.

Their story will inspire you and give you hope that our loved ones who have passed are still with us and will communicate with us when we are open. Whether you have lost a loved one to cancer or not, this book will give you a glimpse into how our loved ones never die and that you are never alone.

Joanne often "shows up" for Linda in unexpected and humorous ways to keep her promise that she would always be around in spirit. Like I did, you will cry, laugh, and feel the depth and dedication that Linda and Joanne had for one another throughout their love story and journey. I highly recommend this book. It is a must-read!

Pat Hastings-Burns
Author, *Simply a Woman of Faith*
Co-author with Larry Burns,
It's Never Too Late for Love

Acknowledgements

In addition to the divine spirit that has pushed me along throughout my life, I want to thank the following people who have provided great assistance with this book project.

To Janice Harper, my tactful writing coach, who also pushed me to write better than I had ever imagined, even when I wanted to quit.

To Pat Burns, fellow author and faithful friend, who shared her writing advice and spiritual messages that kept me afloat.

To Steven Porter and staff at Stillwater River Publishing for their guidance, patience, and expedient service that calmed my first-time author anxiety.

To Christine Skibski, my beautiful daughter, whose love, support, and computer instruction are forever priceless.

To Chris Daley, my devoted little sister and avid reader, who has held me up more times than I ever did for her when we were kids.

To Joanne's loving family, especially Joyce DiBello, Carissa Anderson, Carole Ann Imondi and cousins, who have filled in the gaps of my memory as well as taken me in as one of their own.

To my beloved extended family who seem to love and support me no matter what.

To my army of friends, especially the Joanne Update email list, who have been great listeners during my grief and who have encouraged me to write.

And, finally, to Joanne, my love and soul mate, who planted the seed in the first place.

Introduction

L ate one January night in 1968, as I leaned against the headboard on my college dorm bed studying for an exam the next day, I experienced a spiritual moment I'll never forget. As my roommate slept soundly in her bed across the room, I could almost hear my breath it was so quiet. The wall lamp above my bed provided the only light in the dark room while I balanced my textbook on my bent knees. Every now and then, I would jot down a few words in the notebook by my side. I was focused on the subject.

As suddenly as the flip of a switch, I picked up my notebook and felt compelled to write. The words just poured out of me like a runaway train with no brakes going down a steep hill. I had no control.

What appeared on the paper from my inspired pen was a poem. It began with the title, *A Promise*. The first line under that title read… *"Take my hand and come with me."*

Fifty years later, I made a promise to my wife, Joanne DiBello, before she died that I would write a book about our journey. When she initially proposed the idea shortly after her cancer diagnosis, I thought she was crazy. Even though I had been writing all my life in childhood diaries, travel journals, and Joanne Updates, I had never considered the preposterous idea of writing a book. Now here I am wondering if anyone will want to read it.

Joanne was not the only one to blame for this writing project. Countless others on the Updates email list (you know who you are) encouraged me to continue writing as well. Evidently, the frequent informative emails about Joanne's cancer experience seemed to inspire many readers as I attempted to impart the good and bad during her battle. While this book is intended to expand our story beyond the Joanne Updates, the theme will most likely be familiar to thousands of cancer heroes who have their own inspiring stories to tell. Our fight with this insidious disease was not the first in the world and, unfortunately for many, it will not be the last.

I suppose it's not very uplifting to begin a story thinking about funerals but, despite their hours of concentrated grief, funerals also provide a window into the loved one's life. Introducing Joanne with this scene was intentional in order to focus on the journey, not the final destination. Celebrating the events before and after her funeral transcends that difficult day.

As an avid moviegoer, I have made several references to exquisite scenes and lines from memorable films throughout the book that have inspired me. Although not included in this book, one of my favorite movie scenes is from *Indiana Jones and the Last Crusade* when Harrison Ford attempts to decode several clues in pursuit of the Holy Grail. Faced with a treacherous deep cavern without an apparent bridge, he is instructed to take a leap of faith. Despite great fear and trepidation, he closes his eyes and steps out into space. To his utter surprise, he lands on a solid rock bridge designed to blend in with the scenery. Throughout our life together, Joanne and I took leaps of faith in our God, who always provided a solid bridge despite our limited perception. Writing this book is just another leap.

Throughout my life, one of my inspirations has been my great grandmother, Matie Franklin, who wrote a diary in 1942 about her daily life on a farm in Michigan. Tending animals, collecting eggs, writing letters, caring for her ill mother, caning fruits and vegetables, gardening, and baking pies filled her days with simple, yet honest, hard work and faith. Although I never met her, she lives in the pages of her diary that is a treasure to our family. My guess is that she would be surprised to know how much her writing means to me, and my hope is that I possess even a fraction of her character.

Joanne and I often used the word "forever" to describe our love and commitment. Like infinity, the concept is mind-boggling yet appropriate. Even fifty years ago, the last line of my inspired poem read, *"Take my hand through eternity."* That sounds about right.

FOREVER, JOANNE

CHAPTER 1

The Funeral

Eight days after Joanne died, I drove to the local funeral home with my daughter and sister. It was a hot, sunny Sunday, and everything about me felt numb. With half a heart and my mind on autopilot, I watched myself go through the motions of getting out of the car and walking to the building. I couldn't believe the day had arrived, and my wife was gone.

Comforting hugs at the door with Joanne's sister, niece, and great nephew brought new tears to my eyes as we all strained to ward off our inevitable sobbing. Needing to proceed with the job at hand, we inched our way into the hallway. Even though we walked together, however, my heart was strangely alone.

As I entered the peaceful room that we had set up the day before, I felt Joanne surround me. *This is just what she had in mind,* I thought as I soaked up the light from the windows along the wall at the front of the room. My weepy eyes quickly found the small table with Joanne's container of ashes, her loving picture, and the wild, colorful bunch of flowers from her garden. I smiled when I saw the bright sunflowers that she loved. "No funeral flowers for me!" she had often said. Through the picture on the table, Joanne was looking at me with love and approval.

With a sense of tranquility, the unlikely mix of sadness and celebration filled the air like Greek drama masks. In the atmosphere of open grief unique to funerals, my hope was that Joanne's life and her impact on her corner of the world would be rediscovered and celebrated with gratitude.

The spacious room felt like someone's living room, with cream-colored wallpaper dotted with small purple flowers that she would have loved. As I strolled around the room silently contemplating the pieces of Joanne that were displayed, I tried to forget that she wasn't browsing beside me as we had often done in quiet art galleries. After twenty-one years together, my aloneness felt strange and utterly foreign as if I had been yanked out of my skin.

I smiled faintly when I spotted her small, pastel watercolor painting of our neat, cottage-style house surrounded by flowers and blooming shrubbery standing proudly on an easel next to her table. She'd painted the stairs leading up to the front porch and the "Ciao" sign above the door to be as welcoming as she'd made our home itself. Joanne had loved her house, her garden, and her painting. Living in the house now, alone, tending to the garden and hanging her paintings would be my comfort as well as my sorrow.

As I admired the large professional photo of the two of us that would stand next to me in the receiving line, I could almost hear Joanne protest that she never liked her hair in that picture. At the time, her shorter hair was a light brown, flat style that hadn't yet evolved into the purplish wild spikes she later loved. With our heads tilted together, the photographer had captured our warm smiles and happiness. I had always thought more of the photo than she did and remembered how thrilled I was that we had been treated as a couple during our appointment. Since Joanne was not entirely "out" back then, she was somewhat nervous in front of the camera. However, she had eventually relaxed, especially when the photographer assured her he would photoshop our wrinkles away.

As I came to the end tables beside the couches, the small framed photos of her favorite memories with family reminded me of the stories I had always heard about an epic garden tea party complete with white gloves, milestone birthday parties, and dear cousins' lunches that she often recalled. I loved these images because they were a part of my Joanne.

One familiar picture I spotted made me chuckle. She was holding a small monkey wearing a pink tutu that we'd come across on vacation in the Caribbean. Joanne loved monkeys and in the picture, it looks like she's talking to her new friend. With her sunglasses on, I could only guess that she was promising to take the monkey home. She loved the picture so much that she originally wanted it next to her ashes. With some effort, however, I convinced her that a photo with a more loving smile without sunglasses and without a monkey would reach out to everyone. Nonetheless, I will always love the monkey picture.

Completing my rounds, I came to the table displaying an official declaration from the City of Providence. The impressive list of Joanne's community contributions included founding The North End Girls' softball league in 1974, The North End Girls' Club, and Girls' Ski Club. When I saw the declaration on the table, I knew I couldn't read it right then with my tears ready to gush and my pride in her dedication and energy about to burst.

When the video started to play for final inspection and the songs that she had chosen filled the room, more tears spilled anyway from my eyes as well as my heart. Songs like "Amazing Grace," "What a Wonderful World," "O' Sole Mio," "Wind Beneath My Wings," and even "Margaritaville," made me laugh and cry at the same time. I was not alone.

Joanne's sister, Joyce, was devoted to her older sister and could not hide her broken heart, especially on this day. Neither could Carissa, her niece, who was as close to Auntie Jo as any daughter. I wondered how Jayden, her beloved ten-year-old great nephew, would be able to cope as he hugged me with tears flowing. When he was able to speak, all Jayden could say was, "I miss her so much!" Joanne often said that she hated the idea of leaving Jayden and Alex, his three-year-old brother, hoping she had influenced them enough to make a difference in their lives.

As I surveyed our little group, my eyes found my daughter, Christine, and my sister, Chris, who were trying to keep it together. As a stepmother for Christine and a sister-in-law for Chris, Joanne had been loved as deeply as any family member and would be dearly missed. As their arms encircled me, I felt tremendous love holding me upright. Finally, everyone embraced for a few additional moments as we gathered ourselves for arriving guests.

Just before noon, the funeral director guided us to our places in the receiving line…me, Christine, Joyce, Carissa, and Jayden, who was still sobbing. I had no idea what to expect or how many people would show up. From past experience observing receiving lines, I thought I would be able to take a bathroom break, sit down, or take a drink of water. However, I was to discover that standing on the other end of the receiving line was a different experience altogether.

During the next two hours, there was a constant flow of people showing their love. While I gradually relaxed, I never got that break. It is my nature to be stoic and private when it comes to grief, but not so much on this day. Even though the distraction of shaking hands and greeting the

240 people who quietly stood in line helped me keep it together, the many faces of close family and friends brought the tears. Occasionally, in other parts of the room, there would be quiet bursts of comforting laughter at the mention of a funny memory or long-forgotten connection. At other times, sniffles and sobs reached my ears. A mix of sadness and love saturated my soul.

So often throughout the service, I heard the same phrase, "If it wasn't for Joanne…" Women from the softball league who saw her as a role model when they were teenagers, long-time neighbors who she helped in some way, and coworkers who respected her guidance and high standards would never forget her influence.

Even adult students from the College of Continuing Ed who continued in school because, as Director of Marketing, Joanne had persevered to find scholarships for them, appreciated her compassion. Colleagues who valued her tenacity for excellence, friends from church groups who remembered her strong faith, and family members or friends who shared funny stories of her crazy adventures from kayaking on the swollen Wood River to skiing in the Alps revealed their treasured connections.

As close as Joanne and I were for so many years, I learned even more about her during the receiving line. While many people in the room revealed how much they respected and loved her, I was reminded that Joanne did not belong to me alone.

Halfway through the line, a tall, attractive young woman with tears in her eyes and a slight smile on her face gave me a hug and said, "I'm Maryanne and I have to tell you something."

I was curious about Maryann's story but felt positive energy flowing from her face. I could sense her admiration.

"A few years ago, I was a student intern under Joanne's supervision," she continued. "She was a tough mentor and I worked very hard, but I really respected her knowledge and high standards. When I was about to finish my internship, I heard about a paid position opening up in the same department. I wanted to apply for it, but Joanne discouraged me from taking it and even said she wouldn't hire me. I was so disappointed and surprised."

When Maryann paused in her story, I was surprised about Joanne's decision as well. Feeling as much compassion for her as I could with my weeping heart, I waited for the rest of the story.

Maryann finished by saying, "Joanne explained to me that she saw potential in me for greater things. She said she would love to hire me but knew I would probably delay graduate school if I took the job. She was so right! I took her advice, went to grad school, and it was the best thing that ever happened to me." Maryann looked into my eyes and said with sincerity, "Joanne changed my life."

I'll never forget Maryann's story. Joanne had changed my life too.

When the receiving line ended, the funeral director quietly asked everyone to take their seats. The room was overflowing as everyone settled in where they could. I felt God's peace settle over us as well.

Since the hand of God had been with us ever since we met, the presence of spirit in that room was no surprise. For years, our fire for God was equally matched as we embraced many spiritual paths. Over time, the flame became the steady coals of a cook fire for nourishment or a hearth fire for reliable heat. For Joanne, God was first, then others, and finally, herself.

The Congregational minister who had conducted our marriage ceremony in 2014 and had experienced Joanne's divine spark took her place at the podium. Readings from the Bible, Native American poetry, and eloquent remembrances began to flow according to her wishes.

One of Joanne's assignments was for Carissa, her niece, to read the "Story of the Bell" which Joanne had written for her. Carissa nervously stepped up to the podium, cleared her throat and bravely started to read:

We don't know where this bell came from, but it has been in our family for over twenty years. When my Papa Ralph (Joanne's father) was not feeling good, my grandmother, Annie (Joanne's mother), put it on the table next to his favorite parlor chair and instructed him to ring it when he needed her. She soon realized what a mistake she made, often saying, "That damn bell! If he doesn't break it, I will!" Well, the bell didn't break and Papa passed.

Not even a year later, my grandmother was diagnosed with a recurrence of breast cancer which metastasized to her liver. My mother, Joyce (Joanne's sister), and Auntie Jo took good care of her and at thirteen years old, I did my best to help out. Again, the bell was resurrected. This time, it took its place on the nightstand next to my grandmother's bed. After a couple of weeks, she no longer had the strength to even ring the bell.

The bell then made its way to the hutch at my aunt's house where it remained for twenty years until December of 2017 when my mother (Joyce) had foot surgery. Again, the bell appeared with instructions to ring as needed. I suggested to my mother that every time Auntie Jo got comfortable, she should ring the bell…but that didn't fly!

Earlier this month, the bell was brought out again. This time for Auntie Jo to use…and she did!

Today, we celebrate her victory over her war with cancer. She is free now. She earned her wings, and we ring this bell in her honor.

When Carissa finished reading, she motioned for Jayden to come up to the podium for his task, which was to ring the small silver bell. With amazing poise, Jayden held the bell's handle and announced that he wanted each of us in the receiving line to ring the bell as well. As we followed his lead, the sweet sound of the bell rang out each time, reminding me of both happy and heart-wrenching moments when I had heard the bell years before. Joanne would have been proud of us.

Nearing the end of the service, Joanne's friend and coworker, Steven, rose from his seat with his friend who played her guitar as they sang "Over the Rainbow" in perfect harmony. At Joanne's request, I had asked Steven the week before to sing at her service. Without hesitation, he had replied, "Of course I'll do this for Joanne…I'd be honored." They sang so beautifully there wasn't a dry eye in the room.

In the movie, *Wizard of Oz*, Dorothy wonders whether there is a place with no trouble before she starts singing. As we released the handfuls of shiny balloons outside the funeral home in her honor, I couldn't help but think Joanne was looking at us from her "place with no trouble." I also thought of the time when all the trouble began.

CHAPTER 2

Before the Storm

"Where are you?" Joanne asked me when I took her call on my cellphone. Even though I had just started driving and my focus was on the road, I could tell by her serious tone that something was up.

"I'm on my way home from hand bells," I replied.

"Can you meet me at the East Side Hospital emergency room?" she asked, as if she were asking me to meet her for coffee.

Now I was the one who sounded concerned.

"Sure, but what's wrong?" It felt as if someone had just pulled a switch on my peaceful, routine day with hand bell choir practice and turned it into an unexpected cliffhanger.

"I'm on the way to East Side in a rescue van from the Urgent Care Center," Joanne explained. "I went in to see if I have pneumonia again, and the doctor there thinks it could be something worse. He won't even let me drive myself since he thinks I'll decide to go home."

Wow, I thought in disbelief. With as much calm as I could muster, I tried to reassure her.

"Don't worry, I'll be right there," I said as I shifted into rescue mode.

Joanne hadn't been feeling well for several months with irritable bowel symptoms and, more recently, a lingering cold. Throughout the years, she often developed bronchitis and sometimes pneumonia with a cold. So it was no surprise that she went alone to Urgent Care for such a frequent problem. Joanne would not want to bother anyone anyway.

But I didn't even know that she had left the house, and here we were heading for the ER! As I drove in shock, I thought that the rescue van was probably a good idea because, on her own, Joanne would indeed have returned home, minimizing the fuss, without going to the hospital. The doctor had been right.

Even though my heart was racing beyond any speed limit, I tried to make it to the hospital without getting a ticket. Luckily, it was a clear Sunday afternoon in February. Since the roads were untypically dry for a New England winter day and traffic was light, I sliced through the familiar route with ease. I couldn't imagine what we were facing and tried not to think about it as my car pulled into the emergency room parking space.

Once inside the building, I searched for the receptionist and was guided to the exam room where Joanne was already tucked away. As a rescue van patient, she did not have to wait the usual long hours in the waiting room…another reason to thank that urgent care doctor.

I nervously peeked around the curtain of her exam room, not knowing if I was interrupting any procedure, and found Joanne alone, smiling back at me from her bed. That smile always made me melt. Before we said anything, I wrapped my arms around her and started to relax…a little. At least we were together, and I felt that familiar bond. *This can't be anything really serious*, I thought and hoped.

"So what's going on?" I asked her, trying to be nonchalant. "Is this what you had in mind for us to spend Sunday afternoon?"

"Yes, I thought we needed some excitement," Joanne chuckled. Even though her smiling face was calm, I detected the same hint of concern in her eyes as my own. The ever-present iPad on her lap told me she was already doing research.

The long list of tests and lab work that were performed that day are beyond my recollection. What I do remember is that it was February 9, 2014, and we waited in that emergency room cubicle for seven hours, hoping for answers. But in the end, the only conclusion we heard from the medical staff was that fluid from Joanne's abdomen was seeping into her lungs, and it wasn't pneumonia. We could go home, but more investigation was needed.

After retrieving Joanne's car from the Urgent Care parking lot that night, we finally dragged ourselves into the house at nine thirty. Exhausted in every way, we still didn't know what the culprit was, as if some menacing shadow was lurking behind a heavy door that was now ajar. Appointments for other specialists and additional tests were now on our calendars for the next few days as the unwanted rollercoaster ride began to pull away from the station. Needless to say, we now had more material for our daily prayer time.

Throughout our lives, Joanne and I had connected to God through prayer and meditation, both individually and together. We weren't saints about praying, but we asked for open hearts and minds, recognizing the strength of God's love, guidance, and voice. For me, taking a walk was my best prayer time. Joanne's best time for prayer was in the sunroom looking at her garden. Together, we would often read short inspirations or meditate in silence, finishing with "Namaste," which means, "I bow to the divine in you." But these new challenges and concerns called for deeper prayers.

By Thursday, February 13, we would normally be making romantic Valentine's Day plans. However, Joanne now had an appointment that morning with a gynecological oncologist for more testing at Women & Infants' Hospital which was near my office. With this appointment, we couldn't avoid the word, *cancer,* anymore as it now crept forward into our thoughts. By not uttering the word to each other during the week, we had subconsciously hoped to eradicate the possibility.

Joanne's plan, to which I reluctantly agreed, was that I would go to work while she went for the exam. If there was any significant news, she would call me. Normally, as an itinerant mobility instructor for the blind, I would be on the road teaching outdoor travel lessons. But I purposely planned to stay in the office immersing myself in paperwork as I waited.

The call came around noon. As soon as I grabbed my desk phone, I heard Joanne's voice.

"Hi, honey." She sounded relatively calm as she continued, "It seems there's going to be a meeting here at the hospital about the test results. Can you get here soon?"

"Of course, I'll be right there," I said as I jumped out of my seat. Now it was really time for me to worry as I asked her, "Are you okay?"

"I'm fine, but I'll be better when you get here," Joanne replied.

"Joyce is working here today and wants to be in the meeting, but she's so emotional," she added. "I know she's expecting the worst so I don't think she'll be able to stay. To be honest, I'm not sure I can handle her tears right now."

Joyce was a phlebotomist who divided her time between two hospitals, and she happened to be drawing blood from patients in this building at the time of the meeting. She and Joanne were devoted sisters who always laughed about their different personalities. While Joanne was introspective, composed, cautious, and tenacious, Joyce was exuberant, uninhibited, anxious, and sensitive. Most likely, they agreed beforehand that Joyce would attend the meeting only if she could hold it together.

I felt pretty numb as I mechanically made each step to my car, silently praying, *Oh God, please help us.* The ten-minute drive seemed to take hours. Thankfully, the valet parking service in front of the hospital eliminated the need to search for a parking space. Waiting in line for the hospital security check-in gave me a chance to catch my breath. Once released, however, I quickened my pace to the fourth floor oncology department.

"My name's Linda Skibski, and I'm here for a meeting," I blurted out to the receptionist. Thank goodness I didn't have to wait for anyone in front of me.

"Oh yes," the woman said. "They're expecting you. I'll get someone to bring you there." A pleasant nurse assistant was already at the desk as I turned around and walked with her down the hallway.

As the players in this meeting spotted us and filed into the room, my sense that the news would not be good continued to grow. Joyce was crying in the hallway and greeted me with a hug as she said, "Hi, honey. I'm too upset just thinking about all this. I just can't stay." She then quickly turned and retreated to the phlebotomy lab. I think she knew that she could not be strong for her sister right then.

As I made my way into the room, there were more people than I expected. Despite the cozy décor with plants, paintings, windows and overstuffed seats, it felt more like a summit meeting than a doctor's visit.

When I spotted Joanne already sitting on the small couch, I took my seat next to her, holding her close for a couple seconds.

"Hi," was all I could eke out at first. Then I said, "Sure looks like an audience for the Queen."

"Well, you know me," Joanne replied. As the image of her favorite T-shirt, "The Queen of Everything," flashed across my mind, my adoration grew while I welcomed the diversion.

The tall, attractive man in his fifties stood up from the desk to welcome me and warmly shake my hand. I liked Dr. D. right away as I observed his kindness with his team. When everyone was settled, he introduced Joanne and me to the others in the room…a resident doctor, an intern, and the social worker. Dr. D. conducted the meeting with compassion, respect, straightforwardness, and, above all, a look of hope.

We listened intently as he began to reveal his findings.

"So, after reviewing all the tests and today's exam, I can confirm, Joanne, that you have ovarian cancer." There it was…the monster was revealed as the door swung open. Silence hung in the room.

Joanne and I looked deep into each other's misty eyes. I nodded my head up and down as she said, "We had an idea it wasn't good news."

Until then, however, neither one of us had said it out loud. Everyone in the room seemed ready to catch us, but we didn't fall apart. I don't know why. Maybe it was because we saw the enemy in the imaginary doorway and wanted to kill it as soon as possible, despite our fear.

Joanne's tenacity kicked into gear as she asked, "What stage is it and what's the treatment plan?"

She was no stranger to cancer. Her mother had died from breast cancer in 1998, and Joanne had been a hospice support group facilitator for women with cancer for several years. Asking questions and forming a plan of attack was Joanne's forte, and I was right beside her in full armor.

Dr. D. took our cue and began to answer, "Right now, it's Stage 3, but it could be Stage 4, depending on what we find. The plan would be to begin chemotherapy next week to diminish the cancer as much as possible before surgery, which would take place in a couple months." My brain started to fill up with information, so I asked for all the details in writing. I also vowed to bring a notebook from then on.

At the end of the meeting, Dr. D. said, "We're all going to work very hard to help you fight this disease and will be available to you at any time." With his words of sincerity and hope, I felt that we could depend on him. No one said anything about life expectancy and we didn't ask.

The gracious handshakes and words of support from the medical team helped to ease us into this new family as we made our way to the scheduling specialist. With calendars in hand, we made appointments for intakes at the infusion center and more blood work prior to chemo. New words, new procedures, and new schedules now invaded our private world.

Since we had both cars at the hospital, Joanne and I were alone with our thoughts as we drove home separately. Disbelief overwhelmed me. I couldn't identify any of my feelings as they swirled around and inside my heart. Without warning, a memory about my own breast cancer diagnosis in 1993 popped into my head.

Many times over the past twenty-one years, I had marveled at my ability to forget I even had cancer. Alone with the doctor when I heard the news back then, my reaction had been to shift into action and get the damn thing out. Following a lumpectomy and removal of lymph nodes, only radiation treatments and Tamoxifen, an antiestrogen pill as maintenance, were needed for my recovery. Other than the reminder of annual mammograms over the years, I rarely thought about my ordeal. With Joanne's new crisis, however, my early-stage breast cancer seemed minimal compared to ovarian cancer. That was far more deadly. As my thoughts and fears consumed me, somehow, the car found its way to our driveway.

When I entered the house, Joanne was standing at the kitchen counter near the spot where, in happier times, we sometimes slow danced for no particular reason. Now I took her into my arms on that same spot as we finally allowed ourselves to cry together. This was the love of my life...my heart...my gift from God. I couldn't imagine that she would be ripped from me...not yet, not now. It sure didn't feel that God was on our side anymore as I realized the cancer storm had begun. The day that had started out as any other, had changed our lives forever.

Seventeen years before, another momentous day during more peaceful times had also altered our paths, bringing us together.

CHAPTER 3

❧

Grilled Cheese and Pea Soup

"**Y**ou've got to be kidding me!" I blurted out to my therapist who had just suggested in 1997 that I answer a personal ad in *The Providence Phoenix*, a weekly alternative newspaper. I had been meeting with her for a year following the breakup of my eight-year relationship with Betty. I was forty-eight years old with a beautiful ten-year-old daughter and had never in my life answered one of those "sleazy" personal ads. What was she thinking?

Back then, there was no internet dating. Answering a personal ad in the back pages of a newspaper was considered to be an act of desperation when you were more likely to find trouble, not romance. Generally speaking, there were very few avenues for finding a nice person to date, never mind finding the love of your life. The only options seemed to be risky encounters in bars, blind dates arranged by matchmaking friends, or chance meetings in the grocery store. The process was even more complicated in the gay scene considering the risks of "coming out" at the time. In my circle of friends, any one of us would have been embarrassed to admit even reading personal ads.

Since the usual approaches were not working out for me, I agreed to consider this shopping method, even though it reminded me of searching for a new car. Earlier in therapy, I had already made a list of the qualities I was looking for in my next potential partner, hoping to avoid past mistakes. So I felt I was ahead of the game. Words like dependable, good-listener, honest, independent, and stable were some of the qualities on the list. My therapist was right about the benefit of the exercise because it did provide some clarity—none of the partners in my past relationships had all the qualities

13

I wanted and needed. So, like a reluctant student, I promised to do my new homework and bought the May 23, 1997 issue of the newspaper.

All my life I knew I was different from my girlfriends who were crazy about boys. I did try to fit in and had several boyfriends into my young adult years. But in the end, I was just crazy about girls. I never put a label on my feelings until 1984 when I was thirty-five, trying to decode my ongoing depression. My therapist at the time helped me to "come out" as gay, and it was one of the most liberating times of my life.

Unfortunately, I didn't always make good choices after coming out. My liberation seemed to release an uncharacteristic impulsive streak in me. Like a hormone-driven teenager or a young child in a candy shop, I latched onto the first colorful prospects that came my way. There was the much younger, attractive borderline personality who cut up my clothes in a rage, the straight woman I loved who ultimately, and predictably, chose a man, and the Nervous Nellie who just wasn't a good match. With blinders on, I ignored all the warning signs of major differences and plunged ahead.

The only good choice I made soon after coming out was to undergo artificial insemination to conceive my wonderful daughter, Christine, in 1986. My romantic relationship at that time was one of those impulsive bad choices, but the child that came out of it was and is my joy.

Hoping I had learned some lessons about choosing a life partner, I opened the paper and skipped to the back pages. Under the heading, "Women Seeking Women," I began reading each entry with the thought, *I still can't believe I'm doing this!* The first ad I read did not help to change my perspective. "*Funky, young vegan, 25. I dig butterflies, poetic gestures, sultry starry eyes, fields of flowers and car rides. Looking for everything and nothing. Call back if you called before.*" Much too young for me, and I didn't think I could offer everything, especially sultry starry eyes. My eyes were already a bit jaded. I moved on.

There were others. Phrases such as, "*Must be a muscular female who likes to talk to herself, Let's make it happen,*" and "*Happy, outgoing with slightly twisted sense of humor*" also turned me off to this adventure. Those phrases did not describe me. Even though I was athletic and loved the outdoors, I was not muscular, and talking to myself was not a habit. Even though I am generally a happy person, a twisted sense of humor could mean anything. As I read through the newspaper list, I was searching for someone who would write an ad equal to the one I would submit.

Then, to my surprise, there were some ads that included a few of the words on my "must have" qualities list. However, I wasn't naïve enough to think I could trust the print…oh no, not me. With some skepticism, I circled five entries and rated them to my own interest scale.

Number one sounded promising. "*GWF, young 40s, non-smoker, no drugs, 5', height/weight proportionate, professional, fun-loving, active, sincere, passionate, enjoys outdoors and romantic, quiet times. Interested in friendship/relationship.*" Professional. That was the one word missing from the others. I felt we would be evenly matched somehow. Of course, the word, *passionate*, also caught my eye.

No surprise to me, I procrastinated about calling for a couple days. After all, I had learned a few things about being impulsive. But sometime during the week of May 26, 1997, I found enough courage to take the next step and began reading the instructions for calling. To protect those who placed the ads, it wasn't possible to contact them directly. Instead, I had to call the newspaper's message center and leave a recorded message that the other person could access. Nervous, but determined, I made the call. A recording rambled on but I ignored it, anxious to leave my message.

I'd like to think that my message was witty and charming, but I really can't remember what I said. All I know is that her phone greeting revealed her name…Joanne.

Well, that process wasn't too bad, I thought. Now that I was on a roll, I considered the second ad on my list. "*GWF, young 50ish, seeks spiritually-minded, sincere, loving, uncomplicated non-smoker for friendship and whatever else we wish it to be. Enjoy movies, walks, home, intimacy.*"

I began the second call. The same initial recording came on, but this time, less nervous, I listened to it.

What I heard was, "You will be billed twelve dollars per minute for the call and the charges will be applied to your telephone bill." Twelve dollars a minute! I hung up without leaving a message for number two and promptly forgot about the whole thing.

Two weeks went by. Then, on a Sunday night, the phone rang. "Hi, my name's Joanne," the caller said. "You left a message on my ad in *The Phoenix.*"

In a confused voice, I replied, "I did?" It all started to come back to me as I remembered the ad that I had answered. I couldn't believe I was getting a call back after all this time.

"I hadn't checked my messages for a while since I've had some crazy callers," Joanne explained, "but I decided to listen to them one more time just before my ad expired. I liked your message so I decided to call."

We began a tentative dance on the phone, but it didn't take long before we were laughing and sharing bits of information about ourselves. Joanne owned a small house, I rented a first-floor apartment in a house; she worked in fundraising as the Director of Advancement in Continuing Ed at a local college, I worked for the state as an Orientation and Mobility Instructor for the blind; Joanne loved to garden, I loved birding. Our conversation was easy and flowed as if we had been lifelong friends. We even shared our thoughts on the personal ad.

"I've never answered a personal ad in my life," I confessed to her. "I was so reluctant to even look at them, but I promised my therapist I would."

Joanne surprised me by saying, "I can't believe it! This was the first personal ad I've ever placed, and it's because *my* therapist suggested it to me!

"Oh my god, that's crazy!" I said, thinking we were definitely on the same page. With her ad expiring and me giving up on the calls, I thought this small window of opportunity for us to connect was amazing and almost too good to be true.

After talking for half an hour, we decided to make a date for lunch two days later on Tuesday, June 17. What did we have to lose? *She must be a good person,* I thought to myself. *She even has a bird feeder in her yard!* Sometimes it's the little things that make an impression.

As it turned out, our offices were only a block apart in downtown Providence. It was just before noon on that sunny Tuesday when I started walking to Joanne's building to wait in the lobby as we had planned. My style, like my short, curly blond hair, was a casual, tailored look. So I chose comfortable tan slacks with a short-sleeved print blouse over a black tank top. Though I'm only five foot two with a small frame, sturdy walking shoes were a must for my job and flat feet.

Even though I was excited, I wasn't nervous about meeting Joanne. In fact, I noticed that I was surprisingly calm and confident as I picked up a newspaper to read while I waited, leaning against the wall. Could it be that all that therapy had helped?

Since the lobby became busy with the noon rush, I didn't notice Joanne's approach right away. All of a sudden, she was just there. Short, slim, attractive in a dark brown print, short-sleeved blouse and matching skirt, dark brown hair that came to the base of her neck, and happy brown eyes that matched the best smile I had ever seen. All I could think was, *She's so cute!*

"Linda?" she asked. "I'm Joanne."

When I reached to shake her extended hand, it felt like two strong magnets had finally met. I had never felt such a powerful connection so quickly. "It's nice to meet you," I said as I smiled back. The moment was more than magic.

"Where should we have lunch?" Joanne casually asked.

Since I had already thought about a location close by, I replied, "How about Murphy's Deli down the street?"

"Great!" she said, as if relieved to let someone else make a decision for a change.

We made our way to Murphy's and found a small table near the front windows overlooking the side street. Even though the room was small and crowded, nothing seemed to bother us. We chattered away as if we were continuing our phone call from two days before. I ordered a grilled cheese and tomato sandwich and Joanne ordered pea soup.

"Do you come to Murphy's a lot?" she asked in the mellow voice that I already loved.

"Not really," I answered and explained, "I'm usually on the road for work, eating a yogurt and apple in my car."

"Well, I'm glad you're taking a break from a quick lunch," she said with that beautiful smile showing perfectly white teeth. "What kinds of restaurants do you like?" Impressed with Joanne's ability to keep the conversation going, I noticed her curiosity and focus as if no one else was nearby. I really liked her.

For the next hour and a half we talked and laughed about everything… our lives, our jobs, our families, our interests, our fun, and our relationships. We constantly looked into each other's eyes and found equal ground.

Toward the end of our lunch, Joanne said, "I have a confession to make." I couldn't imagine what she was going to say, so for the first time I was a little nervous.

She continued with a twinkle in her eye, "Before I came down to the lobby to meet you, I circled around a different stairway so I could get a look at you first. But then, I thought, *Oh, she's cute!*"

With relief and laughter, I replied, "Well, I'm glad because that's exactly what I thought about you when we met!" We were definitely on the same page.

As we reluctantly left the deli to return to the reality of work, I wondered if our big smiles were obvious to the strangers on the street. Probably not, but I was certainly aware of mine. On the corner, before we parted ways, we exchanged our business cards with additional phone numbers and said something about getting together again.

Watching Joanne hurry across the street toward her office building, I thought, *Oh, Linda. You're in trouble now!* I was completely hooked. When she reached the opposite curb and turned slightly to look over her shoulder with another smile, I thought I would melt into the sidewalk. The only way I could describe my feeling was to think about Cupid's arrow or even the Holy Spirit and how I had never felt this way before.

All at once I remembered something Joanne had said at lunch. "I have to be honest and tell you that I also responded to another caller named Theresa," she confessed. "I'm supposed to meet her this week, but I don't think she could be more than a friend. Even so, I have to keep my promise to meet her."

Well, that's commendable but not exactly what I wanted to hear. Now I have competition. On the corner, the thought crossed my mind, *I can't let her get away!* So I vowed that I would call her that night…and I did.

CHAPTER 4

꒦꒷

To Be or Not to Be

When I left that corner after meeting Joanne, I felt eight years old again, creeping down the stairs at dawn on Christmas morning, heart pounding with anticipation, eyes open wide, smiling with amazement at the gifts piled around the tree. Now that same joy and excitement filled my heart. I really liked Joanne and was compelled to call her that very night.

With determination, I dialed Joanne's number. "Hi Joanne. This is Linda," I said confidently.

"Oh…hi," Joanne responded with some surprise and hesitation in her voice. I could sense that she had not expected to hear from me so soon. *Oh no,* I thought, *Maybe this wasn't such a good idea.*

I kept going. "I just wanted to call and tell you how much I enjoyed our lunch today. How was the rest of your afternoon?"

"I had a good time too," she said. Joanne seemed to relax and we began to chat about the day. Our conversation was brief this time…I didn't want to overwhelm her. After some pleasant exchanges, we agreed that we should meet on Thursday after work. "How about taking a walk on the Boulevard?" she suggested.

"Sounds great," I happily agreed. "I'll meet you there."

The Blackstone Boulevard is a wide, tree-lined avenue in the heart of a quiet community of large, beautiful homes where generations of wealthy doctors, lawyers, and CEOs reside. The walking path running down the middle of the wide median has been a favorite for runners, walkers, strollers, and nature lovers for years. Despite the one-way suburban traffic on each side, the 1.6 mile long walkway is peaceful and rejuvenating, offering benches along the way for rest or contemplation. The huge oak trees, shrubs, and occasional moss-covered stone structures that frame the walk contribute to the sense of its one hundred-year old history. Best of all, it was within walking distance of my apartment.

If it weren't for my responsibilities at work and home for the next two days, I swear I would have floated away like a hot air balloon. I was so excited. Even my anxiety about the Theresa threat was helpful...the uncertainty of their upcoming date kept my excitement tethered to the ground. I had to prepare myself for the possibility that Theresa could be Joanne's number one choice. But I held out hope that she wasn't.

On Thursday, after making arrangements for Christine to stay at her friend's house for a couple hours, I headed out on foot to meet Joanne at one end of the Boulevard. The late afternoon was sunny, warm and much too nice for driving my car. After all, I was an avid hiker and backpacker. Walking the mile and a half from my house to our meeting spot was just an afterthought.

Joanne was waiting for me on the path. There was that beautiful smile of hers as she said, "Hi," in sync with my own hello. "Where did you park?"

"It's such a nice day, I decided to walk from my apartment," I told her. Her surprised expression told me she was impressed.

"Do you still want to walk to the end of the Boulevard and back?" she asked, knowing that it would be another three miles, round trip, added on to my recent jaunt.

"Sure, no problem. I love to walk," I said honestly. Joanne was definitely impressed.

We began our walk-talk on the stone-dust path, keeping pace with each other, thoroughly enjoying the day and each other's company. I was aware that Joanne walked with small, quick steps, while I walked with longer, steady steps. Despite our different strides, we managed to stay close without either one gasping for breath. Our walking styles meshed just as our personalities seemed to fit like puzzle pieces.

We talked and laughed about how our individual paths had brought us to this path and moment on the Boulevard. Joanne was a native Rhode Islander who had always lived and worked in the Providence area. I was born and raised in Springfield, Massachusetts but later lived in the Philadelphia area and then in Michigan before moving to Rhode Island in 1989. Both of us had already traveled around the country and to exotic places, but we also had dreams to continue exploring.

Joanne and I were the first in our immediate families to go to college. She attended Bryant University as a business education major before working for a year in a public school classroom. It only took that year for her to discover that the chaotic classroom setting was not for her. So she changed direction and attended Rhode Island College for a master's degree in Business Administration.

A few months before we met, Joanne had completed another master's degree from Salve Regina University in Newport. This time, the subject was Holistic Counseling, a totally different field, which expanded her personal, spiritual pursuits. Now it was my turn to be impressed. Her drive and varied interests seemed to reflect many facets of her personality.

My own educational path began when I attended Eastern University near Philadelphia and earned my undergraduate degree in Social Work. After working for three years as a social worker at Methodist Hospital in Philly, I decided to change jobs. That's when I discovered the field of blindness rehabilitation.

I began working as a social worker once more for a United Way agency that provided services to blind and visually impaired individuals. While I was there, I was intrigued with the profession of Orientation & Mobility. The instructors taught independent travel skills, one-on-one, to clients in all environments and in all kinds of weather. The whole idea appealed to my New England heritage of independence and hearty weather. So I too changed direction and completed a master's degree in Education with a specialty in Orientation & Mobility from Boston College. Joanne seemed to be fascinated with my journey, and a mutual respect for each other's grit started to grow.

When we completed our Boulevard walk, Joanne offered to give me a ride home in her brand new 1997 Honda Accord. It was the luxury model in a beautiful, deep eggplant color with a touch of gold trim. "I just picked it up earlier today," she proudly explained. "You'll be the second person to ride in it. My teenage niece, Carissa, had the first ride. Of course, Carissa would rather drive it, but I told her I'd give it to her someday."

"Well, I'd be honored to be even the second passenger in your new car," I said as I climbed in.

There's nothing like a new-car smell. And there's nothing like a new relationship filled with promise. As we pulled away from the curb, Joanne chuckled a little and said, "You know, as I waited for you today, I was wondering if you'd be able to keep up with me," meaning the physical walk. "But I can see I didn't have to worry."

I laughed too and had a feeling that more history had just been made on the Boulevard today.

Meeting was the easy part. We had just found attractive dance partners, but now the question was: *Can we dance together?* For the next four weeks, we tried to find out. Romantic dinners in nice restaurants, lazy days on the beach, comfortable nights at the movies, and homemade dinners at each other's homes. We began to seep into each other's lives as we tried each other on to check out the fit.

One early question had thankfully been answered: *What about Theresa?* Shortly after they had met for lunch, Joanne and I were on the phone. *Should I ask her?* I thought as I noticed my sweaty palms. Finally, I summoned my courage and nonchalantly asked, "So, how did your lunch with 'what's her name' go?"

"You mean Theresa?" Joanne replied. There seemed to be a smile in her voice.

"Yes, Theresa," I said, knowing that she was teasing me.

"Well, she's a nice person but there's no spark there," Joanne answered, and then said something about considering her as a friend, but nothing else. I wasn't listening at that point because my only thought was, *Thank God!* The Theresa competition had faded.

A few days after our Boulevard walk and a dinner in downtown Providence, I invited Joanne over for a backyard barbeque to meet my neighbors and friends from Michigan who were camped out overnight in their RV in my driveway. A small, friendly lesbian gathering seemed right for this "meet and greet" with Joanne and some friends. It was also the first time Joanne would visit my home and meet Christine.

Even though I had already told Christine that I was spending time with a new friend, I also knew that my daughter was not keen about sharing me with anyone. Added to the mix was my knowledge that Joanne had not expected to meet someone with a child. *Would this be a hurdle we could all handle?* I thought. Needless to say, I was a bit anxious but hoping for the best. It seemed to me that if God had any hand in this relationship, things would work out.

The doorbell rang. "Hi, come on in," I said as I opened the front door. Joanne stepped into our living room. She was holding a brown paper bag in the familiar shape of a bottle. Christine was sitting quietly on the couch, cross-legged while she seemed to be focused on drawing. I knew she was actually taking in the scene.

"Hi," Joanne replied with only a hint of nervousness. "I thought you might like this," as she thoughtfully presented her gift bottle of wine. It was Kendall Jackson chardonnay, the same wine she had introduced me to a couple days before during our first dinner out.

"Oh, thank you so much," I said and smiled. "I loved this wine!" I thought of giving her a hug, but decided it was too soon. Besides, young eyes were watching.

I then turned to Christine and said, "Honey, this is my friend, Joanne."

With her long brown hair and beautiful brown eyes, Christine serenely looked up and said, "Hello." Ever since she was born, my daughter had had a mature presence about her. She was always friendly, funny, creative and incredibly kind. Even at ten years old, Christine was polite and confident, so I was not surprised that she greeted Joanne kindly. Whatever negative thoughts she might have had went undetected.

Joanne seemed pleased but a little nervous when she replied, "Hi Christine. I'm very happy to meet you." Joanne came forward and shook her hand. The brief silence that followed told me it was time for all of us to move outside to the small backyard deck where the adults were already gabbing.

I was also anticipating Joanne meeting the smallest member of our little family. Our dog, Buddy, was a young Yorkie-Shih Tzu mix who was a bundle of love. With the face of a Yorkie, floppy ears, and the longer body of a Shih Tzu, we had had him since he was a puppy. Ever since the day he had arrived, he was usually glued to Christine's lap. Many times on a walk, women passing by would admire his frosted tan coat and say to me, "Oh, I wish my hair looked like that." Buddy was smart and lovable and I was hoping Joanne, the cat person, would find room in her heart for our little dog.

As we emerged onto the deck, I could see Buddy was already bathed in affection as he perched on my friend's lap, wagging his fluffy tail when he spotted us. After the introductions to the humans, I added, "And this is the star of the show, Buddy."

Joanne had responded warmly to my friends but was a bit hesitant to approach Mr. Bud. I decided to scoop him up and provide a close encounter that was less threatening. Joanne gently petted his head and softly said, "Hi there, Buddy." She started to relax when he looked lovingly at her and whimpered as if to say, *I love you already.* I had a good feeling about their meeting, especially later on when I found Buddy winning her over as he sat proudly on her lap.

The gathering was cheerful and continued throughout the afternoon. Joanne appeared to have a good time and easily conversed with all my friends. While I cooked chicken and burgers on the charcoal grill, some of us played badminton and softball catch in the fenced-in yard. Christine was at ease, especially since she loved our neighbors and friends from Michigan where she was born. She was so pleased that everyone clapped when she and Buddy entertained the group by performing all the tricks she had taught him. All was well.

After everyone left the house and my friends were settled in their RV, I asked Christine if she had had a good time. "Yes, I did," she replied, but then hesitated as if debating whether to go on. With an honest look in her eyes, she continued "But, Mom, I don't think Joanne's right for you." *Oh no,* I thought. I was crushed.

Christine couldn't tell me exactly why she thought that, so I said something about getting to know her and giving her a chance. She accepted that and went to bed. Later on, when my initial shock subsided, I realized that Christine, at almost eleven years old, was just letting me know that no one would be right for me because she didn't want to share her mom with anyone.

As Joanne and I met more often, I began to experience a hurdle of my own. I started feeling guilty about leaving Christine in the hands of sitters or her friends' parents. We had a very strong mother-daughter bond, especially in the past year when it had been just the two of us against the world. Now I was the rope in the middle of what seemed like a game of tug-of-war. No one was to blame, and neither Joanne nor Christine could fully realize my dilemma. While I struggled to find balance by planning some activities that we could all do together, I hoped that love, patience, and therapy would, in time, do the rest.

By the second week of July, I was definitely in love. The only problem was that Joanne didn't know it. At least, I hadn't told her. Even though I knew she liked me, I was unsure what her reaction would be if I "made a move." Joanne also had a hurdle to deal with and, in some ways, it became my hurdle as well.

When Joanne had placed her personal ad at the suggestion of her therapist, the focus of her therapy was not so much on finding love, as it was exploring her sexual orientation. Even though she had suspected her bisexuality long before, she was just beginning to grapple with the reality in earnest. While she had had several boy/man friends throughout her life, she had secret female attractions as well. In other words, Joanne was not "out" to anyone when we met, and she was afraid. Not only was she getting to know me, but she was also getting to know herself.

Since I was sensitive to Joanne's struggle, I didn't want to push her or frighten her by revealing my strong feelings too soon. Our dance was still tentative and I didn't want to step on her toes. I realized that she was processing a great deal, especially in light of the social climate of 1997.

Back then, LGBT rights and wide acceptance were still in their infancy, and it was potentially dangerous to come out at work, at school, and in families. Even though I was fortunate enough to avoid negative reactions when I came out, I had friends who had lost jobs, were beaten up, or disowned by their family and loved ones. The truth may set you free, but the truth also hurts sometimes. I understood Joanne's fear. In fact, I was still discreet at work.

Joanne also loved her close-knit Italian family who had deep Catholic roots. She couldn't imagine divulging the news and then being cast out by any one of them. Even though she was actively exploring her feelings, she had no plans to reveal them to her family. As a result, I really didn't know if I would ever meet her relatives.

During that second week in July, we were sitting on my L-shaped couch talking and sipping wine after Christine had gone to bed. It was getting late and our conversation was winding down. We were not sitting close but each of us was resting one arm on the back of the couch as we faced each other. Our hands were positioned like those of God and Adam in the Sistine Chapel.

I couldn't stand it anymore...I was about to burst. I surprised myself when I put my hand on hers and said from my heart, "Joanne, I am so attracted to you."

Well, she was speechless. But I noticed she didn't pull her hand away.

"I just had to tell you," I said, waiting for her reaction. As she stumbled over some words, her surprised look was confusing. I couldn't tell if she was happy or scared to death...maybe it was both.

I decided I had my answer when she jumped up from the couch and said something about having to get home because it was late. Before I knew it, Joanne was out the door. I thought, *Boy, Skibski, you really blew it. You scared her off for sure.* I didn't expect to hear from her again.

But to my surprise, she called me the next day. "I'm sorry I bolted out of your house last night. I guess I was just surprised and didn't know what to think. Can we get together tonight to talk?"

"Sure. I'd like that," I responded, so relieved to have another chance. "There's a WaterFire tonight. Let's go down there by the river."

WaterFire is an artistic event in downtown Providence along the river that runs through the city. It was created in 1994 on a small scale for New Year's and has since grown into a much larger landmark event for the city. Circular, three-foot wide, iron braziers anchored in the middle of the river hold the fires that are ceremoniously tended throughout the night by volunteers dressed in black on slow-moving boats. Meditative music is piped through speakers along the river walkways where people stroll or find places to sit. The atmosphere is peaceful, enchanting and romantic, bringing people together and calming the spirit. It was a perfect spot for us to talk.

Night had just fallen as we meandered along the river walkway, listening to the peaceful music that touched the soul like a Gregorian chant. The comforting scent of wood fires filled the air like warm campfires at the end of the day. We hadn't gone very far when we stopped to absorb the scene and claimed our spot on some stone steps. As we watched the crackling fires and people strolling by, Joanne commented about the heterosexual couples holding hands.

"I feel so sad and angry that gay people can't do that," she said. No doubt she was thinking about her former boyfriends and how easy it was to display affection for each other in public. Holding hands where others could see was taken for granted.

"Well, some gay people defy the norm and do it anyway," I said, knowing that most would feel uncomfortable, especially Joanne. I didn't tell her that I was one of those "rebels" at times in past relationships.

After more discussion about the struggle in our society, Joanne concluded, "I just can't do it."

I was heartbroken. My interpretation of her comment was that she was choosing to be with men.

Another hurdle was presenting itself to me. I already knew the pain of women choosing guys over me. In the healing process, I had dealt with it, accepted it, and moved on...or so I thought. Now, the threat seemed to be happening again and an old wound had opened. *Would Joanne be just a dear friend? Could I do that?*

With a heavy heart, I decided to let it go. We ended the evening on a friendly note and returned to our respective homes while I concealed my disappointment. Since I had plans to spend time with my mother, daughter, and her friend at a cabin in New Hampshire for the next few days, I had time to process this new dilemma. A familiar quote kept repeating in my mind: "If you love something, let it go. If it comes back to you, it's yours. If it doesn't, it never was."

A few days later, I returned home from New Hampshire thinking Joanne was out of my life. I was shocked when she called me that night.

After chatting about my trip, she asked, "Do you want to go to the beach tomorrow and then maybe a movie?" She had no idea about my emotional struggle and decision to let her go if necessary. I certainly wanted to see her, but I didn't want my heart ripped out either.

Since Christine was spending the day at the barn for her riding lesson and had plans for a sleepover that night, I was free.

"That sounds like fun," I said, hiding my surprise as best I could. I needed to find out what was going on, but I was on guard. Despite my hesitation, I decided it was worth the risk in order to clear the air.

"I do have a commitment later in the afternoon, but we can reconnect later for the movie," I added.

"Great!" she said, as if nothing was wrong. In fact, she was almost jubilant.

I hung up the phone not knowing what to think. The day together could be really wonderful or a total disaster. At least I felt brave and relatively sure about my own feelings...I thought my therapist would be proud anyway.

We spent a beautiful day at the beach. Since I wasn't inspired to begin any heavy discussion about our status, we just relaxed, read, laughed and played in the ocean. Even our food preferences complimented each other. While Joanne brought coffee and muffins for a beach breakfast, I provided tuna salad on hard rolls for a tasty lunch. Once again, we were puzzle pieces that fit perfectly.

At night, we went to see the sci-fi movie, *Contact*, starring Jodi Foster, which had just come out. Joanne especially loved movies about space, secretly longing to be an astronaut. I loved sci-fi *and* Jodi Foster.

After the movie back at my apartment, I decided to bring up our discussion from the night at WaterFire. Facing each other on the couch, I put my glass of wine down on the coffee table and looked directly into her eyes.

"I thought you were telling me that you couldn't be in this relation-ship...that it was too hard," I began cautiously. "When I was away, I thought it was over so I resigned myself to that idea." I waited for the proverbial other shoe to drop.

"Oh my god," Joanne said with great surprise. "I only meant that it would be hard not to hold hands and hug in public. I'm not brave enough to do that." She took another sip from her glass of red wine and lowered it onto the table.

"Wow, I sure got the wrong message," I said in relief.

Joanne continued, "I missed you when you were in New Hampshire. In fact, I couldn't stop thinking about you and couldn't wait to see you again."

This time, Joanne was the one to "make the move" as she inched closer. We came together in the sweetest moment of a first kiss as our passion for each other was ignited. By letting go in New Hampshire this gift had indeed come back to me.

A year before Joanne and I had met, a song came out that I loved. It was "I Finally Found Someone" by Barbara Streisand and Bryan Adams. Even though I bought the single cassette, I had never opened it, vowing to play it only when I finally found *the* one. I had waited a long time, but now I knew what I had to do.

A short time after that magical night, when Joanne was again at my house, I told her about the song. Without hesitation, I proceeded to unwrap the cassette and put it into the player. When the music started, we began to slow dance in the middle of the living room. As the music swelled, we danced as one.

In the silence that followed with tears in our eyes, Joanne whispered, "Thank you," knowing how much the song meant to me. Then she con-fided, "I have a song too. For years, I would often look up at the stars and pray for *the* one. The song in my heart was "Somewhere Out There." We were definitely meant to be.

Now that we had begun our own beautiful dance on a new path, we thought about where we should go on our first adventure. Both of us had always loved to travel before we met. We agreed it was time to plan a get-away together. *Where should we go?*

CHAPTER 5

Chemo 101

"Is this seat taken?" I asked, pointing to the empty chair beside Joanne. She looked up from the open iPad on her lap with a coy smile on her face. After scanning the large, nearly empty waiting room with plenty of seats, she responded in a sexy voice, "It is now. Have a seat."

"Thanks," I replied as I sat down next to her. I had just sauntered back from a visit to the sterile restroom nearby. "I couldn't help but notice you sitting by yourself. Come here often?" We slipped into our roles with ease.

"As a matter of fact, it's my first time here," Joanne replied and looked deep into my eyes, as if we were in a darkly lit lounge discovering each other for the first time. "Something tells me it won't be my last if you're going to be here," she added with a sultry grin.

"It's my first time here too," I said as I gazed at her beautiful smile. "I'll certainly make a point to be here when you are. Call me crazy, but I'm *so* attracted to you." Our familiar passion crackled, even after all these years, as we laughed together.

"Good," Joanne whispered as her smile faded. She reached for my hand and held it. As I looked down at our hands, I noticed her familiar sexy dark red nail polish that I loved. Holding hands felt like holding hearts.

We had often played this pretend pick-up game. Usually, it took place at a table for two with soft candlelight flickering at one of our favorite restaurants. Either one of us would be inspired to begin the game when returning to our table from the restroom. At other times, we would be sharing a meal at our small, round, bistro-style table in the enclosed sunroom overlooking our backyard garden. We would pretend we were meeting at this cozy bed and breakfast like in the middle of a novel. It was fun ıd alluring to imagine a variety of scenes and act out a fantasy or two.

This time, however, we were in the waiting room before 8:00 a.m. on Monday at the Women's Infusion Center where Joanne would endure her first chemo treatment. We both knew we were pretending to be calm and nonchalant while an undercurrent of anxiety ran just below the surface. Gratefully, the warm reception by the all-female staff and the peaceful surroundings felt like a soft, fleece blanket on a chilly day.

The inside of the building had been newly renovated in muted, earth-tone colors with subtle reminders of nature: bunches of beach grass, butterfly portraits, quiet bubbling water fountains, and a small fish aquarium along one wall in the waiting room. The single cushioned chairs were arranged along the walls with an inviting circle of seats in the middle surrounding a low circular magazine table. The sound of a small TV on the wall played quietly in the background. I couldn't help but notice the contrast between this nurturing setting and the nasty poisonous battle ahead.

It had been eleven days since we had first heard the diagnosis. During that time, our calendars had been filled with appointments for more blood work, scans, fluid removal from one lung, laparoscopic surgery, and an intake meeting to learn about basic infusion procedures and details. A new bizarre world was opening up as if we had fallen into Alice's rabbit hole.

During our induction process, we had learned that one of the requirements for chemo each time was to have blood drawn right after checking in. The platelet count had to be high enough for the infusion to begin. Luckily, the blood drawing room was next to the reception desk. In fact, all the logistics were convenient in that building. The only thing that wasn't convenient was the anxious wait for the results of the lab work to come back. If the platelets, white or red blood cell counts were too low, it meant a wasted trip and a rescheduled appointment.

Finally, Joanne's name was called and the wait was over. We followed Marie, the nurse assistant, down the hallway to a small room for taking vitals—blood pressure, temperature, body weight—another required checkpoint for continuing on to the main event. Always interested in the people around her, Joanne started a light conversation with Marie about the weather, family, and everyone's favorite, body weight. A few chuckles later, we were escorted to the infusion room.

The entrance was located at one end of the large space where the soft décor continued. As we passed two small loveseats in a cozy sitting area on the right just before reaching a kitchen area, I noticed a fresh pot of coffee brewing on the counter to the left. Some tempting homemade brownies had been lovingly placed on a ceramic plate for anyone's pleasure as well. *How inviting*, I thought as I scanned the area.

The large open room was thoughtfully divided by curved partitions that created some private space as well as small group gatherings. Large, comfortable recliners and smaller cushioned chairs filled the spaces while IV poles that looked like saluting soldiers stood ready to serve.

Some patients were already hooked up in their recliners and talking with companions or sleeping peacefully. I particularly noticed those with turbans or hats covering bald heads. I tried not to look. Behind a long nurses' station positioned along one wall sat medical staff in street clothes who smiled as we passed by their computers, plants, and family pictures. Our entrance felt like the first day at a new school as Marie turned to us.

"Joanne, did you request a private space or would you like to join other patients?" she asked as she escorted us to our area.

"Oh, I already asked for a private space," Joanne replied without hesitation. I wasn't surprised. Despite her ease with conversation, Joanne considered herself to be an introvert who needed privacy and quiet as much as she needed air to breathe.

"That's fine," Marie replied cheerfully. " I think there's a spot over here."

She led us to a partially enclosed space on the perimeter of the room near some windows overlooking the sidewalk of the busy street. Joanne's throne was waiting for her along with an armchair for me. With some reservation, we settled in as Marie told us that Joanne's nurse would be right in.

With her dark blue stretch jeans, light mauve mock turtleneck, and lavender sweater jacket, Joanne looked stylishly comfortable for her first round of chemo. Even though her dark Sharon Osborne style hair had been sprayed to stay in place, a few hours in the recliner would most likely flatten her look by the end of the day. Nonetheless, she took pride in her appearance despite the circumstances. As we took our places, we smiled at each other as if to say, *Here we go!*

A few minutes later, a pleasant woman in her early forties appeared at the doorway. "Hi, Joanne?" she asked quietly. "I'm Sarah. I'll be your primary chemo nurse. How are you feeling today?" As she looked at Joanne with respect and protective care, I could sense her confidence and experience. I immediately trusted her.

"Other than being a little nervous, I'm okay," Joanne said in return and then turned to me with a smile. "This is my partner, Linda." Sarah didn't flinch at the revelation of our relationship which I appreciated. As we exchanged greetings, I imagined all of us would see a lot of each other in the months ahead.

Sarah reviewed the details of the five-hour procedure with us. As the self-appointed secretary, I was ready to add any new information to my notes from the previous intake. Not surprising, Joanne was ready to ask questions, especially since she had already pored over this topic online. Curious by nature, she was not shy about gathering information.

"We'll give you the meds for the side effects first," she explained. Since she called them by their medical names, I asked her to interpret.

"Oh sure," she obliged. "The IV cocktail will be Pepcid, Benadryl, a steroid and an anti-nausea med, given one at a time. After that, we'll give you the chemos, Taxol and Carboplatin, separately. They'll take much longer." To both of us, she said, "If you have any questions or need anything at all, push the call button. I'm always nearby."

Sarah moved quietly and efficiently from the computer on the counter in our cubicle to the IV pole with its monitors attached like a totem pole next to Joanne's chair. The temporary IV catheter in her arm had already been set by Laurie, the phlebotomist, who had no trouble finding Joanne's notoriously tiny veins. Despite our anxiety about this poisonous procedure, we were ready to attack.

From the intake discussion, we had already learned about the list of probable side effects…fatigue, nausea, vomiting, neuropathy, itchiness, and, of course, hair loss that was estimated to begin in two to four weeks. Since every patient responds differently to chemo, our fear of the unknown rose to the surface as we watched the IV drip.

For a diversion, I asked Joanne, "Do you want anything from the kitchen?" It felt like our cruise ship had just left the pier.

"Sure, honey," she replied. "Thanks. I'll have a cup of tea. And I think I'll put on one of those TV morning shows for a little while." Neither one of us watched daytime TV very much, so I sensed Joanne's anxiety with this atypical move.

After positioning the small TV attached to the wall by a flexible arm, I headed to the kitchen. Even though there was more activity than when we had arrived, the sounds of conversations, machines, and other TVs were purposely muted. The only exception was the persistent beeping of completed IVs that cried out for attention from anyone who would listen. Warm smiles from the staff were comforting as they performed their tasks.

On this trip through the big room, I noticed the location of restrooms for future reference. Near the kitchen, I also spotted an odd stainless steel box with a glass door. At that moment, one of the nurses opened the glass door to reveal two shelves lined with rolled up linen blankets. Their white and blue trim colors reminded me of Jewish prayer shawls. While the blankets appeared to be thin, it dawned on me that they were also heated. Since I knew Joanne would appreciate those, I made a mental note for later.

Despite her passion for skiing, Joanne hated being cold. For years, we had planned warm weather vacations, usually in mid-winter, so that she could tolerate the New England cold. I tagged along, of course, and loved traveling together, but never felt the need for a winter break as much as she did. Now, the cold chemo coursing through the IV into her veins was creating a new type of cold.

I had found what I needed in the kitchen and headed back. Joanne certainly appreciated the hot tea while we watched TV for a while. Just as she started to nod off from the Benadryl, I told her about the blankets and asked her if she wanted one.

"Oh my god, yes!" she exclaimed. Her face lit up at the thought. "How about two?"

As we turned off the TV and swung its arm back to the wall, Sarah poked her head in the doorway and asked, "How are you doing?"

"I'm ready to take a nap," Joanne replied, and settled into the huge recliner with her pillow.

"Would you like a blanket?" Sarah offered. After I told her I was on my way to get one, she added, "By the way, the recliner is also heated."

To Joanne, those words were magical. Reveling in her queen status, she quickly found the button for heat on the chair. With her sweatshirt hood over her head, the heated blankets covering her body neck to toe, and the recliner heating her back, Joanne resembled a small burrito on a large plate. The colors of the blankets also reminded me of Biblical times and I felt the warmth of God covering my love in her chair.

While Joanne snoozed, I dug into the activity bag I had brought with me. I really didn't mind the long wait. In fact, I was looking forward to reading, doing crossword puzzles, and playing computer solitaire…activities that usually took a back seat to work.

But I also dug into my thoughts as well. *What in the world is going to happen to us?* By God's design, I was born with abundant patience and had learned long ago, by some miracle, to live in the moment. This new cancer threat was a test of those qualities for sure. But the main thought that kept returning to me was that I did not want to be anywhere else. No matter what the course, we were together as a team and I loved taking care of Joanne for a change.

She never liked to be sick. Even with a common cold, Joanne thought illness should be gone in twenty-four hours or less. After all, she had things to do. If the symptoms lingered any longer, which they usually did, she would become very impatient and cranky.

"Don't hover over me! I just want to be left alone," she would bark during illnesses in the past.

"Okay, but I'm around to help if you want," I would usually respond.

With this new disease and even the vague symptoms months before diagnosis, however, Joanne's demeanor had changed. As she accepted my offers of help with greater patience, she also refrained from biting my head off. I'm not sure what deep well she tapped into, but she became a different patient. Now, as I watched her sleeping, I suspected that her fear of the future could be the reason for the attitude change. And perhaps she knew there would be no choice about needing help.

During this initial chemo visit, several medical professionals stopped in to introduce themselves and their services. After her morning nap, Joanne met the social worker, dietician, technician, and a representative from the wellness office that provided yoga, acupuncture, and massage, one of Joanne's favorites. She gathered their information with great interest.

At noon, we were pleasantly surprised by a med tech who stopped by and asked Joanne if she would like some lunch. Her cart was filled with healthy-looking, large round sandwich rolls filled with tuna, egg salad, or ham, along with fruit cups and tantalizing parfaits. The tech explained that after the sandwich cart made its rounds to patients, then visitors were welcomed to check the refrigerator later for leftovers. I didn't mind, but Joanne did. She offered to share half of her sandwich when the tech left our room.

"I can't eat all of this anyway," she whispered so the staff couldn't hear. Unlike me, Joanne enjoyed breaking some rules once in a while.

As the afternoon crept by, Joanne slept most of the time. We were learning a lot in this first chemo class...a new language and new procedures. Throughout the day, we asked Sarah questions, went online, and observed other patients. Even tackling the big event of the day—going to the restroom with an IV pole—was a learning experience. I called it *walking the dog.* Cords had to be unplugged and wrapped carefully around the monitors while the patient had to move slowly, always mindful of the wide base legs extending like a spider. Joanne mastered this technique with pride and reassurance that she could control something else during treatment. Her innate independence would not be denied.

By late afternoon, the infusion was finished and we returned home knowing this day would be repeated the following Monday. That time would be shorter, however, since only Taxol would be given. Always in charge, Joanne had already made plans for her sister, Joyce, to assume chauffeur duty that week, insisting that I return to work.

"You'll need to save that family sick time for bigger events like my surgery," she argued. *Always the event planner,* I thought with admiration. Since her argument made sense, I reluctantly agreed.

Then she added with a strong voice, "I'm planning on beating this thing, you know. I'm not going to let it get the best of me." I was familiar with her determination.

"Well, that sounds good to me," I said. "I'm right beside you on that."

Now at home from chemo, resting on the couch, Joanne snatched her iPad and began checking out funky, buzzed hairstyles in preparation for losing her hair in the following weeks. She also gathered information about wigs—another world to explore. Thank goodness she didn't expect her family and friends to shave their heads in support.

While Joanne did her research, I composed the first "Joanne Update" email to several concerned family and friends. I thought it would be an efficient way to let everyone know about her progress. We certainly needed their support, love, and prayers, while I needed to connect. Despite her need for privacy, Joanne approved of this form of communication after reviewing the email's content. The first of many updates began simply on February 24, 2014.

Hello everyone,
    Since I am now the official scribe (among other things), I'll e-blast y'all every now and then to quickly report on Joanne's progress if you

don't mind. I'm sure there will be individual messages along the way, but this will be an easy way to get the information out there. You are all special to us and can consider yourselves "charter members" of this list. But certainly we will add others if anyone is inclined. Don't feel that you always have to respond if you don't want to…it's mostly fyi.

The message continued to recap the first chemo visit and the planned schedule for surgery and treatments afterward. At the end, we acknowledged our gratitude.

A long haul, but we're ready to do battle and know that we are blessed to have so many family and friends praying and cheering us on. Thank you, one and all. Stay tuned…

Peace and Love,
Linda & Joanne

With the first update sent, I felt that our troops were now gathered for this ominous battle.

It wasn't until Thursday of that week that Joanne began to feel somewhat normal. With extra meds for nausea and constipation, she had some relief as the days passed. But she continued to lack energy and an appetite. We also had to remember some restrictions during chemo treatments such as no dental work, no aspirin, antioxidants, or ibuprofen, and no greasy or spicy foods. Drinking lots of fluids and using hand sanitizer often to avoid infection were important since her white blood cell count—and thus her immune system—would be low. Our heads were spinning.

On Friday morning before I headed out to work, Joanne surprised me by announcing, "I'm going out to do some errands today." She was definitely feeling better.

"Are you sure you're able to drive?" I was concerned.

"I'll be fine. I'm feeling almost normal," she said with confidence and determination. I knew she was on a mission.

"Okay, but call me if you need me," I responded with resignation.

When we had chosen Mondays as Joanne's chemo day, our plan was to manage the side effects during the week so that the weekend would, hopefully, be free for some fun. Our decision seemed to be a good one.

Not that Joanne was ready to party hardy on the weekends. When her energy was spent, the severe exhaustion that followed sent her back to the couch. But she had enough energy to go out to breakfast on Saturday, and even out to a movie on Sunday…just in time to return to chemo again on Monday.

During the second week of chemo, the symptoms were similar to the first, with the exception of increased vomiting, itchiness, and one amazing side effect that we hadn't expected. When she returned home from chemo, her energy level was soaring from the steroids. I watched in amazement at her frenzied pace. She was ready to wash both cars, weed the entire garden, and clean out the kitchen cupboards in two hours. Once she crashed in exhaustion, however, she returned to the couch…her new chemo station. Two days later, she was miraculously back to work at her downtown office. The unpredictable ebb and flow kept me on the edge of my seat.

When Joanne's cousin, Carole Ann, dropped her off at home following the third week of chemo, Joanne reported a disastrous event involving her arm during the procedure.

"Just before the end, I twisted my arm without thinking and felt the IV needle move. Boy, did it hurt!" she exclaimed and continued, "Sarah said the vein leaked and that's what's causing the swelling, redness, and pain."

"Oh my god! What can they do about it?" I asked in disbelief. *What's next?* I thought.

"I have to put ice on it, but it should be okay they said," she explained calmly. "Dr. D. will check it out when we see him this week." Since Joanne didn't seem to be alarmed, I relaxed too.

"At least I'm getting that permanent port put in tomorrow," she went on. "I'll be so glad they won't have to poke around in my arms anymore." *One less pain to deal with* was written on her face.

Even though we had known about the outpatient surgery for the permanent port located on the upper left side of her chest, the date had only been recently set. Since we had learned that chemo affects veins by making them smaller and, therefore, harder to find, it was no wonder that Joanne's already tiny veins would collapse. This procedure would be a welcomed event.

The port was installed the next day without incident. Since Joanne requested minimal anesthesia, her recovery was less intense. I couldn't help but think how tough she was. She was focused on fighting and healing while I was focused on caring for her when she needed me. This time, Joanne appreciated the help.

My own feelings were a jumbled mess. While I kept a lid on my worry and fear, I used love and hope like a spear, ready to destroy the next threat in order to protect her. I loved taking care of Joanne and embraced my new purpose. Even though I felt powerless to remove the cancer, at least I could ease her way. I also had faith in our strength to overcome obstacles. For two decades, we had built a solid foundation of love as we had tackled the challenges of our relationship. But now we faced a new formidable enemy as if it was the mythical Kraken rising from the sea. Some days, I was afraid and exhausted.

Despite her fluctuating side effects that now included diarrhea, lackluster appetite, and general malaise, the doctor was satisfied with Joanne's tolerance for the treatment now that the first three-week cycle of chemo had been completed. The next obstacle presented itself on the Friday before she was scheduled for round two.

While we were watching the news at dinner time, the phone rang.

"Hi, Joanne? This is Sarah from the Infusion Center." We were surprised to hear from her and looked at each other with concerned faces.

"Oh, hi," Joanne answered with some apprehension in her voice.

"I'm calling to tell you that your blood work this week shows your platelets are low. If they don't increase over the weekend, you might not be able to have chemo on Monday."

"Oh no," she said with disappointment. "Is there anything I can do to bring them up?" Joanne did not want to delay this fight.

"Actually, no. I'm afraid not," Sarah answered and then added, "Just try to avoid infections, and don't worry. The platelets should increase on their own. I just wanted to give you a heads-up." She tried to be reassuring.

Joanne hung up after thanking Sarah for calling. Not to worry? Of course, that's exactly what we did for the next two days. We avoided possible germ contact, spent time in nature, and rented movies.

By this time, I had decided I would not miss any more of the chemo days. My mind wasn't on work anyway, so I figured I needed to be with Joanne. When I told her, she didn't argue.

When we arrived at the Center that Monday, our anxiety had multiplied. The routine blood draw was completed by Laurie, Joanne's new friend, and sent to the lab. Like before, we waited forever to hear if the blood levels were acceptable. When we finally heard the good news that we were on, we were walking down the hall once again with a sigh of relief.

Ironically, we were quickly learning that having chemo was better than not. Chemo was the weapon we needed.

Hours later, when we returned home, Joanne headed to the couch while I retrieved the mail. One handwritten envelope addressed to Joanne caught my eye. It was from one of my Michigan friends who had met Joanne years before on the back deck of my former apartment.

"Hey, honey," I called out. "There's a card for you from Kathy in Michigan." I walked to the TV room and handed it to her."

Almost asleep, Joanne raised her weary head and said sincerely, "Oh, that's nice." She raised herself part way to a sitting position and opened the card.

Inside the envelope was a cute card and a printed insert that fell out. Joanne read them and said, "I love this! It needs to go on the refrigerator."

As I took the paper insert, I read the quote in white letters on a lavender background. "*BE FEISTY, BE A WARRIOR. Go to War With Cancer and KICK ASS!*" I thought it sounded like a great motto.

Two days later, almost five weeks since chemo began, Joanne stepped out of the shower in the morning and called me in. Wrapped in her towel with her hand extended to me, she said, "Look."

Inside her hand was a fistful of her dark wet hair.

With tears in our eyes, I wrapped my arms around my honey. The next class was about to begin.

CHAPTER 6

Provincetown

"Are you sure you can take a walk right now?" I asked Joanne as she rose to a sitting position on the antique, beige velvet couch in her small, uncluttered living room. Now ten weeks after we met, we were in love and taking care of each other. Her longhaired calico cat, Cara Mia, sat motionless on the floor in the next room watching her adored human with intense interest.

"Sure I can. My wrist doesn't even hurt," she answered with assurance.

Earlier that morning, she had undergone outpatient surgery on her right wrist to remove a painful ganglion. Joanne had never had any type of surgery before this. Now she was yawning after a nap and eager to resume normal activity by announcing her intent to get outside.

"Maybe you should take it easy," I warned. "I bet the anesthesia hasn't worn off yet." I was talking from experience as I remembered recovery from my own surgeries several years ago. "How about if I come with you?" I thought she might be a little wobbly at least.

"No, thanks. I'll just walk in the neighborhood. I won't go far," she replied. Joanne was determined to put this idea into motion.

"Well, at least walk on the sidewalks," I said with a smile as she chuckled. I was learning that for some reason Joanne preferred to walk in the street, despite the presence of nice, smooth sidewalks. Her defiance of the rules was becoming a joke between us. Actually, I was beginning to love that part of her but did not want to reveal that secret too soon.

I was also learning that helping Joanne was a fine art. Not only did she break the rules of suburban walking, but she also defied the expectations of recovery from illness. Too much help made her grumpy and too little help made her sad. Since this minor wrist surgery was not a big deal to her, she did not expect to be dependent in any way. She put her comfortable walking sandals on and went outside.

Less than five minutes after Joanne left the house, I heard her return by the backdoor. As I went to greet her in the kitchen, she looked up at me from the mudroom steps.

"Whew!" she exclaimed. "I'm exhausted! I walked to the third house and just had to come back. Guess you were right." She plopped into the nearest chair and looked so surprised that this medical procedure could affect her stamina so much.

"Well, you just need to relax and take it easy," I replied without judgment. "Just pretend you're the queen and I'll wait on you." I was also thinking of our trip to Provincetown in two days…our first real getaway…and hoping she'd be well enough to go.

"Okay, I could get into being the queen," Joanne added, "I'll even let you drive my car to P-town," Despite her apprehension about our destination, she wasn't about to stay home due to her bandaged wrist.

For years, Provincetown has been known as *the* gay mecca of the Northeast. Located on the tip of Cape Cod, Massachusetts, the historic Portuguese fishing village and art colony is a favorite destination for diverse people, especially the gay community. Freedom of expression and creativity are hallmarks of the P-town scene. In less than three hours, drivers from Rhode Island can be transported to a welcoming town where two women holding hands in public was incidental rather than shocking most everywhere else in 1997.

Especially in the summer, P-town's population swells with visitors of all ages from around the world, and the activities are as diverse as the people and their pets who stroll the narrow streets. Whale watching, sailing, people watching, beaching, biking, listening to street musicians, kayaking, walking the dunes, shopping, browsing art galleries, dancing, catching a drag queen show, eating in fine restaurants or grabbing a lobster roll on the go contribute to the merry scene both day and night.

As native New Englanders, both of us had visited Provincetown in years past with family and friends. I could even remember spending a day there with my mother long before I came out. At the time, I was oblivious to the gay community as we focused on historical sites and eating out. Later on, when I visited P-town with new lovers and gay friends, I saw the place with new eyes, of course. I thought I was in heaven!

Joanne had been to P-town throughout her childhood and college years, also with family and friends. She even had a friend from college whose family lived and worked there. However, her view of the town would be different on this trip. Not surprising to me, now that we were a couple in love, she was anxious about going there.

Identifying our first getaway destination had involved some constructive compromise. When I first suggested this trip, Joanne had said, "Sure." Then she thought about it.

"Well, I don't know," she hesitated. "I don't want to run into anyone who would recognize me. And I don't think I could stay right in town." Even though our relationship was beginning to feel like a secret affair, I understood her fear.

"That's fine," I said, knowing she needed to wade into the water. "Whatever you feel comfortable with is okay. At least you can walk in the streets with everyone else." We both had to laugh at her aversion to sidewalks. "Where do you want to stay?" I asked.

After some thought, she had named the Shoreline Motel.

"I've stayed there before and it's right on the beach," she offered. "It's quiet and comfortable and only a few miles outside town." I could only guess at the courage she had to muster for this adventure as well as this relationship.

"Sounds good to me," I said honestly, just thrilled to hear she would go.

Whereas I love to be in the middle of the hoopla, Joanne, like Cara Mia, preferred to observe from the sidelines before easing into the fun. On this trip, we would share the noise and excitement of the crowd as well as the peace and serenity of the motel. Out of love and respect, we flexed our ability to compromise.

The day to leave had arrived. After gathering my maps and reviewing the directions, which I loved to do, we were ready to embark. Joanne's new car was packed, Christine was settled at her friend's house for the weekend, Buddy was safely tucked away at a favorite kennel, and the late summer sun smiled down at us. Since my old Ford station wagon with encroaching rust was no match for Joanne's chic ride, it stayed parked in my driveway. As we pulled away from the curb, I reached for Joanne's unwrapped left hand, and said, "Here we go!" We couldn't help but smile at each other, knowing we were headed for three days of fun.

The motel was indeed situated on a wide section of beach overlooking Cape Cod Bay less than five miles from Provincetown. With two stories, the building had a redwood façade that created a distinct, welcoming look. We turned into the crushed stone parking lot and pulled into a space near the front door. A few minutes later, we entered the front door to register before unloading the car.

The décor of the lobby was clean and inviting—nothing too fancy, but relaxing. When the desk clerk informed us that our room was on the second floor and there was no elevator, we didn't flinch. Feeling physically fit, two flights of stairs certainly didn't bother us, especially when Joanne insisted she could carry light items with her sore wrist. So we collected our belongings and quickly found our room. It was perfect. The small terrace with its table and chairs called to us as we opened the sliding doors and breathed the salt air.

A couple hugs and kisses later, I naturally started to unpack since I always made any space my home wherever I roamed. Preferring to live out of her suitcase, Joanne decided to check things out in the lobby. Half an hour later, she returned laden with brochures, guidebooks, and some notes she took from her conversation with the front desk clerk.

"I thought we could plan an itinerary," she said as she presented the brochures and coupon books. Since Joanne seemed to be a great activities director, I agreed to follow her lead. While my forte was maps, directions, and getting there, Joanne's forte was planning events. I sensed that we were a talented travel team.

Leaving some room for spontaneity of course, our list included a whale watch, spending time at the beach, taking in a couple shows, dancing at a women's bar, shopping, and attending the Unitarian Church service on Sunday morning. Since the word for the weekend was *comfort*, the itinerary was subject to change, especially *holding hands in public* that was only on my mental list. What we did know for certain was that renting bicycles and/or kayaks was out of the question this time due to Joanne's recovering wrist. She knew her limits.

Since it was still afternoon, we decided to drive into town, park the car, and gradually make our way to whatever casual restaurant caught our fancy for dinner. We had already made reservations for the next night at a restaurant for fine dining, knowing how crowded it would be. As we started strolling with the crowd on Commercial Street, I felt as if we were getting our feet wet at the ocean's edge. While I was excited, Joanne was nervous.

The festive scene was familiar—a colorful mass of tourists, shopkeepers, entertainers, locals, flamboyant drag queens, bicyclists, dogs on leashes, and the occasional vehicle inching its way through the crowd on the one-way street. People of all shapes and sizes spilled out of shops with their bagged purchases, ice cream cones or boxes of homemade fudge. Many couples, both gay and straight, were holding hands, talking and laughing as they headed to their next destination.

No matter which direction we walked, a view of the harbor was only a turn of the head away while small alleys provided some respite from the congestion. The buildings lining the main street were a mix of quaint bed and breakfasts with beautiful gardens, art galleries, restaurants, souvenir shops, jewelers, bookstores, and entertainment bars. Completing the heart of the town were the practical establishments, including local pharmacies, grocery marts, banks, and hardware stores.

Benches under trees and outdoor eating areas provided rest for weary walkers and a chance to listen to sidewalk musicians whose music filled the air and calmed the soul. In front of the town hall, horse-drawn carriages and open trolleys stood ready to offer relaxing tours of the historic area as well. A long wharf extended from the center of town where boats of all sizes waited patiently for fishermen, sailors, and boat tourists. To me, the atmosphere was both chaotic and soothing at the same time.

I allowed Joanne to lead the way as she immediately relaxed into shopping. Browsing in and out of small, interesting shops took skill, and she was an expert. While I didn't mind some shopping, after a while I needed to find one of those inviting benches outside. As I sat there watching people, I decided that shopping with Joanne was like watching a butterfly in a garden. It was best to wait and let the butterfly come to me.

I really didn't mind waiting. Watching people passing by has always been relaxing and interesting to me. I often compared it to my love for fish aquariums. Ever since childhood when I had watched the fish in my grandmother's small fish tank, I've been fascinated with the variety of colors, shapes, and motion of aquarium inhabitants. P-town's streets had an abundant mix swimming by.

After what seemed like a long rest, Joanne approached the bench with a shopping bag in her hand and sat down.

"Hi," she said with a smile and a look of triumph. "Look at the new top I found on sale…fifty percent off!"

"Great," I exclaimed as I looked at the pale lavender jacket from the clothing store, *Fresh Produce*. "That'll look nice on you." With her dark hair, loving dark eyes, and petite frame, I thought anything would look nice on her.

I already loved Joanne's girlie-girl style with her flowery tops, makeup, and nail polish. Most people would think she was straight and that we were just girlfriends on a shopping spree. Once again, that feeling of hiding a secret affair crept to the surface and I felt sad that I still couldn't be myself.

"How about getting a drink before dinner?" I suggested. "There's a nice bar and restaurant with an outdoor porch near the center of town." Since Joanne was definitely on the same page, we walked and talked our way there, weaving around people and bikes.

After finding our way to the porch bar and settling in with our drinks overlooking the parade of people, I was wondering what she was thinking about her new perception of the crowd, especially the gay couples and drag queens.

"I'm so glad to be here with you," I said as we toasted to each other. "I can see you studying everyone. What are you thinking?"

"Well, it's so different for me now." Joanne looked deep into my eyes. "I love being here with you too, but I'm just trying to figure out how I'll fit in with all of this." I could almost hear her mind whirling with the thought of change.

Even though she had visited P-town before, she was now facing a new chance to be her true self. From my own experience of coming out, I knew that the consequences of honesty could be daunting.

"You don't have to be a drag queen or a butch dyke with a buzzcut or anything you don't want to be," I offered with empathy. "Just be your honest self and everything will fall into place at the right time. Remember, it's all about *comfort*." As we continued to look deeply into each other's eyes, I was reminded of our first lunch at the deli when our hearts connected.

"Thank you for understanding," she said quietly. "I can't believe how patient you are. It means a lot." Then she added, "I'll get there." At that moment, I could sense her confidence and commitment.

"I know," I said and meant it. My initial worries about her backing out of the weekend had faded as my faith and trust in our new love had grown.

After a pause, I turned our attention to the glamorous drag queens as they cheerfully called out to passersby, hawking their shows scheduled for later that night. Their sparkling bright colors, gold lame, flowing gowns, six-inch heels, XXL boobs, gorgeous makeup, and two-foot high wigs could not be ignored. I loved their artistry and creativity, especially their show names…Ginger Snap, Kim Chi, Sham Payne, and my personal favorite, Hedda Lettuce.

Usually seen during the day on a small, motorized scooter riding down Commercial Street, Hedda Lettuce, was tall and beautiful as her lime green dress and the feathery boa wrapped around her neck flowed behind her. Her huge wig was coiffed to resemble, not surprisingly, a head of iceberg lettuce that was also lime green, of course. I thought her concept and image was outstanding. I suppose it also helped that my favorite color was green.

"You could try to look like Hedda Lettuce!" I exclaimed to Joanne. She started to laugh and before we knew it, silent tears of laughter spilled out of us. We almost rolled out of our seats at the thought of Joanne, the introvert, on that scooter dressed in lime green.

After a second glass of wine, we decided to avoid wobbling back to the car by staying put on the porch and ordering dinner. At least we knew the food was good and the view was interesting. Our timing seemed to be perfect for catching one of the drag shows that happened to be in the same building as well.

"Do you want to go inside and see the drag show?" I asked while we were paying the tab. "It seems appropriate I think," grinning at her.

"Oh sure, what the hell!" Joanne was loosening up it seemed.

Waking up the next morning without the usual responsibilities of work and home was luxurious. Our peaceful room and the calming ocean view were unforgettable. We couldn't resist a short walk on the beach before looking at our itinerary. Of course, we had choices on that list, depending on the weather and our energy level, but we wanted to make the most of our time together.

Since we both loved the beach and Joanne's wrist could be protected from the sand with extra wrap, we decided to grab hot coffee and breakfast sandwiches on our way to relax on the beach for a couple hours. However, with reservations for a three-hour whale watch around noon, our beach time would be limited. For efficiency, we packed extra clothes in our packs in order to meet the boat on the wharf directly from the beach.

There are several beach choices in Provincetown. Race Point Beach was the largest beach on the ocean side with big waves and wind. Lighthouse Point Beach was across the harbor, requiring a boat taxi during high tide. Herring Cove Beach was on the bay side with usually smaller waves and calmer wind. While this beach was closer to town, there were additional choices at the entrance.

Even though there were no signs to designate a choice once the fee was paid, in 1997, everyone knew. To the right was the *straight* portion of the beach and to the left was the *gay* side. Even beyond the gay beach was the rumor of a nude beach. Needless to say, Joanne felt most comfortable with the *straight* side of Herring Cove Beach. My choice, of course, would have been the gay beach so that I wouldn't have to pretend…again.

From my perspective, there was little difference in appearance between the two beach sides. On each beach, people were sitting in low chairs with umbrellas or not, reading books, swimming in the water, laughing or sleeping. Both sides looked like typical beach scenes, other than the mix of couples. I was looking forward to the day when Joanne would discover this comparison for herself.

The whale watch boat tour was spectacular, with several close sightings of humpback whales showing off their black and white tails. Even though we had been on whale watches separately in the past, sharing this first tour together was special. After the boat docked, we had time to return to our motel to dress for dinner.

So far, Joanne had not run into anyone she knew despite the remote possibility of a familiar face on the wharf. Since she had a wide circle of friends and acquaintances who had often crossed our paths in Rhode Island, her concern in P-town was somewhat realistic. Consequently, her reluctance to show her true colors continued as we prepared for an evening out.

Since the restaurant we chose had a wonderful reputation for excellent food and a romantic atmosphere, it did not disappoint. A cozy table for two, a dimly lit room with natural stonewalls, glasses of fine wine, the freshest fish on the planet, and candlelight softly glowing around my new love's face. We were lost in each other.

As we enjoyed our scrumptious meals, we talked about the day, our lives, and our plans for the rest of our weekend. To my surprise, Joanne had agreed to go to another show after we ate. This time, it was Kate Clinton, a well-known lesbian comedian, who was appearing at a women's bar down the street. There would also be dancing afterward. Needless to say, I was looking forward to the chance to be ourselves.

After paying the restaurant bill, we headed outside back into the quiet night. By this time, the crowd on the street had thinned out as it usually did by mid-evening. While a soft breeze from the ocean pushed the clouds away every now and then to allow a few shy stars to peek through, I felt happy and content in the moment.

As we started walking, without a word, Joanne slipped her left hand in mine. I looked at her grinning face with surprise and a broad smile as we continued walking in the middle of the street, holding hands in P-town.

The next morning was Sunday, our last day. The plan was to have a nice breakfast by the water, attend the church service, and then complete some souvenir shopping in town before heading back home. While we sipped our first cup of coffee in the room, we haphazardly turned on the TV to see what the rest of the world was doing. Immediately, we saw that *Breaking News* had interrupted regular programming.

When we heard the shocking news, our jaws dropped...Princess Diana had died in a terrible car crash.

"Oh my god!" we both exclaimed at the same time. Like everyone else in the world, we couldn't believe it. Here we were on August 31, 1997, enjoying our weekend and anticipating a new beginning together while a beautiful life had suddenly been cut short. The contrast was overwhelming.

Since we continued to watch the TV longer than we had expected, we decided to skip the church service. Still reeling from the news, we packed our belongings and checked out as we headed into town for breakfast.

Everywhere we went we overheard people commenting about Princess Diana. Even in festive Provincetown, the atmosphere was subdued. After eating a delicious breakfast where we quietly gazed out at the harbor, we wandered into a gift shop to browse among unique greeting cards and photographic artwork on the walls. All of a sudden, we heard a shout.

"Joanne!" A guy in his early fifties with glasses and salt and pepper hair approached with a huge smile on his face. *Who in the world is this?* I thought with a little trepidation.

As she turned to look in the guy's direction, Joanne also shouted, "Steven! What are *you* doing here?" She was obviously happy to see him.

"I was going to ask you the same thing," he said as he gave her a big hug.

"I'm here with Linda…my partner," she motioned for me to come over. I certainly noticed her words, *my partner*.

Steven's smile widened in surprise as he shook my hand and said, "So nice to meet you. I'm here with my partner, Bill." Bill calmly came forward for hellos as he smiled warmly. His friendly blue eyes were direct and kind.

When Joanne saw the question on my face, she explained, "Steven's my cousin who lives in Washington. We hardly ever see each other and now look! We had to come to P-town to connect." Her face was aglow.

Since neither Joanne nor Steven had known for certain about the other's *secret*, we all chattered in amazement about this new revelation and expressed our happiness with our new bond. Despite the desire to find a café to share our stories, a meal or coffee, we had to part ways. Most certainly, we would make a date in the near future when Steven and Bill would be visiting family again in Rhode Island.

As we drove home, we recalled the wonderful moments and unexpected surprises of the last three days, especially meeting Joanne's cousin. For me, that surprise was almost too good to be true. Now I had to see how I would fit in with the rest of her family. I kept thinking about one of my favorite quotes, *"Change how you see…see how you change."* Changes were definitely in the air.

CHAPTER 7

✦

Meet the Family

"So what do you think?" I asked Joanne who was hanging out at my house on Halloween. She had dropped by right after work to help with the festivities.

Since it was our first Halloween together, I was showing off the wild black and orange wig I loved to wear on one of my favorite holidays. The wig was fashioned after those worn in the original Broadway play *Cats*. Since 1984, I had donned the wig each year at work and whenever I handed out candy at my front door.

"Oh my god, that's crazy," Joanne exclaimed with some reservation.

Even though she was not wild about Halloween, she was willing to accept my enthusiasm. She had even agreed to attend one of my friend's annual parties in costume the following night as long as she could be an elegant cat. I suspected that she would have preferred to skip the costume and observe others from the sidelines, but her all-black cat costume with full makeup also provided some anonymity. In contrast, I would be dressed like Roy Rogers, my favorite childhood TV cowboy, complete with cowboy hat, checked shirt, chaps, and a tiny mask that hardly hid my true identity.

"Do you want to try it on?" I took off the wig and handed it to her.

"Yeah, sure," she said as she reluctantly took the wig. "But I'm not really into wigs."

When she put the wig on, we laughed together at her image in the mirror. Although the spikey wig had a drastic effect, transforming her into a cool punk rock star, pretending did not seem to be one of her favorite pastimes.

"I like to wear it when I hand out candy to the kids and see their shocked faces when I open the door," I explained. "Sometimes one of them will ask me if the hair is real. I tell them *Sure, I just had it done today. Do you like it?*" We both started to laugh at my playful side.

"You're nuts," she informed me as she took the wig off. "But you know I'm not wearing that tomorrow night at the party, right? I'll be uncomfortable enough being in a house full of lesbians."

At least she laughed a little. Days before, she had already expressed her reticence about the event, despite my reassurances that she would be among very interesting and fun-loving women.

But I understood her message about wearing the wild wig. Even if it had been from the Broadway show, she would never choose to be the kind of cat that stood out in a crowd. Thoughts of the showy drag queens on our Provincetown weekend came to mind when Joanne had been content to observe from afar.

Christine loved Halloween as much as I did. Along with collecting candy, she always loved the homemade costumes I had created for her since she was able to walk. Now, at eleven years old, she was creating costumes on her own as her artistic talent bloomed. This year, she wanted to be a dead jockey. How she came up with this idea was a mystery, but her theme was not too surprising considering her passion for riding horses. At least she already had the riding helmet.

As Christine was getting ready to join her fellow goblins that would soon swarm the neighborhood en masse, Joanne was watching her apply gory makeup with the help of the bathroom mirror. Fake blood, green eye shadow, and black scars on a white foundation amazingly transformed her beautiful face to a scary spectacle in minutes. Joanne was genuinely impressed.

"Christine, that's excellent," she told her. "Would you help me with my makeup tomorrow night?" While her request was genuine, I sensed that her ultimate goal was to bond with my daughter and I loved her even more for her kindness.

From Christine's beaming face, I could tell she was happy that Joanne had asked for her help. They had recently exchanged makeup and nail polish information like girlie-girl cohorts. Even though she was too young to wear daily makeup, she was absorbing cosmetic tips for future use. I was just relieved I was off the hook with this part of her education. Our first

Halloween together turned out to be a huge success for all of us, including the dead jockey.

It had been four months since Joanne and I had met and we were crazy about each other—mind, body, and spirit. Despite our individual responsibilities at home and work, we created time together in every way possible. Whether it was a short phone call after work, a quick walk in the neighborhood, or longer hours for dinner and a movie, we loved sharing every minute.

As we began weaving our lives together, we did not dwell on any possible obstacles ahead since this relationship felt different from the others when I had been wearing blinders. This time, the foundation was being laid with equally solid bricks that seemed strong enough to withstand whatever challenge came along. We couldn't imagine otherwise.

Part of the tapestry we were weaving had to include our families. Since both of us had strong ties to our immediate and extended families, we were certain to meet everyone eventually. Joanne's family lived locally while most of my relatives lived at least two hours away in Massachusetts. So far, we had had only quick introductions to Joanne's close family members when our paths happened to cross and one gathering in August with my family in Massachusetts. The occasions when we would meet more relatives, of course, would be during picnics, birthday parties, and the approaching holidays. Despite the smooth waters so far, I remained apprehensive as this new phase continued to evolve.

"Do we have everything?" Joanne asked as we gathered the last tote bags from my spacious kitchen. It was a hot humid day prior to our Province-town adventure. With her white, V-neck cotton top, light blue-stripped capris and sexy sandals, she looked as enticing and fresh as clean sheets.

"I think we have everything," I said as I made my way to the front door with Christine close behind. "The salad and brownies are already in my car."

The day before, I had made my legendary mandarin orange tossed salad and Nana's brownies for my family's annual end-of-summer picnic. We were headed to my brother Ray's house in western Massachusetts where he and his family hosted the gathering every year. As this trip would be Joanne's first, I was looking forward to sharing my family with her.

"Aren't we taking Joanne's car?" Christine asked hopefully as we descended the porch steps. She thought Joanne's new car was pretty cool…much more so than my boring station wagon. She also disliked the long drive, especially without Buddy who was content to stay home curled in his bed.

"No, my dear," I replied as I chuckled to myself. I often thought Christine had been a princess in another life, enjoying the finer things in life. "At least you'll have the whole backseat to yourself." She moaned a little.

"Maybe next time we can take my car when I know the way," Joanne told her as we approached my car. Even though I already had no doubt she would make this trip many more times, I also loved hearing her comment about our future together. In just a short time, we already felt bonded enough that I couldn't imagine a future without her.

We piled into the car and headed out. Once on the highway, Joanne turned to me.

"So tell me again who's going to be there?" she asked. Since I had been out to my relatives for several years, Joanne was only slightly nervous about meeting them. She already had a sense that they would welcome her with open arms.

I went through the list of relatives gathering today. My younger brother, his wife, and three young daughters were hosting the party at their rural house with an aboveground pool. My younger sister, her husband, and three older children who still called me *Auntie Loop*, would travel an hour from their home on a lake. Fortunately, my mother and her brother, our Uncle Ken, were visiting from Florida to join us as well. Four of my cousins and their two adorable toddler girls would round out the lively group. I was proud of my family and knew Joanne would fit right in.

While the long drive began on the highway, we eventually cruised on winding country roads through wooded mountains that made my ears pop. As the car droned and conversation ceased, it wasn't long before Christine and Joanne nodded off while I enjoyed the ride. When my passengers woke up from their snoozing, they loved watching the cozy houses and large fields pass by with the occasional grazing horse or cow. Serenity and peace prevailed outside as well as inside the car.

When we finally pulled into Ray's crowded driveway, we could hear the laughter and chatter coming from the backyard. Splashing in the pool had already commenced. Not only was I excited that Joanne was meeting my family, but I was also proud to introduce her.

Loaded down with our belongings and food, we made our way into the house and then to the back deck where everyone had gathered. As the seated adults gabbed away, my brother puttered with the grill while the kids yelled "*Marco...Polo!*" from the pool on the lower deck. Christine quickly joined her cousins.

"Hi there," I announced to the group as I put my arm around Joanne. "We finally made it." To my surprise, her body seemed to stiffen at my touch as if any display of our affection was forbidden in front of family. I hoped she could eventually relax.

A boisterous *Hello!* chorus sounded as everyone stood up for greetings. Joanne hung back a little until my sister came up to us, hugged her and said, "Welcome to the family."

Despite their reserved New England nature, all of my relatives echoed the same message to her with their kind words and welcoming gestures. Joanne's anxiety level seemed to drop as she melted into the party.

From then on, the festive picnic carried on with warm conversation, bursts of laughter, and the happy noise of a good time. At times we would reminisce about Ken's wife, my Aunt Millie, or my father, Ralph, affectionately nicknamed *The Ralphers*, both of whom died from cancers in recent years. Their spirits hung around us like soft whispers.

Joanne talked with everyone and easily engaged in conversations whether we were standing together or not. Every now and then we would catch each other's eye and smile with love. I was happy that she was having a good time and even more pleased that we could be ourselves. As I enjoyed introducing her to my family, however, I imagined that the scene might be different with Joanne's family since she preferred to hide in the closet. While I had played that game for years, I did not look forward to the familiar pretense.

My family gathered again at my house on the Sunday before Thanksgiving because some of my relatives could not make it on the holiday itself. This schedule change left it open for Christine and me to attend Joanne's family celebration on the holiday at her sister's house nearby. Although I already knew they were a loving family, I was still nervous about meeting them.

"I'm sorry I'm not out to my family, honey, but I just can't right now," she said as we talked about the gathering planned for the next day.

She had already confided in her cousin Carole Ann, but she was fearful about revealing our relationship to anyone else in her family. Since Joanne had preferred to keep her love life separate from the relatives most of her life, even her boyfriends had rarely met her family.

"I have to go over to Joyce's house early to help her set up," she explained. "So I'll meet you and Christine there." Although I wasn't exactly happy about this arrangement, I accepted her decision with love.

"Okay," I replied reluctantly. "I understand but I can't say it's going to be easy to pretend I'm just your friend." We looked at each other with serious faces, trying to respect each other's position.

While I felt sad about having to hide again, I knew I could play the role. After all, I had had plenty of practice for years. But even though Christine would be with me, I was already feeling lonely just thinking about the charade and driving over there in separate cars.

With Joanne's large family, there would be a full house for Thanksgiving. In addition to Joyce, her husband, and fourteen-year-old daughter, Carissa, Joanne's mother, Anita aka *Annie,* would be there at least for part of the time, depending on her father who was chronically ill at home. Eight of their respected aunts and uncles would grace the large table while several cousins, including Carole Ann, would either come for dinner or later for coffee an'. Thanksgiving for Joanne's family was traditionally an open house so the guest list was fluid.

On the day of the holiday, Christine and I dressed in our church clothes and drove over to Joyce's house, not really knowing what to expect. Parking on the street lined with cars, I gathered my bag as Christine carried the small colorful flower arrangement we brought as a hostess gift.

As we approached the ranch-style house and the sound of voices and laughter grew, Joanne's smiling face appeared at the door that led into the kitchen.

"Hi," she said as she opened the door and gave us quick hugs. "C'mon in and meet the family." She looked at me with an extra shot of love that melted some of my anxiety.

The crowded house was filled with a happy chaos of people talking, dishes clinking and pots clanging as the meal was prepared. Every available space was packed with additional small tables and chairs while relatives inched their way around speeding children, barking dogs, and people planted in conversation. The delicious aromas of Thanksgiving dinner tantalized my appetite.

"Joyce, come over here a minute," Joanne called out to her younger sister who looked like a mini tornado of activity.

"Okay," she called back and hurried over to us. Slightly taller than Joanne with longer wavy dark hair and a round attractive face, Joyce was a bubbly personality.

"This is my friend, Linda, and her daughter, Christine," Joanne explained to her younger sister.

"Oh hi, welcome," Joyce smiled and shook my hand. Christine handed her the flowers.

"Oh thank you! These are beautiful," she exclaimed to Christine. "Come on in and make yourselves at home." Then she was off and running to the next task as one of the kitchen crew asked her a question.

Joanne continued to introduce us, but we didn't get far before we were stopped by a tiny, elderly lady with big glasses. With the biggest smile and hands extended to cup our faces, she joyfully said, "I am so glad to see you again. Where have you been? I haven't seen you in ages." It was the best greeting Christine and I had ever received at any occasion.

Joanne put her arm around the little lady's shoulders and told her, "Auntie, this is my friend, Linda, and her daughter, Christine." Auntie's eyes looked a little confused but she kept smiling with genuine love.

We later learned that she had early Alzheimer's disease which explained her initial confusion about our identities. Nonetheless, her exuberant kindness meant a lot and was just what we needed at that moment.

With every introduction and conversation, I felt that we were being enfolded into this large Italian family like chicks under mother hen's tender wing. I could see that these people were accustomed to welcoming close friends and more of my anxiety melted away. However, I still wondered if the reception would have been different with the truth revealed.

Before the dinner courses began, Carissa was kind enough to take Christine under her wing for kid fun while the grownups chatted over glasses of wine. Laughter and love filled the air while I sipped my wine and watched my new love out of the corner of my eye. As soon as Christine returned to her seat beside me, Joanne stood near the big table and raised her voice to quiet the noisy group.

"Settle down, everyone," she announced in her director's voice. "We're ready for the prayer." She waited until it was quiet. "Uncle Al, would you like to say Grace?" As the oldest among the aunts and uncles, Joanne recognized Uncle Al's respected status in the family.

"No, you go ahead," he said as he waved his hand for Joanne to have the honor. She didn't hesitate.

"Okay then," she replied, almost eager to move the day along. In a strong voice she spoke from her heart.

"Our heavenly Father, we come to you today in gratitude for the people around this table and the abundant food before us. Thank you for all your blessings as we enjoy this day together. We also remember the ones we love who can't be here with us, but we're glad they're here in spirit. Thank you for your love and grace always. Amen."

As heads lifted and cousins rose from their seats to serve food, the sound level started to rise as if a volume dial was being turned up. In no time, Italian wedding soup with fresh crispy bread was served. Then salad. Then pasta. I was already stuffed and these were just the first courses. There was a whole Thanksgiving dinner ahead.

With a break in the action, everyone settled back in their seats. During the lull, I overheard some conversation at the big table while the aunts and uncles paused between courses.

Auntie Sue, married to Uncle Mario who was one of the brothers, said to Joanne's mother, "Annie, how is Ralph doing?"

Like my father, Ralph was also the name of Joanne's dad who was not joining us, as he was ill.

"He's as mean as ever," she replied with exasperation in her voice. "I know he's not feeling well, but he drives me crazy." Auntie Sue nodded knowingly.

Everyone in the family was sympathetic to Annie who seemed to have the opposite personality to Ralph. I had already heard stories that he had also been particularly hard on Joanne throughout her childhood. Annie, however, was active, kind, and loving to everyone.

"Joyce," Joanne called out as she gathered dirty dishes from the tables, "is the gravy still on the stove? Turn it off before it burns," she directed her sister who seemed flustered with too many things to do at once.

In the next minute, Joanne told Carissa, "Help Auntie Gen back to her seat next to Uncle Gene. And then see if anyone needs anything to drink at that table." Carissa did not hesitate to respond.

Observing that Joanne was clearly in charge, my admiration grew as I watched her operate. Her family, especially her sister, seemed to appreciate her ability to organize and expedite every course. In the months since we had met, I often glimpsed her take-charge attitude when making decisions, solving problems, or confronting difficult people. She was definitely a woman of action.

In no time, a full turkey dinner with all the trimmings was set before us. Despite my already full stomach, the display of colors and aromas on our plates tempted both Christine and me once more and we ate as if we'd been fasting all day. Everything was delicious.

Despite Joanne's silent concern for my comfort throughout the day, she, along with all the cousins, was constantly bobbing up and down serving food, clearing plates, and offering wine or coffee, especially to the aunts and uncles. I tried to do my part with cleaning up but was reassured that I should sit and relax.

At one point, Joanne sat down at the big table for a few minutes to visit the aunts and uncles.

"So Joanne, are you dating anyone?" Auntie Mickie, Al's wife, asked her. My ears perked up.

"Oh Auntie, I don't have time for that," Joanne laughed it off.

Since no one else continued the questioning, I had the impression that privacy was highly respected among this family. When no further information was offered, it was time to move on to a different topic. I felt relieved for Joanne, but uncomfortable for myself as I was bursting to let them know how much I cared for her.

Carole Ann, who sat at my table, caught my eye and smiled knowingly. Throughout the meal, she had been gracious and gratefully kept me company as dessert was served. The mouth-watering array of desserts also brought Christine back to her seat.

As her eyes widened with delight at the sweets, Carole Ann told her, "You really should have the cherry cheesecake. Uncle Gene makes it every year and it's the best." That's all she had to hear as she reached for a piece.

Christine was hooked on this family as if she had Italian blood running through her veins. I could see she was having a good time and, like most kids focused on their own world, did not seem to notice any pretending going on at all.

Throughout the day, I was grateful for the loving atmosphere and warm reception of Joanne's relatives, despite the pretense of her current dating status. When asked how we became friends, her clever pat answer was, "Our offices are only a block away," implying that our jobs were entwined. While I wondered how long we would keep up the façade, I also knew my love for Joanne was greater than these minor discomforts.

Feeling as stuffed as the turkey when it was time to leave, we made the rounds for our goodbyes and thank yous. Warm smiles and good wishes from everyone. As Joanne gave me a quick hug, she whispered that she would stop over after she was done helping her sister clean up. That news warmed my heart because I had reached my limit with pretending.

With our coats on waiting by the back door, Joyce came over, gave us big hugs and said, "I'm so glad you could come. Hope to see you again."

I'm sure you will, I thought as we headed out the door.

A series of first holiday celebrations with our families followed in much the same manner with some creative scheduling in order to balance our time. With Christmas approaching, we looked forward to our favorite family traditions such as the candlelight service at my church and Joanne's Italian seven fish dinner, both on Christmas Eve.

The seven fish dinner tradition comes from Southern Italy but has evolved in America as a fish and seafood dinner with family and friends on Christmas Eve. In Joanne's family, the menu usually included smelt, baked scrod or whitefish, snail salad, spaghetti with clams and baccala, which is a dried salted cod. Christine loved everything while I loved the gathering… and maybe the scrod. With these family feasts, honest communication, and equal sacrifice, Joanne and I were slowly learning to share our time with the people we loved.

Attending family group events, however, was not conducive to getting to know individual relatives. One-on-one encounters happened more often with Joanne's immediate family than mine, since they lived nearby. More advanced planning would be necessary for Joanne to get to know my mother, for instance, who lived in Florida at the time.

Even though Joanne had told me stories about her parents, I had only met her mother briefly at that Thanksgiving dinner and a couple of birthday parties that followed. She was always pleasant toward me and I could see the kindness on her face as she interacted with everyone around her.

I already knew she worked hard, especially caring for Joanne's father, and had sacrificed much for her family. Anita was also a legendary shopper, always finding the best bargains. Joanne usually went shopping with her on Sundays and, most likely, honed her own shopping skills during these trips.

One day, Joanne told me a story about her mother that was not well known in her family circle but that touched me deeply.

"My mother had a difficult time when she was pregnant with me," Joanne explained. "I don't know what the exact problem was, but the doctors told her that she shouldn't go through with it." Her face was serious. "They told her she could die if she had me." Now I was serious too as I listened intently.

"My mother thought about what they told her but she was determined to have me," she continued. "So against the odds, she essentially told them to go to hell. After that, she made it through the pregnancy without a problem. I'm here only because my mother was tough."

Joanne's eyes filled up. So did mine. In the following silence, I rested my hand on hers.

"I'm so thankful to your mom," I whispered. I had seen her only a few times, but I already loved and respected Annie.

I had never met Joanne's father, Ralph, and of course she never met mine, who had died from bladder cancer years before. From the stories I had heard, her father, unlike mine, was a very cranky patient whose health was rapidly declining from a myriad of ailments. Even before his illness, he had a reputation for being a mean bastard so his current pain only added more barnacles to his attitude. The only person who seemed to melt any corner of his heart was Carissa, his only grandchild, who loved taking care of him. Nonetheless, Joanne did not intend for me to meet him, fearing he would say something hurtful or make a scene. I didn't want that either.

Little did I know how fate would bring her father and me together for our first meeting. The scene was not what I had expected.

CHAPTER 8

∞

No More Tequila

After our first holidays, we decided we needed a break from family obligations. Despite her father's declining health, Joanne's family encouraged her to keep her vacation plans. Since a trip to an all-inclusive resort in Cancun at the end of January had seemed like a great idea, we switched gears and focused on fun. I collected the maps and Joanne pored over the guidebooks for possible activities. When the day came, we took a Greyhound bus from Rhode Island to Boston's Logan Airport as we looked forward to a new exotic adventure together. It felt like a honeymoon.

After a long travel day that included a small bus ride through poor, run-down neighborhoods of Mexico, we arrived at our resort. In contrast, the grounds were breathtakingly beautiful with tall palm trees, gentle breezes, fine-trimmed green lawns, tropical gardens bursting with color, and hammocks swaying over white sand beaches. The low buildings were immaculate inside and out. Narrow winding terracotta pathways connected the buildings to the sparkling pool areas where white-coated staff tended to guests in lounge chairs.

Feeling that we had been transported to a new tropical heaven, we quickly settled into our room on the second floor that overlooked the courtyard and ocean beyond. In Cancun, unlike Provincetown, Joanne was less inhibited about showing her affection, so the masks were off. Since we certainly did not want to be arrested in a foreign country, however, holding hands in public was not always a good idea. But we generally felt free.

Our week was filled with sipping pineapple drinks on the beach, snorkeling, zooming on jet skis, visiting Mayan ruins where Joanne tried to make friends with the iguanas, eating out, taking the local bus into town, and even taking risks dancing the night away at a remote gay bar.

Before we left Rhode Island, I had investigated the possibility of a gay scene in Cancun.

"Honey, I have a list of gay bars and even a gay beach. Would you want to check them out?" I asked one snowy day while we perused our trip information.

"Maybe. Let's see when we get there," she had said with a sense of adventure. As our love deepened, Joanne had been increasingly open to new possibilities.

After a couple days in Cancun, we had settled in and were feeling confident about finding our way around the resort and in parts of town. One afternoon as we lounged under the palms, Joanne turned to me.

"So where is this gay beach? Have you found it on the map?" she asked. I was absolutely shocked to hear her question.

"Well, the directions in the guidebook are a little vague," I replied. "I think I found the name of it on the map but so far, I haven't seen any signs along the road."

"Maybe if we find that gay bar tonight we could ask about the beach." Joanne was smiling as if she were the Cheshire Cat. I looked at her with my jaw hanging open like a codfish.

Thinking the tropical air had affected her brain, I was a bit stunned that Joanne was the one to make such a daring suggestion. Even though she accepted her bisexuality, attending gay venues had not always been comfortable as she had one foot in each world. This turn of events was a pleasant surprise.

"Sure," I said without hesitation. "I've already looked at the address and closest bus stop." Thank goodness I loved maps.

That night after dinner at the resort, we hopped on the local bus and headed out on our adventure. Although the bus brought us to the stop we wanted, we didn't expect the neighborhood to be so deserted. While some cars rolled along on the four-lane street, only a handful of pedestrians were on the sidewalks. At least there were streetlights. It was only then that we looked at each other wondering if this was such a good idea. But we were determined to find our destination.

"Here it is," I said as we looked at the sign on the stone building. I had to admit I was a little nervous.

"Well, we're here now. We might as well go in," Joanne decided as she led the way.

When we opened the door to the dimly lit bar, the blasting music told us we were in the right place. As our eyes adjusted to the lower light, we observed that the lively crowd was mostly men sitting at tables or at the bar, talking and laughing. Many were dancing to the loud music and some spotted us as we joined the scene. Friendly smiles and greetings made us feel right at home. The only problem that seemed to slip our minds was that we didn't speak Spanish.

Luckily, we knew *cerveza*, the word for beer, and *por favor*, so we ordered a couple beers and found seats at one of the large, round tables. "Do you want to dance?" I asked Joanne.

She didn't hesitate as we pushed our chairs back and found some space on the dance floor. Even in a foreign country, letting loose in a gay atmosphere felt liberating.

Returning to our table, we found a young man sitting with us who was eager to say hello…in English. With a mix of communication, he explained that he was so happy to find us so he could practice the few English words he knew. His partner sat quietly next to him as we tried to connect. Unfortunately, he had no information about the gay beach we were looking for, but we enjoyed the effort. Seems we both needed more language practice.

As we stepped back into the night after our bar encounter, Joanne exclaimed, "I can't believe we did that! We must be nuts." Now there were even fewer pedestrians on the street which added to the eerie atmosphere.

"I know," I said. "But it was fun, wasn't it?" With inflated confidence, we chose to ignore the quiet streets as if we had just climbed Everest.

"Yes, it was and I loved doing it with you," she answered as she took my hand while we walked to the bus stop. Joanne's true colors as a daring partner and explorer were showing and I loved that spicy side of her.

Every day in Cancun we were careful to drink only bottled water, avoiding salads that might be rinsed in tap water and using hand sanitizer. By the end of the week, we were pretty proud of ourselves for avoiding Montezuma's Revenge. Everything quickly changed, however, on Friday night, the day before we were leaving.

Earlier that night, we had taken the bus into town for dinner at a nice restaurant and then hopped to a couple bars for drinks. Since I was pretty loose and filled with bravado by the time we reached the last crowded bar, I accepted a tequila Jell-O shot from the waitress who was passing them out like candy.

It was on the bus ride back to the resort when I knew I was in trouble.

"I'm not feeling so good," I slurred as I started to feel my legs giving out. We were at our stop and the door was open for us to disembark.

"Here, let me help you," Joanne said as she reached for my arm and helped me with each step down off the bus. Somehow I walked into the resort and up to our room holding onto her.

"I'm sorry," I kept repeating as I landed on the bed. I was vaguely aware that Joanne was helping me undress and get under the covers. Sinking into oblivion, I was soon gone.

But not for long. The next few hours felt like a continuous push through a revolving door from the bed to the bathroom and back. I had never been so sick—in every possible way—and it just wouldn't end. Whether I slept or not was just a blur.

When the alarm went off early the next morning, I was not much better.

"Lin, we have to get up and pack." Joanne was gently shaking my arm. "We can't miss the bus to the airport."

I just moaned. The thought of moving my body, never mind preparing for travel, made my stomach churn.

"I'm going down to get some coffee and a muffin or something," she said. "Try to sit up and drink some water. Can I get you anything?" Joanne heard me moan again before she left the room for a few minutes. I didn't know how I would survive the day. This curse had to be more than a hangover.

Returning with her food and a ginger ale for me, Joanne sighed at my sorry state knowing what she had to do. After reviving herself and without any complaint or judgment, she went to work packing both suitcases and helping me get dressed. Even though I could not eat a thing, I did manage some sips of the soda. Finally, by the grace of God and Joanne's help, I made it down to the lobby to wait for our bus.

"I don't know how you're going to ride on the bus," Joanne said as I slumped on the couch with my eyes closed.

"Maybe you should just let me die here," I responded and tried to smile. "Or just pull me along like the luggage and I'll have to follow." Joanne smiled too and put her hand on mine.

The rest of the travel day was a blur of bumpy bus rides, waiting in the airport either in a seat or in a corner on the floor, and sleeping on the plane. Miraculously, I did not get sick. Even Joanne marveled at that.

By the time we reached Boston and the interstate bus terminal, I was still weak but more alert. My constant thought was that if it hadn't been for Joanne I would still be in Mexico. While I thanked her profusely all the way to Rhode Island, I vowed to never sip tequila again.

It was late at night when the bus pulled into the terminal in Providence. To our surprise, Joyce was waiting for us. She was angry as she approached.

"Joanne, you have to come with me," she said curtly. "Dad died yesterday."

Joanne put her hand to her mouth. "Oh no," she cried as the tears formed in her eyes.

"I had no way to reach you." Joyce was upset and looked at me as if I was to blame.

Before I had time to express my condolences, Joanne and her suitcase were whisked into Joyce's car and they were driving away. As I stared at them leaving the parking lot, I couldn't believe how lonely I felt after such a wonderful week. Even my excruciating intestinal plague didn't matter anymore.

As I slowly made my way to my car and drove home, I had no idea what would happen next.

During the next week, I did hear from Joanne who apologized more than once for the abrupt departure at the bus station. She also explained how her father had died at home and that everyone in the family considered his death a blessing in light of his suffering.

Even though I realized that the funeral would be another event when I would be Joanne's friend, not her lover, I wanted to express my sincere sympathies to her family. Attending the wake was certainly more important to me than my own distress.

After driving to the funeral home alone, I entered the building with the usual gracious greetings from formally dressed staff at the door. Not recognizing any familiar faces as I made my way to the correct parlor, I continued to the guest book table outside the doorway where I signed in.

Entering any funeral room always brings tears to my eyes even if the deceased is a stranger. This time was no exception. I quickly spotted Joanne across the room as she stood in the receiving line with her family. But she did not see me until I was standing in line to visit the casket. When we locked eyes, she smiled that beautiful smile.

Studying the picture collages on display along the wall, I continued to inch my way toward her father. To me, pictures at a funeral honor and summarize the person's years of joys and tears. In a few short minutes, I was taking a glimpse of Joanne's father and getting to know him just by looking at his family photos. With his family around him, he displayed a reserved smile. But in other shots, he was working in the garden, hugging Joyce or holding baby Carissa, showing a softer side.

When I reached the open casket, I knelt down and folded my hands. Gazing at his serene facial expression, I noted the physical resemblance to Joanne.

In my mind, I said *Hello Ralph. I'm Linda. It's strange that I'm saying hello and goodbye to you in one breath. I didn't know you but maybe you know me now. If you do, you know I love your daughter and that it's okay. Rest in God's peace. Amen.*

I rose from the kneeler and proceeded to the head of the receiving line where Joanne's mother stood to greet me. After a brief hug and a few sincere words, I went down the line thinking I would like to get to know her. No one could have guessed that I would have that chance in the months to come.

CHAPTER 9

Wigs and Hair

For several days after the fateful shower and first clump of hair, Joanne's hair now appeared on the floor, on her pillow, and in the bathroom sink. Mercifully, it was a gradual process, but her hair was definitely falling out every day. It was as if there was a third cat shedding in the house. The other two cats, longhaired queen tabby Rosie and younger black and white jester Charlie, were surprisingly oblivious to the extra hair in the house.

"I guess it's time for me to make an appointment at that wig shop," Joanne announced one day, knowing that step also meant having her head shaved.

We already had a recommendation for a good shop and a prescription for a *cranial prosthesis* that sounded as if she would receive a new head. The insurance company required those specific words in order to pay for a basic wig. The cost could be anywhere between two and five hundred dollars.

"It sure looks like the time has come I'm afraid," I said. "I'll take time off from work and come with you no matter what day it is." We both knew how traumatic such an event could be.

"Well, I want to make sure the appointment is after Uncle Al's birthday party on Sunday," Joanne added. "I don't want him to know I have cancer, and a bald head would be too much of a shock." Even though her hair was thinning, she was confident in her skill with gel and hairspray to create her normal look…at least through Sunday.

Joanne loved all of her ten aunts and uncles, especially Uncle Al who was turning 102. He had remained active all of his life and was known as a savvy investor who loved to advise Joanne about the stock market. Also an avid golfer, he and Uncle Gene had played a round with Joanne and me when Al was ninety-six. The two uncles beat us easily but enjoyed handing out appreciated golf tips to us along the way.

Even though Uncle Al's mind remained alert and engaged with current events and email, his body was now wearing out from chronic congestive heart failure. With the loving care of family, he was able to stay in his home with the determination to attend his big birthday party on March 23. Joanne did not want to worry Uncle Al with her diagnosis. She figured his heart was weak enough without additional heartache.

Whether Joanne would feel well enough to attend this party, however, was uncertain. During the past month, we found ourselves in a weekly routine of sorts with chemo infusions. Our new normal now included days of manageable symptoms, lost days sleeping on the couch, good days for driving into the office, and fun days for short visits with family and friends. Time for blood work, acupuncture, and massages filled in the spaces. We could never really predict Joanne's stamina for anything so our schedule was always tentative.

The day of the party had arrived. Since she hadn't slept very well the night before, Joanne was dragging herself to get ready.

"Are you sure you can make it today?" I asked, concerned when I saw her struggle.

"I have to go," she said with the same determination I imagined Uncle Al felt. "And besides, I can always leave early if I have to." Joanne had learned more than stock market advice from him. "At least my appetite is better today."

"And I have to say your hair looks great," I added as she smiled in the mirror.

About forty friends and family were expected to arrive at a favorite local Italian restaurant that was well known for its homemade-style dishes, friendly wait staff, and comfortable large event rooms. Several family functions had been held there in years past, including Uncle Al's seventy-third wedding anniversary with Auntie Mickey who had since died.

The room for his birthday party was actually a large space off the main dining area that had been decorated with balloons and flowers. I especially liked the gigantic balloon arrangement of three separate Mylar balloons in the shape of the numbers, one, zero, and two. We were all gathered and chatting at the tables, waiting for the centenarian star to arrive. Other patrons in the restaurant occasionally glanced over and smiled as they were swept into our excitement and anticipation.

Finally, someone announced that Uncle Al was on his way from the parking lot. Even though this wasn't a surprise party, it sure felt like one. As his wheelchair was rolled into the restaurant, everyone in the building started clapping and cheering. I tried to ignore the wheelchair that signified how weak he really was. Until recently, he always had a quick step and would have waved a wheelchair away. Now I had an ominous feeling that his time was short. The concerned looks on his family's faces told me I wasn't alone.

As he approached the party room, Uncle Al's face was radiant with a huge smile and laughing eyes. Someone had placed a cardboard birthday crown on the top of his full head of hair. With all the excitement, he could have been Jesus on Palm Sunday.

As everyone settled around large round tables, an atmosphere of love and laughter also settled on Uncle Al's nieces, nephews, and close family friends. We spent the next two hours honoring a much-loved patriarch of Joanne's family. Despite the fatigue on his face, Uncle Al soon offered a few words to the group, thanking everyone and expressing his love for his family.

At one point in his speech, he said, "I'm so glad I made it here today." Then, with a chuckle he continued, "You know, anyone can get to 101…I was determined to make it to 102 and I did," he said proudly. Everyone smiled as another round of applause exploded around the tables.

Throughout the celebration, Joanne ate more than usual and waited on Uncle Al whenever she could. I knew she was exhausted, but she hid it well. Even though some of her close family members knew about her illness, they did not discuss it during the party…at least, not within earshot. If Uncle Al had suspected Joanne's condition, he never let on. Her focus was on her family, not herself.

Two days after the party, Joanne and I arrived at the Golden Rose Wig Shoppe for our appointment that had been arranged after hours allowing for privacy. We had learned online that the small business was owned and operated by a mother-daughter team who catered to women with cancer. The reviews had been glowing.

We pulled into a parking space in front of the shop that was located on the end of a small strip of stores on a busy commercial street. Feeling somewhat anxious and afraid about this next leap into the unknown, Joanne forged ahead with the inevitable bald head.

But she was on the fence about the wig. She knew she would probably use one for special occasions and, of course, visiting Uncle Al whose health was failing more each day. But wearing a wig every day was questionable. Fortunately as an option, she had also discovered many attractive head coverings online that spoke to her feminine style.

Before we got out of the car, I put my hand on hers and squeezed it as she held mine tight for a moment. We looked at each and took a deep breath. At the last minute, Joanne smiled and said, "I just hope my head is a good shape." I had to laugh to myself. While I had been worried about her emotions, I had forgotten her concern about the shape of her head.

As I opened and held the shop door for Joanne, we entered a new world of Styrofoam heads covered in wigs of every style, shape, and color. Hues of brown, blonde, gray, and black in styles that were wavy, straight, curly, short, long, and shoulder length gave the impression of a hairdressers' convention.

Some heads were sitting on three-tiered shelves along the walls on our left, many heads hung from the ceiling, and even more wigs adorned tall hat-tree stands that stood proudly for inspection. On the right side of the room, two empty hairdresser chairs facing large wall mirrors were poised for wig fittings and, of course, hair removal. We started to browse through the aisles just as the owner's daughter came out from the back of the store.

"Hi, I'm Michelle. Are you Joanne?" she asked calmly. In her early forties with dark medium-length hair and compassionate eyes, Michelle shook our hands and encouraged us to look around while she gathered the required paperwork Joanne had brought with her. She had also brought pictures of her usual hairstyle knowing that the chosen wig could be cut and colored to match.

After Joanne had asked some questions about the procedure, choice of synthetic or natural materials, and of course, cost, she told Michelle, "I'm not really sure how often I'll wear a wig, so I'm also interested in the head coverings you have here." An array of turbans, scarves, and hats were on display in the glass counter case and along the back wall.

"Certainly," she replied. "I can show you how to wrap them so they'll stay on and look nice too." Joanne's face lit up as if she had just won the lottery.

As we perused the sea of classy-looking wigs, I leaned over to Joanne and whispered, "I think you should get a wig like Hedda Lettuce." An image of the green drag queen on a scooter flashed in my mind.

"Okay," she chuckled, "but I don't think we'll find one here."

She was right. There were no funky wigs on display like those found in a Halloween store or a shop in Provincetown.

Joanne's current hairstyle was like the celebrity, Sharon Osborne: dark brown with reddish highlights, layered and feathery, longer in the back to the base of her neck, and somewhat spiked on top. It looked good on Sharon, but even better on Joanne.

"I'm sure we have one like that," said Michelle as she examined the pictures we brought. "And we can also adjust the color and trim it to your style and length on the next visit."

Michelle located a couple wigs that came close to Joanne's hair, but the fit could only be made after her hair was buzzed. The time had come for her to climb into one of the chairs by the mirror. I sat in one of the waiting room chairs by the door.

Joanne seemed nonchalant as she chatted with Michelle who expertly prepared her tools and kept the conversation going. Her compassion and understanding were evident when she shared personal stories of close family members who had also endured cancer treatments.

The quiet buzzing of the trimmers began as the conversation continued. Joanne stared intently into the mirror as I kept my eye on her. A few minutes later when the buzzing stopped, Joanne had a fuzzy head. The conversation stopped as we absorbed the shocking moment.

Here was the same face I loved, but she looked so different without hair. I was amazed at the transformation. She put a hand on her head and lightly rubbed her new look.

"Wow," was all she could say as she turned to look at me.

The deed was done.

In that second, we knew her cancer was real and the battle was on. Joanne had just joined an army of cancer patients as if she was starting boot camp. *GI Joanne*. Her identity had just changed. She was still the same strong person, of course, but different now…a tough cancer warrior.

Unlike Samson in the Bible who lost his strength when his hair was cut, Joanne was gaining hers by joining other bald sisters for support.

"I can't hide now," Joanne said to me as our eyes locked. In that moment, I felt that she had crossed a line. Commitment to honesty, the strength to be herself, and a pledge to the cause all shown in her glistening eyes.

Michelle told us that dying the wig would be done quickly and that the trim appointment could be made in the next couple days. Joanne decided to wait and investigate the headscarves on display when she returned for the second visit. After expressing our appreciation to Michelle for her compassionate service, Joanne put the warm hat she had brought with her on her head as we walked out the door.

"How does it feel?" I asked back in the car. Meaning both physically and emotionally, I couldn't imagine the feeling.

"It's so weird," she said. "I can't even describe it." She was still in shock. "I'm just glad you were here...and I'm glad I brought a hat because I'm cold," she smiled.

"At least my head is a good shape," she added with glee. I chuckled with her.

"I can come with you for the wig trim if you want," I offered while looking forward to seeing the finished product.

"Thanks, but I think Joyce would like to come with me next time," she replied honestly.

I didn't mind. By this time in our relationship, Joyce and I were good buddies who called each other *Honey* whenever we greeted each other. Years before, I had been uncertain about her acceptance, but it hadn't taken long for us to form a loving sister-in-law bond. We had learned to share Joanne with love and respect. It made sense that she should go with Joanne on the next visit.

As a young adult, Joyce had completed courses for hairdressing and had maintained her license even though she was now an experienced phlebotomist. Naturally, she was interested in Joanne's hair. She also loved her sister very much and wanted to support her in any way she could. Although Joyce admitted she was an emotional person, I often observed her strength and sense of purpose when caring for others. When she accompanied Joanne for the wig trim appointment, I knew the experience meant a lot to both of them.

After I came home from work that day, Joanne presented the new wig and tried it on for show and tell. "What do you think?" she asked.

"Wow, I love it," I exclaimed sincerely. "I can't believe how much it looks like your hair." I thought it was amazing.

Joanne then surprised me by saying, "Now I want you to take a picture of me with my bald head and then with the wig on for your book."

"What book?" I said incredulously. *What in the world is she thinking?* I thought.

"The book I want you to write about us and my cancer journey," she said as a matter of fact.

I just rolled my eyes and decided to humor her, "Yeah, right," I murmured as I took the pictures. *That'll never happen.*

For the next half hour, she explained about the special wig shampoo and cap needed for a snug fit. To Joanne, the cap was especially important. With her concern about style, worrying about a roving wig on her head was not about to happen. So she remained skeptical about this wig business.

By the end of the week when she was feeling better, Joanne visited Uncle Al a couple times at his home and then at the hospice center where he had been transferred. He was getting weaker and weaker. Despite her new sense of openness, she wore the wig for each visit and he was never the wiser. Whether she ever revealed her cancer to him during those visits remains unknown.

On Monday night, March 31, only a week after his birthday party, we received the inevitable phone call that Uncle Al had passed away. Despite our sadness, we knew that he had accomplished his goals: to reach 102, attend his party, reunite with his wife and, undoubtedly, meet his God.

After the wake on Friday night, the funeral was held the next day. Ironically, the collation after the cemetery service was served at the same restaurant as his birthday party. In a more private function room this time, the familiar crowd gathered once again, connecting with love and affection for Uncle Al.

Joanne continued to wear her wig throughout the funeral events even though the wig made her head sweat one minute and freeze the next when she went outside into the cold spring air. At one point, while she was making her way to visit everyone around the tables in the restaurant, she stuck her hand to her head and looked at me in panic.

I knew what had happened…the wig had moved.

Not much, but enough for her to be concerned. She scurried off to the ladies room and later returned with a look of relief on her face. Luckily, she had saved the day but I knew she wasn't happy...no matter how good the wig looked.

As soon as we returned home, she was adamant.

"That's it with the wig. I'm not wearing it anymore," she declared as she removed it from her head, putting it back on its permanent Styrofoam head. No more pretending.

After that near disaster, Joanne's quest for attractive head coverings began in earnest. She found warm caps for winter and lightweight caps for summer, pastel coverings with flowers, sparkling scarves for dress, bright colored toppers tied with a knot on the side, and fleece sleeping caps for nighttime.

One day while we were getting ready to go out to dinner with friends, I watched Joanne expertly tie a fancy mauve scarf that naturally matched her outfit perfectly.

"That looks so nice," I said with affection. I had always been impressed with her appearance and coordinated details.

"Well, you know what my mother always used to say, *Accessories make the woman*," she replied proudly. I had heard this quote many times, especially when my well-meaning wife scrutinized my attire before heading out.

Some of Joanne's mentors for head coverings also included women from the cancer support group she had facilitated at the Hope Center. Since they wore their turbans, large earrings, and beautiful makeup with pride, Joanne followed suit. She may have given up some individuality with her bald head, but she regained it with those stylish headdresses.

As the days and weeks went by, the chemo rollercoaster ride continued speeding toward surgery, the next station. We were operating as if cancer was an uninvited lodger who we tried to ignore as we went about our lives. Sometimes, however, this pest demanded attention that we reluctantly managed with as much combined strength as possible.

On Monday after Uncle Al's funeral, Joanne was scheduled for her seventh chemo infusion. Each week since the end of February, she had received a treatment. This was the week for a double dose again that would mark the final three-week round before surgery. After waiting once more for the platelet count that had to be 100 in order to proceed, we were surprised when the nurse assistant did not collect us. This time, it was Sarah, her chemo nurse, who approached us with a serious face.

"I'm so sorry, Joanne," she said with sincere sympathy. "Your platelet count was only 47. I'm afraid you can't have chemo today."

Our faces dropped as we stared at Sarah. This was the first time we were facing a delay.

"Oh no," Joanne replied. "What happens now?" We really didn't want to postpone anything that might affect the schedule for surgery. No treatment meant the cancer was free to grow. I was afraid to think that the enemy would have the upper hand.

"Don't worry," she replied. "Even though you'll have to wait a week, the next three infusions can be given right up until the surgery date. And even then, the date can be changed. Just try not to get a cut or bruise this week because your platelets are so low." *Yikes*, I thought. *Any infection now could be disastrous.*

After Sarah left the waiting room, I turned to Joanne, "So, I still have the day off. What do you want to do now?"

"Let's go have an early lunch with burgers and beer at that new Irish pub around here," she said without hesitation. Her message was loud and clear: *Carpe diem.*

"Well, the beer is for me...I don't think you should have any."

"Party poop," she replied with a fake scowl.

The rest of the day unfolded without a plan. After lunch, we headed to one of our favorite wooded parks to sit by the lake reading the books we would have read at the infusion center. Since Joanne was feeling energized without chemo, she then suggested we go to the movies, one of my favorite things to do. A day of fun rather than frowns suited us.

When *Captain America* ended and we returned to the car, she finally thought she should return home. While the lesson of the day had been to make the most of every moment, we concluded that we were becoming experts.

Ever since we met, we had operated with a sense of gratitude for each day and moment. Meeting during the second half of our lives when time is more precious no doubt helped to shape our attitude. But I think we knew God gave us a gift that we couldn't waste. Every day was a special holiday together.

Without the negative effects of chemo that week, Joanne's schedule was packed. While her energy level did not match her pep before cancer, she was still able to go to work some days, conduct business as executor of Uncle Al's will, shop for a two-hour stretch, attend a wedding, and help me celebrate my sixty-fifth birthday with takeout and cake at home. Despite what I thought was an amazing week of activity, she was still disappointed that she had to rest while Christine and I went to the golf driving range on my birthday.

Sometimes I appreciated my own space or hours spent with Christine when I allowed myself to forget about cancer for a while. But I missed Joanne on my special day playing golf. I also missed her when I would go to the grocery store alone because she was too tired to walk far, when I watched a movie on TV as she slept soundly on the couch, or when I ate dinner alone when she was too nauseous to eat. With every adjustment, I was missing a part of *us*.

Our cancer education progressed as we experienced each new test result, procedure snafu, and change in side effects. With Joanne's connection to an online blog specifically for women with ovarian cancer, she was learning about different chemo treatments and surgeries as well as how other women coped with their disease. They were becoming online friends as well as advocates for ovarian cancer awareness and research that seemed to need support. As a result, we both started wearing teal-colored wristbands that represent ovarian cancer and recognized September as its designated awareness month, in the same way that October was for breast cancer. In Joanne's heart and mind, her cause had expanded to include the globe.

After the last chemo treatment in late April, we were headed to Dr. D's office for another routine follow-up visit armed with the first question we always asked. *Is the chemo working?* The two tests that usually provided the answer were the CT scans which revealed tumor size and location and the CA 125 blood tests that essentially measured the protein from ovarian cancer cells. If that number went up, we knew the cancer cells had increased. When Joanne was first diagnosed, her CA 125 count was 2,770.

By now, the oncology department was our home away from home. Staff called us by name and we knew the way to several offices, labs, and cafeterias. Joanne checked in at the desk and a few minutes later, we were waiting in an exam room. One of our familiar nurses had already taken vitals and asked Joanne how she was feeling. Now we were anxious to see the doctor.

"Well, good morning," Dr. D. said as he breezed into the room with his warm smile and hand extended to shake hands. Always upbeat, he quickly sat down on the small stool across from Joanne and seemed ready to have lunch with us.

"Fancy meeting you here," Joanne smiled, grateful for his cheerfulness.

"I know...it's such a coincidence," Dr. D. took her cue. "Since I'm here, let me tell you about your recent tests." We had already known that some progress was being made, but we didn't know how it looked for surgery.

"Your CT scan shows that the tumors have decreased in size, and your CA 125 count is down to 222," he continued. "It looks like the chemo has done its job as we had expected." If Dr. D. was pleased, we were too.

He went on to explain that surgery would be extensive in order to remove as much cancer as possible. Joanne would have a complete hysterectomy along with removal of the omentum, which is a fold of abdominal tissue encasing the stomach and other organs. Dr. D. also prepared us with the possibility of a bowel resection if they found cancer cells there. Joanne was not happy with the prospect of needing a colostomy bag. Unbelievably, this would be the first major surgery in her life.

"When is it scheduled?" I asked after I put down my pen and notebook.

Dr. D. looked at his paperwork to be accurate, "It's next Tuesday, May 6, but it depends on the blood work the day before." Those words *it depends* were always popping up and added to the feeling that we were sitting on the edge of our seats. *Lord give us strength* was my daily prayer.

Even though Joanne had other questions about recovery after surgery and the schedule for resuming chemo, we knew some of the answers from our previous discussions with Dr. D. We continued to trust his expertise and optimism.

As the visit ended, Dr. D. said, "So where are you two traveling to next?" He knew we loved to explore new places and we were always after him to tag along.

Joanne was the first to respond, "We're determined to go camping in our RV in July...Boothbay Harbor, Maine. We always go away somewhere for a week for my birthday. Want to come along?"

"How about a cruise? I'll come along for that instead." We all laughed at his more luxurious choice. The truth was, we really liked Dr. D and under different circumstances we would probably be friends outside the hospital.

When the laughter faded, he said, "I know it's been a difficult road, Joanne, but you've done really well tolerating the chemo. I'll do my best for you and we'll get this nasty stuff out."

We both thanked him and trusted him completely. Unless we heard bad news about the upcoming blood work, the next time we saw Dr. D. would be in the hospital on the day of surgery. But, of course, *it all depends.*

CHAPTER 10

❦

A Mother's Love

"I think you should go to the doctor," Joanne scolded me as if I was her ailing child, lying in a feeble state on my couch. "You might have a slight fever," she concluded after placing her hand on my slightly warm forehead.

"I suppose I should call," I replied in a resigned voice, looking up at her concerned face. "I was hoping this would just go away on its own." I was rarely sick so I had hoped to push through this lingering stomach distress, diarrhea, and low-grade fever. My appetite was practically non-existent.

Ever since we had returned from Mexico, my symptoms hung on as if Montezuma wouldn't let go of my coat. I had tried to ignore the signs that something was wrong, especially during the funeral for Joanne's father. But now I was willing to take Joanne's advice. I couldn't blame a tequila hang-over any longer.

"Well, you look pretty moosh to me," Joanne used the word she claimed was Italian for something like muddy or sloshy. I always thought it sounded appropriate for feeling under the weather, no matter what the real definition might be.

Within the next couple days, I visited my doctor and the lab work she ordered revealed that I had contracted *shigella*. The name sure sounded nasty, and the information about this bacteria was even less appealing. The printed medical summary the doctor gave me said it was rod-shaped and closely related to E. coli. My first thought was, thank goodness it hadn't spread to anyone close to me. My second thought was, will I have to spend the rest of my life in the bathroom?

The treatment was a round of antibiotics and strict dietary instructions, if you could call sipping Jell-O water for ten days a diet. I had to laugh at the irony. A Jell-O shot was my undoing and now Jell-O was my cure. Even though I was weak, I could still function well enough at home, vowing that I would never return to Mexico again.

As the year unfolded, Montezuma's Revenge long behind me, I was keenly aware that there is always something special about *firsts*. Joanne and I had already spent our first Thanksgiving and Christmas holidays together with our families. Now it was time for our first Valentine's Day and, unlike the others, this romantic holiday would be just for us. Since planning surprises was my favorite way to celebrate, I tried on a few ideas before finding the right fit for our busy schedules.

The first hurdle was finding the appropriate greeting card. Although my heart was full of love, most of the cards did not exactly reflect my feelings for another woman. There were several that read *for my husband* or *my wife* with pictures of a loving heterosexual couple on the front. Even the cute cartoony bear couples on some cards depicted boy/girl accessories. I finally settled for a beautiful card *To The One I Love* that seemed generic enough. I would have to write a meaningful message inside, however, in order to personalize this first Valentine's Day card.

Before the day arrived, I was on the phone with Joanne.

"Don't make any plans for Saturday morning or night, honey," I told her. "I have a couple surprises for you." I'm sure she could feel my excitement over the phone.

"Okay, but how do you know I won't be seeing my other girlfriends?" she responded coyly.

"Well, you'll just have to cancel them." I didn't even flinch like I would have months ago. I was now confident in our love. "How about I pick you up at nine? Oh, and don't eat breakfast."

"Okay, but what should I wear?" Not surprising Joanne wanted to be coordinated whenever she left her house.

"I think comfortable sweats would be just fine." I didn't want to reveal too much by telling her to dress warmly, especially since she hated the cold.

After completing a couple errands on Saturday morning, I drove to Joanne's house with enough excitement to lift the car off the road. Standing on her doorstep with a dozen deep red roses and a smile that almost wrapped around my head, I rang the bell.

As she hurried down the steps from the kitchen to answer the door, I caught a glimpse of her open jaw as she said, "Oh my god, those are gorgeous!" Hugs and kisses followed as soon as I stepped into the mudroom.

Joanne loved flowers and her talent for arranging them in vases was amazing to me. At the kitchen counter, I watched her expertly place the roses and baby's breath in a tall glass vase as she asked me, "So where are we going?" She also loved surprises, and the joy of letting someone else take charge was written on her face.

"I can't tell you now but you'll probably guess by the time we get close." It would be a forty-minute drive and, unless blindfolded, she would know our destination after thirty minutes.

The drive was uneventful as we chatted like two excited kids going to the beach. It certainly wasn't beach weather in February, but at least it wasn't snowing. Sure enough, after thirty minutes, Joanne guessed it. "Are we going to Beaver Tail?"

She was referring to a favorite Rhode Island state park on the rocky coastline that offered beautiful vistas overlooking rough ocean surf pounding the rocks below. Many visitors walked the grassy paths or climbed over the enormous rocks to commune with the ocean in warmer weather. Our view on this chilly day would be from the car due to the typical fierce wind coming off the water.

As I pulled into a parking space overlooking the mesmerizing ocean, I confessed, "You were right of course." We took a few minutes to take in the gorgeous view. Then I reached behind me to grab the case I brought from the backseat. It was filled with a thermos of hot coffee, freshly baked blueberry scones from our favorite bakery, and containers of mixed fruit I had filled at home.

"Oh, this is wonderful!" she exclaimed as her face lit up like twinkling Christmas lights. "You know how much I love these scones...this place... and you." She leaned over for a thank-you kiss. "What a great way to start Valentine's Day."

We relaxed at Beaver Tail for a couple hours, taking a short walk to the lighthouse, using the binoculars to spot birds, talking and laughing about a million things. The plan was to return to our home duties for the afternoon before meeting again for the next surprise that was a fancy dinner out. Even though Joanne knew what we were doing, she didn't know where.

Our Valentine's dinner took place at an exquisite Newport restaurant overlooking the bay. With our dressy attire, posh surroundings, and soft candlelight between us, this romantic stage was quite different from the romantic morning with coffee and scones. While we loved both events, the evening setting required an unspoken need for secrecy as if fine dining on Valentine's Day was reserved for straight couples. Consequently, there was no leaning over the table for a thank-you kiss, no holding hands on top of the linen tablecloth, and no lingering looks of love. We were not in P-town anymore where we could be open. Nonetheless, I had the feeling we were setting the tone for romantic Valentine's to come.

Late spring had arrived and Joanne's backyard garden was brimming with new color. Yellow daffies, pink and red tulips, purple coneflowers, black-eyed Susans, blue cornflowers, and white cascading bridal veil bushes lined the perimeter of the lush lawn. The infant grass looked good enough to add to a salad. New dark green leaves already filled the grapevine that seemed to swallow the entire back fence and the wisteria covering the arbor near the house provided shade for the brick patio underneath. Even though the yard was small and the neighbors close by, the tall stockade fence and beautiful flowers created a peaceful secret garden. While I was impressed with Joanne's gardening skill, I discovered I had a knack for certain gardening jobs as well.

"So, do you want to shovel the mulch from that pile into the wheelbarrow and then I can spread it around?" Joanne was in director mode as if she were the queen and I was the worker bee.

"Sure, I don't mind being mulch mama," I said honestly.

I actually preferred the mindless physical part of this mulching chore. Since the only gardening I had ever done was to plant flowerpots on my deck, I was content to learn from Joanne. With her floppy straw hat, old T-shirt, and dirt-streaked tan capri pants, she looked like a garden expert who loved to spend hours digging in the dirt. I thought we made a great team.

But there was another queen in the yard as well. Cara Mia, her long-haired calico cat, was luxuriating in her favorite spot under the huge bridal veil bush. Observing her human with adoration while tolerating me, Cara was feigning nonchalance by blinking her eyes shut every now and then. In reality, she was waiting for her chance to saunter down the driveway.

"Cara!" Joanne shouted as she noticed her feline escapee halfway to the street. "Get back here right now." Believe it or not, Cara stopped in her tracks, debating her next move.

"Cara?" she repeated with authority. I was astounded to see Cara pirouette in the driveway and head back to the yard at a trot like an obedient dog. She knew who the alpha was in this pack and I could see they were another formidable team.

Even after mulching for a couple hours, Joanne wasn't about to stop. During a water break, I foolishly thought we might be finished with garden chores.

"How would you like to trim the wisteria?" she asked as she looked at me with the long-handled clippers extended in my direction. I could see that *no, thank you,* was not an option.

"Okay, but how do you want me to do it?" I had the distinct feeling that my garden boss had standards along with endless energy.

"Use the ladder and trim these new sprigs." She was pointing to the new growth and exactly where to cut.

"I don't want it to look too neat, though," she continued, "My father always had everything trimmed too much and he lined up the same color geraniums all in a row." Since Joanne preferred the wildflower look with lots of multicolors, I concluded that her garden style matched her multicolored personality.

Halfway through the sunny afternoon, we heard a visitor walking up the driveway to the backyard.

"Hi there," Joanne's mother called out to us. She was smartly dressed in a casual blouse and slacks, coordinated with her jewelry and bag. With her softly coiffed hairstyle and makeup, she certainly did not appear to be almost eighty. I admired her more each time our paths crossed.

"Hi Ma, what are you doing here?" Joanne stood up from the rich dirt and came over to greet her smiling mother. "I'd give you a hug but I'm filthy," she added as I watched them from the ladder entwined with the monster wisteria.

"Oh, I don't care about that." Her mother came over and gave Joanne a warm hug and kiss. "I've been out shopping—what else?" Shielding her eyes from the sun, she lifted her head in my direction with a smile.

"Hi Anita," I called out. Since I had only met her a couple times, I didn't want to presume using her nickname.

"Oh, please," she said and waved her hand. "Call me Annie." Then she sat down in one of the lawn chairs and chatted with Joanne as she gazed upon the flowers. Their love for each other was shining on their faces as they fell into easy conversation. I quietly resumed my work, honored to share the scene.

While they gabbed away, I thought how the interaction would be different if my mother and I were sitting there. With her reserved English heritage, Dottie's expressions of love were more controlled. She certainly could be chatty, but a little distant at the same time. Nonetheless, I knew her love was there.

When Annie was ready to leave, she said her goodbyes to Joanne and entered the house for a pit stop. By this time, I was back in the kitchen refilling my water bottle. As she headed to the front door, I walked with her to see her out.

Just before she reached for the doorknob, she turned to me and said quietly, "I'm so glad Joanne has a friend like you." She looked deep into my eyes with a slight smile as if she wanted to say more. However, her expression said more than the words she kept to herself. In that moment, we both knew what she meant. I believe Annie knew her daughter's heart and she was happy I was part of Joanne's life. And that made me happy too.

By mid-September, we had planned a tent camping getaway to a favorite state park on Cape Cod. I had all the equipment and enthusiasm while Joanne had a little of each. To sweeten the start of our trips, I was now in the habit of presenting her with a small bouquet of travel flowers in a vase that would decorate our picnic table, bed and breakfast room, or wherever we landed. She was always surprised and delighted to find the cheery flowers on the car seat or on the kitchen table before we headed out. But this time, I wasn't sure the flowers would help with Joanne's recent worry.

For a few weeks, her mother had been feeling tired along with losing her appetite. In other words, she was feeling *moosh*. Both Joanne and Joyce urged Annie to call the doctor, but she minimized her symptoms and postponed calling for an appointment. They were especially worried in light of Annie's past history with breast cancer ten years earlier. When she finally made the appointment, however, it was unfortunately during our camping trip.

Even though Joyce planned to be the one to accompany Annie to the doctor, she reassured Joanne that she would provide the results when we called from the campground. In the age before cellphones, the plan was to use the payphone next to the camp office. Knowing that her sister was a trusted caretaker, Joanne had agreed to be away despite her concern.

Joyce also had a reputation in the family for having a sixth sense or a unique spiritual connection. Her dreams and premonitions often came true. Since an ominous vibe about Annie had recently nagged at her, she insisted that the medical staff order additional tests, including an MRI. Unfortunately, her strong premonition proved to be accurate once again.

While our long weekend on the Cape was relaxing and fun, a dark cloud followed us everywhere. When the day and time had come for Joanne to call Joyce for the full report, only one of the payphones was working. With perseverance at the busy phone, Joanne finally got through to her sister.

"Hi Joyce," I heard Joanne's frustrated voice from inside the phone booth. "What's going on?" I felt her anxiety through the glass.

After several minutes of short conversation with her sister, she hung up the phone and took a deep breath before opening the folded booth door. With emotion in her voice, she explained what was happening.

"Her cancer's back," she blurted out in disbelief. "It's in her liver this time and who knows where else." Joanne's eyes were filling up but she was angry as well. When I attempted a comforting hug, she waved me off. "We have to leave and get back there."

I knew she was angry about this news, not angry with me. All I could do was agree to pack up and offer whatever help she needed. Now it was my turn to take care of Joanne who was crushed with this devastating news.

Without surgery as an option, the doctor's plan for Annie was strong chemotherapy right away. The prognosis was grim with an estimated time of a few months at the most. Even though Annie reluctantly agreed to start chemo, the attack on her body was much too violent for her to continue. With tremendous conviction, she told her family that she wanted to use her remaining time for connecting with the ones she loved. Annie's plan did not coincide with that of her doctor.

Despite her deteriorating strength and noticeable weight loss in the following weeks, Annie was determined to celebrate her eightieth birthday in October and travel to Florida to visit her niece, Gloria. In order to include Disney World, one of her favorite but physically demanding destinations, Joanne and Joyce convinced her that renting a wheelchair would enable her to revisit "It's a Small World," and the "Tiki Birds." When she reluctantly agreed, the decision to travel was set in motion.

While Joanne focused on her mother and the trip to Florida, I hovered in the background ready to pitch in whenever I could. Sending balloons for Annie's birthday or fixing dinners for Joanne were small tokens of support. I often told her I would be glad to serve as chauffeur, reader, or cook for her mother as well. While she appreciated my offers, she wasn't ready to relinquish her responsibility as primary caretaker. She wanted to fix things on her own before delegating tasks.

From all accounts, Florida was good medicine for Annie. Even though Joyce and Joanne worked hard in the hot sticky weather, they were happy to share this journey with their mom. While I tended the fires at home, however, I had no idea that one event on the trip would be good medicine for me as well.

When Joanne returned home, she called to let me know.

"Hi Lin," she said over the phone. "I'm back safe and sound." All I heard was the exhaustion in her voice.

"Hi, how did it go?" Even though I had missed my honey, I didn't want to seem selfish by barging over to her house.

"It was a good trip but I'm *so* tired," Joanne replied.. " I can't talk long, but I have to tell you something." I was intrigued.

"I came out to my sister while we were at Gloria's," she announced.

"You *did?*" I was sideswiped as if a car had just run a stop sign and slammed into me. "What did she say?" I asked while sitting on the edge of my seat.

"She was so mad," she sighed on the phone. "She started yelling at me and everything." Since they had been alone for this monumental conversation, no one else was aware of the revelation.

"I don't know what's going to happen next," she said. No wonder she was exhausted.

We talked for a few minutes before Joanne had to end our conversation and get some rest. All I could do was ponder this news and wonder about the next time I would encounter Joyce.

Everyone in the family rallied in loving support around Annie despite their simmering frustration that the universe was so unfair. She had only a few months of freedom after caring for Ralph. Now her time was being snatched away and everyone was angry because she deserved more.

Everyone was angry except Annie. She was using her time to think about others and not feel sorry for herself. Unbeknownst to most, she began Christmas shopping early for her family…just in case she didn't make it to the holiday. She also wrote individual letters to her daughters to be read after her death. Annie was determined to tie up loose ends and make her peace.

During November, Joanne decided to accept my offers of help and asked if I could drive her mother to her acupuncture appointment. Annie had accepted Joanne's suggestion for this type of treatment since it was less invasive and she accepted my chauffeur service as well.

Our time together was spent in easy conversation about family and memories as we drove to her appointment. After returning home, despite her fatigue, Annie offered a cup of tea that I felt was an important gesture of hospitality. While sipping tea at her kitchen table, we chatted some more before she needed to rest. Even though the spring day at Joanne's front door was never mentioned, we were comfortable with our level of friendliness. My only frustration was there would be no time to know her more deeply.

As Annie grew weaker, even lifting the silver call bell took too much effort. Joanne was naturally spending more time at her mother's house along with other family members who performed house chores, errands, and meal prep. Joanne also provided the luxurious service of rubbing her feet. Even though the hospice nurse was very helpful, the care of her loving family could not be matched.

A devout woman of Catholic faith, Annie loved having her devotionals and prayers read to her. At one point, I was called upon to fill in for this honorary job. In a small way, I felt part of the team. With her eyes closed and a slight smile on her face as she listened, I had the sad thought that this could be the last time I would see Anita DiBello alive.

Joanne called me late at night on December 10. When the phone rang, I could almost feel the sadness emanating from the sound.

"Hi honey," she sobbed. "My mother died tonight." She could hardly get the words out.

"Oh honey, I'm so sorry," I said as my heart sank. My eyes were blurry in seconds. "What can I do for you?" We were both crying now.

"We're here at the house waiting for the funeral home people to get here," she managed to explain. "I'll be here for a while with Joyce and Carissa. Carole Ann's here too."

"Do you want me to come?" I would have done anything for her. Both she and Joyce had been staying at Annie's house all week without much sleep so I knew she was spent.

"Can you come over to my house tomorrow morning?" she whispered. As she thought about what she needed, she had regained some control.

I was at Joanne's door early the next morning and found her at the kitchen counter. Without saying a word, she collapsed in my arms while her shoulders shook from sobbing. Her heart was broken and mine ached for her.

With coffee steaming from our cups as we sat on the couch a few minutes later, she told me what had happened the night before. Annie's last twenty-four hours were filled with moments of ups and downs, lucidity and confusion, visions and words of love. While Carole Ann had stepped out for an errand to retrieve some medication for her, the hospice nurse was nearby ready to help. But at the final moments just Joanne, Joyce, and Carissa were around the bed. Annie was able to speak and seemed aware enough to tell them, "Your father's coming." Then, a moment later, "Am I dead yet?"

Surrounded by her family's unselfish love and reassurance to let go, Annie told them all, "I love you," before she breathed her last.

After Joanne finished her account, she said to me, "It was beautiful. I'll never forget it." Then she added, "That's how I want to go." I listened but didn't want to think about it.

"I want to be awake enough to tell you what's happening," she continued. Even though I wasn't surprised about her wish to control her last hour, I still didn't want to think about it.

Before Anita's funeral, I found myself wandering in a local department store trying to find a nice sweater for my outfit. My loathing for shopping must make the shopping gods cringe because they rarely help me with this task. After pawing through some sweaters on several racks without success, I was about to give up. It could have been only thirty minutes but my search felt like hours. Finally, out of frustration, I said out loud, "Annie, you have to help me."

Two minutes later, on a rack I'm sure I had just examined, I spotted the nicest cream-colored, mock turtleneck sweater with fine cable knit down the front. It hung by itself two feet away. I couldn't believe it. But I had to check the label. With my mouth hanging open like a bass on the line, I discovered it was exactly my size. *This was definitely meant to be,* I thought to myself. *Thanks, Annie.* I felt like I had found a new shopping buddy.

The wake or visiting hours at the same funeral home for Ralph had already been well attended the day before. Now, the church was filled for Annie's funeral Mass. Joanne and Joyce had been busy all week with the preparations but experienced some snags with the church protocol. While Joanne was adamant that the song, "Wind Beneath My Wings," should be played, the Catholic church would not allow secular songs during the Mass. With the persistence of a tiger, however, she would not back down. Finally, the priest agreed that the instrumental version could be played before Mass started while the casket waited inside the doorway. Joanne was somewhat satisfied and I was proud of her tenacity.

Once again, I was sitting without Joanne in a pew halfway to the altar, aching to be close to her on this day of sorrow. While the quiet organ music played softly in the background, the remaining mourners found their seats. When the music stopped, the casket rolled into the doorway at the back of the church and stopped as the familiar "Wings" music started to fill the sanctuary. Moments later, the sound of loud sobs mixed with the notes. When I turned to look, I saw Joanne draped over the back of the casket as she cried uncontrollably. Now I ached even more.

At the end of the song, Joanne regained her composure and walked with her family as they followed her mother's casket down the aisle to the front altar. The rest of the day seemed like a blur but the scene before Mass became etched in my heart and memory forever.

A couple weeks later, close to Christmas, I was helping Joanne string lights in her house. Despite her lack of enthusiasm for celebrating, she admitted that her mother would have liked to see the sparkling decorations. At one point during our task, I was on the backyard brick patio when I happened to notice an astounding sight. I ran into the house to summon Joanne.

"Joanne," I called out to her. "You have to come outside to see this." I was trying to keep a lid on my excitement as if it were a bouncing jack-in-the-box. "Put your coat on. It's very cold." She came running.

"What is it?" Joanne was totally perplexed as she swung her jacket on.

As she turned the corner, I pulled her over to the patio and pointed to the small rosebush next to the house. Her eyes burst open as she stared at the large, single yellow rose with delicate red trim.

"I can't believe it," she exclaimed. "It's winter. This shouldn't be blooming now." I immediately thought of her mother.

Then she added with more astonishment, "But you know, yellow roses were my mother's favorite flower." Not surprising that Joanne and I had the same thought.

We continued to stare at this beautiful flower until the cold settled into our bones, forcing us to return to the warm house. I couldn't help but think about the day in June, only months before, when Annie had walked up the driveway as we worked in the garden. With this rose, she was still connected, providing another reason to believe that spirit lasts forever.

CHAPTER 11

Surgery and Rice Krispies

My filthy car inched its way in line at the enclosed carwash as if it were one segment of a huge caterpillar heading into the dark mouth of a hungry cave. Keeping an eye on the attendant's hand motions for alignment, I had no problem easing my fourteen-year-old Honda Civic onto the tire guide. Joanne sat quietly in the passenger seat, pensive with her thoughts. As I handed the money through my open window and prepared the car for the wash, I wondered if she was thinking about the cute story we often mentioned when the loud machines started the spray and the swishing strands of sponge.

Years before, when Carissa was four or five, Joanne was in the driver's seat as they prepared to enter the noisy carwash. With anxious dark eyes, Carissa turned to her and blurted out, "Auntie, hold my hand." The car continued creeping toward the ominous spray, foam, and whirling brushes, all threatening to gobble them up. She added nervously, "I'm scared."

Naturally, her loving aunt reached out and held her hand throughout the frightening experience that probably, in her young mind, seemed to take hours. Once they were out into the sunlight, safe and secure, Carissa dropped her hand and smiled with delight. "That was fun, Auntie!" In a few short minutes, she had learned to slay her fear with the love and support of her auntie's hand.

We had just left the hospital where Joanne had her blood taken in preparation for major surgery the next day. If the lab results were less than acceptable, however, surgery would be delayed. Once again, we had to wait on the edge of our seats to find out. Echoes of Dr. D.'s familiar phrase, *it depends*, still floated in our heads, adding to our anxiety.

"Well, there's nothing we can do right now until we hear about the blood work this afternoon," Joanne had stated matter-of-factly when we left the hospital. Also thinking about her fatigue and safety, she couldn't afford any other bug, infection, or mishap. Despite shaking off a recent head cold, the stress of further complications weighed heavy. Even a sprained ankle would delay the schedule.

"You're right," I said. "Live in the moment," I quoted our worn out mantra.

"Do you mind if I go through the carwash on the way home?" I added, changing the subject. "It won't take long." Sometimes I welcomed the mundane activities of our lives as a diversion.

"Go ahead, should be fun anyway," she joked wearily. "Before I forget, would you put air in my tires while I'm in the hospital?" Both of us were control freaks when it came to caring for our cars, and after those hospital visits, I always felt the need to control *something*.

As my car crept into the soapy cavern, I turned to Joanne and as Carissa had said so many years ago, I smiled and asked, "Do you want me to hold your hand, honey?"

She smiled back and said, "Yes, I'm scared."

I had a feeling she was referring to more than the carwash as I took her hand in mine. I also remembered what she had asked me to do a few days before.

Even though she tried to keep her anxious thoughts about the impending surgery to herself, Joanne had made a request that revealed her anxiety. I had been composing another "Joanne Update" when she asked, "Honey, could you ask everyone to pray or send positive thoughts at the exact time of my surgery?" Normally, she let me create the email updates, so I was surprised at her comment.

"Sure, I'd be glad to." I loved her idea and added the paragraph.

Joanne does have a request of all of you if you are willing and able. No, it doesn't involve shaving heads anymore. She would be so touched if we all could say a prayer or send a healing thought on Tuesday, the 6th, at 2:30 p.m. when her surgery is scheduled. We'll be at the hospital before that of course at 12:30, but they say she'll be on the table by 2:30.

At church last Sunday, we heard a comforting thought about angels surrounding her bed and she thought it wouldn't hurt to have all of us there too. The surgeon might need extra help as well.

Joanne felt fortified by the thought of our army of angels coming along in spirit. The power of group support and love was like another hand reaching out to help steady our unsettled minds.

The afternoon phone call that day after the carwash brought welcome news. The lab work was satisfactory and the surgery was scheduled for the next day. Despite our initial joy, however, mixed feelings of fear and doubt quickly fell like volcanic ash. We wanted to proceed with the new phase of attack but feared the unknown surprises that could be lurking inside her body. Since it was Joanne's first major surgery, she was also nervous about the pain and recovery. Nonetheless, the cancer train kept chugging ahead.

The day before surgery reminded me of a moment during a weeklong backpack trip in New Hampshire in the seventies. I was hiking with a diverse group who loved the rugged White Mountains as much as I did. With our experienced guide, we trekked from hut to hut each day, exhausted but challenged in body and spirit.

At mid-week, we were facing a big test the next day. The experienced hikers were discussing the scary details of the ridge that loomed before us. Our guide, however, described an easier alternate route for those who wanted to, essentially, chicken out. Since I admitted to myself and to one of my hiking buddies that I was afraid, the easy path was tempting. With the encouragement of my friend who had faith in me, however, I decided to face my fear and hike the difficult trail.

The views from the ridge the next day were glorious and I discovered untapped strength in myself. The lessons I learned on that hike about fear, challenge, faith, and hope became lifelong pearls I carried for years. Now I had to take those pearls out, dust them off and share them once more before Joanne's surgery.

Early in the morning on the day of surgery, Joanne and I were sitting in our large master bedroom in the attic where we often shared prayer and meditation time. At other times, we used the spacious, peaceful sunroom overlooking the backyard. But today, we chose the more intimate sitting area looking out through the small window. With the inviting mauve and sage green décor and peaked roof, we had always considered the fully carpeted space to be our private bed and breakfast. Today, we needed the peace of this space before facing a difficult day.

Our sweet longhaired tabby cat, Rosie, lay beside us on the floor tucked into a perfect package. She always loved to be with *the girls*, no matter who they were. A perfect hostess, she had found us four years before when she was a stray and rarely let us fend for ourselves. Our younger second cat, black and white Charlie, preferred to stay downstairs, guarding the house from his window perch in the living room. They both lived in kitty paradise.

"Do you want to read today's *Daily Word?*" Joanne asked as she handed the booklet to me. She sat in her mother's maroon wingback chair while I sat in my great grandfather's rocker, drawing strength from our ancestors. My coffee was balanced on the hassock in front of us. Unfortunately, Joanne had to refrain from anything more than water as required for surgery.

"Of course I'll read," I said, although I could see she was already tired as she handed me the booklet. I quickly glanced at the day's topic, "Heart Matters," and scanned some of the text before adding, "I'm not sure this is a good thing to read today."

"Why not?" She was settled into her mother's chair with one of the prayer shawls donated by caring church ladies draped over her shoulders.

"Well, it talks about heart attacks…and then, spiritual heart attacks." I was thinking about surgery.

"You're right. I don't want to hear about heart attacks today." Joanne shuddered and continued, "What about something from one of Gary Zukav's books?" It had been a while since we had read anything from this spiritual teacher so I wasn't sure where the book had landed.

As I searched the nearby bookshelf, I thought fleetingly about Joanne's collection of books and how they reflected her interests and expanded mind. Several versions of the Bible, Jewish devotionals, *The Koran*, Tibetan prayer books, Reiki books for the certificate she achieved, books by Joel Osteen, the TV minister she thought was cute, Native American poetry, and even Wiccan stories all spoke about Joanne's spiritual quest. We had read from all of them over the years, allowing our thoughts to expand like a fistful of natural sponges heavy with water.

"I can't find any of his books," I concluded and didn't want to waste time looking any further. "How about the old standby, the twenty-third psalm?"

"Okay, that never gets old." Joanne listened as I began, "The Lord is my shepherd…"

With quiet hearts, we eased into our routine of silent prayer and yoga *ujjiayi*, or ocean breath. After a few minutes with eyes closed, Joanne said, "I might fall asleep here."

Without a word, we assumed our hands in prayer position at chest level, turned to each other and said *Namaste*, honoring the divine spark within. This time of connection always opened our hearts and minds to give us strength to face all kinds of challenges, whether it was an argument between us or, this time, surgery.

Before we rose from our seats, Joanne looked out the window and seemed to ask the trees when she said, "If I die during surgery, do you think I'll go to hell?" *Where was this coming from?* I thought.

"Why would you think that?" I couldn't imagine.

"Oh, I don't know. I just thought that maybe because I'm bisexual," she added. Despite all the expanded ideas and open minds, Joanne still hung onto some old religious guilt from childhood. I could hear the struggle in her voice…even now.

"If you really want my answer to your question, it's no," I replied with conviction. "I don't think you're going to hell." Joanne had turned to look at me.

"You're one of God's most loving, generous, and caring creations I've ever known and He knows your heart." After a pause, I couldn't resist adding, "Although, you used to have a pretty short temper, so maybe…." I smiled in her direction.

"Yes, but I'm much better now, don't you think?" Joanne laughed as I nodded in complete agreement. I used to compare her to a porterhouse steak, tender with a streak of gristle. Over the years, she had learned to mellow out.

"And anyway," I continued more seriously, "I don't need to tell you this, but I'll remind you. God is much too big to keep in a church box for only a select few who get to go to heaven…little minds imagine a little God." Joanne smiled as she absorbed the words. "I think what matters most is that God put us together for a reason, and you are definitely one of God's lights in this world."

"I hope so. Guess I had a weak moment." Joanne confessed, "I'm just a little afraid I won't make it through the surgery and what they'll find." I wouldn't allow myself to think that far ahead. "Like Zukav says, *love and trust*, not *fear and doubt*, right?"

"Right," I said. "And anyway, if you think you're going to hell, then I suppose I'll be going too." I grinned. "So I'll meet you there." Actually, the only time I thought I might deserve that fate was when I was trying to be straight.

By noon that day, we were heading up the elevator to the surgery floor of the hospital that was our proverbial home away from home. Even though Joyce and Carissa were working, they would be stopping by whenever possible during the wait before surgery. With my activity bag loaded, I was ready to camp out for the duration. We were in battle mode as Joanne made her way through the check-in process.

Once she was settled in bed with her hospital gown and cap, our anxiety began to rise again as we waited for the parade of medical staff. Even without makeup and the girlie *accessories* her mother prized, I thought Joanne looked cute. The surrounding curtain walls did little to muffle the sounds of a full house, so we were forewarned of each person's approach. Nurses, technicians, anesthesiologists, and even housekeepers came and went, sometimes asking questions or providing information. Joyce and Carissa popped in to show their love and support but could not stay long. Finally, Dr. D. arrived in his scrubs.

"We meet again," he said cheerfully. "We're just about ready. Do you have any questions?" Since the summary of work to be done was etched in our minds, we only needed reassurance that all would be well. While just his presence and positive manner had a calming effect, his words also added comfort.

"Everything will be fine and you'll be camping in Maine before you know it," he said with a smile. I loved that he remembered those things.

Just before Joanne drifted off from the IV med, I leaned over for a quick kiss, squeezed her hand and said, "I love you honey. See you soon." She whispered the same as her eyes closed in sleep. In the next moment, she was rolled away like Cleopatra on her barge. I also thought I saw a few angels floating by, ready to flood the operating room.

Since I'm not one to worry until I need to, the next few hours were spent in relative calm in the main lobby. Seated at her circular desk nearby, the patient liaison was ready to relay messages to family and friends who were also camped out in the cushioned chairs. Confident that I would get information when available, I settled in and realized I was now an expert at waiting.

Whenever I had had enough of reading or crosswords, I would take a walk to the gift shop, the indoor Au Bon Pain for coffee, or spend time at the saltwater aquarium, hypnotized by the fish that resembled Disney's Nemo and Dory. I didn't wander far in case the liaison came looking for me or if Joyce or Carissa happened by.

As I continued to watch the people aquarium passing by, I periodically texted Christine and my sister like a play-by-play sportscaster. My intermittent prayers seemed like texts as well even though God was sitting right next to me.

Eventually, my thoughts wandered back to the morning when Joanne pondered hell and guilt. Raised Catholic, her spiritual foundation was laid early with all those rules and tenets, including definitions of sin. In the early seventies, she had been swept into the Charismatic Renewal, a Holy Spirit movement that spanned all denominations. With a fiery faith, her life was filled with a new zeal as if a door in her mind had blown open. Although, when the wind eventually blew in a different direction and the movement faded, Joanne settled into living with God, not preaching about God. I suspected that her current ideas about guilt and sin still lingered from her past.

My mind scanned Joanne's good works and how she expressed her love for others with a listening ear, a welcoming smile or time sacrificed. After college and throughout a productive working life, Joanne's faith had sustained her and even propelled her into compassionate pursuits like starting the girls' softball league and facilitating the cancer support group for women. *How could she think she'd be heading for hell?* I thought with disbelief.

Both of our spiritual journeys had led us to each other at the right time. While working on her master's degree in holistic counseling a year before we met, Joanne's mind expanded even more. This time, she discovered an array of spiritual paths and, like a painter with a loaded palette, she took a dab of each color to create a new mix. This spiritual blend offered different ideas about sin and hell, God and Goddess, and divine light in all creatures. Not only did her mind open about spirit but also about herself. New growth allowed her to examine her sexual identity and meet me. As I sat in the lobby, I marveled again at God's timing.

Attending church as a child was a natural part of my life. Even my ancestors included American Baptist ministers and missionaries. So when the time came as a teenager to consider my future in a whirl of idealistic fervor, I wanted to be a minister. For many reasons, the ministry was not my destiny and my churchgoing vacillated for decades. Even so, I was always aware of God's hand and stability in everything I attempted, whether I went to church or not.

Like Joanne, I also experienced Holy Spirit moments and sometimes felt carried on the crest of a wave, ready to change course. But after years of trying on different churches as in a boutique and listening to heated debates about God, I finally concluded that my only judge was the God in my heart. My religion became *God is Love* and, like Joanne, I preferred to live with God, not preach. When we met, my mind was ripe to join her in a spiritual quest before returning to a more solid foundation. At this moment in the lobby, God was part of the family.

Carissa arrived just as the liaison approached and relayed the news that surgery was over and the doctor would be down shortly for a conference. Now I could worry. Until I knew the outcome, my fear of the unknown settled into my bones. I was so grateful that Carissa could attend the conference. Despite my confidence with meeting Dr. D. alone, I couldn't depend on my weary brain to function properly. Her expertise as a licensed practical nurse would certainly be a plus.

For years, I had watched Carissa grow into a sweet, compassionate young woman who worked hard to accomplish any goal set before her. In many ways, she embodied several of her family's traits. While caring and generous, she was also assertive and savvy about finances and investments. She rarely procrastinated. Even though she could be stubborn and sometimes over-reactive, Carissa usually kept a cool head when needed. And in the footsteps of her grandmother, she was also an excellent bargain shopper. Like Joanne, I could always depend on Carissa.

Dr. D. found us in the lobby. His positive vibe was now mixed with fatigue after hours of surgery. As soon as he directed us into a small conference room nearby, he wasted no time getting to his report.

"Everything went well," he said warmly. "She's in recovery and is doing fine." He noticed our sighs of relief. "We did the complete hysterectomy, installed the IP port in her abdomen for the next chemo, and removed the omentum and all the small tumors that looked like Rice Krispies. I believe we got it all." A little red flag popped up in my head, however, thinking how impossible it would be to remove so many tiny tumors resembling cereal.

As I made some notes and before we could ask questions, Dr. D. added, "We also had to perform a small bowel resection where a tumor was hiding in her large intestine." *Yikes*, I thought as I looked at Carissa who was looking back at me.

"What does that mean?" I eked out the words. All I could imagine was the threat of a colostomy bag.

"It's not a big problem," he said quickly. "She won't need a colostomy." With honesty, however, he continued, "The only thing we have to look out for in the next few days is leakage. If that happens, then it could be a problem and we'd have to do a repair."

Carissa started asking questions as a medical professional and ended with, "Do you have any idea how many years she has?" I interpreted the word *years* as a sign of hope.

"Well, I usually don't like to say since there are so many new drugs being developed these days," he replied. I already knew that Dr. D. was up to date on this topic. "But right now with ovarian cancer, it's usually four and a half to five years."

At that moment, I vowed to myself that I would never relay this prediction to Joanne. Although, a part of me suspected she had researched the details months before. My guess was that Carissa would never tell her aunt as well. In silence, we had made a pact in order to keep hope alive.

A groggy Joanne was eventually transferred from recovery to a private room on another hospital floor where she was expected to remain for a few days. Even though she knew I was there, conversations would have to wait until she was coherent. The morphine pump was a savior for pain management and would continue for as long as needed. Every time the nurses quietly came in and out of her room like a revolving door, they always asked me if I needed anything as well. In my own groggy state, I appreciated their concern. When I started to slump into the visitor chair, however, I realized I was fading into exhaustion. With pure adrenaline pushing me along, I made my way home to an empty house where I fed two very hungry kitties and then plopped into bed.

After morning chores the next day, I began my new routine of home, hospital, home, sleep, and repeat. When I arrived at the hospital, I was shocked to find Joanne sitting in her recliner using her iPad as if she was sitting in the sunroom at home.

"Well look at you," I said, unable to contain my surprise. "I can't believe you're sitting up." Memories of her expectations about recovering from a cold within twenty-four hours flooded back.

"Hi honey," Joanne replied, still sounding *moosh*. "It's all about the morphine pump." With the reminder about pain meds, I knew this miraculous recovery wouldn't last long. "They even had me walking my IV in the hallway a while ago."

Joanne went on to say she didn't sleep very well and that her weak appetite didn't mind the post-surgery diet of light, bland food. We chatted about her pain level, the caring staff, the kitties at home, and the family and friends I had contacted with updated news. Even though Joyce, Carissa, and Christine stopped by briefly for individual visits, Joanne requested that everyone else wait to visit until she was settled at home. She may have wanted angels around the operating table, but not in person until she felt better.

Joanne's hope for a quick recovery was dashed the next day when a fever spiked and fluid filled her lungs. She was in a nosedive with everything and the nurses were concerned, especially regarding a possible bowel leak. With the help of critical care staff, however, her condition stabilized and all was well…until she tried to return to bed.

While I stood in the hallway waiting for the aides to complete their duties, I heard Joanne scream in pain.

"Oh God!" she cried out as she was halfway onto the bed. I quickly stepped into the room ready to help, but the nurses were already lifting her legs onto the bed. Evidently, Joanne had tried to get into bed on her own without knowing the proper technique. Familiar with her defiance of many rules and instructions, I wasn't surprised at her attempt to *just do it*. Needless to say, from then on she was very receptive to learning a new procedure and vowed she would obey good patient rules.

With every passing day, the threat of a leaky bowel resection lessened and Joanne continued to make slow progress. Since she disliked taking more pain medication than necessary, she was relieved to discard the morphine pump and worked diligently to regain her strength. I admired her perseverance and felt certain that her determination alone would make her victorious in this battle with cancer.

By mid-week, I was sitting in the hallway visitor's area waiting for Joanne to return from X-ray when Joyce approached holding a small plastic bag.

"Hi honey," she greeted me with a hug and kiss on the cheek. "How're you doing?"

"I'm okay, just waiting for Joanne to get back from X-ray." I was happy to see her. "What's in the bag?"

"This is for you," she extended the bag to me. "I was just in the gift shop and found it on the sale table. I thought you might like to give it to Joanne." Feeling a bit awkward with her presumption, I waited for more explanation. "I would have just told you about it but it was the only one left and I was afraid it'd be gone." *Okay*, I thought. *That makes sense.*

Her purchase was a small stuffed bear, about twelve inches from head to toe, with soft tan fur and small black shiny eyes. She was wearing a small white T-shirt with red letters that said, *You know it's Love when forever is not enough.* The word *Love* looked like a square pin on the front. A broad-brimmed, white felt hat with feathery trim sat coquettishly on one side of her head while a double strand of choker pearls completed the ensemble. I knew at once that Joanne would love this stylish bear—it was perfect.

"That's not all," Joyce added. She quickly found the bear's left paw with a red circle that said *Squeeze On/Off* and pressed it. Immediately, the square Love pin started flashing and a jazzy song came on.

> *L is for the way you look at me,*
> *O is for the only one I see...*
> *V is very, very extraordinary,*
> *E is even more than anyone that you adore can*
> *Love....*

I was delighted and very touched that Joyce would give this to me for Joanne. My initial guarded reaction turned to love for my sister-in-law and her generosity. Now that her anger about Joanne's coming out was ancient history, our alliance had only grown stronger over the years as we had learned to share Joanne. I was grateful for the bear, and also secretly thanked Annie who might have influenced this one-of-a-kind bargain.

Joanne finally returned home after six days in the hospital with the Love Bear always perched nearby in a place of honor. Even though she was thrilled to be home, she had mixed feelings. In the hospital, there was safety, structure, and quick responses to medical questions and concerns. At home, she was initially insecure about walking, showering, climbing stairs and taking orders from me, her new Nurse Ratched. But Rosie and Charlie made her homecoming well worth it. Under the pretense of not caring that she was home, I often spotted them curled next to her as she slept.

Joanne was definitely on the road to recovery despite her low energy and struggle with pain. During the day, she adapted to the recliner and slept well upstairs with properly placed pillows. By eating small portions several times a day, her appetite improved as well. As the days melted together, I welcomed my familiar caretaker role even when Joanne's gristle occasionally popped out.

One afternoon, she was resting at her recovery station on the couch in the TV room with the essentials nearby on a tray: a glass of water, the cordless house phone, her iPad, and the small silver bell from her mother's house used for summoning me if needed. She had been napping with her favorite sleep shade that had two big green eyes painted on the front. Whenever she wore it, I called her *Nancy* after an old comic strip character who resembled the mask. While she rested, I was busy with a project at the other end of the house.

All of a sudden I heard her yelling, "Lin! Linda!" She was definitely mad. I ran to the TV room expecting a tragedy.

"What's the matter with you?" Joanne barked. "I've been ringing this goddamn bell like crazy!"

"Well, I didn't hear it." I tried to be patient. "What do you need?" Joanne still had the sleep shade on and I tried not to laugh at the fake green eyes staring back at me. As she simmered down, I asked again, "What do you need, Nancy?" Now I could laugh because she was laughing too.

"I'm sorry," she replied softly. "I just wanted another blanket and some more water." Her tenderness had returned.

When I came back with the water and blanket, I offered a possible solution. "Why don't you call my cellphone from now on? That bell is too soft and my hearing is too far gone." Not all our problems were huge.

Four days after returning home, we saw Dr. D. for general follow-up and removal of Joanne's forty-four stitches. From the favorable report and our comments from home, he seemed pleased with her progress. Even though a leaking bowel resection was no longer a concern, he warned her to avoid lifting or straining the IP port. Not wanting any delays in this cancer fight, Joanne was more than willing to comply.

The next round of chemo would be a combination of familiar Taxol and Cisplatin that required a slow infusion through the new abdominal port. Starting in a couple weeks from our visit, the treatment schedule would be two weeks on and one week off. Rounds of chemo would continue until her CA 125 test was at 20 or less. Since the count after surgery had been 112, there was still work to do. Evidently, some of those Rice Krispies had been hiding.

In the next two weeks before chemo would commence again, we often reflected on the concept of time and normalcy. By the calendar, our journey with ovarian cancer had begun only three months before. The actual experience, however, felt like three years. Our crash course in cancer demanded that we throw time out the window and focus on each day's lesson, for better or worse. Since time was out of our control, we tried not to think too far ahead.

The only exception was Joanne's decision to complete her funeral arrangements. Not wanting to admit that dying could be part of this fight, we rarely discussed the reality in detail. One day, she simply made an appointment at a local funeral home, went by herself, and announced her intentions after dinner. After revealing her instructions as if she were showing me how to feed the cats, she encouraged me to make my final arrangements as well. Not afraid of death and its uncertainty, Joanne had taken control of planning the event despite her hope to delay the date. Unlike my love, I shuddered at the thought of losing her.

During this waiting period, we also had to redefine normal which seemed more like an amoeba, always changing shape. Our normal now included slowing down, isolating ourselves due to low energy or fear of infection, scheduling CT scans, blood work, lung taps, chemo, and learning to switch gears at the drop of a hat. However, all these new additions to our normal life could not stop us from having fun. We were determined to look cancer in the eye and say, *No, you can't take that!*

Joanne was not about to stay home for two weeks, just waiting for chemo. As her strength slowly increased, we hauled our camper van out from storage and scheduled a weekend camping trip with two of our RV buddies. The destination was a popular family campground close enough to home so we could return quickly if needed. Needless to say, we looked forward to a change of scenery.

As dusk quietly fell on our wooded campsites, the four of us gathered around the struggling campfire, watching it grow with each new log. Relaxing in our chairs with glasses of wine, we quietly settled in for a peaceful night and warm conversation. Bundled up with a warm hat covering her fuzzy head, Joanne raised her glass and said, "Now this is what I call normal."

"Amen," we all agreed in unison.

While the discussion around the now blazing fire did not dwell on chemotherapy, I silently contemplated the next round of chemo and what new side effects lurked around the corner. As I glanced at Joanne's peaceful face next to me, however, those anxious thoughts finally shifted to thinking about a much happier event coming up: our wedding ceremony. With crickets chirping in the background, I finally decided to throw *Fear and Doubt* into the fire and postpone making my funeral arrangements for another day.

CHAPTER 12

No Mud, No Lotus

Christine was guiding me by the hand through our house. With strict instructions to keep my eyes closed, I stopped her after a few steps into the hallway and said, "Honey, you know I should take your arm if you're going to be my guide." We both chuckled. As a mobility instructor for the blind, I had taught her how to be a sighted guide almost as soon as she could walk.

"Oh Mama," she said with the exasperation of a budding teenager, "I know, I know. But we're just going to the front porch. Then you can open your eyes." My daughter stood eye to eye with me these days and her confidence was already soaring over my head. She loved surprises as much as I did.

With all traces of winter behind us, the fresh spring air greeted us as Christine slowly opened the front door. It was late Saturday afternoon and one day after my fiftieth birthday in 1999. The night before in my dining room, I had been surrounded by smiling faces topped with party hats, who belted out a boisterous rendition of "Happy Birthday" around a glowing cake. During the festivities, Joanne revealed that a fancy surprise would take place the next day, extending the celebration. I was instructed to dress up but that was all. Christine's grinning face at the party told me she was delighted to be a cohort in this secretive plot.

Finally, we came to a stop on the wide front porch. "Okay," Christine said with glee, "you can open your eyes!" Before looking up, I noticed a camera in her hand as well.

"Oh my god," I managed to say with one hand covering my mouth. In front of our driveway sat a long ebony limousine, quietly idling as if it were waiting to whisk me away to the Oscars. An elegantly dressed chauffeur, complete with traditional cap and a pleasant smile, held open the passenger door at the back of the car. My beautiful Joanne, grinning with joyful satisfaction in her sexy black dress, stood on the other side of the gaping door as if she had already won an Oscar.

"Surprise!" she exclaimed. I wondered if she knew I had never ridden in a limo before. "Are you ready for anything?" By this time, she knew I loved adventures.

"Sure!" At that moment, I decided that turning fifty wasn't such a bad thing after all.

I gave Christine a thank-you hug after she took our picture and entered the posh limo with delight. There was even a bottle of champagne waiting on ice.

"Where are we going?" I asked as our driver deftly popped the champagne cork. In all honesty, I was excited to be with Joanne even without knowing our destination. If we went around the block, I would have been happy.

"You'll have to wait until we get there." She was crafty. "It'll take about forty minutes so let's have some bubbly." Since I always tried to enjoy any journey, I had no difficulty sinking into the soft leather seat as I sipped my champagne.

After our carefree ride and an empty bottle, the limo pulled up in front of a restaurant in Wellesley, Massachusetts. I was thrilled to read the striking blue and white sign, "Blue Ginger," hanging above the extended blue awning. One of my favorite TV chefs, Ming Tsai, owned the new restaurant that was on my list of longings. I was also thrilled that Joanne remembered.

She had made reservations, of course, and we were quickly seated at an intimate table and tended to by unobtrusive waitstaff. I soaked up the elegant black and adobe tan décor in anticipation of an exquisite meal. Already mellow from the champagne, we threw caution to the wind and ordered fancy cocktails. Original names like Lion's Tail and Burnt Orange Negroni seemed appropriate for a special celebration. After all, we weren't driving and fifty comes only once in a lifetime.

As we pondered the menu, I thought about our first Valentine's Day dinner in Newport two years before. Back then, our anxiety about being out as a couple weighed heavy on our meal. Now, with confidence in our love and more alcohol than usual, we didn't care what anyone thought. Joanne even moved her hand to mine on the tablecloth. My heart fluttered.

As we savored what I considered to be the best meal of my life, even without a fuzzy head, our conversation settled on our relationship and what comes next.

"So honey, what can we do about living together?" she asked as we laid our forks down. Now that it had been two years since we'd been together, Joanne wanted a plan. During the past few months, we had talked briefly about the next step as if we had laid a jigsaw puzzle on the table before fitting the pieces together.

"I don't know," was my first response, then, "I guess we have to think about where and when."

It sounded simple and complicated at the same time. One thing for sure, it made no sense for Joanne to sell her house and move into my apartment with less room and investment. Moving into Joanne's house was an option but we had much to consider, especially for Christine and Buddy as well. Without a doubt we wanted to live together, but the best solution could be to wait for a while.

"On one hand, it would be great if we lived together now because I feel bad about leaving Christine so much." I continued to feel pulled in two directions. "But I don't want to change her school and neighborhood." Even though Christine was a joy, the unpredictable teen years loomed ahead. And I had no desire to churn the waters any more than our boat could handle.

"Well, I don't know if I'm ready for a houseful now anyway," Joanne said honestly. "If you moved into my house, I'd have to have some work done to make room." An image of the old woman who lived in a shoe flashed across my mind for some reason. So far, her small house was perfect for one, but it would take more than a shoehorn to stretch it for more.

"What about looking for another house?" I continued bravely. "I know how much you love your house, but maybe it would feel more equal in a different place." I could almost feel Joanne squirm.

"I suppose it wouldn't hurt to look," she finally replied as I sensed the wheels turning. Once a real estate agent, Joanne's interest in properties had not waned over the years. Many times when she drove, I would remind her to watch the road while she scanned the roadsides for unique houses.

With more drinks and bravado, I added, "I have to admit that the idea of moving into your house would not be easy for me." I felt like a crock-bound plant that would resist being transplanted, even if a new pot could provide more healthy growth.

"Really?" She seemed genuinely surprised. "You know I would do everything I could to welcome you." Thoughts of renovating the basement for Christine and redoing the attic for ourselves resurfaced from earlier discussions.

"I know you would," I could say with reassurance. "But I don't know if I'd ever feel like it was my house." We sat in silence for a few minutes as we empathized with each other's position.

As we looked deeply into each other's eyes, once again over soothing candlelight, Joanne said, "Well, let's plan to plan, okay?" I nodded in agreement as we finished our meal. This birthday not only ushered in a new decade for me but a new phase for us.

The next few years could be compared to the formation of a pearl. In an oyster, an irritant enters the shell and in defense, the oyster produces layers around the invader to create a precious pearl. This transformation could take from five to twenty years. Even though Joanne and I had fallen in love with a bang, like any couple over time we had discovered irritations with each other that began to invade our happiness and future. Without some protective layers to form the pearl, our love would never make it. Thankfully, the effort to save it didn't take twenty years.

"Are you ever going to make those shelves?" Joanne was hounding me again. "It's been weeks since Kyle finally finished the basement and I need those shelves you said you'd put up." We were sitting on the couch in the TV room at her house and I started to cringe as soon as she spoke.

"Yes, I'll do it," I responded without hiding the exasperation in my voice. "I could come over tomorrow I guess." Even though I enjoyed woodworking projects, I had little confidence that I could live up to Joanne's standards. Her impatience with my methodical approach was often displayed with a quick push of my hand as if to say *get out of my way, I'll do it*. My response was usually silent anger and retreat.

"Okay, that'll be good." She had simmered down. "I'm just so frustrated with Kyle and the horrible job he did with the basement." The slipshod renovation to make a small living space for Christine had taken six months, although we wondered if Kyle, the contractor, would be the one to actually move in.

The next day, I focused on building the new shelves that would store piles of Joanne's serving plates, odd bowls, and seasonal dishes next to the dryer in the basement. The shelves didn't need to be fancy, just sturdy enough for a heavy load. I cut three boards and fastened them to the drywall with brackets. After completing the job, I was satisfied with the result and the dishes were stacked.

Two days later, I was in Joanne's kitchen while she tended to her laundry. All of a sudden, I heard a loud crash from the basement and a blood-curdling scream. As I ran down the stairs, I heard the worst stream of swearing ever. Even though Joanne was unharmed, she was exploding with anger. Plates, dishes and bowls lay on the cement floor, some, in pieces, at her feet.

"*Fanculo!*" Joanne slipped into Italian but I knew what it meant. "What a fucking mess!" She shouted at me as I attempted to pick up the pieces. "I can't believe this. You're just like Kyle!" When I first saw the disaster, I reprimanded myself for not reinforcing the shelves but when Joanne compared me to our nemesis, I was hurt.

"I'll clean it up," I tried to appease her. But Joanne's rage continued. At one point, I thought she might throw one of those plates at me, adding to the broken pile.

"Just get out of here!" she screamed. I was more than glad to retreat. As a full-fledged people pleaser, I was more inexperienced with confrontation than making shelves. I went upstairs, gathered my things and drove away thinking *this is never going to work.*

We didn't contact each other for a week. In my stubbornness, I vowed I would not be the one to make the first move. Memories of all those romantic getaways and candlelit dinners seemed to shatter in the air like burst balloons caught in a shower of razorblades. I felt sad and angry for being such a wimp. After years of avoiding confrontation, I needed to find my voice in this relationship. But I didn't know how.

Despite the love and laughter of the past few years, the incidents of conflict had increased during our *planning-for-the-future* phase. Joanne seemed to grow more impatient with me and her bursts of anger always burned me like a hot poker. Even though God's voice told me, *Hang in there, it'll be worth it,* I was in a quandary about how to feel better. As my mind churned, I finally decided that an extra counseling session wouldn't hurt.

Just as I was about to call my therapist the phone rang. It was Joanne.

"Hi." She sounded almost shy. "I don't know if you want to talk to me but I just wanted to say I'm sorry I blew up." She waited a few tentative seconds. I could only listen while she continued. "I was just so mad I couldn't stop."

"Joanne, I'm sorry about the shelves," I said finally. "I don't really know what to say but I think we should talk about all this." She was listening and agreed.

Since we were savvy about the benefits of therapy, we concluded in the next few weeks that couples' counseling could help us with our derailed relationship. Despite our solid foundation, the irritations were increasing and threatened to chip away at our love. Fortunately, we both recognized our need for help. After all, we had originally met at the suggestion of our individual therapists several years before. It made sense that another perspective could help us again.

A couple weeks later, we found ourselves in a small cozy office located in a renovated Victorian house near my apartment. In her sixties with short gray hair and glasses, Margaret was an experienced professional recommended by Joanne's therapist. Despite her mild demeanor, we soon learned that her insight and challenging questions found their mark like an expert archer.

After listening to our story in brief, Margaret stated with clarity, "It sounds like you are both dealing with several major changes." Joanne and I nodded. "But you both seem committed to making this work."

"Yes, we are." We replied in unison as we looked at each other with smiles.

"We're just not sure how to overcome these obstacles," Joanne added just before the same words were poised to spill off my tongue.

"I think it would be helpful for you to think about what brought you together in the first place," Margaret offered. "What did you find attractive?" She was providing some focus and much appreciated homework. "Then try making a list of the things that irritate you about the other or even what you think the other might write down about you."

"That's ironic that you should say list," I said and smiled at Joanne. "Before we met, we had made lists of what we wanted from a partner." I thought that it might be a good time to look at those old lists again.

Joanne and I were optimistic about counseling with Margaret in the following months, and we took our assignments seriously. After we had made our new lists, we planned to discuss them with each other at home during our prayer time. Since we felt that God's hand had brought us together, we should at least focus on our faith to keep us together.

With the completion of the renovated attic bedroom, which we'd decided upon even before living together, our spacious carpeted master accommodated our new king-size bed as well as a cozy sitting area that was perfect for quiet discussions. Even the bed reflected our differences coming together. Joanne's twin mattress was firm, mine had more cush for my new lower back pain, and the long sheepskin strip covered the split in the middle. Our attempts to find perfect harmony knew no bounds, even with furniture.

"So what's on your list?" I asked Joanne as we sat upstairs in the new bedroom. We had been reading a daily devotional and meditating silently.

"Okay, I'll just read my list," Joanne said without thinking of a better way to begin. "First, your procrastination drives me crazy." We looked at each other and smiled. After fifteen years, I still hadn't put curtains up in my living room, opting to use only the apartment's venetian blinds.

"Second, I wish you were more proactive and not so reactive…like… just do things without my prodding." I wasn't sure I understood that one.

"And third, I wish you would tell me off once in a while." We chuckled at that one since I recognized my fear of confrontation. Now it was my turn.

"Well, here's my list," I said nervously. "I really have a hard time with your fits of anger." I glanced at Joanne who was looking out the window with apparent remorse. Her outbursts were so uncharacteristic of her loving nature that I sensed her struggle with that part of herself.

"Second, I'm frustrated with the way you take over and get impatient with me." Joanne nodded her head in agreement.

"And third, I don't know if you understand how hard it is for me to share my time between you and Christine." We looked at each other with the spark of love that kept the pilot light on. And since we had also been reading from the Buddhist monk, Thich Nhat Hanh, I repeated one of his quotes, "No mud, no lotus."

I could picture the gorgeous lotus flower rising from the muddy water at its base just as the soul blossoms through its difficulties and trials. Without the muck, there can be no beauty.

Later that day as we contemplated our earlier discussion, Joanne found me plopped on the couch in the TV room.

"Hi, honey," she greeted me as I looked up at her standing next to the arm of the couch. With her hand extended toward me, I noticed the envelope. In a soft voice, she continued, "This is for you but I don't want you to open it now."

"Oh…okay," I said, not knowing what mystery the envelope represented. "What is it?" My curiosity grew.

"It's just something I want you to put away for later," she instructed. "You can open it whenever I'm gone," she continued as I looked puzzled. "You know, if I die or something." With eyes opened wide, I took the envelope with apprehension at such a morbid thought.

Without further comment, Joanne left the room as I wondered how our earlier prayer time had influenced this move. Out of respect for her wishes, however, I placed the unopened letter in a box and forgot about it.

Changes did not happen overnight, but we felt hopeful in our commitment to make compromises that would keep us together. Noticing our differences and communicating on equal terms became easier with practice. We even became aware of our dynamics during a series of dance lessons.

We were excited to join a small group of gay couples at a private dance studio offering weekly ballroom dancing lessons. Since we loved to dance, we wanted to improve our moves. Naturally, the first question was *Who was going to lead?*

As Joanne and I faced each other, I said without hesitation, "I'll lead." Joanne was a little surprised but pleased as well. "After all, I'm two inches taller," I added. We chuckled at the constant joke between us.

"Okay, no problem." Joanne assumed her follower position.

As the dancing began, leading was easy. As we learned more demanding steps, however, Joanne took over. At one point, she said in exasperation, "Will you please lead?" I stopped and looked at her.

"I would if you'd let me," I said with quiet confidence. To my surprise, Joanne immediately relinquished the lead and seemed content with following from then on…at least when dancing.

We learned more than the cha-cha or swing during those lessons. I learned to speak up more often and she gradually learned to back down. And we both learned that there is a time to take control and a time to let it go.

With the help of Margaret, spirit, and dance lessons, we gradually recognized how we could change our behaviors for greater balance. Like breaking in new shoes, our comfort level grew and our future looked more hopeful. As the months passed, the prospect of moving in together was a much happier thought despite the sacrifices that loomed ahead.

Even during our difficulties, we had been looking at a variety of houses on the market. Unlike dancing, I gladly followed Joanne's lead when attending open houses and reading descriptive ads in order to learn the lingo. She was an expert in the world of real estate and I was impressed with her wealth of knowledge and insight. Again we were making lists, but this time we enumerated the pros and cons of each new property.

I also examined my reasons for never owning a house at this point in my life. Apartment living had always suited me, despite the lack of investment opportunities. Calling the landlord about a leaky pipe, a broken step, or a fallen fence was worth the rent. While looking at prospective houses was interesting, I had always felt I could lay my head anywhere and feel at home. Whether I snuggled in a sleeping bag or luxuriated under a satin comforter, I embraced the adage *Home is where the heart is.* Owning a house for security was never my priority.

Yet the wheels of change were slowly grinding toward a decision. Financially and logistically, a move to a new house made little sense. The renovations to Joanne's house created the space, waiting four years for Christine to graduate high school created the timing, and our healing relationship created the confidence to make the move to Joanne's house. We were ready to make the sacrifices and meet the challenge of melding our different house styles.

Even with new appliances and countertops, my older kitchen with high ceilings resembled a Victorian-style home. I rented the first floor of the house that was as comfortable as an old shoe. While interior decorating was not my priority, I loved the unique built-in bookshelves, bay window, and my hodgepodge belongings that were full of sentimental value. Joanne's cottage-style house, on the other hand, was nicely coordinated with family antiques and floor-length lace curtains that showcased her Italian heritage. Somehow we would have to compromise.

The wall phone rang in my kitchen as Buddy rose from my lap in the living room. It was late at night in May 2004, and I was relaxing after a hectic day helping Christine prepare for her senior prom. In her floor-length deep red gown with beading on the strapless bodice, she had looked stunning as she posed on the front porch with her date. With her long brown hair coiffed high and her confident poise, I imagined her ruling a country somewhere. Best of all, Christine's heart was as beautiful as her serene face.

"Hi Mama," she said with excitement. "Guess what?" Her happiness was catching.

"Hi honey," I answered, relieved to hear joy, not trouble, on the other end of the phone. "What's up?"

"I was chosen Prom Queen!" She could hardly contain her joy and surprise.

"Oh that's wonderful honey," I said with delight. "But I'm not surprised." Not only was I being truthful, I was also proud to think she would call her mother with the news. With every year that her maturity grew, I knew it wouldn't be long before she'd be moving out on her own.

Christine had certainly been included in the discussion about moving. Despite her excitement about house hunting, however, the idea of changing schools and neighborhoods had not crossed her mind. Once realized, she agreed that waiting until college would be the best for her and the timing would then be right for me to make the move. When home on school vacation, she planned to use the new basement guestroom at Joanne's house, even if she had to duck from the low ceiling. That part of the puzzle fell into place with ease.

"So what are you going to do with the asparagus fern?" Joanne asked me as I arranged some Tupperware containers on the bay window seat in my old dining room.

Surrounded by piles of my dishes, appliances, folding TV trays, and wall hangings, we were setting up for the next day's moving sale at my apartment. Small chairs, a tall linen closet, and even my old bulky computer were lined up for a new home. Fifteen years of accumulated stuff were being filtered through an imaginary sieve and the task seemed daunting. Since I hated conducting yard sales anyway, I was glad for Joanne's help.

"Oh, *Fern* is going to my brother's along with this ponderosa pine." I couldn't hide my sadness as I gazed fondly at my twenty-year-old fern. The feathery strands draped over the wide pot and almost touched the floor. Not having been transplanted in years, *Fern* was as crock-bound as I felt. Unfortunately, despite the renovations there would be no room in Joanne's tiny house for large plants.

"Maybe you should move it into your bedroom during the sale so no one takes it." Joanne used a softer director's approach these days. In the past, she would have cursed my damn procrastination for not moving it sooner.

Scheduled to arrive the next day with his pickup truck, my brother would, fortunately, keep many of our family heirlooms that would not find a place at Joanne's. My grandmother's metal top kitchen table, the large deer wall hanging, and my heavy oak dresser and vanity were priceless to me. At least they would stay in my family. I could almost feel my roots pulling away from the side of the pot.

As strangers filed slowly through my house handling my belongings, I felt invaded. My mind told me I was doing the right thing and that physically letting go was a healthy exercise. But my heart was not in sync with my head. Even though the process had begun months before, letting go en masse was unsettling.

In order to cope, I reminded myself of the purpose and final outcome of this sacrifice. Joanne was on my team as we steamed ahead toward our goal of sharing lives. Along with spending thousands in renovations, sharing her private sanctuary, and weeding out her own belongings, Joanne had even sacrificed the coveted first-floor closet for my convenience. Compromising at this stage in our lives was not easy but the beautiful lotus was about to bloom. As I continued to walk a mile in her shoes throughout the day, my anxiety turned into unexpected relief and a feeling of accomplishment by the end of the day.

There is an old joke in the lesbian world that by the second date, a U-Haul truck shows up at the door. Since it took seven years for us to live under one roof, we became examples of the unconventional among our peers. No matter—our patience and preparation added cement to our foundation when the time came to rent the truck.

Moving day was surprisingly uneventful as moving days go. Since we had already moved a great deal by car and our new camper van, only a small U-Haul truck was needed for the rest of our belongings. As I closed the door of my apartment, my thoughts were a mix of sadness and excitement at the same time. Christine and I had spent fifteen years in this old comfortable house, living and growing. Now we were both headed in new directions, still living and growing.

As I opened the front door early the next morning with Buddy on a long leash, I thought of Dorothy's familiar quote as she opened the farmhouse door and stepped into a new world, *Toto, I've a feeling we're not in Kansas anymore.* This certainly wasn't our first time heading out for a Buddy Walk from Joanne's house, but our new status as permanent residents gave me a new perspective.

Even though I liked this quiet suburban neighborhood with its flat sidewalks, I felt a pang of longing for the older, bumpy sidewalks of the Victorian-like neighborhood I had just left. I had especially loved taking Christine around on Halloween as the spooky old houses transformed the streets into a haunted dream. Now I felt like a stranger on this new block. Buddy didn't seem to mind though.

He trotted ahead on the long extendable leash without a care in the world. The only time Buddy seemed irritated was when he looked back at me as if to say *Hurry up! Why are you so slow?* With his cute Yorkie face and shiny tan coat, Buddy was irresistible. Even though he was small, he considered himself to be a Great Dane. Naturally, we wondered how he would adjust to living with a cat.

As we climbed the front porch steps after our walk, I noticed black and white Oliver in the window watching us with interest. I could almost hear him saying, *I'm not sure but I think I like this dog creature. I wonder how long he's going to stay.*

We had found Oliver a year before at a shelter after Cara Mia had died from mouth cancer. He was the only cat in the "Let's-get-acquainted Room" who wasn't in a frenzy. Since he was older, he nonchalantly watched the youngsters leaping and rolling as they vied for attention. Now in his new home, Oliver acted like our perfect butler and had quickly latched onto Joanne's heart.

Buddy's heart was not so easy to win over. Most of the time, he quietly moved from his napping station any time Oliver crept close for a snuggle.

Whether this retreating behavior would change was undetermined. At least peace reigned…for now.

As I unleashed Buddy and settled into the warm house, I found Joanne standing at the kitchen counter. At the sound of my steps, she turned and smiled. "Hi honey, welcome home."

"Boy, that sounds good." I quickly wrapped my arms around the love of my life. At that moment I felt transplanted and my roots were stretching out into new soil, ready to grow some more.

CHAPTER 13

❧

Wedding Bells

"It feels like I've never left," Joanne said as we followed Marie, the nurse tech, down the familiar hallway to the infusion room. Although the décor was the same, the pumped up air conditioning almost convinced us we were now entering a refrigerator.

"Well, believe it or not, it's only been about four weeks since your surgery and the last time we were here," I responded with the obvious. Since time had taken on a bizarre meaning altogether, it felt like four years, not weeks, to me.

Marie turned to Joanne, "So I think you know that with this new chemo and IP port, you'll have to lie down, right?" Joanne nodded as Marie continued. "We have a couple private rooms for that next to the kitchen area if they're available."

Joanne smiled as we approached the room and found it empty. She loved her privacy. We already understood that the new chemo drug, Cisplatin, was very strong and would be administered directly to Joanne's abdomen through the new port. The familiar drug, Taxol, would also be given in combination during these first two weeks. The third week would be a free week, like a vacation of sorts. Depending on test results, another round could follow throughout the summer.

Within minutes of settling into our new room, we heard a familiar voice.

"Well, look who's back." Sarah, our chemo nurse, swept into the room with a cheery smile. "Did you miss me?" After months of sharing cancer and camping stories with Sarah during these visits, we had become almost family.

"Yes we did," Joanne confessed honestly. "But we sure didn't miss chemo." Now that she had regained some strength, it didn't seem fair that she was about to be blasted again with these nasty chemicals.

"I'm afraid this chemo will probably do a number on you with nausea and fatigue." Sarah was now serious, "And it's very important that you take in lots of water...drink, drink, drink." I knew what Joanne's scrunched facial expression meant. Unlike me, she absolutely hated drinking water.

"Drink, drink, drink would sound good to me if it was something stronger," Joanne added. I nodded my head in complete agreement as we all had a laugh.

"Well, if you don't think you can drink enough water, you can always choose to do a home IV." Sarah went on to explain that a visiting nurse would come to the house and teach me how to set it up. Despite Sarah's reassurance that it would be easy, however, I couldn't ignore the slight fear and trepidation that washed over me. I should have paid more attention to the IV procedure after all these months.

Even with the help of anti-nausea drugs, the side effects from the Cisplatin were the worst yet. As predicted, Joanne's nausea and exhaustion walloped her all week. Finding foods that were agreeable, even in small amounts, was a monumental task. Clear soups, saltines, and some puddings made a hit until she graduated to my Christmas raspberry/lemon Jell-O mold. With her depleted appetite and affected taste buds, my legendary side dish was as prized to her as the meal we'd had at the Blue Ginger years before. Mingled with my worry and helplessness about her sorry state was the joyful thought that I could at least make something she would eat and enjoy. After all, my culinary reputation had always been as a comfort food cook—never a gourmet chef—and Joanne needed comfort.

Learning how to set up and dismantle the home IV saline solution became a new skill that I could proudly add to my Nurse Ratched resume. Even though using the original IV port in her chest eliminated sticking a needle in her arm, Joanne seemed to enjoy referring to me as the sadistic nurse from the movie, *One Flew Over the Cuckoo's Nest*. In response, I often called her Patient Ratched.

We continued to be amazed with our ability to cope with these unexpected curveballs hurled our way. However, we also looked forward to the day when we could hang bird feeders or plants on the IV pole instead of saline solution. At least the effort to provide extra water was helping her recovery from these wicked side effects of poisoning her body in order to destroy cancer.

By the weekend, Joanne had miraculously bounced back from the unrelenting stretch of exhaustion and discomfort. I was amazed when she began making lists of chores to do and errands to run as she ignored cancer in favor of life's ordinary tasks. Less ordinary, however, were the preparations for our wedding ceremony that was coming up in two weeks.

The struggle to legalize same-sex marriage anywhere in the world had always seemed like a futile effort. Building the Great Pyramid of Giza would have been easier. Even the slightest progress toward new laws felt like those enormous stone blocks inching along on log rollers as Egyptian slaves pulled the ropes. Like most people, I never entertained the idea that I would ever witness such legislation in my lifetime. Then, with the same surprise as a lifting fog that reveals a burst of sunlight, the law giving us the right to marry was passed in Rhode Island in 2013, less than one year before Joanne's cancer journey had begun.

Weeks before her surgery, we had occasionally broached the subject of legalizing our marriage but hadn't formalized any plans for a ceremony. After seventeen years of living and loving together, our commitment to each other and God was granite solid. We never felt a need to don white gowns or tuxedos and dip into our savings for a wedding. With the intrusion of cancer, however, our thoughts drifted toward some practical applications and peace of mind.

According to some experts, there are a thousand and one benefits to the institution of marriage. Not everyone would agree with greater happiness, longer life, and less depression, but the legal advantages that straight couples take for granted cannot be denied. For years, horror stories of loving gay partners losing everything still haunted those of us who could be denied visitation during sickness or even the final moments before death.

When Joanne and I considered legal marriage, our impetus was initially health insurance. Since she was not yet eligible for Medicare at sixty-four and was now considering retirement, the idea of an easy transfer to my health insurance at work was appealing. Other benefits came to mind as well. As Joanne's wife, there would be no question about my access to medical information, visitation at the hospital, or even filing taxes.

Another important benefit that we didn't like to think about was easier access as executor of our wills.

We had Edith Windsor, the gay rights activist, to thank for our full benefits. After her wife of forty years had died in 2009, Edith was forced to pay an exorbitant inheritance tax because her legal marriage was not recognized by the federal government. Straight married couples did not have to pay the tax. After a relentless battle, the Supreme Court ruled in her favor in 2013, paving the way for greater acceptance of same-sex marriages. Now that the law had been passed, Joanne and I agreed to legally tie the knot. Our cancer journey was difficult enough without worrying about our rights as a couple.

"So, honey, let's get our minds off cancer and plan our wedding," Joanne announced three days before her major surgery in early May. She was ready to use her iPad for research as she perched in her usual dark brown wicker rocker in the sunroom. There were no nameplates on our favorite seats but I imagined a "Director" sign on the back of hers.

The newly constructed sunroom was the largest room in the house. As wide as the house itself, it extended into the backyard another twenty feet and felt like a sanctuary. Tall double windows flooded light into the room from three sides and a glass sliding door gave access to the back steps and garden. An iron gas fireplace in one corner provided cozy ambiance and heat with the touch of a switch while a tiled, round bistro table and chairs sat ready for an intimate lunch along one wall. Solid beige walls, light pine trim, and a hardwood floor added to the cheery atmosphere. The four armed wicker chairs lined up in an arc facing the backyard on top of a Navajo style rug were well used.

"That sounds like a great idea," I agreed, "especially since we only have a few weeks." We had become a formidable planning team with complimentary skills, ready to focus on a new, happier goal. Finding a window of opportunity when she would feel her best after surgery would be tricky.

Our relationship had evolved from the days of counseling when the pendulum of emotions had swung in opposite directions. Over the years, we had used our improved communication skills to compromise and solve problems so that now the pendulum rarely moved from the middle. Like the Serenity Prayer, we had changed what we could in ourselves but accepted and appreciated our differences. Love and understanding had grown as beautifully as our garden and we couldn't imagine life without the other. Getting married would be the icing on the cake.

To say I was anxious about pulling off such an event in a short time was an understatement. I may have looked relaxed with notepad and pen next to my favorite light brown wicker throne, but my mind was racing.

"I guess the first thing to think about is a date." Joanne zeroed in with her electronic calendar on her lap. "Since chemo is starting up again in early June in a three-week cycle, I think we should pick that weekend just before my free week." She was on a roll. "By then I should be feeling somewhat normal."

Even though cancer wasn't invited to this wedding, it still influenced our planning for the ceremony. We knew that new chemo side effects, Joanne's stamina, and unexpected surgical delays could change things in a hurry. But we were determined to squeeze out every normal moment possible. Once again, we were learning that weaving life's events into a cancer frame would always be a challenge.

"Hey," I exclaimed as I looked on the calendar for the date she had just mentioned. "That would be Saturday, June 14. It's close to our anniversary." We both smiled at the thought of the day we had met years before when I had answered her impetuous ad. Even Charlie and Rosie raised their heads with sleepy eyes from their separate napping chairs as if to say, *What's all the fuss?*

Under the circumstances, the option of going to city hall with witnesses and using a justice of the peace crossed our minds...but only for a second. Neither one of us had walked down the aisle as brides before so this was our chance. Spiritually, our first choice was a church if one could be reserved on short notice and if one would accept a same-sex ceremony. Our second choice would have been a peaceful outdoor setting like a garden or beach, but adding extra plans for unpredictable weather seemed crazy.

After deciding on the date and probable setting, our wedding to-do list grew. For practical purposes, the guest list would have to be small. Only a few close family and friends living nearby could be included. Fortunately, we enlisted Christine to quickly produce "Save the Date" notices and invitations. As a professional graphic designer, she had exceptional artistic talent. And now married, Christine's husband agreed to be the photographer. For flowers, there would be one large display for the ceremony, and for the reception, we could rent one of our favorite cozy Italian restaurants. With her connections as an event planner, Joanne also had a reference for a small bakery whose owner produced beautiful cakes. My anxiety had turned into excitement as I imagined our special day and forgot about surgery and chemo for a while.

"At least we already have our rings," I said as I wracked my brain to remember the traditional items on a wedding list. "Although, it's hard to get mine on and off now because of my knuckles." These days, my arthritic hands looked more like my Nana's whose fingers had become gnarled over the years.

"Mine comes off okay," Joanne replied, "but we can do something else with the rings for the ceremony." Joanne was thinking ahead but then recalled a memory. "Remember when we got these rings, honey?" Of course I remembered as we reminisced once more.

One early January, a couple years after I had moved in, we were bundled up in Provincetown walking briskly along the shops. After countless getaways to our favorite escape over the years, Joanne's initial discomfort with being "out" had dissipated long before. We had often enjoyed the offseason peace and tranquility of P-town as much as the warm festivities of summer.

While enjoying a bed and breakfast stay over the weekend, we intended to marry ourselves on this trip since at that time gay marriage was not yet legal in Rhode Island. Even though Massachusetts had passed the law, we preferred our home state for any ceremony. No matter what, we were determined that our impromptu, two-person wedding would include buying rings in a town where the clerk would smile with us, not frown in judgment.

When the rings in the window of a fine jewelry store caught our eye, we sauntered in, preparing to browse. Not surprising, we comprised the entire winter crowd in the small store as the elder jeweler waited on us himself. After we found the rings we liked in the case, the jeweler proudly presented them to us.

"Oh, I like this one." I quickly decided on the small gold ring. The slender band separated at the top like a divided parkway where three diamonds sparkled in a row. The rounded lines indicated a feeling of softness that suited me.

"I like this other one." Joanne picked up a ring that was similar but different. While hers also separated at the top with four small diamonds lined up in the middle, the top of the design was squared off on one side, creating an angular line and a feeling of strength. I thought the rings perfectly represented our similar tastes but different personalities.

The jeweler seemed pleased that we liked his designs and explained the rings would be ready the next day after sizing them for our left pinky fingers. Despite her coming out progress, Joanne did not want the rings displayed on the traditional ring fingers that would tell the world we were married. Even though a familiar pang of sadness about secrecy lingered for a moment like the flashback of a bad dream, my deep love for her allowed and accepted her innate need for privacy.

"Do you remember when you proposed to me honey?" Joanne grinned in the sunroom as we continued to recall that weekend in P-town.

"Ummm, I remember when I asked you to marry me at Beaver Tail," I hesitated to say. I was referring to one of the local trips to our favorite ocean view years before. The day had been magical because, miraculously, we had the entire park to ourselves. The peace and stillness had been a gift from the heavens.

"Oh my god," Joanne said sheepishly, "I really don't remember that." I was shocked as she continued. "I just remember when you proposed in P-town on the bike path."

"I can't believe it," I said, as I started to laugh. "I really don't remember the bike path." Now we were both laughing but I managed to add, "But I do remember finding that plaque in the gift shop and thinking *how appropriate*." We glanced at the small narrow quote on the sunroom wall that read, *Grow old along with me, the best is yet to be.*

"Well, it's a good thing you proposed twice then," Joanne concluded. "One for you and one for me."

"And it's a good thing our minds work...or don't work...the same," I added as I rose from my chair heading to the kitchen. "Can I get you anything?" I asked, bending over for a kiss. At that moment, our love, not our memory, was all we needed.

While Joanne was still in the hospital recovering from surgery, I continued making phone calls to secure the restaurant for the reception as well as consulting with the minister who would conduct the ceremony. Incidentals like choosing music, writing vows, and deciding what to wear danced in my mind as well. Despite the unpredictable cancer backdrop, our wedding plans were gratefully turning like well-oiled gears. But our greatest relief was scheduling the church sanctuary.

After years of sampling different denominations, we had landed at a huge Congregational church where we felt equally accepted and inspired. The tall gothic structure was usually filled on Sunday mornings, the music was exquisite and the sermons were always thought provoking. When thinking about our wedding, however, the large sanctuary would have swallowed our tiny group. Thankfully, an intimate chapel off to the side of the main area would be perfect.

Without hesitation, we had asked Rachel, the minister, to conduct our ceremony. Our interaction with her had always felt warm and compassionate and we were thrilled when she expressed her delight with our request. By God's hand, the date was free and the wheels continued to turn.

The day of the wedding in June began early with love in the air amid partly cloudy skies. As planned, Christine arrived at the house early for makeup duty, especially for me, and general bridesmaid assistance. As she walked through the front door, I thought of the first time I had walked into Joanne's house so many years before.

As soon as Joanne had opened the door that day, I had been impressed with the cozy, yet elegant, décor of the living room. Even though the antique, tawny velvet couch and two comfortable armchairs had been reupholstered with cornflower blue over the years, the house now looked very similar to that first visit. The long lace curtains, light floral wallpaper, and large Mediterranean painting hanging over the faux fireplace mantel loaded with family photos enhanced Joanne's Italian heritage. The sage green wicker coffee table perfectly matched the colors of the large Oriental rug surrounded by glossy hardwood floors.

As Christine and I passed through the house, memories jumped out to remind me of our already married life. Glimpses of our travels together could be seen on the walls in the dining room. Sitting under the crystal chandelier at the rectangular oak table, our dinner guests were always surrounded by colorful paintings from several cruises and watercolors from talented friends. As an avid photographer, Joanne had collected stunning works by coworkers as well. Though the rooms were small, the spirit of peace, love, and adventure filled every crack.

Getting ready for the wedding was hectic but not overwhelming. Since Joanne was already exhausted, her pace was slow and steady. She chose to wear an artsy sundress with large red, orange, and raspberry flowers bordered by a small black jacket. Her raspberry headdress with a side knot perfectly matched the colors in her dress. Despite how miserable she felt physically, I thought she looked fabulous.

Less concerned with my outfit, I had chosen my comfortable linen tan set with pants and flowing jacket over a dressy black top. With Joanne's help from her private boutique the night before, a Native American style necklace and earrings would accessorize my outfit. I thought I was set… until Christine and Joanne ganged up on me in the small dressing room.

"Mom, why don't you wear this beautiful brown paisley scarf instead of your jacket?" Christine was taking her bridesmaid's duties seriously.

"Yes, absolutely," Joanne joined in. "It's wide enough so it can be tied in the back." Now I was outnumbered.

"Oh, I don't know," I whined. "That's not really my style." Even though I tried to be strong, I knew I was overruled. With a sigh, I let them fuss over me while I stood like a mannequin. Together, the two artists created their masterpiece and I eventually agreed to the new look.

"Okay," I conceded. "But I'm going to wear my jacket at the restaurant." At least I had some say in the matter.

After Joyce, our second bridesmaid, arrived in her yellow print dress and jacket, matching Christine's yellow sundress, pictures were taken in the backyard and garden. We decided to keep some wedding traditions like picture taking while certainly abandoning the groom doll on the cake.

As we drove to the church and our waiting guests, our excitement bubbled while holding hands in the car like teenagers, not sixty-year-olds. My concern for Joanne's wellbeing weighed heavy on my mind but I was glad we decided to have chairs handy during the ceremony. If at all possible, cancer was taking a back seat on this day.

We were giggling inside and out when we arrived at the church and saw family and friends entering the church from the side entrance that led to the chapel. My eighty-eight-year-old mother looked stunning in her royal blue dress and jacket contrasting with her snow white short wavy hair. She was flanked by my younger brother, Ray, and sister-in-law, Ann, who were also dressed in their Sunday best. Looking as chic as her aunt, Carissa and her boyfriend were entering the doorway and waved as they made their way to be seated. Having our families present for such a non-conventional event was heartwarming and I was filled with gratitude.

"Hi, my sister," I greeted and hugged Chris, my younger sister, who was standing with her husband, Mark, at the back of the chapel. Despite her hidden anxiety, she had agreed to read a scripture during the ceremony along with Carissa who would also be reading. Their participation and support meant the world to both of us.

"Hi sister and sister-in-law," Chris responded with a radiant smile. As loving comrades, she and Joanne would have started gabbing on the spot but we had little time before Rev. Rachel came by in her clerical robe to move us along. It was time to begin.

With everyone seated, Joanne and I stood hand in hand at the back of the chapel facing the front altar that held our beautiful spray of flowers. Tall, stately Roman-style pillars stood on each side of the altar with a striking stained glass portrait of a biblical family that seemed ironically different from our own. Dark wood and adobe tan walls surrounded us with strength and grandeur. My heart was filled with joy as I turned to Joanne and smiled.

As Christine and Joyce began their cadenced walk in front of us, I whispered, "Here we go." Joanne squeezed my hand and when the recorded music, "Perhaps Love," began to play, we walked together down the aisle, savoring every slow step. Tears of happiness welled up as we met Rachel at the altar.

Years before, John Denver and Placido Domingo had recorded the song as a duet. We loved the lyrics. "Perhaps love is like a resting place, a shelter from the storm. It exists to give you comfort, it is there to keep you warm…" In our planning, the song seemed perfect for the wedding so we convinced one of our friends to operate the music device at the right moment. As we all listened to the beautiful words, we knew the right choice had been made.

Facing the love of my life and holding her hands, I flashed back to our first lunch with grilled cheese, pea soup, and the deep connection I had immediately felt looking into her eyes that day seventeen years before. Despite our rolling journey, the pilot light never went out. I was proud of our determination to work together for so long in order to reach this moment. Joanne looked back at me with the same message in her eyes. Although the threat of losing her tugged at the back of my mind, the ominous thought flitted away like a hummingbird as the ceremony began.

Words of love and commitment, prayers of thanks, affirmations of support and blessings for peace filled the sanctuary as everyone participated in our renewed promise to love and cherish each other forever. We read familiar scripture from the Bible, "*Let the peace of Christ rule in your hearts,*" and "*For where you go I will go.*" But a Native American wedding blessing also defined us, "*Now you will feel no rain, for each of you will be shelter for the other, Treat yourselves and each other with respect, and remind yourselves often of what brought you together.*" With these basic tenets, our relationship had thrived and flourished.

The minister's poignant blessing touched our hearts, "*May each day unfold into a new and beautiful adventure for each of you. God bless you with a long life together surrounded with those you love.*" Our ceremony, like every day, was filled with hope no matter what defined a long life.

Neither one of us knew what the other would write for vows. Not surprising, they were similar but different, like our rings and our personalities. As the sanctuary seemed to fade away, leaving only the two of us, Joanne began reading part of a poem.

"*I was always yours to have. You were always mine. We have loved each other in and out of time.*" Our connection was so strong that we had often felt like time travelers, knowing each other in another life. Joanne continued to read.

"*From the moment I spoke to you and later met you, my heart leapt with joy. You are the answer to my prayer as I looked up at the stars so, so many nights and asked God to send me my soul mate...You are the love of my life.*" As we beamed at each other, it felt as if we were standing alone with God's hands resting on our shoulders.

My vow to Joanne echoed the same thoughts about our divine gift and forever commitment as well as additional words about our unique journey.

"*Throughout these years, you have been my friend, my love, my fellow spiritual seeker and my daring playmate. We have shared easy fun days as well as difficult, sad days...always with an equal commitment to work things out and grow together...I love you with all my heart and soul...*" Although my voice cracked toward the end, we kept beaming as our minds returned to the ceremony.

The minister's final words were the pronouncement that we were married and partners for life. After a kiss to seal the deal, we faced our families hand in hand and almost skipped back down the aisle.

"So, honey, do you feel any different?" I asked my new wife as she lay on the couch in the TV room, propped up with pillows behind her while I rubbed her feet, resting in my lap. The wedding and reception were over and Joanne was exhausted.

"Not really, how about you?" she replied honestly. We had to chuckle about our wedding night locale in front of the TV.

"Me either," I said. "Maybe I feel a little closer to you if that's possible." My thought was that we should feel something anyway.

"It sure was a beautiful ceremony and everyone seemed to have a great time at the restaurant," Joanne commented with a sigh. Despite her own fatigue, concern for the guests was her constant priority. Twenty of us had filled the cozy dining room with laughter and raised glasses.

"I loved the cake," I said, picturing the exquisitely piped one-tier creation topped with real asters and hyacinths cascading from the top along one side. Two entwined silver hearts sat on top where the traditional bride and groom replicas usually stood. The light lemon cake with raspberry filling melted in the mouth.

"I was so glad that Christine, Carole Ann, and Joyce gave toasts," Joanne said thoughtfully. "It meant a lot to me." I remembered when Joanne came out to her sister years before and how attitudes had changed and healed.

"You know what I really liked?" I looked at my honey with a twinkle as she nodded for me to continue. "I liked when someone clinked a glass for us to kiss." Now we were both smiling as I got up and kissed her mouth as sweetly as the very first time.

"I'll tell you what I really like, honey," she replied with a smirk. Joanne was in the moment. "I really like you rubbing my feet." I took the hint and returned to my seat and old job.

We had no plans for a honeymoon, of course, until cancer allowed another window of opportunity. But the idea remained in the back of our minds. In some ways, we had already traveled on many romantic honeymoons and every day, even in the sunroom, was like a holiday.

CHAPTER 14

Tree of Friends

"What time are Mary and Eileen supposed to get here?" Joanne asked me from the royal blue couch in our cozy camper van. With her legs stretched out to the end of the couch and an AARP magazine in her hand, she rested contentedly after a simple oatmeal with blueberries breakfast.

I looked up from my crossword book and thought about our friends for a moment as I reached for my steaming cup of coffee waiting patiently on the nearby shelf. I was completely relaxed in the cushioned passenger chair that was swiveled away from the dashboard, facing Joanne.

"I think they said mid-afternoon, depending on traffic and how much they meander along the way," I replied. We admired our slightly older friends for their spunk and appreciated their support. Over the past fifteen years, we had often said, *If Mary and Eileen can do it, so can we.*

Having left Rhode Island three days before, we were now in Boothbay, Maine, nestled in our favorite campsite overlooking a peaceful cove. The tall grasses among the blue water swayed gracefully with the breeze as the mix of aspen, birch and pine trees surrounded our home in the woods like old friends. Looking out at our view always reminded me of the Twenty-Third Psalm, "He leadeth me beside still waters, He restoreth my soul."

Joanne certainly needed restoration of both body and spirit after enduring two grueling weeks of chemo and a blood transfusion following our wedding. Whether she could manage this ten-day camping trip was a question we pondered even as we made our way along Maine's rocky coastline road taking in the breathtaking ocean views. Our new modus operandi had become *Try it and see what happens*. At least our little RV provided more comfort than our aging cabin tent years before.

For the first five years after we met, we had used the tent and air mattress whenever we camped. After sacrificing her comfort for so long, however, Joanne finally had enough. In research mode before the age of the internet, she had scanned the newspaper ads for camper vans for weeks. As a former backpacker who had scorned RVers and their need for creature comforts, I was momentarily appalled at the idea until the arthritic pain in my lower back reminded me that creature comforts may not be so bad.

Unfortunately, the attractive used RV described in the ad that Joanne circled had already been sold. With determination, however, she continued the search for another month until one Friday night she came running into her kitchen where I was cooking dinner for us.

"I can't believe this," she exclaimed. "That same ad for the van we wanted is back in the paper." Before I could respond, she reached for the wall phone and stated, "I'm going to call right away."

"Great idea," I said honestly. I knew she was on a roll as her excitement swept me along like a leaf on a swift stream.

We learned from the owner that the van was indeed available since the first sale had fallen through. As we slowly approached the manicured suburban home the next morning, we spotted the nineteen-foot 1989 Ford Econoline camper in the long driveway and felt another love-at-first-sight moment. Despite the van's age, the white exterior with navy blue trim was in mint condition. All the creature comforts were there in miniature: kitchen sink, two stovetop gas burners, sleeping quarters over the cab, wood cupboards, royal blue curtains, and a convenient toilet in the back. I decided that my backpacking days were definitely over.

After a successful test drive, the owner said to us, "It seems like this van was made for you." Since we had the same thought, the papers were signed and our deposit check exchanged hands. The sale would be complete in a few days following a systems inspection but we knew our new girl would pass. As we drove away, I had the feeling that we had just bought a house together.

"I think you should register the van in your name, honey," Joanne said thoughtfully. "We can share expenses, of course, but it'll be your baby." She knew I was sensitive about the upcoming move into her house that, to me, would always feel like hers alone. The van represented a way for me to feel some ownership, even if it was a house on wheels. Through the efforts of counseling, we had learned to respect each other's position which often meant letting go of control.

"I like that idea, thanks." I could sense Joanne's love and trust as if we were back in the dance studio taking lessons for the cha-cha, swing, and deciding who should lead. "And I think we should name her, *Minnie, Meant-to-Be,*" I added. We loved the name almost as much as we loved each other.

As we waited for the arrival of our friends in their own fancy camper van, I thought about the past two days of heavy rain. Since Joanne was weak as a newborn kitten, we didn't mind staying put the first day, reading, resting, and eating soup. By the second day of rain, however, Joanne was ready to ignore the weather, ride the shuttle bus to town for some homemade chowder by a fire and browse through a few unique gift shops. I knew her strength was improving when she started collecting brochures for a Puffin cruise, a Schooner sail, and a Harbor lobster lunch cruise. Her ability to bounce back after the ravages of chemo always amazed me.

"I'm really surprised that I'm able to walk on these hills," Joanne confided. After walking back along the gravel road from the shuttle bus, our camper was coming into view. Even though the wooded campground was relatively quiet during the weekdays with sites spaced well apart, we anticipated the noise level to rise over the weekend.

"To tell you the truth, I didn't think I could do it at first," Joanne said quietly. I just listened as she continued. "This really gives me some hope that I'll recover when chemo stops." I knew she was anxious to resume a normal life and kick cancer to the curb.

"You'll get there, my honey lamb," I said, putting my arm around her shoulders as we approached our folding chairs under the awning. "I think it's time for wine. Do you want some?" Even I was ready to relax.

"I think I'd better stick with a cup of tea for now," she replied. "Then maybe a short nap before dinner, okay?" Joanne may have felt like Wonder Woman earlier but her tired body was calling for a timeout.

Surrounded by chirping birds and raindrops on the roof, the relaxing rainy days were perfect opportunities to share long conversations about ourselves, our relationship and this frightening cancer journey. Our devotional books as well as our garden flowers for the picnic table were as important to bring along on our travels as toilet paper. After reading a daily inspiration and then meditating, our hearts were opened to sharing deeper thoughts that connected us as much as locking eyes.

"Honey, I'm so grateful to God that I have you while I go through this," Joanne said after *Namaste*. "I just wouldn't be able to do it…no way." With an adorable navy fleece cap covering her smooth bald head, she looked at me intently as she leaned against the couch pillows.

"Joanne, I would do anything for you…I love you so much." My eyes never left hers. "If I could take your place, I would." I was serious. My tendency was to fix things and find solutions to the problems standing in the road. With her insidious cancer, I felt helpless and I hated to see her suffer. Taking her place seemed like the only fix.

"Well, I wouldn't want you to go through this hell," she continued. "Right now, I'm still hopeful and I'll keep fighting and pushing myself no matter what." From her stories about growing up with rowdy kids near her house, I imagined her taking on this cancer as a tough big sister, defending her family and honing her grit.

"Are you afraid, honey?" I whispered after a pause. I had often watched her staring at the garden or pensively gazing at the ocean. Joanne did not usually talk about her fear with me in order to spare me from worry. Perhaps she was also afraid of falling apart.

"I'm not afraid to die because I know God is with me and I saw how it was with my mother, but I don't want to suffer." Joanne's eyes were filling up as she added, "It's like I have to keep letting go while holding on at the same time."

I got up from my comfy chair and sat next to my wife, whose tears trickled down her cheeks. As I wrapped my arms around her, I could feel the warmth of her divine light while our quiet sobs mingled with the rain.

"Hey there," Mary called out as she and Eileen sauntered into our campsite in the afternoon. They had just maneuvered their camper into the site across the road. With Mary's no-nonsense approach and Eileen's quiet demeanor, they fit together like puzzle pieces. Despite graying hair and older physiques, they looked younger than their years. We were genuinely happy to see them as we exchanged warm hugs.

Although we had known our friends for many years, I could not remember the exact day and circumstance of our meeting. Like most friendships, they seem to evolve from other connections like a chain reaction. When Joanne and I melded our lives together, we brought along not only our family trees but also many dear friends who filled their own tree. As we interacted with each other's friends, new branches grew from the old. By the time Joanne's cancer journey began, our tree of friends was a solid oak with deep roots.

"How's the old married couple?" Eileen asked as they found seats around the picnic table where we would later play Rummikub, one of our favorite games, with drinks and snacks.

"We're the same as always," Joanne responded with a smile from her folding chair in the sun. "When are you two getting married?" We all chuckled knowing that, like us, Mary and Eileen already felt married. But, unlike us, they had no plans to legally tie the knot.

Not one of us had been married before, although Joanne came close to considering marriage when she dated Rob for three years in college. At least, everyone expected them to marry until their lives went in different directions. She often told me she could imagine herself with a child more than with a husband.

My own brush with a straight marriage happened during my trying-to-fit-in phase of dating, long before I officially came out. Even though the guy had asked me to marry him and I had agreed, I knew something was missing. Shortly after the faux proposal, we broke up. Walking down the aisle as a bride in a white gown toward a tuxedoed groom was never my dream. I would have preferred to wear the tuxedo.

Our campsite was located at the end of a peninsula next to the accessible boat launch. At times, the area was busy with boaters but we had also appreciated the small access for dipping our kayaks. Years before cancer, we loved bringing our toys that included bicycles and hiking boots as well as our kayaks. We were always on the go.

While paddling one year in the cove, a seal had popped his head out of the water and followed us with as much curiosity about us as we had for him. As usual with all animals, Joanne paddled as quietly as she could in order to get as close to the seal as possible. I imagined St. Francis, the patron saint of animals, patiently doing the same. Watching Joanne also reminded me of the saint's quote: *Preach the Gospel at all times and when necessary use words.* I loved her example and appreciated her steadfast St. Francis statue in our garden.

In the early years of friendship with our camping buddies, we had paddled a few times on rivers with Mary while Eileen preferred to meet us at the boat takeout spot ready to serve a tasty homemade lunch. Division of labor worked for them and we were all too willing to partake of Eileen's culinary delights. Even though our common interests with them had not included many sports other than golf, we had always enjoyed campfires, browsing gift shops, dances, and eating out. Joanne especially loved to discuss house projects and financial matters with Mary.

In the early days of counseling when we examined our personalities and focused on growth, Joanne's comfort level with my tree of gay friends coincided with her acceptance of her own bisexuality. Initially, she seemed almost shy and even annoyed at lesbian events. Over time, when her confidence in her identity and our relationship grew, she opened up and relaxed among my friends. Without knowing it themselves, those friends provided the rich soil that helped Joanne and me grow stronger together.

"So, I take it you didn't bring your kayaks on this trip?" Mary stated the obvious but was also fishing for Joanne's present state of health.

"Good god, there's no way I could even lift a paddle," Joanne replied. "I'm just happy I can walk around the campground and shops or sit around the fire." Any sign of normalcy these days kept us afloat more than our boats could.

Before we owned kayaks, we had learned a lesson or two about ourselves and how to compromise when we attempted to paddle a canoe with my backyard friends. Often paddling in a friendly group of avid canoeists, these women welcomed us despite our clumsy canoe strokes.

Paddling a canoe is a team effort of course. One person has to artfully paddle at the stern, or back, providing direction and the other paddler at the bow provides power and warning about dangers ahead. After many unsuccessful attempts, Joanne and I concluded that this type of teamwork would not suit our relationship. Our canoe trips usually ended with both of us barking at each other and stomping off to the car for a silent ride home. We recognized our success when working together at home or when traveling but realistically decided we had our limits. At least we noticed that I was finally barking back.

One summer day, Joanne suggested we rent kayaks on one of Rhode Island's saltwater ponds. She had been kayaking before with her long-time friends, Mary and Joe, but I had only dreamt of trying the sport. After one quick lesson, I gleefully adjusted the footrests, positioned the paddle at shoulder height, and took off from the shore as if I had been born in a kayak.

Joanne smiled with delight as we peacefully paddled on the huge pond together, but steering our own boats. While learning to kayak, we also learned how to accept our differences. We discovered that paddling in different boats was much more interesting than matching strokes.

That Christmas, to my great surprise, I found the same rental kayak with my name on the tag under the tree in Joanne's living room. She had secretly purchased the white boat for me and a yellow one for herself after the season had ended when the rentals went on sale. For years, they always symbolized our separate journeys together.

"Are you thinking of a honeymoon someday?" Eileen asked as we sat around the crackling campfire watching the sparks float into the blackness. With drinks in our hands and only peaceful murmurs of other campers in the distance, we considered the happy prospect.

"Well, we don't know when of course because of stupid chemo," Joanne replied, sounding tired and disgusted at the thought of cancer. "But someday I'd like to go back to Hawaii…this time with Lin." Several years before, she had visited her former neighbor and close friend, Pat, in Maui where she experienced a spiritual island connection. With persistent hope in her heart, Joanne was determined to share this special place with me and her friends. But, as Dr. D. had said, *it depends.*

We left Boothbay in the rain once more but not with heavy hearts. Despite nature's peace, the abundant lobster and sweet blueberries, we were anxious to return home to our furry friends, Phoebe and Charlie. Between my daughter and Joanne's sister, the kitties had been well cared for during our absence.

As we opened the backdoor, however, Phoebe screamed to the contrary. *Where have you been? I'm starving! Can't you see I'm wasting away?* Her original name, Little Miss, had evolved into Little Miss *fill-in-the-blank.* This time, she was dubbed Little Miss Piggy. Her roly-poly body could hardly be described as wasting away despite her constant pleas for food. Since our response to her complaint was unacceptable to her, she turned her back while we unloaded Minnie.

Charlie's initial response was a skittish run downstairs until he recognized his mommas. With our identities revealed, his greeting was soft and sweet. His impeccable manners would not allow such a display as his little sister's. We often wondered how he coped with her shenanigans.

Our tree of furry friends had grown many branches over the years and we were grateful for their spirit, antics, and affection. Like Oliver, our former black and white, Charlie couldn't get close enough to Joanne when she was sleeping, providing another comforting warm body when chemo chilled her blood. Crazy Phoebe made Joanne laugh as she chased her big brother through the house like the bicycles in the Tour de France. We needed these treasured friends for healing as much as we needed our human friends for support.

The routine of chemo resumed until mid-August when Dr. D. announced that the latest CT scan revealed no sign of cancer. We sat frozen in his office with our mouths agape as his words sunk in. However, he tempered the good news by saying, "I'm in a quandary. The CA 125 still shows a count of 107." With that many lingering cancer cells, we had many questions for Dr. D. as he discussed possible causes. But, in the end, he valued the CT scan readings more than the blood test. With his recommendation that Joanne take a two-month break from chemo, we felt like the cage door had opened and Joanne was set free.

Naturally, additional blood tests and CT scans would continue periodically, but life without chemo seemed like winning an Oscar. Joanne deserved an award for her endurance. As she felt stronger and could say, "The more I do, the better I feel," she began composing more lists of possible activities. My list included kayaking, biking, hiking, and golf while her list added shopping, weeding the garden, and cleaning the closets. In our individual ways, we happily tackled both lists together just like paddling our kayaks.

By mid-September, I was able to include the following paragraph in my Joanne Update,

During these past few weeks, we have been living an almost normal life. Joanne has been feeling like her old self more than ever…stronger, more active, and less tired with more appetite. Although, now she thinks

she needs to go on a diet! We've done some weekend camping with the RV on the beach and in the woods and have been able to meet more often with friends and family. That has been the best medicine! In fact, some days we have even forgotten about cancer…although, her cute, still fuzzy head is an obvious reminder. She has been continuing to work part-time which can still wear her out. But she's definitely looking forward to retiring on Oct. 16. Who knows what projects the "Queen" will insist we tackle! One piece of good news we just heard is that her CA 125 is down to 20! Thank you, God, and all of you for your prayers. The next CT scan will be on Oct. 14…so we'll see what that reveals.

Most of the time I referred to the massive list of Update readers as family and friends, belonging to separate groups. In reality, everyone on the list had lovingly merged together. The tree branches had overlapped on each tree. Relatives were as supportive as friends and loving friends were as close as family. We needed them to restore our souls like still waters.

In 2014, five and a half months after diagnosis, Joanne was declared N.E.D., no evidence of disease, following a clear CT scan in October. The news was an even better gift than the balloons and good wishes she brought home from the office on her last day of work. The IP port in her abdomen was removed in November and Joanne resolved to make the most of her joyous retirement. Her first plan was to take a watercolor painting class at a local senior center that was a longtime dream. Not surprising, the second item on her to-do list was to visit her hairdresser.

As her hair grew back, she transformed from gray to dark purple like the eggplant color of her faithful Honda that continued to run like a top ever since our second date on the Boulevard years before. By the end of December, Joanne was back with a stronger body and a stronger divine spirit. Even that nagging twenty-cancer-cell count couldn't dim her hope for a healthy life with her new wife. With our annual downhill ski trip in Vermont scheduled for the end of January, we were whistling down a new road.

Every year around Christmas, Joanne invited her circle of friends from the former Charismatic Renewal over to the house for a casual gathering of meditation, and homemade soup and salad. In time, they had become my friends as well. Someone in the small group eventually dubbed us *The Church of the Little Women*. Every November, Joanne pondered a theme for the little service and often felt led by the Spirit in unexpected ways.

"Did you get the mail today, honey?" Joanne called out from the sunroom. I was in the TV room watching golf, one of my favorite pastimes.

"Not yet, but I'll get it now." I opened the front door and shivered with the cold autumn air. After gathering the mail, I made my way to Joanne. "Here's something for you from Unity." We often used their *Daily Word* devotional that planted a thought for the day for some focus in our foggy heads.

After opening the envelope, Joanne looked at the contents and said, "Wow. Look at this." She held a three-by-five transparent decal that said, "*Be Still…and know.*" "This is my theme for the service." Then she added, "And I think we should put it on the window in Minnie."

"Sounds perfect," I whispered as I kissed the top of her purple head that would soon be covered with a ski helmet.

CHAPTER 15

∝

Spirit Quest

The wide snowy path through the quiet forest was marked with several long ski tracks that stretched as far as the next bend. Some were evenly spaced and parallel while other imprints ran helter-skelter like the thin sticks dropped randomly in the game of Pick Up Sticks. The tracks were phantom reminders that other skiers had passed this way before us.

"Joanne, what do I do when we come to a hill?" Christine was alternating her arms, poles and cross-country skis as she awkwardly followed Joanne, our graceful leader. I took up the rear in our little line-up with only slightly less flailing than my daughter.

The early spring day in New Hampshire was crisp with the sun peeking through the clouds and trees as if it was winking at us in amusement. With daypacks strapped to our backs, we were on a weekend adventure in 2003 that included Christine's first cross-country ski lesson. Still in high school, she had agreed to leave her friends and horses behind in order to share some fun with her two mommas. After six years of bonding, Christine now referred to my love as *Momma Joanne*. She always added sparkle to our adventures and we felt honored that she chose to spend some time with two old grownups.

Deftly maneuvering her skis to a gradual stop outside the tracks, Joanne partially turned toward Christine who had also managed to stop on the flat snow. Even though I had learned the basics years before on several XC ski outings, I slowly joined them, ready to audit the class for any new information I could use.

"So, when you're going downhill, remember to bend your knees and keep your upper body slightly forward like you were going to sit on a chair." Joanne was a natural teacher who exuded patience with her students. She genuinely wanted them to excel.

"Stay in the tracks or keep your skis parallel if there aren't any tracks," she added. Christine was practicing the bending and tucking while she remained in place. I couldn't help but mimic the moves as well.

"Of course, if you're going too fast, you can snowplow the ski tips in for more control," Joanne advised. That move would require more practicing.

Around the bend, a small descending slope presented itself. Joanne smoothly sailed in a straight line down the hill but Christine's knee bends, tucks, and snowplow position were forgotten as she veered off course into a bush. Luckily, she was laughing her head off as she rose on one elbow while we gathered around to assist.

"Of course, downhill skiing is easier," Joanne consoled her. "This is much more work." We continued through the woods, falling and laughing our way from one rest stop to another.

Whenever Joanne spoke of her downhill ski adventures during college years and into adulthood, her face would glow as if skiing had been a spiritual experience. Her stories were filled with challenging conditions on black diamond trails, moguls and beautiful views in the Alps. Even though I had never seen her on downhill skis, I could imagine her expertise and joy as she carved the snow from side to side. She had stopped skiing years before we met since she could no longer rally her former skiing buddies as they joined the world of work and home ownership. My one experience on downhill skis years before ended in disaster as I vowed to never attempt such a foolish sport again.

As the three of us recovered from our wintry day in the woods back at the bed and breakfast, Christine moaned a little about her sore muscles. Even a hot shower and Tylenol weren't enough to ease the pain.

"Maybe I should do some Reiki on you," Joanne offered. "It couldn't hurt and I need some practice." Christine appreciated any promise of relief as we chuckled again about bending knees and tucking butts.

Several months prior to our ski trip with Christine, Joanne had completed her second-degree Reiki (pronounced *ray-key*) training with John Harvey Gray and his wife, Lourdes, both Reiki Masters, in New Hampshire. Through this Japanese technique of laying on hands, life force energy is spiritually guided through the body for stress reduction, relaxation, and healing. Through her holistic counseling courses and connections, she had learned about Reiki as an alternative medicine and had been eager to sign up.

When Joanne practiced the technique on me, the treatment felt like a wonderful glowing radiance flowing through and around me. Resting or circling her hands slightly above me, her palms were almost hot with energy. With my eyes closed, I was amazed to sense so much light from head to toe. Along with helping her other friends and family, Reiki also seemed to help our relationship by opening more doors of understanding and connection to our spirits. Her commitment to this compassionate practice became another step on her spirit quest journey and also added to mine.

Even before we met, we had both been receptive to exploring less conventional spiritual paths and were curious about other cultures. We began our childhoods with Western Christianity but, as adults, we longed to expand our experiences. While moving my belongings to Joanne's house, we noticed duplicate book titles that reflected similar interests. My thinking had expanded years before while reading *Seven Arrows* and *Black Elk Speaks* as I connected with Native American culture. I had smiled when I found the same books on Joanne's shelf.

The idea of a vision quest had always intrigued me as I learned that, in some Native American cultures, it could be a supernatural experience of interacting with a guardian spirit animal for advice and protection. My intrinsic connection to birds was as close as I would get to such a supernatural experience other than my spirit connection to my dog, Buddy. There were even times when I felt I had been a bird in another life, especially when I could fly in my dreams.

As a rite of passage, a vision quest often helps to develop survival skills, gain maturity, and connect with nature, the Creator and ancestors. At an early age, I had connected spiritually with nature on church retreats or weeklong camps. As I grew, I increasingly felt God's presence when ensconced in the woods, sitting by the ocean, or hiking in the mountains. My vision quest was not one week, month or year. I realized my spirit quest was my lifetime.

Along with her charismatic renewal experience and innate curiosity, Joanne had connected with mentors who taught her about sweat lodge cleansings, deep meditation, and chakras. At times, she would burn sage for cleansing a house or room of negative energy. Of course, the social backdrop in the 1960s and 1970s, including sensitivity training and encounter groups, also became fertilizer for expanding spirit experiences.

We both wanted to sample alternative connections to the divine in the world and in ourselves. No matter where we had travelled, near or far, we always searched for spirit as if we were on a scavenger hunt and we inevitably found it in others and within. When our lives entwined, our individual spirit quests met side by side like meeting on the river in our kayaks.

Prior to Joanne's Reiki classes, at some health store she had randomly picked up a catalog of programs at the Kripalu Center for Yoga in the Berkshire Mountains of western Massachusetts. When she brought the book home one day, we perused the weekend retreats that were offered.

"Are you interested in any of these?" Joanne asked me. We were standing shoulder to shoulder at the kitchen counter like two kids reading a comic book. After turning a page, I pointed to one program description.

"Maybe we should think about this one...Introduction to Kripalu Yoga," I responded. *It makes sense to start at the beginning,* I thought. "I'd love to try it." Neither one of us had taken yoga classes before but we were open to the idea, especially as a shared adventure.

The pictures in the catalog were inviting. A large stone facility set high on a wide grassy hill surrounded by deciduous woods overlooking rural mountains certainly appeared peaceful. Although the private and dorm style rooms looked sparse, they complemented the yoga focus on spirit, not luxury. The schedule summary was packed with yoga classes, vegetarian meals, relaxation and options for chant sessions, massage treatments, spiritual dancing or guest speakers. The drive would be only a couple hours from home.

"Let's do it," Joanne said with enthusiasm. We loved the process of planning, packing, and traveling to new places. To me, the journey was always a welcomed part of the destination.

As we drove to Kripalu on a Friday afternoon, we gabbed away on familiar New England roads near my hometown area. The yoga center was also near Tanglewood, the summer home of the Boston Pops orchestra that was near and dear, so we weren't worried about getting lost. Occasionally, I would reach over to hold my best friend's hand until I needed two hands for the wheel.

"I'm looking forward to the food too," Joanne said in anticipation. "I hope we have some of those dishes from our cooking class." For some weeks, we had been attending a small vegetarian cooking class in the instructor's home. To my surprise, my taste buds had been delighted to discover tempeh, seitan, and tofu variations that were absolutely delicious when combined with complementary fresh vegetables and spices.

"Me too," I agreed as my stomach growled. "I'm also looking forward to not cooking." We turned and smiled at each other, knowing that a week-end getaway free from responsibility would soothe our spirits.

After slowly driving up the long winding driveway, the beige stone and brick building with four stories came into view. Resembling a sprawling modern church and seminary, its parking lot and entrance were at the back where we parked beside other guests who were unloading their cars.

As soon as we carried our bags through the glass doors, we felt it. The peaceful spirit of the place seemed to cover every piece of furniture, every pen on the register counter and every person walking by. The unspoken message was that, in this space, we wouldn't need to run to get anywhere or talk loudly to be heard. The journey in the car had been pleasant but this destination felt like Mecca.

After settling into our private room, we briefly browsed the tiled hall-ways, cozy lounge areas, and front patio before the dining room opened for dinner. With a high cathedral ceiling and full-window back wall providing a view of the woods, the dining room was filled with rectangular wood tables and chairs to the right and left. A long metal buffet table loaded with an array of colorful fresh food stood in the middle of the quiet space. Soft meditative music floated above the muted voices of hungry guests. I felt like we were eating in church and realized that spirit was indeed everywhere.

Our first yoga class began the next morning in a large open room with a mix of twenty-five people. Sunlight poured through the windows as we gathered on the floor with individual mats in a communal circle. In her fifties with light brown hair and a serene face, our instructor was already sitting with her legs crossed and palms facing upward on her knees. Like children entering a new classroom, we followed the teacher's cue and emu-lated her position. Joanne and I sat together like best friends on the first day of school.

After introducing herself and the basics about this yoga class, the instructor taught us how to breathe. With eyes closed, my breathing slowed and deepened, allowing my body to relax completely. I discovered that *ujjayi* (pronounced oo-jai) breath, or ocean breath, felt so powerful and rhythmic that I could almost touch my soul. Only the faint sound of the ocean filled the room as all we breathed together.

When the instructor called for the sound of a communal *ohm*, I initially felt a giggle rise from within. I couldn't believe I was sitting in this circle sounding out a chant so often heard in comedy skits. If I imagined my giggling sister sitting next to me, I would have laughed out loud. Luckily, I refocused in the nick of time and embraced the new breath and chant. A quick, one-eyed glance at Joanne told me she was much more serious than I.

The weekend was filled with learning. Unlike other types of strenuous yoga, our introductory class was a gentle, compassionate yoga. I loved the child pose with knees bent to my chin on the floor and forehead touching the ground as if in a womb. For strength and courage, the warrior pose with arms stretched forward and behind like a fencing lunge tapped into my sometimes hidden Amazon. Even the chanting and free-flowing dance classes added new awareness to the divine spirit within our hearts.

Joanne and I became hooked on yoga. When we drove away from Kripalu, we knew we would return. We also vowed to seek out the Kripalu yoga classes near home that we learned were available. The spirit of the weekend followed us home and whenever we received future catalogs in the mail, I felt the spirit again as soon as I opened the pages. Our fervor for yoga did not replace our God. Yoga helped us to expand our God and compassion for ourselves and each other. We had found a new tool in our quest for spirit.

"I really love this journal Chris gave me for Christmas," I stated to Joanne as we continued to pack our suitcases. "I'm going to start writing in it on this trip." Joanne was half listening to me as she focused on what makeup to bring.

The four-by-six dark burnt orange leather book was bound by thin leather strips and contained rough linen pages. One long thin leather strip could wrap around the smooth middle several times to keep it closed. It reminded me of the journal Kevin Costner used out West in the movie, *Dances with Wolves*. The color of the book resembled the red rocks of our destination and the sound of the leather when I opened it made me think of a saddle when mounting a horse. Bringing the journal would be an inspiration.

We were headed to Sedona, Arizona, this time for a business/pleasure trip. Joanne would be attending a marketing conference in Scottsdale after we visited Sedona and the Grand Canyon. We had been living together for five years, the sunroom addition was completed, and we were ready to escape the February cold for some desert sun.

After using our timeshare points to secure a reservation in Sedona, we were excited to explore a state neither one of us had been to. Our research told us about the spectacular red rock landscape, huge saguaro cacti, and vortexes that are thought to be swirling centers of earth's energy for healing and meditation. We made notes to visit Cathedral Rock, Bell Rock, and other vortexes with open minds and hearts.

The journey to Arizona was long but satisfying as soon as we saw the irregular rocky views from the rental car as we sped to our resort. Dotted with the quintessential image of cacti whose curved arms reached toward the blue sky in praise, the ancient land's spirit seemed to rise and greet us even before we stepped out of the car. The feeling reminded me of Kripalu.

Our resort was nestled in the heart of Sedona's main street with low buildings, gift shops, and adobe-style restaurant fronts. The entire town was wrapped in the arms of spectacular red rock formations of every hue and shape. From our balcony, we could sit with our coffee or glass of wine and stare at the craggy line of rocks in awe. We swore one of the rocks on top was a statue of Mother Mary.

The morning after we arrived, as we gathered brochures from the town information center, we asked the clerk about going to the Grand Canyon. The cool day was sunny and our schedule was flexible.

"If I were you," he said urgently, "I'd go right now." He went on to explain how fickle the weather can be at the Canyon and that most visitors are disappointed with clouds, fog, and rain. The ride would take three hours north toward Flagstaff.

"Right now?" we said in unison. "Today?" Since the clerk was insistent, we agreed that we would grab some snacks, jump in the car and follow his directions…*carpe diem*.

If we hadn't been open to the spirit of the moment, we would have missed one of the most spectacular days of our lives. Since visiting the Grand Canyon had always been on my Life List, the excitement oozed out of me and spilled into Joanne. Once again, we were little girls laughing on a school field trip.

Despite the cold wind as we stood overlooking the expanse and glorious beauty of the Grand Canyon, the air was crystal clear and the sun sparkled on the palette of rusty colors as far beyond our view as we could imagine. We held each other close for warmth, for sheer joy and with gratitude to God, for each other and especially for the clerk who urged us on. This place was a big find on our spirit quest.

After strolling the paths and historical landmarks along the rim, we watched the sun set over the wonder before us. Quiet with our thoughts, I felt my journal calling me. While Joanne warmed up in the nearby visitor center, I sat bundled up on a rock and penned my thoughts of blessings and awe in the leather book from my sister.

Each day in Sedona presented unexpected carpe diem moments. While still glowing from the Grand Canyon, we used another break in the weather the next day for a Jeep Tour ride over the red rocks. For whatever reason, we were the only customers waiting in line. After allowing time for others, our driver, Bob, decided to take us for a private tour.

"I'll be your chauffer for today." Bob smiled as he introduced himself and explained what to expect on the three-hour tour. We strapped in and felt honored to be his only riders.

"Where are you from?" he asked as we engaged in friendly conversation.

"We're from Rhode Island," Joanne answered before I could. "How about you?" Joanne may have been an introvert but she excelled at conversation with a genuine interest in others.

"I can't believe it," he turned around excitedly. "I'm from Cranston." We were dumbfounded that Bob was from our home state. At that moment, we felt another unexpected spirit encounter tied to this incredible place.

The Jeep took us up, down, and over the red rock formations on a thrilling ride. Despite the vertical slants, we trusted the sturdy vehicle and our trusty driver. Bob was a sensitive teacher, filling our minds with history and spiritual connections. We learned that Sedona had unique features that were found only in places like Jerusalem and Tibet. Although we never experienced the touted vortex energy, we concluded that Sedona itself was a vortex.

At sunrise on the day before we left Sedona, we drove to the rendezvous spot west of town where we had reservations for a hot air balloon ride. Neither of us had been in a hot air balloon before and we were determined to make the most of our time. While we had already hiked on the red rocks, now we would float above them for a different view.

At the end of a dirt road, we found the crew, four other passengers, the deflated balloon and basket waiting for us. After introductions, the procedure of filling the green and yellow balloon began. I jumped at the chance to volunteer holding the rim of the balloon as the deafening fire blower pumped hot air, causing our ride to take shape. Joanne, the avid photographer, took at least a million pictures.

The takeoff was as silent as a whisper and as peaceful as a prayer. We hardly realized we were in the air until the objects below suddenly looked smaller. As we floated up and up, letting the wind take us, I felt no fear. Unlike an amusement ride or even an elevator, there was no odd feeling in my stomach from sudden motion. Joanne and I looked at each other with broad smiles the entire flight as we communed with the rocks below. After a soft landing, strawberries, croissants, and champagne topped off a perfect ride.

Exhilarated from the ride, we headed back to the resort to relax and consider our options for our remaining hours in Sedona. Adjacent to our building was a unique gallery of shops and restaurants that we hadn't explored.

"Let's check this place out," Joanne said eagerly. Knowing that she was a shopper par excellence, I acquiesced at once. But I also wanted to find a gift for her.

As we strolled through the shops, we came to a large open gallery of bronze wind sculptures of all shapes and sizes twirling gracefully in the gentle breeze. Some were as tall as an apple tree while others were tiny and delicate.

"Oh my god, these are beautiful," Joanne exclaimed. "I think we should get one." She was constantly thinking of additions to the garden.

"They are beautiful," I replied. "But they cost so much." I had noticed the price tags were in the hundreds of dollars range.

"Well, we should seize the moment like we've been doing all week." What she said made sense all of a sudden. "And they'll ship it to the house," she added, sealing the deal.

The sculpture we chose stood five feet tall on a thin but sturdy rod. The wind-catching blades extending from the top third of the pole resembled a section of DNA strand that tapered at the top and bottom. The swirling, never ending motion was smooth and graceful like two dancers moving in harmony. The piece, aptly named "Wind Dancers," reminded me of us. After making the purchase, I forgot about the price.

When we left Sedona and the red rocks, our prayer was to carry its spirit with us. Despite our withdrawal, we felt renewed and energized just as the brochures had described and then some. The gift I found for Joanne, a metal sculptured heart the color of the red rocks, would hang in the sunroom and remind us of our love for Sedona and each other.

Sometimes during our lifelong quest, spirit found us when least expected. A year after our Sedona trip, we were visiting a nearby botanical garden in the summer with my daughter and sister. Living in Massachusetts, my sister Chris often came for a short stay at what she lovingly called "The B&B." We loved having her and Christine usually joined us for fun outings.

We had just finished browsing the huge tropical greenhouse and were walking down the main winding path toward the parking lot. Other visitors strolled ahead of us as staff were preparing for closing. As we approached some low bushes and a short stonewall on the left, a small animal boldly left the underbrush and came toward us. At first, we thought it was a squirrel.

"Well, look at this!" Joanne exclaimed. "It's a cat." Chris and Christine gathered around the friendly animal who quickly reveled in Joanne's loving touch.

Despite the cat's long hair and extremely bushy tail, its body was very thin. No wonder we thought it was a squirrel. With evidence of having recently fed a litter of kittens, we concluded this cat was definitely a she. The sound of her purring reached me long before I approached the enamored group.

"I wonder who she belongs to," I said practically. "I'll find someone who works here and ask." I could already sense Joanne's connection to this cat.

"I don't think she has a home," Chris chimed in. "She's so skinny." By this time, Christine had joined the worshipers and I felt outnumbered.

When I finally found a couple workmen, neither one could tell me a thing about the cat. One of them suggested it might be a barn cat from across the street. It was late in the day and there was no one else to ask.

"I think we should keep her," Joanne said as I returned. "I don't see any kittens and she's obviously hungry." Chris and Christine were no help as they both agreed with her.

"We don't need another cat," I said emphatically. We already had our black and white Oliver, and I was still grieving over Buddy's death from congestive heart failure three years before.

After some discussion, we all agreed to bring her to a familiar animal shelter for examination and any treatment. We wanted to protect Oliver from potential disease and we needed a realistic plan considering our impending Alaska cruise the following week. At the shelter, we told the vet we would adopt her if she hadn't been released to someone else while we were on vacation. We left the decision in God's hands.

When we returned from a glorious adventure in Alaska, we found the cat was still available. Keeping our promise, we adopted her and welcomed her into our kitty paradise. We named her Rosie. She could have presented herself to any number of visitors at the botanical garden that day, but she had chosen us. Her spirit seemed to say *You need me just as much as I need you.*

Shortly after Rosie became a member of the family, I was facing a medical issue with my right shoulder. Months before, I had often felt shooting pain during some mundane tasks but tried to ignore the signs of a major problem. Finally, a searing pain during a routine twist while backing up my car prompted me to call the doctor. The tests that followed revealed at least two long tears in the tendons of my shoulder. Presented with the choice of physical therapy or rotator cuff surgery that would guarantee greater results for my golf swing, I chose surgery despite the warning about a difficult recovery.

In June 2011, the operation was performed, unbelievably, at an outpatient clinic, not the hospital, and took only two hours. With five incisions in my shoulder, my arm in a block sling, and plenty of pain meds in my system, the nurse tech rolled me to Joanne's ageless dark purple car. She would play nurse for a while as I figured out how to manage without my right arm. Since I had rarely been sick, my new role as patient would be a new experience for both of us. Hopefully, we wouldn't forget about spirit.

As Joanne gently helped me out of the car and into the house, my foggy brain told me I was home and needed to find the recliner. As the nurse in charge, she already knew the list of instructions for food, medication, and rest.

"Can I get you anything, honey?" she asked as I settled into the recliner. Considering the Percocet for pain, I didn't need much else.

Rosie decided she needed to investigate as she jumped up on the footrest. Even though she had filled out since arriving, she was still lightweight so she was no bother on the chair. Having grown into a longhaired beauty, her manners were almost as impeccable as Oliver's. She loved playing hostess and caretaker.

"Just some soup and crackers I guess," I replied. "And some tea if you don't mind." I knew how to be a considerate patient.

"Okay, coming right up." Joanne kissed me on the forehead and bustled in the kitchen with her task.

Joanne waited on me with great patience and kept me company in the TV room as she read. Whenever I felt like watching television she complied, and when I needed to rest my eyes she let me doze. Pillows propped my arm and shoulder and a cute circular neck pillow resembling a dog supported my neck.

Strange dreams from the meds plagued my sleep. Convoluted and stressful treks through crowded rundown buildings or frightening faces glaring through glass windows remained vivid even after waking up. I hadn't anticipated this unnerving part of recovery.

For the next few days, I was in excruciating pain and could not get comfortable, even with Percocet. As the pain subsided, the meds were reduced and the strange dreams, thankfully, faded. Sleeping, however, continued to be a problem. Even in the recliner and taking Vicodin for a change at night, my maximum sleep time was an hour and a half.

Adding to my sleep deprivation was painful physical therapy. Passive exercises had begun soon after surgery and my physical therapist, who must have been a drill sergeant in another life, increased the intensity of the exercises for reaching full range of motion. As a dutiful PT patient, I performed my home exercises five times a day despite the pain and urge to quit.

Since Joanne always encouraged me to keep going, I had no excuse or escape. My routine was to use the master bedroom upstairs for most of the exercises as well as the bathroom hallway and door for using therapeutic bands and pulleys. My nurse Joanne had become my recovery coach, especially when I became discouraged.

Upstairs, Rosie, my constant companion, lay on the bed in her tucked position watching me on the floor as if to say, *You can do it because I'm here.*

Sometimes, I had tears in my eyes from the pain. But other times when I looked at Rosie, I thought about when I initially said we didn't need another cat. What I hadn't realized at the time was that I needed *this* cat.

For four months, I had to sleep in the recliner. Even though my shoulder was improving, my attitude was spiraling downward. I was surprised with my crankiness.

"Do you want to go out for lunch, sweetie?" Joanne thought I could use a change of scenery.

"Now why would I want to do that?" I barked back. I couldn't believe the words that had just spilled out of my mouth. Joanne looked at me with a blank face.

"Oh, I don't know, Linda Crablegs, maybe so you'd sweeten up a little," Joanne said jokingly.

She was referring to one day years before when she had written a note on the table as a reminder for me to pick up some crab legs for dinner. The note simply said, *Linda crablegs.* When I saw the note, I had asked her if it was my new name. We had had a good laugh and the name stuck. The incident always reminded us also about Joanne's nickname, Crabby Cakes, when she had found a tank top in P-town with the same name silkscreened on the front. During her grumpy years, the cute top seemed appropriate.

The recovery after my shoulder surgery taught me a few things about myself, including my vulnerability when faced with chronic pain and sleep deprivation as well as my need for perspective and humor. I also realized how quickly I could forget about spirit and ocean breath.

CHAPTER 16

Downhill

"Hey there, my snow angels," Dave called out as he cautiously walked up our snowy driveway toward my Honda Civic with the hatchback propped open like a baby bird's gaping mouth. Suitcases, bags, skis, and snowshoes had already been neatly stacked with just enough space for his skis and belongings. Joanne's old faithful purple Accord was tucked away in the garage since my car handled well on snowy roads, especially in Vermont.

"Hi neighbor," I answered with a smile. "Right on time as usual." With his multi-colored ski hat complete with earflaps pulled tight over his full head of snow white hair, I could almost imagine Dave as a little boy racing up the drive with excitement. Despite his eighty-six years, his sparkling blue eyes and kind smile still held that boyish charm.

Joanne had just placed a tote bag full of snacks in the backseat and quickly found Dave for a hug. "Hi Dave, so nice to see you." Joanne's voice became muffled as her head squished into the chest of his down jacket. Hugging Dave, who was over six feet, was like hugging a tree for us five-footers.

Having been close neighbors for twenty-five years, Joanne and Dave had always shared house and yard advice as well as current events in the hood. When his wife's health spiraled downhill from cancer seven years before, we often secretly shoveled his driveway in the winter. It was the least we could do. Ever appreciative, Dave referred to us as his snow angels even after he moved to another town.

It was a late, partly cloudy Sunday morning at the end of January 2015, and the three of us were preparing for a three-hour drive. Ever since she had been declared N.E.D. weeks before, Joanne had been gaining strength and a renewed appetite. Now she was positively spunky about resuming her activities, especially downhill skiing.

Looking forward to our fourth time attending this annual event in Vermont, we had Dave to thank for inviting us in the first place. As an elder hostel group of energetic seniors, the thirty attendees met every year for a week at the same cozy inn for ski lessons, three scrumptious home-cooked meals per day, and usually an evening around the piano and fire-place for an American Theater program that I loved.

Dave's first recommendation about this trip years before had enabled Joanne to return to a sport she adored. To her delight, it took only five min-utes to find her ski legs again despite a twenty-five-year hiatus. From then on, she skied in the advanced group every year and I loved to watch her strong, free-flowing body eat up the snow as she tackled every scary drop with ease. Her smooth motion on skis was as beautiful as an operatic aria.

For the first two years in Vermont, I had used my snowshoes as an alternative to the ski experience. Since my one disastrous ski lesson years before still haunted me, I was content to watch skiers instead. During the mornings, I would usually snowshoe alone in a variety of nearby wooded areas, all the while missing Joanne as she enjoyed her lesson. Even though I didn't mind being alone with nature, I had appreciated the stray attendee who would occasionally accompany me on my strenuous adventures.

Right after the second trip, Joanne insisted that I put my fears aside and take ski lessons again. She seemed to sense some hidden ability in me despite my sixty-three year-old body and mind. After all, my shoulder was fully recovered and recent knee pain was only sporadic. I also had to admit that every time I watched the skiers float down the slopes, I thought, *How hard can it be if all these people can do it?* I had decided I was up for the challenge.

To my utter surprise, the lessons at a less intimidating local ski area were a success. With perseverance and Joanne's additional guidance, I even graduated to a blue-dot or intermediate trail once in a while. When I brought my new skills to Vermont and joined the beginner group, I felt like a grownup. I never dreamt I would own my own ski helmet that cov-ered my head in anonymity with the other skiers.

With Dave in the front seat for legroom and Joanne in the backseat for nap room, we left Rhode Island behind. The drive to Vermont was care-free as we drove through the familiar New England countryside edging our way closer to the snow-covered mountains. As always, the familiar psalm came to mind, *"I will lift up mine eyes unto the hills, from whence cometh my help?"* The line always seemed appropriate, especially now that we needed help more than ever on our cancer journey.

Whenever my passengers dozed, I thought about last year's trek that was B.C., Before Cancer. I recalled how Joanne would be surprisingly out of breath as she made her way to the ski lift and now concluded that her lungs must have been filled with fluid even then. I wondered about her endurance on this trip and couldn't help but worry a little.

Finally arriving at our destination, the colder Vermont air blasted our faces as we opened the car doors and gradually unloaded our bags like ants with breadcrumbs in front of the two-story inn that resembled a quaint motel. Others in the group were doing the same as we greeted them with smiles, laughter and compassionate hugs. Many members of our tenacious ski family already knew about Joanne's cancer struggle from the updates I posted. Thankfully, the hardy spirit of the elder group, who often skied into their nineties, matched our own grit for adversity. There would be empathy this week but no pity party, just the way Joanne liked it.

With a large, circular braided rug in the middle of the lobby and maple benches and chairs along the windows, the warm space was inviting and functional but not fancy. Behind the check-in desk on the right was an open door to the small innkeeper's office that bustled like control central. Guests and their luggage moved in all directions. On an opposite wall stood an open, spacious wooden cubby for storing skis, snowshoes, and poles. We felt like we were home again.

Beyond the desk was an open stairway leading to the private guestrooms. Luckily, our room was on the first floor, eliminating the need to haul suitcases upstairs. Despite her renewed strength since chemo had ended, gliding on skis would be easier for Joanne than climbing stairs that still left her winded.

After signing in and collecting our name badges and schedules, we trudged our belongings to our neat and tidy room. We would see Dave throughout the week at meals and on the slopes. Per usual, I loaded the dresser in our room with every stitch from my suitcase while Joanne kept her case flat on the stand for daily use. One queen and one large twin bed laden with our extra ski duds filled the small room. At last, we felt as though we had escaped life with cancer.

The schedule was the same every year and I loved the consistency. A homemade turkey dinner on Sunday night, a full breakfast every morning at seven, ski lessons at the mountain at nine, lunch transported to the lodge at noon, free ski in the afternoons, BYOB drinks and snacks by four thirty at the inn, and a scrumptious dinner at six. The relaxing program around the piano capped off the evening while many friends, including Dave, started to doze on the couches by the glow of the fire. Occasionally, a light snow could be seen from the windows that often rattled with a gust of bitter cold wind adding to the Vermont ambience. I always savored every minute of this peaceful scene.

For some reason, I felt comforted, not bored, by the same predictable schedule. The months before we arrived had been filled with unexpected twists and turns forcing us to sit on the edge of our seats as we waited for cancer's next move. At least here in Vermont, we could count on something: the schedule.

Perfect weather for skiing continued throughout the week. Joanne was in her glory on the slopes and I was holding my own on the easy trails that I concluded were comparable to the blue-dot trails back home. Then, without warning on the last day of skiing, the proverbial monkey wrench was thrown into our perfect week.

After returning my rented skis and boots at the hut outside, I was heading into the lively lodge to find Joanne for our scheduled group lunch upstairs. Skiers, in all stages of preparing for or returning from the slopes, were scurrying in every direction. Some teenagers were already wolfing down pizza slices at small lunch tables while other skiers lounged around a blazing fire to warm their icy bones. Navigating the lodge always required alert dodging skills but the atmosphere was merry and intoxicating.

I found Joanne sitting on the stone wall by the huge stone fireplace where several tired skiers struggled to unload their heavy boots by the crackling fire. She was accompanied by an official staff person and one of her skiing buddies who all seemed to be waiting for me. Their serious faces conveyed an ominous sense of urgency.

"Hi," I said tentatively to the small cluster. "What's going on?" Joanne started to respond but was quickly interrupted by the medical person, deduced from her badge at close range.

"Joanne's been in an accident on the mountain during her ski lesson," the woman explained. "I think she needs to go to a hospital to get checked out." Since her arm wasn't in a sling, she wasn't on crutches, and no bruises were showing, I was confused about the problem.

"I think I'm okay but they want me to go," Joanne said. She did seem a little groggy. Then her friend, Mary, spoke up.

"We were high on the mountain, just starting to go down, when one of the guys in the class skied over her skis causing her to crash." I looked at Joanne who lifted her open hands and shoulders as if to say, *Go figure.* "I think she hit her head really hard," Mary added.

"I don't remember too much about it," Joanne explained. "Just bits and pieces like trying to get up and then the instructor trying to help." She still seemed okay to me but then she continued.

"The thing I remember the most was coming to in the first aid station and asking, *How did I get here?*" Her voice sounded frightened. Then her eyes fixed on mine.

"Honey, the instructor told me I skied all the way down the hill on my own but I don't remember a thing about it," she said quietly. This new development was definitely not on the schedule. But the sinking feeling I had was more familiar than I wanted it to be.

Thank goodness I had taken my car for the snow because we were heading for the hospital emergency room an hour away and the hilly roads were slick. Knowing that Dave would be concerned, we texted him periodically for updates. As we drove, Joanne recounted as much of the accident as she could remember but her downhill descent remained a mystery.

"I just can't imagine how I did it," Joanne repeated again. "It was a black diamond hill too." She was quiet for a few minutes before continuing. "Maybe I had help from God…or Jesus…or Mary…or even the Wiccan priestess." We both started to chuckle.

"Well, I can't imagine any of them on skis," I started to laugh and Joanne chimed in.

"Oooh, I'd better not laugh too hard…my head," she warned herself as her laughter subsided. Another thing we needed to be serious about was not allowing her to fall asleep. The medical tech at the lodge had made that clear.

With the mention of the Wiccan priestess, my mind flashed back to a class we had taken years before when we explored the idea of past lives. In an historic village next to a calm harbor in Rhode Island, the small group had met upstairs in a Victorian house that served as a holistic health center. I had been skeptical about the meeting but Joanne was enthused.

After discussing the possibilities of past lives and explaining the group process for the class, the instructor led us in a guided meditation. Deep into the quiet, the only vivid image I connected with was a tall, lean African man running gracefully on the plain with a long spear in one hand. I felt his strength and confidence but could not determine if this was a past life or just a movie in my head. Joanne's experience had been more consequential.

Her connection was with a Wiccan priestess or witch. From her description afterward, the image was not the negative stereotype of black hats, nose warts, and cackling over a black cauldron. Instead, she felt attuned to the earth with positive power to engage in all of nature's movements. Joanne saw herself on the rocky edge of the roiling ocean as the waves crashed around her feet with arms stretched above her head, commanding the water and sky. The feeling had been strong enough for her to pursue the possibility of a past life.

Later on, she naturally researched everything Wiccan and had even bought a book on Italian witchcraft. One fall, Joanne suggested we spend a Halloween weekend in Salem, Massachusetts, in order to attend the sacred Samhain (pronounced *sah-win*) ceremony. There had to be more to Wicca than the children's story of *Strega Nona* and her never-ending pasta pot. Joanne was determined to find out.

With pagan Celtic roots as a harvest festival that included connections to other worldly spirits, the Wiccan ceremony we attended was surprisingly beautiful, not scary. Honoring the four corners of the earth, recognizing the spirit in each other and chanting to all ancestors was respectfully performed in a large circle with candlelight in a remote field. Even if Joanne hadn't been a Wiccan priestess in another life, the experience satisfied her curiosity and opened our minds to an interesting spiritual path. Whether the priestess helped her on the ski slope would never be determined.

Waiting in the Vermont hospital emergency room for something other than a cancer-related issue seemed like a welcome change of pace. While we would have preferred something like a sliced finger or broken toe, a possible concussion was small potatoes when compared to the cancer monster. Joanne was nonchalant about the whole event as she sat propped on the bed in the draped cubicle, doting on her iPad. I sat in the hard chair beside the bed wishing I had my phone charger and the novel I had left waiting on the nightstand in our room.

With the procedures and tests completed, we were anxious to see the doctor and be discharged. Actually, we were hoping to return in time for happy hour at the inn. Finally, the young doctor pushed the curtain aside and came over to the bed.

"Hi, Joanne," he said pleasantly. "It looks like you have a slight concussion." We weren't surprised with the formal diagnosis, but we were relieved to hear there were no unexpected twists and turns.

"The only treatment will be rest for the next few days," he continued. "And no TV or computer screen time so that you can rest your brain." At the mention of screen time, I shot a sideways glance and smile at Joanne who returned the look. The iPad would have to rest as well.

Other than a headache, fatigue, and occasional dizziness, Joanne returned to the inn practically unscathed. However, she opted for a rest, not wine and cheese, before dinner. Our compassionate friends greeted her with open arms and hearts, and more than one commented on the merits of a protective helmet. Dave was especially happy to welcome his snow angel who, thankfully, hadn't become a heavenly angel. Joanne was grateful for a full week of skiing before she was decommissioned and I was thankful she had a hard head. I also wasn't surprised when she told me to sign our names to the roster for next year.

On the drive home with my passengers in their favorite seats, my mind wandered to Joanne's ordeal on the mountain and her miraculous downhill run. Once again, I thought of the same psalm, but this time the second line seemed to pop out at me: "*My help cometh from the Lord who made heaven and earth.*" Maybe God knew how to ski after all and had led the way.

"How are you feeling, Joanne?" Dave asked as we zoomed along on the highway. Even though Dave usually socialized with the guys during our ski week, we had always looked out for each other as good neighbors tend to do.

"Other than a little tired and dizzy sometimes, I feel fine," Joanne said honestly. "I don't know if it's the concussion or just me." Sometimes her cancer symptoms vaguely resembled other issues, leaving us in a quandary about actual causes.

"Well, at least you knew the way to the hospital," Dave smiled as we all remembered the year before.

While skiing that week, Dave had experienced symptoms that could have been a heart attack. Despite his independent spirit, he agreed to take a rescue van to the hospital for reassurance. As soon as we had heard the news, we drove to the emergency room to support him and, of course, to provide a ride back to the inn. Luckily, his episode was a false alarm and he was back around the piano that night. Dave was a treasured friend.

With the one-year anniversary of the cancer diagnosis fast approaching, I also wanted to believe there could be a cure just as miraculous as Joanne's ski run in Vermont. She had recovered from her concussion and continued to function with as much normalcy and resolve as possible. Any celebration of the anniversary would focus on the absence of cancer rather than the day we heard the diagnosis. And since Valentine's Day had been forgotten in the wake of that dreadful news, we were determined to acknowledge some romance this year.

"Where would you like to go for Valentine's Day, honey?" I asked Joanne as she studied her latest watercolor class project in the sunny dining room. With her paintbrush poised in her hand for the next stroke, she had been sitting at the sturdy oak table totally immersed in her creation for over an hour.

"I don't know...nothing fancy," she answered as the sun glistened on her purple hair that had grown long enough after chemo for her favored Sharon Osborne look. "How about sushi and a movie?" Our favorite Japanese restaurant was consistently scrumptious with efficient service, allowing for guaranteed movie times.

"Sounds great," I quickly agreed as I put my hand on her back and looked over her shoulder. Her painting of an unfinished rooster against a black background popped out at me and almost crowed it looked so real. "This is beautiful, honey." I was genuinely impressed with Joanne's budding talent in the two watercolor painting classes she attended after retiring four months before.

"Thanks, but I didn't draw it...this is one of those transfer sketches," she said modestly. "You should see how good some of the others in the class are." All I knew was that her colors were vibrant and gorgeous. Joanne continued, "For my next freehand project, I want to try a picture of the front of our house." I could almost imagine a framed likeness on our wall.

After our relaxing sushi dinner and movie, I presented Joanne with two Valentine gifts rather than one. The first present was a delicate silver ring with a central ruby heart surrounded by another heart of tiny diamond chips. In my attempt to embellish its symbolism, I wrote in the card about two hearts coming together as one, her ruby birthstone speaking to our passion, and the diamonds, my birthstone, adding sparkle and strength to our love. Joanne loved the ring and vowed to wear it forever.

But it was the second gift that almost brought tears to her eyes. Now that she was able to resume her gardening ventures and I had greater confidence in my woodworking skills, I would construct two raised flowerbeds along the sunny side of the house for the vegetables she kept talking about. Despite her returning strength, bending over was still a chore and the raised beds would provide a great assist. Joanne was as excited about my present as if it were Christmas, not Valentine's Day. I never knew flowerbeds could be so romantic. I also realized that we had come a long way since that day years before when the basement shelves collapsed and the dishes crashed to the floor. I was sure these flowerbeds wouldn't fall apart and neither would we.

As winter came to a close and spring nudged its way to our door, we continued to ignore cancer by taking weekend ski getaways, planning summer vacations, and preparing the garden for inevitable blooms and promising vegetables. Ever diligent about home improvements, Joanne made arrangements for a total front porch renovation in the next few months as well. The old cliché about no moss growing underfoot certainly applied to her.

Without advertising her impetus for completing these house projects, I knew Joanne wanted to make life easier for others, namely me, just in case the chemo didn't work. I usually detected a sense of urgency from her whenever she conveyed her plans. Even though she would often say, "After this is done, that's it for the house," I would respond with a, "Yeah, sure," knowing that another idea wasn't far behind. Whenever she challenged my innate procrastinator, I did my best to keep up while admiring her drive.

In April, three weeks before a major earthquake struck Nepal killing close to nine thousand people, Joanne and I felt the ground crumble around us as we convened with Dr. D. for the scheduled three month blood test and CT scan. Prior to the visit, we had already received word that her CA 125 blood work had risen from 17 to 63, indicating cancer cells were on the rise. As we entered his office, our sinking feeling was like gripping the bar in that familiar rollercoaster car perched on the top, ready for the first long downhill drop.

After our usual pleasantries, Dr. D. confirmed our suspicions. "Well, it looks like we have some work to do," he continued with the facts. "The CT scan shows three small tumors in the upper abdominal area…one in a lymph node above the kidney and the other two are in the lining out-side the stomach." As we listened with worried faces, he discussed possible chemo combinations and answered our questions about surgery that he thought would be unnecessary. The rollercoaster was starting its descent.

"When will treatment start?" Joanne asked cautiously. "I'm supposed to go on a Disney cruise in a couple weeks with my family." I knew her plans with her sister, niece, and great nephew were as important as any treatment.

"Treatment can wait until you get back," the doctor reassured her. *What?!* I wanted to scream. Since I was ready to attack those nasty cancer cells with guns blazing, I didn't see the wisdom in waiting.

"The tumors are very small and I think *carpe diem* can help you as much as any chemo," he continued as his concern for body, mind, and spirit reminded me to focus on trust. "Of course, I'll be coming along," he joked as Joanne returned his smile.

"You better think twice about that…kids on a Disney cruise?" Joanne quipped. I could see they were in cahoots with their optimism.

Knowing about Joanne's penchant for researching options, Dr. D. also gave us his blessing for seeking a second opinion. Since we had trusted his knowledge and involvement in new research, we had never considered another opinion. At his suggestion, however, we decided to seek out the head of medical oncology at the Dana Farber Cancer Institute in Boston in order to explore new clinical trials. We thought it certainly wouldn't hurt to take this side trip on our cancer journey.

A week before Joanne's Disney cruise, we made the trek to Boston. Everything about Dana Farber was easy. The drive, the parking garage, clear signage to the departments, and helpful receptionists all contributed to a positive experience. Even lunch in the bustling cafeteria was like an organic gourmet meal.

Our visit with the doctor was as comfortable and reassuring as a visit with a close friend. Despite her status as head of the department, Dr. M. had entered the room without an entourage and spent half an hour with us providing clear information and respectful answers to our questions. She agreed that the new tumors were too small for surgery and the next round of chemo was appropriate. When we left Dana Farber, we felt relieved to be on the right track and fortified for the next battle.

While Joanne was cruising in fantasyland on the sea, I kept the home fires burning while working, feeding Rosie and Charlie, and balancing my emotions. I could have tagged along on this cruise but sensed their need to share family time alone. Having already been on several cruises with Joanne, I wasn't jealous. To be honest, I was content to spend a quiet week with only my thoughts before the chemo chaos resumed.

Throughout this first cancer year, my mixed emotions sometimes swirled around like a gust of autumn wind catching dry leaves in a flurry. Anger, fear, depression, sadness, love, compassion, joy, trust, and surprise churned together in varying proportions. In order to function with some control and be supportive to Joanne, I often put these emotions in imaginary boxes on a shelf. Whenever I needed one, I took the box down and lifted the lid. At times, however, some of the dangerous inhabitants that I didn't like escaped on their own.

With the latest recurrence of Joanne's cancer, I initially let anger and fear escape and mingle together. Without really knowing who to blame, I had shouted at God in anger that she had had only seven cancer-free months, and I was afraid to imagine my life without my wife. We had had eighteen years of laughing as friends, loving with passion, exploring with wonder and crying when lost, both side by side and as one. I wasn't ready to let go. For a short time, my faith, my trust, and my optimism were barreling down that first long hill.

Intellectually, we knew that ovarian cancer often returns. Even though we had discussed the possibility, there was always the hope that the other shoe wouldn't drop until years later. Joanne expressed her anger and fear with me at first, but she quickly regrouped with the evidence from the medical field and other patients that remission and recurrence were merely a part of life with ovarian cancer. As she pulled me along a more positive road, I put anger and fear back in their boxes in order to gear up for the next fight.

Some of my thoughts during my bachelorette week drifted to the state of our spirit quest. I wondered why I wasn't angry with the Wiccan priestess for this cancer news…or Buddha for that matter. We had spent years exploring other spiritual paths as if we had traveled around the world spending time in exotic countries, only to return home again. In the end, we had returned home to our Christian God who had expanded outside the box. We hadn't gone to church more, we just loved more. My anger toward God wasn't really fair but God was my anchor spirit who could take a punch every now and then.

Joanne returned from her Disney cruise whistling "Hi ho, hi ho…it's off to work we go," as we returned to the infusion center. This time, she would receive six twenty-one day cycles of Taxel, Carboplatin, and Avastin, a new addition that decreases the blood supply to cancer tumors. The side effects of the three drugs were familiar but also included annoying restless legs. While at chemo, her legs would flex and struggle to stay put as Joanne's face screwed up in discomfort. Reluctantly, she often accepted another drug to combat the restless leg effect. My thought was how ironic that these legs that had carried her downhill in Vermont only three months before were now so beyond her control that she needed to medicate them into submission.

The slow administration of all three drugs meant long hours at the center, but we felt like sophomores returning to school with more confidence and swagger. Longer hours in the recliner while chemo dripped meant that Joanne had more time to plan her vegetable garden now that the raised beds were constructed and waiting. If all went according to plan, chemo would continue through the summer.

During the first three weeks of chemo, Joanne's symptoms intensified. She experienced greater muscle and joint pain, shortness of breath, and intense fatigue. However, she was grateful that her appetite remained intact and that she could push herself to complete tasks on less intense days. Joanne always knew how to grab onto life and whip it around by the tail. And I was her willing partner. As long as we had a glimmer of hope that the chemo would help, we lived stubbornly in the moment. I was impressed with her fortitude despite ongoing pain and discomfort and she was impressed with my patience and flexibility as a caregiver. Once again, we were a team fighting to stay alive together.

On Wednesday night two and a half weeks after the first round of chemo, we were watching the news after a grilled chicken dinner when Joanne turned to me on the couch.

"I've been noticing a few extra hairs on the bathroom sink since Monday," Joanne said tentatively as she put her hand to her full head of hair. "I think I'll brush some out." She lifted herself from the couch.

"Okay, honey. Do you need me for anything?" I really didn't know what I could do other than stand by for moral support.

"Not really." Both of us had conveniently forgotten about hair loss this time around.

Joanne started to brush her hair in the bathroom and decided she would go outside onto the front porch to minimize the mess. I watched her walk through the front door with her purple head as I flipped on the porch light switch from the inside. In the kitchen, I started washing some grapes for a snack.

Ten minutes later, the front door opened.

"Lin, come here quick," Joanne yelled. "You've got to see this." As I approached the living room, my jaw dropped in amazement.

Joanne stood at the front door with a completely bald head.

"Oh…my…god," I exclaimed. I couldn't believe my eyes. Joanne had left the house with a full head of hair and returned minutes later with her hair lying in a heap on the porch. This was an old familiar look so we weren't as emotionally distraught as before, but we were definitely shocked with how quickly it had happened.

"Well, at least I don't have to go to the hairdresser this time." Joanne's practical reaction to this surprise set the tone for taking things in stride. "I think I need some Ben & Jerry's Cherry Garcia, honey." I could tell what was coming next.

"Would you go and get some…Pleeease?" She was giving me that look I could never resist.

As I headed out for the ice cream, the thought occurred to me that Joanne's downhill miracle run in Vermont could turn out to be an easier feat than this downhill slope with cancer. Even so, with hope in my heart, not in a box, I looked forward to next year on skis.

Joanne's cruise photo
next to her funeral ashes

Our professional portrait
(Photo by Sebastian Studios)

One of many cousins' lunches

The professional at work, 2006 (Photo by Nora Lewis)

Joanne's Caribbean monkey friend

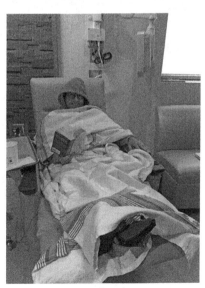

Wrapped at chemo

Legendary orange & black
Halloween wig, 1997

My family's Annual Picnic,
Jo and Lin on right, 2017

The new couple at the first Annual Picnic, 1997

In love in Ogunquit, Maine

Playing in Cancun, 1998

Joanne with cousin, Carole Ann

First bald head, 2014

Joanne's new wig

Uncle Al at 95, Jayden at 2 months

Gardener par excellence

Joanne and her mother, Annie

Cara Mia and her human

Linda, Christine, Joanne and Buddy at Christmas

Carissa, Rory, Joanne, and Joyce at our wedding

Camping at Little Compton beach

River kayaking

Joanne on cross-country skis, 2000

Joanne and sister-in-law, Chris

Auntie Jo and Jayden at 6 years   *Lovely Rosie*

With Pat and Larry in Maui, 2016   *Hawaiian chapel
and cross blessing*

Possible refugee in the rain?   *On our first Olivia cruise, 2005*

Miracle sign in San Juan, 2017

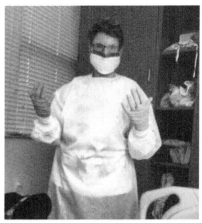

Unexpected Orlando vacation outfit, 2018

Recovering from Crisis #2 in ICU

A loving visit from Joyce

At the diner before tackling the DMV

Last good day at Water's Edge, July 12, 2018

CHAPTER 17

Cats, Chemo, and Plan B

"Oh no…I can't believe this," I blurted out loud to no one in particular as I stood in front of the stove in our compact kitchen.

The speckled salmon-colored counter was a mess with dirty mixing bowls, measuring spoons, and assorted utensils that included dripping hand mixer beaters. I was standing with one hand inside my favorite lobster claw oven mitt holding onto a round cake tin filled with batter. The door to the oven was open and ready to receive my offering but something wasn't right.

"What's the matter?" Joanne called out from her chemo station, which is to say, our couch in the TV room. It had been two months since her dramatic hair loss and the four chemo treatments since then had required more downtime than she experienced the year before.

After closing the oven door and returning the cake tin to the counter, I headed to her couch to explain my tale of woe.

"I've had that oven preheating for forty-five minutes and it's still only warm," I lamented as I stood in the doorway. "I can't believe it's conking out today of all days." My volume was rising while Joanne listened and commiserated. Normally, she'd be cursing at the damn thing and another probable house expense, but all she could muster was a subdued reaction in light of her fatigue and pain. Joanne's current priorities had little to do with broken appliances.

"Did you check the temperature, honey?" She tried to be helpful despite her weakness. Hearing her soft voice, my irritation dissipated and I quieted down. Normally, I would have reacted to such a glitch with greater patience but the cancer ride seemed to be taking its toll on me as well.

"Yes, the temperature's set right but the oven isn't getting hot enough." I concluded I would have to either attempt the bake anyway or go to Plan B...whatever that would be.

It was a Thursday afternoon at the end of July in 2015 and Christine's twenty-ninth birthday. Having left work early, my plan was to bake her cake prior to the informal dinner party we usually hosted at our house for the event. Along with balloons and our old, much-loved rainbow birthday ball as decoration, the tradition also included baking her favorite Funfetti cake that still satisfied her inner child. Luckily, my daughter's love for sentimental attachments matched my own so we both looked forward to the same birthday cake every year.

My delight was to decorate the top of her cake with a different imaginative creation each year and her delight, besides eating the cake, was to assess my design. This time, my idea was to construct a camping scene complete with green icing, broccoli trees, tiny woodland creatures I found at a unique toy store, and a miniature campfire formed out of wooden matchsticks. Since Christine also shared my love for tent camping, I thought she would appreciate the themed masterpiece.

As expected, my attempt to bake the already mixed cake in a slow oven proved to be disastrous. The two, round flat discs that came out of the oven could have been used for track and field events but not for a birthday cake. While it had been baking, however, I had conjured a new plan that Joanne agreed would be awesome.

Thankfully, one of our favorite Italian bakeries, only two minutes from the house, still had the items I would use for my alternate birthday dessert. With glee, I constructed the unique array in the kitchen just before Christine arrived. And throughout dinner, I could hardly contain my excitement as if I, not my daughter, were the birthday girl.

Finally, the moment arrived. The lights were out, her eyes were closed, and we sang "Happy Birthday" with gusto. When Christine opened her eyes, her jaw dropped as she giggled with the delight I had hoped for. On the table was a campfire replica made from long chocolate eclairs propped together as logs to form the outside teepee shape with smaller ricotta-filled cannoli lying as coals on the inside. Birthday candles on the top ends of the eclairs provided the campfire's flame. Everybody loved the edible campfire that later went down in family history as a memorable one-of-a-kind cake. What I remembered the most, however, was the recurring lesson about switching to Plan B without moaning, realizing that a change in plans could turn out to be a godsend.

We never found out what had happened to the oven because the next day when I turned it on to investigate further, it preheated perfectly. There hadn't been a problem before the bake and the oven continued to operate normally after that night. Apparently, I needed yet another reminder from the universe about the art of changing plans that would be tested time and again.

Despite the familiarity of chemo treatments, the new rounds that had started in mid-May produced greater challenges, including schedules more unpredictable than the year before. Usually Joanne could count on two days of unbelievable steroid energy that she loved for gardening, attending her art classes, lunch with friends or days at the beach. But even those two days were now filled with sudden crashes of fatigue.

Predictably, the next seven days were spent in exhaustion on the couch with leg pain from neuropathy and occasional shortness of breath. I hated to see her ashen face grimace with pain as she tried to sleep, but I was helpless to fix it. All I could provide was love, comfort, and frequent back rubs that she never refused. Joanne often said to me, "This is more than just being tired…more than feeling *moosh*. It's like a sick tired."

"Do you want me to leave you alone, my sweet?" I would ask her as she lay on the couch. Knowing how much she needed her privacy during illnesses in past years, I didn't want to hover.

"No, I love having you here," she would whisper. "Can you stay here and read your book?" I would always comply. Joanne's shift from cranky patient to subdued patient became more apparent with every week.

Sometimes her sister would come over for short visits while I reluctantly went to work, but Joanne generally preferred phone calls and email contacts with others when she felt so awful. Whenever possible, she called anxious friends and family to allay their fears and share a laugh. Thinking of others was never far from her mind.

Despite her malaise during the second week, also known as the bad week, Joanne was able to fend for herself for light meals and a cup of tea on most days. So she insisted that I continue working in order to save my family sick time for treatment days when she relied on my presence at the infusion center. Thankfully, I could focus on teaching a lesson at work, but she was never far from my mind when I was driving alone in my car to the next client.

During the third or good week of each round, Joanne usually felt almost normal. As if in a frenzy, we would seize the small window of opportunity for assorted getaways, mini-vacations, or overnight visits from Jayden, her great nephew. Planning for these escapes required short notice, however, since chemo was often delayed due to a drop in white blood cells or platelets. Blood work on the Fridays before treatment determined whether Joanne would receive chemo on the following Monday. If the answer was no, then she had to wait a week for treatment, sometimes requiring a three-hour blood transfusion as well to boost her blood count.

These unexpected glitches threw our plans and emotions off like the old round compass mounted on the dash in our camper van. Over the years, the device had lost its fluid so that the needle inside spun around with only a random chance of pointing in the right direction. Trying to focus and get back on track emotionally was a challenge as we changed any reservations we might have made for fun during our *good* week. The constant surprises kept us ready for anything. Needless to say, we often switched to Plan B.

One vacation we hated to change was our annual RV camping trip to Provincetown in mid-July that included Joanne's birthday. The reservations at Coastal Acres campground had been made prior to the cancer recurrence news in April and the deposit had been sent. Joyce was available to feed Rosie and Charlie while we were gone with Christine as her backup. Despite the arrangements, however, the impending treatment schedule forced us to consider more realistic options.

"What do you think about the Cape, honey?" I asked Joanne as we relaxed in the sunroom with our dozing kitties before dinner. I took a sip of wine and turned toward her blue bandana-covered bald head. She had been engrossed in her iPad connections and I thought I would call the campground in the next few days..

"I don't know," she sighed. "I've been thinking about how I might be able to manage, but..." Joanne thought a moment before continuing. "I really don't think I'll be able walk into town and that means we'd be stuck at our campsite...unless we constantly unhooked the van."

In past years, we had always walked or biked the half mile or so from the campground to Commercial Street for the restaurants and shops.

Admiring the tidy gardens and cozy bed and breakfasts along the way to town was half the fun. If Joanne felt sick on this trip, nothing would be much fun for her.

"That's okay," I sympathized. "You probably wouldn't enjoy the beach either." I was thinking about our favorite beach activity. We would often take the van to the "straight" side of the parking lot where we could park the camper all day next to our chairs facing the beach and water. Having the convenience of the camper's toilet and serving lunch from the side door like a vendor overruled my former preference for the "gay" end of the beach where cars had to park far away from the water.

As societal norms had changed over the years since our first P-town trip, there seemed to be less distinction between the gay and straight sides of the beach. We could be ourselves in either space and felt comfortable holding hands whenever we felt like it. Even Joanne had boldly commented to me a few times, "It's Provincetown for God's sake. I don't really care what people think." Her tune had definitely changed since that first getaway.

"I hate to say it but I probably couldn't sit at the beach for very long," she agreed. "Maybe we can think about a B&B in P-town for New Year's instead." Joanne sounded excited with the thought of celebrating something after chemo. Cancer may have kept her on the couch more often, but not much could prevent the event planner from thinking ahead.

"That would be awesome, especially since we've never been there for New Year's," I said while thinking it would be a welcome escape…something to look forward to. We both liked the sound of Plan B.

"I was also thinking that it might make more sense to spend a few nights over my birthday at Little Compton." Joanne would not be denied her birthday celebration.

For several years, we had been using the overnight camping arrangement at the Town Beach in Little Compton. Being in Rhode Island, the pristine beach was only a short drive from our house and provided an unprecedented camping-on-the-beach experience.

During the summer, two far ends of the stony dirt parking lot were roped off for RV users with permits. One row of spaces faced the long beach with dramatic waves while the other row faced a grassy lane lined with tall swaying reeds and a distant pond. An adjacent Audubon sanctuary contributed to the natural peace of the area that was devoid of buildings and fancy facilities.

Despite the summer daytime crowd and close camp spaces, I never tired of drifting off to sleep with the sound of breaking waves in my head or sipping a mug of hot coffee while sitting on a rock watching the morning sun create sparkly diamonds on the water. As we looked out the window of the van with the decal, *Be still…and know,* we always considered the spirit of this beach to be our refuge.

The rules and regulations for using the camp spaces were a perfect fit for our wacky, unpredictable schedule. Reservations could be made only on the Monday of the desired week and upcoming weekend, and the maximum stay was three consecutive nights. Since planning on short notice was our expertise, we had often used our permit during chemo treatments. The required limited stay usually meant greater availability, and we could hurry home if necessary.

This year in July, we spent our three nights celebrating Joanne's birthday with a full moon over the never-ending waves, gazing into a magical campfire while I blew bubbles in the queen's direction. We may not have been in P-town, but we were gratefully together by the sea. As we drifted off to sleep, our bodies molded into one S-shape, I couldn't imagine anything better than this change of plans.

Throughout the summer of 2015, the looming question was whether the chemo was blasting those new tumors or not. Like a fulcrum that determines the seesaw's balance, the answer to our question came in August with only two more treatments to go. Our hope and future plans hinged on the answer.

On a follow-up visit to Dr. D., we heard the good news: The CA 125 was down to 11 from over 200 when the rounds of treatment began in May. Since he was encouraged that the combination of drugs was doing its job, so were we. Even his recommendation that Avastin continue as a maintenance drug was not enough to dampen our optimism. The plan was that Joanne would receive an infusion of Avastin every three weeks, perhaps for the rest of her life. Undaunted, Joanne's spirit was lifted into outer space with the news and I noticed she was researching cruise deals for a warm-weather getaway.

By October, we heard the words *"No evidence of disease, N.E.D.,"* once again. The CA 125 was down to 8 but the maintenance drug would continue. Despite the good news, however, the thrill was gone. Some firsts just can't be duplicated, like the first day of school, the first baby, or the first view of the Grand Canyon. Even though our emotional skin had been toughened by the mountainous terrain of this cancer journey, we operated with some hesitation about the future. Nonetheless, we had hope that our plan for life after treatment could be better than expected.

"Hi, honey," Joyce bubbled as she wrapped me into a hug and planted a big kiss on my cheek. My sister-in-law had just arrived by our back door to join us in the sunroom for a cup of celebratory tea.

"Hi, honey," I returned with a smile. Despite the fall weather, Joyce's suntan and flowing blonde hair streaked with pink maintained a summer look. She handed me a Ziploc bag filled with a small stack of blue rectangles.

"I brought you some more masks from the hospital." Ever thoughtful, she was keeping us supplied with whatever we needed to keep infection away.

From the start of chemo, we had been warned that Joanne's immune system would be compromised. With hand sanitizers in every room of the house, we had incorporated safety precautions as a way of life. Never wanting to draw more attention than her bald head, Joanne had reluctantly donned a mask occasionally in a crowd or around sick kids. Otherwise, the masks remained stored for future use.

Joyce's exuberant entrance had sent young Charlie running down the stairs into his man cave in the basement. Seven-year-old Rosie, on the other hand, sauntered up to Joyce like a perfect hostess and waved her longhaired tail as a generous hello. She waited for the customary lift into her human aunt's arms for a squeeze and raspberry kisses. A visit from Joyce was always a whirlwind event.

"Hi sister," Joanne lifted her head from her favorite rocking chair for a quick kiss from her sister, who plopped down into the empty rocker beside her.

"I'm so glad you're done with treatment," I heard Joyce remark as I put the kettle on in the kitchen. "How are you feeling?" Her concern for her beloved sister ran deep.

"I'm feeling stronger every day I'm away from chemo," Joanne replied. "But it looks like I'll have to live with Avastin…maybe forever." Joyce's smile faded. "At least the side effects are just some pain in my joints and feeling tired...nothing new."

"I just hope and pray I'll have a long remission," she continued. "I have to take whatever God gives me and plan some vacations for a change." Joanne still believed in a miracle cure but was realistic about the nature of ovarian cancer. Even though she was encouraged by survival stories, she had already made her arrangements with the local funeral home.

"Well, I want you around forever." Joyce looked at her sister with tears brimming. I handed her a mug of tea and hesitated about joining them in case they wanted sister time. When they both motioned for me to sit, I appreciated the gesture and found my favorite chair.

"I'm not afraid to die, Joyce, but I'm not ready to give up either," she said with fierce determination. I could sense the spitfire grit from her childhood that seemed to fill Joyce and I as well. Our mutual love for Joanne had cemented our bond over the years but this cancer threat was extra glue between us. "So my plan is to be around as long as possible," Joanne added.

Whenever I heard Joanne utter the words, *not afraid to die*, I had absorbed them intellectually, but my heart always cringed. I refused to let the scary thought penetrate too deeply and too prematurely. Our quiet talks about death had usually ended with resolve to tackle it later when the battle became lost. I wasn't afraid to die either, but I was afraid to accept the reality of losing her.

"Okay, well, I'm glad you're not giving up," her sister agreed wholeheartedly. "I can't even talk about it or I'll start bawling." Joyce was ready to change the subject so she did.

"Don't forget I'm available to feed the kitties whenever you guys take off," she said eagerly. Even though Joyce was an avid dog lover with three small pups of her own, she smothered all animals, including cats, with love.

"Just pick a place where you won't get another concussion," Joyce added with a laugh. She had her sister's number when it came to daredevil escapades. As we reminisced about the ski trip in Vermont that started the year, we had no idea we'd be facing a different cancer enemy at the close of the year.

A couple weeks after Joyce's visit in October, we took Rosie to the vet for her routine checkup. Ever vigilant about suspicious lumps, Joanne was concerned about two new small lumps on Rosie's belly that she had recently discovered while brushing her one morning. Having lost her beloved Cara Mia thirteen years before to mouth cancer, Joanne realized that cancer stalked felines as well as humans.

While Rosie was lying on the vet's exam table, we asked the doctor about the lumps. As a precaution, Dr. V. suggested that they be aspirated for lab testing. After two worrisome days, the tests revealed abnormal cells requiring expedient biopsies and surgical removal if necessary. Just when we thought we had left cancer behind for a while, the growling threat was again nipping at our hearts.

With the possibility of major surgery looming ahead for our faithful Rosie, we met for a consult with the surgeon, Dr. S. Despite showing him an expressive mad-face, Rosie allowed him to examine her belly thoroughly without a fuss. We were very proud of our obedient patient.

Dr. S. clearly defined our options which included doing nothing, removing only the lumps, or removing the entire right side of mammary glands where the lumps were located. Even without having the biopsy confirmation, he explained that there was an eighty percent chance that cancer was present. We braced ourselves for the inevitable choice. Since he was encouraged with Rosie's early detection and hopeful that surgery could be the cure, we decided to give our girl a chance with the complete mastectomy.

Thankfully, our friendly, curious, playful, and comforting Rosie survived a successful major surgery in early November and the prognosis was positive. Recovery and rehabilitation for a cat, however, proved to be as daunting and challenging as any concussion or chemo treatment.

"Boy, I wish she could talk," I said to Joanne as I carried a limp Rosie into the house. We had just collected our patient two days after surgery and were anxious about the list of instructions we needed to follow.

We had almost laughed at the nurse who emphasized the words, "*Keep her quiet and confined.*" Our minds were ticking away with ideas for accomplishing such a task with a cat. Despite her usually sweet demeanor, Rosie was not compliant if she had other plans. The list of instructions also included warm compresses on the incision and the dreaded white cone collar around the neck to prevent her from licking her wound. We naively thought that a team of two humans could outwit a subdued feline.

"I know," Joanne agreed with my wish but quickly added, "Maybe we wouldn't want to know what she had to say right now." We both laughed at the thought of her probable displeasure.

For whatever reason, Joanne had always felt a deep spiritual connection with cats, and they seemed to feel the same toward her. She would often be a magnet for the shy ones and was called upon by family and friends to assist with trimming nails or administering medication. Before cancer, she had even attempted to start a private business called Kitty Kare, with calling cards designed by Christine, for providing services when owners would be out of town. I wouldn't be surprised if Joanne really did know what Rosie was thinking.

Sometimes her connection with cats went beyond the physical world. When Cara Mia was diagnosed with cancer in 2002, Joanne was devastated. After fourteen years together, she had considered Cara to be a sweet friend, teacher, and companion who had been devoted to her only human. For a month and a half, Joanne doted on her ailing cat, used Reiki, and prayed to God and her mother's spirit for a miracle.

During their last week together, she had experienced moments when Cara placed her paw on her hand as if to comfort Joanne as she cried. Despite her pain when climbing stairs, Cara went up to the attic anyway to sleep with Joanne at night. Before taking her to the vet on her last day, they spent time in Cara's favorite garden where she had loved to watch her human digging in the dirt. As Cara deteriorated, her intention became a prayer for release rather than a miracle.

A few nights after Cara died, Joanne told the story about an unexpected visitor in the backyard. After waking up in the middle of the night and deciding to go downstairs for a drink of water, she stopped at the top of the stairs to look out the window at Cara's burial spot below. On the trellis, Joanne spotted a cat with similar coloring watching something in the leafy wisteria.

After a couple minutes, she called to the cat who looked up at her, jumped down, and began patrolling the yard the way Cara used to do. She thought, *Could this be Cara making a visit?* After sitting contentedly by a bush for a while longer, the backyard visitor scurried off, leaving Joanne with some peace that Cara remained connected.

For Rosie's rehabilitation, our creative minds had constructed a confined space in the corner of the dining room using the oak table and old screen doors for walls. Bedding on the inside of her cave provided some cozy comfort as well as an open cat carrier for additional privacy. A tiny litter box in the corner completed the interior design. Our pride had shown on our smiling faces the night before we brought the patient home.

As I placed Rosie with her white cone framing her sleepy mad-face into her new digs, she began to walk gingerly onto the bedding before plopping down again. Through her haze, she appeared to be dumbfounded with the setting and completely nonplussed with the cone. Both Joanne and I sensed some rough days ahead as caregivers and I secretly wished Joanne really could communicate with her cat friends.

Our first mistake with Rosie was to forget about Charlie. After slinking back upstairs from his basement man cave, he had watched our efforts with suspicion. The day before, he had already inspected the new rehab center with interest, but now he had doubts about what he thought was a new creature invading his domain. After all, she smelled different. After spending two days at the vet, she had lost her Rosie odor.

As we spoke softly to Rosie inside her safe house, Charlie crept closer and let out a threatening hiss. Rosie twitched with fear and scampered as best she could to the back wall as her cone banged the leg of the table.

"Oh my god," Joanne yelled, adding to the confusion. "Get him!"

I quickly scooped up Charlie and returned him to the sunroom where I could close the glass French door in the kitchen. After a few minutes, calm returned to the house as we realized we had to orchestrate a gradual meet-and-greet as if they were strangers. This chore hadn't been on the list of vet instructions.

Our nursing duties commenced with hesitation about Rosie's needs but we did our best to utilize any trial and error methods we could imagine. The warm compresses on her incision were a hit after she realized the wet cloth would feel soothing. We had our doubts about the white cone collar, however, as we turned off the lights for the night.

The next morning when we came downstairs, we found Rosie outside the makeshift house asleep on the living room carpet without her cone collar. One screen door of the rehab center had collapsed to the floor and appeared to be her great escape route. How she wriggled out of the cone around her head remained a mystery. Needless to say, we needed several Plan B's.

After reconstructing the screen door walls more securely and returning Rosie to her space, we phoned the vet's office for advice. To our relief, there was an alternate plan for preventing wound licking. They suggested using a baby's onesie, obviously trimmed to size for allowing use of the litter box. Since we were open to any wild suggestion, we gathered a couple onesies from Carissa who was happy to help. Fortunately, Rosie accepted her new garment as a cute accessory. In fact, she seemed to relish her new role as our longhaired baby doll, complete with screen house, while she continued on the road to recovery.

By the end of the year, we were thrilled to be told that both Rosie and Joanne were cancer free. I'm sure Rosie was glad she wouldn't have to suffer through chemo treatments and I know Joanne was glad she hadn't had to wear a white cone collar after her cancer surgery. At least their futures were brighter than a few months before. Since we had canceled a mini vacation in Florida when Rosie's health changed our plans, we were more determined than ever to plan our own great escape in the months ahead.

CHAPTER 18

Normal is a Mixed Bag

Joanne's great nephew, Jayden, was lounging on the couch in her chemo station, totally immersed in the iPad screen he gripped on his lap. Rosie was sandwiched quite contentedly between his left leg and the couch cushion without a second thought about her past surgery. Glancing at Jayden, I wouldn't have been surprised if his body was suddenly sucked into the computer game that held his focus. I imagined the young Alan Parrish fading into another world in the movie *Jumanji* and marveled that his computer obsession was now the norm for this generation of nine-year-olds.

With his black hair and dark eyes, Jayden could flash a charming smile to melt the heart whenever his face wasn't glazed over with his games. He had been a frequent visitor to our house since his birth and his beloved Auntie Jo had doted on him as if he were a little prince. For balance, however, Joanne also prodded him to complete his homework assignments anytime he stayed under our roof. She always encouraged him to do his best and in fact, expected him to reach for the moon. Now that she was feeling stronger, an overnight at our house felt like part of the normal routine.

Jayden knew she had cancer but, like most kids and cats, he lived for the present moment. He rarely offered his thoughts about the difficult topic of her health but we remained patient and open to any potential discussion. Since Joanne was in the kitchen per usual rustling up some grapes for his dessert, everything in his world felt normal.

Sitting on the opposite end of the couch, I quietly finished my pasta on the folding tray while the local TV news summarized the day's events. As the light snow occasionally caught my eye through the dark windows, I noticed Jayden's feet encroaching into my couch potato station as evidence of his growth over the years. While he wasn't a baby anymore, he still loved his regal status at Auntie's.

Joanne loved having Jayden visit, but I worried that she would become overly tired. I knew she pushed herself to assume her role as teacher and mentor, so I was on guard for signs of fatigue. Taking care of him seemed more important to her than ever for maintaining her identity as a caring aunt and providing proof that she was still capable. Being in the kitchen as a provider was evidence that she was still in control.

Throughout this cancer journey, I noticed that I had become protective of her even during remission when she amazingly accomplished her long list of activities. Over time, I had learned to offer help at the right time without sending the underlying message, *I don't think you can do this*. I respected her need for normal independence as I would with my visually impaired clients, but I kept a watchful eye for any sign of trouble.

Being a teacher, I also looked for opportunities to nudge Jayden toward life lessons of thoughtfulness and respect. When he was younger, he liked to work with me on projects in the basement workshop and even though the airplanes and wooden cars didn't last, our bonding time was permanent glue between us.

"Hey, Jayden," I attempted to get through his fog. No response. I tried again more forcefully, "Jayden!" To my surprise, he lifted his head in my direction on the second try, not the fifth.

"Huh?" he managed to utter through his open mouth. I thought he might already be practicing for his teen years.

"How about bringing your dirty dishes to the kitchen for Auntie Jo?" I had resisted my automatic motherly maid response to pick up his dinner plates that remained on his tray.

"Oh, yeah…in a minute." Jayden's primary focus was winning the next round in his computer game. My own love for games surfaced for a second as I empathized with his response, but my inner adult took over.

"C'mon Jayden, you can pause it." I continued next with the coup d'état, "Auntie Jo needs you to bring them out now because she's tired." Despite his apparent indifference to the situation, he would do anything for her. In a flash, he rose from the couch and willingly brought his dishes out to the kitchen where I heard a loving exchange between them.

As they returned to the TV room and took their places with Joanne in the recliner, she made a familiar request.

"How about we all watch a family movie or show?" Joanne's tone was more than a suggestion. She valued sharing time together, not just sitting in the same room, and wanted to impart another valuable lesson to her nephew.

"Oh, all right," Jayden sighed in compliance, knowing any argument was futile. Despite his protests that were typical of his peers, he was a good boy who was smart enough to recognize the true boss in our house.

After sifting through the possibilities, we all agreed to watch the original version of *Mary Poppins* that I had tucked away in my collection. Even though he considered the film to be too *girlie*, Jayden thought it was a hoot that Joanne and I had seen the movie in theaters when we were teenagers. At least we had his attention.

As the movie played, I occasionally glanced at Jayden who was just as engrossed in the story as he had been in his computer. As I watched quietly, I didn't want to break the spell of this normal moment so I kept the comparison in my head. About the time Julie Andrews was ready to open her carpetbag, I noticed Joanne was closing her eyes for a doze and probably nighttime slumber.

Despite my familiarity with this movie scene over the years, I watched with childish delight as the items were magically pulled from Mary's small bag. One by one, a coat rack, an ornate mirror, a huge rubber tree plant, a Tiffany floor lamp, and even a tape measure to see how everyone *measured up* emerged from the carpetbag. Mary Poppins was nonchalant about each belonging, as if it was normal to her, while the two children were filled with wonder and amazement.

Now that our new year had just begun, I thought of that bag and wondered what might be pulled out in the months ahead. We had experienced enough of life to know that each year promised a mix of the usual routine as well as unexpected surprises. Even before cancer, changes like arthritis in the knees and less energy for marathon chores had altered our old normal. With the greater challenge of adapting to cancer changes, we searched for a way to accept this unwelcomed part of our lives.

In January 2016, we celebrated the New Year in Provincetown as planned and almost forgot about cancer. Our stay at yet another quiet, charming bed and breakfast had been rejuvenating enough, but our reservation for a prepackaged New Year's gala dinner transported us to a new level of normalcy that we hadn't experienced in what seemed like years.

Located in an older quaint two-story building overlooking the harbor in town, the restaurant entrance was on the side away from the street. Bordered with tiny, twinkly white lights, the narrow cobblestone walkway invited bundled customers to come out of the bone-chilling night into the cozy atmosphere of the holidays. With a low ceiling and three separate dining areas, the space could accommodate a crowd while still providing an intimate setting.

For the holiday celebration, small linen-covered tables had been pushed together to form seating for six where we spent the evening toasting each other, laughing with new dining friends, and eating a scrumptious meal of fresh jumbo lobster tails and filet mignon. Tom and Jeff, a couple who were regulars at this New Year's event, shared their life stories and delighted Joanne with real estate talk. She showed little sign of slowing down.

With party hats and noisemakers supplied by the waiters, we brought in the New Year in the warm circle of revelers who didn't care about our lingering kiss at midnight to the tune of "Auld Lang Syne." Without warning, however, a penetrating thought stabbed my mind: *I sure hope this isn't our last New Year's.* Unfortunately, those thoughts sometimes haunted me during normal moments like these and I realized that Joanne must be haunted as well.

As we hurried back to the car with my arm around Joanne's shoulders for warmth, we passed the old spired town hall building with its double-wide cement walkway leading to the equally wide front stairs. A quick glance at the building brought back sweet memories.

"Jo, remember when we went to the prom here?" I gave her a squeeze as she looked up at the town hall.

"Yes," she replied emphatically. "I still can't believe you made me walk up there in front of everybody." Even though her words said she was annoyed, her tone said she really hadn't minded at all.

One year shortly after I had moved in with Joanne, we had camped for a week at Coastal Acres with the RV in early October. The theme in town was Women's Week and we had agreed to attend prom night at the town hall. The event was a chance for gay couples, who never had the chance in high school, to attend a prom with their chosen loves. Years before, any gay couple brave enough to show up at their high school dance would have been turned away at the door. In P-town, we all had the chance to relive the scene the way we would have liked.

After dressing up in the van, we had ordered an open aired bicycle cab as special transport to the building. With her sparkling v-neck top and fine-knit black sweater over flowing black crop pants, Joanne always dazzled me. Her long-spiked dark brown hair, perfect makeup, and red nails were accented by a diamond-like necklace and matching earrings. To me, she was already a sexy prom queen.

Not wanting to revive my high school prom dress, I chose a tailored white shirt opened at the neck, a trendy loose tie, and print suspenders over black dress slacks. A fine gold neck chain and gold stud earrings added some minor bling while my sage green leather jacket added some protection from the elements. Function over style was never far from my mind.

Despite the chilly autumn air, our spirits were high and our love warmed us as we huddled together in the cab cart. As the driver pedaled in front, we decided to use this novel mode of transportation on the way back to the campground as well.

The entrance to the hall was crowded with prom-goers on either side of the wide walkway. As couples arrived in their finery and paraded to the building, the crowd would cheer, clap, and holler with a loud greeting of support. After completing the ascent to the top of the stairs, each couple would stop and kiss their partner to even louder cheers from the crowd. While I loved the scene, Joanne was hesitant at first. After watching the parade for a few minutes, however, she mustered her courage and we joined the parade hand in hand toward our prom as if it was the most normal thing to do.

The sounds of the DJ's music filled the air as we approached the spacious auditorium decorated with autumn colored streamers and balloons. Folding chairs lined the walls and a rainbow photo op backdrop with tripod cameras had been set up in one corner of the room where happy couples posed. Unlike high school, the crowd was a mix of ages and styles and our excitement surpassed our expectations.

After checking my jacket, we proceeded to dance the night away. As I held Joanne close and smiled into her eyes, I marveled at my transformation from high school to middle age. I felt so blessed to have found the love of my life, but also to have found my true self after all those years. The prom experience had finally been magical and right.

"You have to admit it was a fun night," I offered as we reached the car on New Year's with frozen faces. "At least we had our clothes on," I smiled. "Remember the nude beach?" Joanne had to laugh as we settled into the car.

"Oh yes, I'll never forget that day!" She turned to me for a kiss. From her tired face, I knew her energy was finally fading for the night. On the cold drive back to the B&B, we reminisced about a hot summer day years before.

Not long after the prom, we had been exploring the Cape on one of our summer adventures when Joanne, the event planner, decided we needed to find the mysterious nude beach we had heard about. It certainly wasn't marked on a map but somehow she had managed to collect vague directions to its whereabouts. Supposedly, the nude beach was an extension of a well-known public beach in a town mid-Cape. Personally, I hadn't been anxious to find it since the idea sounded like nails on the chalkboard of my reserved English upbringing. Parading at our prom was one thing, parading at a nude beach was another matter.

With large canvas totes filled with towels, sunscreen, and snacks, we headed out as if on safari to find the lost city. The beach crowd sunning in chairs with umbrellas began to thin out as we passed the boundary of the public beach. Despite the beauty of the grassy dunes, white sand, and foaming waves, the hot sun was sapping our energy. I was ready to end our quest, plop down on the sand and bask in the sun where we were.

"So, where do you think this nude beach is, honey?" I hinted at my secret wish to stop. So far, only an occasional beach walker had passed by, clad in bathing suits.

"I think it's up here a ways," she said confidently. "I think I see a small sign." Sure enough, I spotted the rectangular sign that said something about clothing not required beyond this point. *Oh shit*, I thought. *She really wants to do this.* Joanne was full of surprises... and spice.

After walking another quarter mile, Joanne pointed to a low dune and suggested we camp there beyond the swaying grasses. At least we wouldn't be on display in the center ring at a circus. I reminded her that our chosen spot would also be safer than open sand. Despite the quiet stretch of beach, any crazy gawker could decide to cross the line.

Since this was one of those *"living on the edge"* moments that Joanne seemed to enjoy, she minimized the stranger danger with assorted reasons. She pointed out that we were hidden and wouldn't be staying long anyway. As I recalled her reluctance to hold hands in the streets of P-town years before, I thought about the saying, *Be careful what you wish for.*

As I discretely peeled off T-shirt, shorts, and bathing suit, I couldn't help but look over my shoulder for onlookers. Once settled on the blanket, however, I had to admit that the warm sun felt soothing on my birthday suit and the dip in the dune provided relief from the strong breeze off the water. But I couldn't say I was completely relaxed. Being physically exposed to the world was completely foreign and uncomfortable to this Baptist New Englander. Just when the hot sun had baked us enough, Joanne announced another idea.

"Let's go skinny dipping in the ocean!" She was on a roll. I thought she must be nuts as I looked at her with a speechless face. "No one's around and we can just run into the water," she added. Incredibly, she was serious about leaving our dune cover and plunging into the cold waves.

"Okay, let's do it," I heard myself say. If I had hesitated, I certainly would have declined.

Before I knew what had happened, we were running hand in hand toward the water like two giggling toddlers who had escaped their parents sitting on a beach blanket. We jumped into the water with delighted screams at the brisk cold on our warm bodies. As we paddled in the waves up to our necks, our faces crinkled with smiles and laughter at our bold move. Joanne was definitely my daring playmate and I marveled how my love for her could expand more than I ever expected. Even on a nude beach, I found myself thanking my God for her.

After timing our escape from the refreshing ocean when no one was in view, we hurried back to our dune to dry off before heading back to our normal life. Just as Joanne had decided the prom parade wasn't so bad after all, I concluded that our nude beach day was an exciting memory I would never forget. I also realized that if it hadn't been for Joanne, I would have missed it.

With the New Year and chemo treatments behind us, we steamed ahead with living in 2016 while accepting Avastin infusions every three weeks as just another companion on our road. Sometimes her neck and shoulder pain kept her up at night and fatigue forced her to nap more often, but otherwise, she attended her art classes, shopped with her sister, planted vegetable seedlings and had as much fun as she could. Whenever anyone would ask Joanne how she could maintain her positive attitude, part of her answer was that she was living with cancer, not dying from cancer. Together, that was how we rolled.

After the screened feline rehab center had been dismantled, Rosie rapidly recovered from her surgery and wary Charlie happily accepted her identity when her scent returned. She had shown no signs of discomfort in the four months since her ordeal and she had continued to eat, play, and cuddle like normal. We were as delighted with her remission as we were with Joanne's.

At the end of January and after Jayden's overnight, we trekked once again to Vermont with Dave for our Senior Ski Week. Per usual, Joanne skied in the advanced group, sans concussion, and soaked up every minute of her favorite sport. My beginner slope had been waiting for me and I carved the snow as best I could until the last day. In a freak move, however, I fell on my right side, twisting my already arthritic knee and ankle. With impending knee surgery scheduled for March, I had an ominous feeling that my skiing days could be coming to an end with that fall. What I couldn't know was that recovering from physical pain would be nothing compared to the emotional pain that waited ahead.

During that week as our ski friends learned about Joanne's remission, more than one person had asked if life had returned to normal. In order to answer that question, I often thought about Dr. D's words: *It depends*. Our responses varied, of course, according to our interpretation of the word at the moment. Our life this year certainly was not the same as the year before cancer.

Defining normal is as difficult as trying to hold onto falling snowflakes, none of which are the same as the other. Just when you think you've collected some lacey flakes, they melt. They can change in a second, an hour or a day. If a routine is performed long enough, it becomes the normal thing to do. As soon as there's a change, then normal simply changes shape like those snowflakes.

With cancer, our typical routine was constantly shifting. Infusions, blood work, good days, bad days, hope, and fear rolled around like the numbered balls in a bingo bin. Even during remission, the only normal thing about our days was that a change was bound to be around the next corner. When something in our lives remained steady, like our love, faith in God, or even a ski week schedule, we latched onto it and held tight to keep us from being swept away.

In early March, prior to my knee replacement surgery, Joanne's routine CA 125 blood work revealed a slight rise from 11 to 29. Although quick to blame Avastin for everything that went wrong, we waited anxiously for the CT scan results. With the good news that the scan was clear, we raised our hands in the air rejoicing that we could carry on without chemo. However, the disconcerting rise in numbers continued to follow us like an annoying mosquito.

The day before my surgery, I had just returned home from the lab for routine blood work of my own to find Joanne hovered over two trays of tiny cups filled with black dirt and elf-like green sprouts popping up from the middle of each cup. She loved planning, preparing, and tending her garden, especially the vegetables easily reached in the two raised beds I'd made for her.

"Hi, honey lamb, what're you doing?" I came over for a kiss. She wore our favorite house uniform of sweat pants and a gray hooded zip sweatshirt.

"Just giving these babies a little drink," she responded while concentrating as if the sprouts were precious jewels. I loved watching her perform such normal tasks.

"What're you planting this year?" My expertise was planting flower boxes on our front porch that Joanne appreciated, but tending a vegetable garden was not my forte. Although Joanne secretly longed to live on a farm with chickens and sheep, growing vegetables in the suburbs had to suffice.

"Well, I'm doing two or three different tomatoes, lettuces, arugula, carrots, yellow squash and green peppers for you." Joanne smiled with affection for her wife who appreciated her thoughtfulness. But then her smile faded as she returned to her rocker.

"I got a call from Rosie's vet while you were out." Her tone had changed as I remembered the routine blood work two days before. I braced for the news.

"Her cancer's back," Joanne announced as she looked at me with resignation. "They said it's aggressive but they can't predict how long she has." The news came as a punch to the gut.

"I hate cancer," Joanne whispered with anger.

As we both focused our gaze onto our sleeping Rosie beside us in her own rocker, I thought about cancer's eroding effect on our spirits. Despite our efforts to rise above the negative in the past two years, part of Joanne's spirit had been worn down like stones smoothed round from the ocean's constant force. Some of her edges had been ground off as she searched for meaning. While her body had been hammered by cancer, her spirit was in transition during this remission. The news about Rosie was another big wave pounding the stone that was taking a new shape.

In contrast to Joanne, my spirit seemed to be growing edges I never had before. I had become more spontaneous, more proactive, and more anxious. Whereas I had often looked up with my head in the clouds before cancer, I had changed my focus down to the physical details of the road ahead. Joanne, on the other hand, seemed to increasingly gaze upward toward the divine, becoming more tolerant and serene. The only exception was any time she heard that cancer had returned.

After the bleak news, we decided to let Rosie enjoy her life with us without further surgery or treatment, hoping and praying that she would beat the odds. Like many pet caretakers, we were grateful we had the option to honor her quality of life. After all, Joanne had also been honoring her own quality of life whenever she had the chance.

My knee replacement surgery in March was almost a blip on the radar screen compared to the greater concerns in our household. The operation was successful, my pain was manageable, and physical therapy began the day after I returned home from the hospital. Comforting once again, Rosie also reminded me that it could be worse as I imagined she had been thinking about her cone collar.

Unlike the recovery for my shoulder repair, however, I did not have to spend four months sleeping in the recliner and I fully recovered in four months, not twelve. My diligence with home exercises was driven by my desire to play golf as well as to care for Joanne.

Her anxiety about other realistic concerns had been evident even before the day of my surgery. Despite her clear CT scans and days of normal activity, Joanne continued to experience incapacitating fatigue and discomfort which reminded us that the monster still lurked in the background. Caring for me this time would be different than years before cancer.

"Make sure you use that walker they'll give you when you come home," Joanne had told me as we relaxed on the couch before the scheduled day. We had been discussing the packet information I received about surgery expectations and recovery.

"I don't want you to lose your balance and fall," she added. "I might not be able to help you." I could feel her anxiety about our house becoming an infirmary without nursing help.

"Don't worry, honey," I had reassured her. "I'll be a good patient and I'll work very hard to get back to normal." I rubbed her extended painful leg as she sat in the same spot as Jayden not too long ago. "And besides, we can always call Joyce or Christine to help."

"I know." She motioned for me to rub her feet as well. "I'm just nervous that something will happen to you because I just couldn't manage without you." The past two years had also increased her vulnerability, revealing a big change from the carefree days of nude beaches and skiing black diamond slopes.

"Well, I'm not planning on going anywhere and we'll be in Hawaii before you know it." We had vowed that nothing would keep us from our planned trip in September.

On May 11, two months after Rosie's cancer returned, I sent another email Update about Joanne's recovery that included Rosie's journey as well.

...With a heavy heart, I have to tell you that our beautiful Rosie is gone. For a few weeks, she had been slowing down as the tumors grew, but last week her breathing became more labored. We had considered putting her down then, but in typical Rosie fashion, she rallied over the weekend, enjoying my family's visit. By Sunday night and Monday morning, she quickly deteriorated and was struggling so hard to stay with us. We couldn't let her suffer any longer. So we arranged for a very compassionate mobile vet to come to the house on Monday afternoon. Even then, Rosie presented herself as a beautiful, gracious queen. As heartbreaking as it was, we are relieved that she isn't in any more pain.

Her incredibly sweet, brave, and generous spirit had encouraged us when we were recovering from illness or surgeries, and her playful kitten antics had delighted us every day. I do believe that animals, especially our pets, teach us many lessons about life if we only pay attention. Rosie was on a mission to knock some sense into our heads about what is really important…love, bravery, relaxing, and play. We miss her so much, as does her younger brother, Charlie, but we feel grateful and honored that she chose us to be her family.

By July, our normal routine almost resembled life before cancer. I had returned to work and golf and Joanne bustled with gardening, art classes, and shopping. Despite the Avastin schedule, we continued our getaways to the Cape and Little Compton with the camper as often as weather and health allowed. We even considered resuming our annual bike trip to the quaint town of Bristol, Rhode Island, for the spectacular July 4th parade.

Founded in 1785, the nationally known Bristol parade is the oldest July 4th parade in the country and is attended by thousands of spectators and marchers each year. The scene on parade day is electric as flag-waving crowds and TV cameramen gather on the two-way street through the usually sleepy town by the harbor. Most locals set up their chairs and blankets by 5:00 a.m. to secure a spot along the grassy curbside where huge maple and oak trees provide some shade. For out-of-towners, the challenge is to park as close as possible before the roads close to traffic.

For several years, Joanne and I had looked forward to the parade, but planning our strategy to get there was more like a science. We would drive to Warren, a nearby town along the East Bay bike path that lead to Bristol, park the car, and bicycle four miles to the parade. As we approached the town, picking up coffees and donuts at our favorite shop, we locked the bikes on an iron fence, and walked to the main street. As we scanned the curb, we always found enough space on the cement for two medium-sized butts and our portable cushions. While my heart would swell with pride when the bands played, I was just as proud of our ingenuity.

On a good day during this year of remission, Joanne considered the bike trip. With some reservation, we pulled the bikes down from their hooks in the garage, pumped up the tires, and shakily mounted our ten-speeds. After a short run around the block and a soft fall when Joanne lost her balance, we concluded that we would need to train for next year rather than attempt the challenge this year. As we put the bikes away, that nagging thought stabbed me again, *I wonder if this is the last time.* On parade day, we watched the broadcast on TV and even caught a glimpse of the curb we used to call our own.

Even with healthy days, the nagging rise in CA 125 numbers continued to pervade the summer since the count had grown to 200. Other than signs of a hernia and some fluid in one lung, the CT scan revealed no sign of cancer. Every time the scan result came up negative, we felt like dancing down the hospital hallway. As long as the doctor reassured us there was nothing to treat, we gathered our belongings from his office and went on our way. Our prayers still included images of a miracle cure, beating the odds, and complete healing. Why not?

Right after the Fourth of July, we were sitting on the front porch with our morning coffee before the sun became too hot and the pesky bugs invaded. Joanne lounged on the cushioned couch with a large pillow propped behind her back as she scanned the internet for Hawaii information. I was content with my bird book in a similar chair next to her as our sea glass wind chime from Maine tinkled softly overhead. On the opposite side of the porch next to a beach-themed sitting area with a different mellow wind chime, we heard Charlie at the open window quietly meowing for attention.

"Hi, Charlie," I called out. "We hear you." After Rosie's passing, Charlie often wandered the house apparently looking for her. We could only guess what he was thinking and wondered if he was lonely for another playmate.

"I think we should go online and find him a new friend." Joanne had already switched from Hawaii to Pet Finder on her iPad. Other than Rosie who found us, we usually searched for rescue kitties in order to save a tenuous life.

"Okay, we could even go today if it works out." My lack of hesitation surprised even me. While the birds chirped and our large wind chime provided its meditative tone, Joanne revealed her findings.

"In East Providence there's a new momma and her litter of kittens that just arrived from Florida." Joanne smiled as she showed me the cute fur balls on screen.

"Ooo, look at that tiger's cute little face," I cooed. "It looks like Rosie." I was hooked, but I should have remembered those words, *Be careful what you wish for.* It seemed that a new bundle was being lifted from Mary Poppins's carpetbag that could change the meaning of normal forever.

CHAPTER 19

Mother Maui

"Which one should we take?" Joanne asked me as I faced her in the middle of the bustling kitty room at the no-kill shelter. She was attempting to hold onto a frisky tiger kitten that seemed a bit neurotic. The lookalike bundle of joy I held lay peacefully in the crook of my arm, purring like a Cadillac. The choice seemed obvious to me.

"This one seems quiet and sweet," I answered. "I think we should take this one." As a shorthair gray tabby, the kitten's appearance was cute but ordinary. She did not compare with the longhair elegance of Rosie but I thought I detected potential for a loving soul.

After standing in line on a busy Saturday morning in July and filling out the three-page application on a clipboard, we watched the volunteer attendants assisting everyone with their possible pets. Enduring the wait was difficult for my arthritic left knee that had been screaming for the same surgery given to the right one months ago. Between Joanne's fatigue and my old knee, we felt we had already paid the price for a new pet.

All around us, large and small wire cages lined the walls while others stacked in three layers formed walls of their own in other parts of the tiled, well-lit room. Cats of all shapes, colors, and sizes filled each cage and Joanne wanted to rescue every fur ball she laid eyes on.

The kittens in our arms were part of a litter whose mother rested quietly in a cage on the floor beside us. Since her mostly black fur coat did not resemble a tiger, we assumed the dad must have looked more like the kitties we held. Not surprising, the momma cat appeared exhausted and ready to release her little charges, two of which still pounced on her head. As I watched their antics, I thought, *All mothers need a break.*

For the arrival of our newest family member, we had set up the basement guestroom for her initial quarantine as suggested by the vet for a gradual introduction to the house sounds and scents. Even though Charlie was intrigued with the closed door, there were no violent exchanges from either side. We were hopeful that our new addition would blend in without a problem.

What to name our little friend became our focus. The shelter volunteers had dubbed her Little Miss but my first thought was Abby because she had seemed as serene as a monastery. As we spent time with her, however, we quickly discovered that her quiet demeanor at the shelter had been a ruse.

Like one of those Transformer cars in the movies, she revealed her true identity while climbing the guestroom curtains, pouncing on everything in sight, and constantly looking for trouble. While she made us laugh with her twitter sound, not a meow, and skinny upright tail in the shape of a question mark, her fearless attitude warned us that she had no time for reprimands. Names like Trouble, Wild Woman, and Too Much quickly rose to the top of the list. I liked the idea of Little Miss *Fill-in-the-blank*, depending on the moment.

For whatever reason, we finally chose the name Phoebe. The kooky character from the TV sitcom, *Friends*, seemed to be part of our inspiration since she was always getting into trouble. As Phoebe gradually found her way into our family and hearts, I decided I had no right to complain since I was the one who chose her. At least she had seven weeks to settle in before we took off for Hawaii.

My diluted image of Hawaii had always been taken from movies and brochures of Honolulu, Waikiki Beach, and pineapple farms that had never impressed me. Consequently, I had little interest in going with Joanne five years before in 2011 when she decided on impulse to visit her friend, Pat, on Maui. Since I had just returned to work after my shoulder surgery, I also couldn't justify taking more time off back then. However, when she came home exuding a spiritual high and a vow that we would go back together, I had been certain that I would eventually set foot on Hawaiian soil.

For the next five years after her trip, I had heard Joanne and Pat talk about Mother Maui as if she were a friend. They were referring to the loving energy and feminine force that surrounds the island of Maui, one of eight major Hawaiian Islands. Now that my interest in this spiritual and historical side of Hawaii had been piqued, I was eager to share an adventure that would also feel like our delayed honeymoon.

With our luggage packed with summer clothes and the same leather-bound journal I had used in Sedona, Joanne and I left our house in early September, 2016, for a two-week trip to Maui. Despite her chronic neck and shoulder pain and sporadic fatigue, Joanne was holding her own and ready to ditch the home front for paradise. Even a fifteen-hour plane ride, hopping from Providence, to Detroit, to Seattle, and then Maui, wasn't enough to dampen our spirits. My upcoming second knee surgery in October and all health-related issues would have to wait because Mother Maui was calling us.

"Oh, wow!" I exclaimed with my face inches away from the airplane window. Joanne's neck was stretched to peer over my shoulder but she had viewed the tropical scene before and had insisted I enjoy the coveted window seat.

"Isn't it gorgeous?" she said as she put her hand on my thigh with a familiar tenderness that never got old.

"It's absolutely beautiful," I whispered. "And the view is nice too." Joanne responded to my line with a *humpf* and a loving squeeze.

The first surprise we encountered as we looked out the window had been a vibrant rainbow that the parting clouds revealed as we began our descent. The second jaw dropper was dramatic tall mountains forming a craggy magnificence in every direction. Despite the typical flat landing strips of the airport, the surrounding lush grassy fields and palm trees only hinted at the rich terrain waiting beyond the airport boundary. The view took my breath away as I felt spirit say to me, *Welcome, my child.*

Flying so high above the ground had always taught me to look at the big picture before looking at the details of a place or even a problem like cancer or our wobbly relationship years before. The hackneyed phrase, *don't sweat the small stuff,* usually came to mind. Each time I had flown, a new perspective presented itself as a reminder to keep an open mind.

Our aerial approach to Maui began with the feeling that the island would not be like any other tropical place I had visited in the Caribbean. My stereotyped image of Hawaii had suddenly changed with that first view from the airplane window high above the ground. I sensed that this was a dramatic place as I reached for Joanne's hand.

"Are you excited, honey?" Joanne asked me. The light in her eye and broad grin on her face told me all I needed to know about her own answer. She seemed to have put cancer in a box on a shelf for a while.

"I'm very excited," I said emphatically as I pressed her hand. "I'm glad this all worked out." I didn't know what to expect about our adventure or about the future for that matter. But I loved the moment in the plane and vowed to ignore cancer as well. This trip was our time to laugh, not cry.

After a successful landing and deplaning process, we collected our belongings and rented a cute economy car before shopping for groceries to share at Pat and Larry's house. The plan would be to stay at their lovely home overlooking the ocean for five days before heading to our reserved condo on another part of the island. Being independent and respectful guests, we would explore Maui on our own while spending some time with our friends for a few meals and outings. Like prepared girl scouts, we had researched our guidebooks and taken notes from Joanne's previous trip. Unfortunately, I had forgotten about jetlag that could descend when least expected.

After driving past miles of open fields once used for sugar cane, we arrived at Pat and Larry's home set high on a hilly street in the early evening which, for us, was one o'clock in the morning Rhode Island time. I think our adrenaline kept us standing.

As we slowly trudged up the small stone walkway to the house, we caught the sound of greeters coming to the door.

"Aloha, girlfriend," Pat exclaimed as she grabbed a smiling Joanne for a loving hug after placing a flower lei over her head. With a flower in her short brown hair, perfect makeup, and a blue/purple tie-dyed sundress, Pat looked much younger than her early seventies. Outgoing and energetic, she connected with everyone heart-to-heart.

I was next in line as we entered their airy, inviting house. As Pat greeted me in like fashion, Larry waited patiently behind her for introductions. Up until now, we had only heard about her loving soulmate since they had met on the island after Joanne's first visit.

"Hi there, I'm Larry," he said as he bent to meet us for hugs. Tall and slim with wire-rimmed glasses, trim gray hair and a moustache to match, Larry's kind and gentle face beamed down at the three short women in front of him. I liked him instantly.

After a few moments of chatter, laughter, and brief details about our flight, we retrieved our bags from the car and settled into our guest quarters on one side of their delightful house. Our cheery room with a long row of small windows captured the gentle breezes and birdsong while the double bed in the middle of the room seemed to promise a good night's sleep. With our long plane ride now forgotten, we were looking ahead to our relaxing but long delayed honeymoon.

The spirit of Maui seemed to reside throughout the house with the colorful décor and meditative flavor of paintings and treasures peeking out on tables and shelves. The open sliding doors and windows looking out onto a wrap-around deck pulled us to go outside for the view of palm trees and the distant blue ocean.

With love for us and each other, Pat and Larry also exuded the calm peace I already felt on the island. Both retired and in fairly good health, they were active, playful, and great listeners. Since Pat and Joanne regularly connected by phone, our friends were also up to date with her cancer journey—which thankfully meant that questions about her health on our first night were brief. After a light supper and warm conversation, we finally trundled off to bed.

The early morning sunlight and cacophony of unfamiliar bird song woke me with a start as we began our first day in paradise, whispering on the deck in our bare feet. Even with a slight breeze, the air was already humid as I detected the faint perfume of exotic flowers bursting on vines and trees off the deck.

"How did you sleep, Jo?" I whispered. I had been worried that her chemo neck pain would keep her awake as it had at home.

"I slept like a log," she said with relief. "How about you?" She knew my left knee pain occasionally stabbed me at night depending on wonky sleep positions.

"I slept okay but my back wasn't happy." Despite general good health for years, my old body felt like a vintage car needing irreplaceable parts. Back exercises for sacroiliac joint dysfunction had become part of my daily routine while a visit to the chiropractor provided monthly maintenance like an oil change. With the creeping effects of weight-gain, arthritis, and even the battering ram of cancer, however, we remained grateful that our bodies felt strong and alive.

While Joanne videoed our panoramic view and good morning hellos to future viewers, I kept my binoculars glued to the nearby mix of parrots, parakeets, and assorted new birds that I could add to my life list of bird sightings. My initial thrill was looking at them in their natural habitat, not in a pet store cage. It struck me that Joanne and I had left our cancer cage behind for this natural beauty.

"Thanks for inviting me, honey," I said to her as I smiled and put my arm around her shoulders. She looked at me and chuckled.

"Well, I'm just glad you were available," she responded coyly. "You were first on my list." Now I was laughing too.

"Fancy that." I thought of my list of personal want ads from years before. "You were literally first on my list from the start and I still have the newspaper clipping if you want proof." Her eyes met mine before we shared a kiss in the morning sun.

"I love you so much," she said softly. "I'm so happy I can finally share this with you." I thought about our journey over the past nineteen years and felt so much gratitude for everything, including the ups and downs. I wanted to soak up every ounce of love I could.

"I wouldn't want to be anywhere else," I replied. "But you know, this is only paradise because you're here with me." As a tiny ray of sadness pricked my heart, the birds continued their twitters and chirps. Without a sound, a flashy green Gecko lizard appeared on the deck rail for inspection.

"This is a gorgeous place, but I also feel like we're in paradise even in the sunroom at home," I added. We had often commented on the holiday feeling of sharing every day together.

"I know what you mean," Joanne paused before switching gears, "but right now, let's get moving and see some more of Maui." As event director, she had a long list of activities waiting.

Despite my lackluster history grades throughout school, I had developed a penchant for history in my adult years. On every adventure, near or far, I eagerly sought out the history of new places in order to imagine myself transported in time. While I didn't read every word on every statue plaque, I loved to discover the true history of traditions and myths. My first intention on our journey was to experience authentic Maui, not the tourist version. Fortunately, Joanne shared my interest so her event list reflected those choices.

My second quest was to find a special ring. Over the years, my attachment to rings had become an obsession so that I gravitated to the ring case in every gift shop and unique jewelry store. With a ring on almost every finger, I had room for one more and wanted to find a special ring on Maui for my left ring finger in honor of our honeymoon. My small wedding ring only fit on my little finger.

The third pursuit was for my sister. Before we left home, Chris had requested that I bring back an interesting rock from the ancient isle. Of my three challenges, I suspected this request would be the easiest one of all. But it turned out that Mother Maui had other plans.

Our first full day on Maui felt like a meet and greet with the area. Still functioning with extra adrenaline, we tagged along with Pat and her girlfriend on a coastal walking path for a couple miles, hopping from one fancy resort to another. Despite the humidity and long walk that dragged me down, Joanne seemed stronger than ever as we gazed over rocky cliffs to the pounding surf below.

One of our favorite stops along the way was a small stone chapel where we found some respite from the heat. As we entered from the back of the pews, our attention rested on the contemporary stained glass window behind a polished altar at the front of the chapel. Rather than traditional Biblical scenes filled with men, the window depicted the three women who went to the tomb after Jesus's crucifixion. The focus on feminine energy in the chapel had been a welcome change of spirit that felt as refreshing as the shade.

"Let me take a picture of the two of you," Pat offered eagerly. Since we were already positioned in front of the altar, admiring the window, we turned to face her as she stood in the aisle.

"Okay, that's a great idea," Joanne agreed. "Take it from the waist up and try to get some of the window too." Being an avid photographer, she was always considering the best shot.

"Yes ma'am," Pat obliged. She knew her assertive friend well.

After the picture was taken, Pat came closer to show us the result. She had captured our best smiles with the altar and window behind us in perfect light. As we inspected the shot, we all seemed to notice the same thing at the same time.

"Oh my god...and I do mean God too," Pat exclaimed. "Look what's over Joanne's head." She took the words right out of our mouths.

The small altar cross that seemed to glow with the reflecting sunlight was perfectly poised above her spiked purplish hair with a white flower over her left ear, radiating a golden aura. The coincidence appeared to be an anointing.

"Wow," Joanne whispered humbly. "I feel like it's a blessing." She was genuinely touched. I felt it was a sign of hope that God's hand was hovering over her throughout the darkness.

As a surprise treat that evening, Pat and Larry brought us to a special event at the Maui Arts Center that included a delicious buffet under the roof of an enormous outdoor patio. As we feasted around circular tables, live local musicians and elegant hula dancers provided additional flavor to the mixed crowd.

The main event inside the center was a greatly anticipated show of traditional Hawaiian music and dance. Even though we could hardly pronounce the name of the group, we enjoyed the dramatic numbers and interesting history of Maui before jetlag hit us both at the same time. Halfway through the production, we could not keep our eyes open. I could have melted into the floor I was so tired. Consequently, we left the show before it ended and retreated to our bed where we crashed into deep sleep. The adrenaline had finally worn off.

Thankfully, Sunday was a day of quiet activity that included attending a Unity church service, brunch at a nearby golf course café, and a visit to Pat's friends, Gary and Allen. A couple for many years, they had helped Pat when she first moved to Maui and remained spiritually connected to her. Their huge contemporary home was filled with quiet peace as they gave us the tour. A bubbling fountain here and there added tranquility to the inside as well as the outside garden that resembled a rocky gully filled with fruit trees, dramatic blooms, and even a cotton plant. I felt the spirit of Mother Maui in every corner.

The next day would be a long one for the two of us. Our plan was to explore the famous Road to Hana that all the guidebooks recommend for its spectacular rainforests, abundant waterfalls, and winding roads through those craggy mountains seen from the plane. The two-lane road extends from the northern side of Maui clockwise around the eastern end where the town of Hana is located to the south coast, opposite the start. Our big decision had been whether to drive our rental car or take a mini-bus tour. Either way, the trip had been estimated to take ten to twelve hours.

Initially, our younger selves thought we would be fearless and drive the car. Our old lady selves decided to seek out a reputable tour. With numerous warnings about the treacherous road, steep cliffs without side rails, and my desire to enjoy the view rather than spend the day gripping the wheel, our choice seemed reasonable. We had also heard that the town of Hana was a sleepy town, not an outstanding destination. So, this trip would be all about the journey that was already a familiar lesson for our life together.

We met the mini-bus tour at 7:00 a.m. in the parking lot of a tiny outdoor mall and quickly discovered that most of the twelve passengers were younger than we were. At least we didn't feel like total wimps.

"Good morning everybody," a short, middle-aged man said joyfully as he hopped off the modern bus with his clipboard in hand. "It's a beautiful day for our trip to Hana. Have your tickets ready and I'll find your name on my list." As we gathered our day bags, a handful of waiting passengers joined us in line.

"I never had the chance to do this last time," Joanne said as we waited to board the bus. "I'm so glad I'm feeling good now." Even though she wasn't about to dance a jig, her face and quick body movements revealed a stronger Joanne than two months before.

"Me too, honey," I replied. "You're probably in better shape than I am." And I wasn't kidding. With my painful knee, her pace usually surpassed mine as she regained strength without chemo.

On the air conditioned bus, we quickly learned that our driver was a native of Hana who had fourteen children and a wealth of knowledge about his land. It would have taken years to pronounce his birth name correctly so we called him Walter as he suggested. We could manage *mahalo*, which means thank you, but other street names and locations remained a puzzle.

Since the tour included a continental breakfast and later a lavish baked chicken lunch, our only concerns were to relax, enjoy the views, and take pictures. As we pulled out from the café after the tasty breakfast, we grinned at each other with delight. Whether we were at Beaver Tail, in P-town, Sedona or Maui, our joy continued to be sharing adventures next to each other.

"I feel like we're in one of those old Bob Hope and Bing Crosby movies," I compulsively remarked. "You know the ones that start, *Road to Rio, Road to Morocco*." Joanne looked at me with a pathetic smile like I was a nut. And to think she loved me anyway.

Lush rainforest and jungle described the northern side of the island, with high waterfalls around every corner. Deep ravines with crashing waves provided a dramatic backdrop to every view. Our trusty guidebook had been correct when they described newly paved roads on the north side, and Walter prepared us for the south route after Hana that would include some jostling on gravel stretches.

Along the way, our cheery driver would occasionally locate a patch of wide shoulder on the road for a brief photo-op. We took pictures of each other, the waterfalls that started to look alike, unique tropical flowers, trees with multicolored bark, and the ever-constant ocean. Whenever Walter had to squeeze over to let cars pass on the narrow road or navigate hairpin turns, I silently said a *praise Jesus* that I wasn't driving.

A unique experience along the way was the black sand beach at Wainapanapa. We had learned that the sand was actually fine volcanic rock but were surprised that it felt soft and somewhat oily. No time for a dip, however. Our sampler tour would have to suffice with the hope of returning another day.

While tempted to find a rock for my sister on this unique beach, I remembered multiple warnings from locals who said that Mother Maui would not be pleased. If a rock is taken from the island, bad luck will follow. I chose to obey the mother and decided my quest would have to be some other meaningful memento.

By the time we approached Hana, I truly understood that the beautiful journey on the mountainous road was the main event. The peaceful town by the water was mostly flat and dotted with small houses and signs indicating paths that lead to town beaches. Without reservations to stay or relatives to visit, there was little reason to linger.

After we blinked through Hana with its one gas station, two restaurants, and one school where Walter's fourteen children would have been the size of the graduating class, we looked forward to a possible swim in the Seven Sacred Pools at O'heo Gulch. Unfortunately, the pools were closed due to heavy water flow, wind, and who knows what else. Even in Maui we all had to accept Plan B that became hiking some nearby scenic trails rather than a swim. With occasional bench rests, Joanne kept pace.

After a delicious outdoor lunch that marked the southern route of our tour, the ride became predictably bumpy. Since I wasn't standing or climbing stairs, my knee was content as our bodies swayed in our seats with the rocking bus on uneven road.

"How are you doing, Jo?" I turned to the window where she sat next to me. As if she were the fighter, Rocky, absorbing numerous blows, Joanne wasn't one to complain about chronic pain.

"I'm fine, honey," she said somewhat annoyed. "You know, Lin, you don't have to keep asking me. I'll let you know if I need to rest or anything." I realized that Joanne did not want any reminder about cancer on this trip.

"Okay, just checking," I replied. In the past, I would have been upset with her rebuke but over the years my emotional skin had toughened. Apparently, I had learned to respond like the shock absorbers of the minibus.

As I tried to soak up the history of each notable landmark and unique Maui feature, my mind came to rest on the bigger picture. How the aloha spirit of the island affected everyone seemed to be the priority. From my observation, people treated others with kindness and respect for all spiritual paths. Everyone seemed to be on equal spiritual ground and I realized that this spirit is what Joanne had brought back from her first trip to Hawaii.

Similar to Sedona, Maui seemed to be another vortex where even celebrities found solace. Charles Lindberg was buried there, Oprah owned property, and Willie Nelson is said to frequent the quaint town of Paia. I imagined they could walk the streets without fanfare or hassle from paparazzi. On Maui, everyone was a celebrity with a divine spark.

Our honeymoon bus tour ended late in the day but thanks to Walter it had been a rich experience of sights and sounds. Back in our car, Joanne was already consulting her notes for the next day's trip to the Haleakala National Park and Crater.

Early the following day, as we drove along the smooth twisting route I had dubbed Road to the Crater, our ascent brought us closer to the clouds. We were heading to the summit of Haleakala at over ten thousand feet above sea level, where we would visit the enormous crater described in the guidebook as spectacular. We had passed a few turnouts with views but waited for those further up the road.

"Let's pull over there," Joanne suggested as she pointed to a flat space bordered with a low stonewall. I turned into the empty space.

"Oh wow," I exclaimed as we piled out of the car. We hadn't even reached the top and here was a spectacular view all to ourselves.

"It looks like the same view from a plane," I said as we stood in awe above a sea of white clouds stretched over mountain ridges.

"Quiet, for a minute," Joanne raised her finger to her mouth. "Listen." We stood still for a few minutes. There was no sound...at all. No wind, no traffic, no voices...just absolute silence. We looked at each other in amazement. It was the most silent moment we had ever known. As we held hands lost in our thoughts, I wanted to bottle the moment to keep forever.

The crater was indeed spectacular. From the parking lot along with other trekkers, we walked the paths to the various lookouts where we scanned the rust-colored volcanic expanse. Despite the high steps, my knee, thankfully, did not give out. However, if I forgot to adapt my first step up, a sharp pain quickly reminded me to use the new knee. The body always had a mind of its own.

The view of the crater reminded me of the Grand Canyon on a smaller scale and I marveled at the comparison. Even the strong Hawaiian wind and the memory of the chilly Arizona gusts seemed to connect the two panoramas. Ironically, my leather-bound journal had begun with our trip to Sedona and would end with this trip to Maui.

While we hiked along the paths to the rocky summit of the ancient volcano, Joanne suggested I take a picture of a rock to send to Chris rather than disturb Mother Maui by pilfering one. Problem solved. My wife was full of good ideas.

As I wandered near the visitor center, taking pictures of the view and looking for the perfect rock, I often glanced at Joanne who was exploring on her own some yards away. Not surprising, she seemed to be intrigued with a particular creature. A few minutes later, she returned to me.

"Look what I was watching," she reported with satisfaction. Her face was shining with love as she handed her phone to me. "I took this video for you, honey. I figured you'd know what it was."

"Oh thank you," I smiled back at her as I watched the scene play back. The video was of a Chukar, a bird similar to a quail that was poking around the vegetation where Joanne had been roaming. She knew the bird would be gone before I had a chance to join her so she had used her phone to capture her find.

"I love it," I exclaimed. "It's a new bird for my list." Joanne seemed proud of herself since she knew I would love her gift. No matter what cancer concerns she might have had at any moment, she never forgot about me, even above the clouds.

Our stay with Pat and Larry was coming to an end and we were gearing up for our next adventure at our rented condo. Before we said adieu, however, Pat came with us to the quaint shops in Paia where I hoped to find a ring. One unique gift shop, Maui Hands, caught my eye.

As we browsed the aisles in the upscale shop, I gravitated to the jewelry counter and scanned the case for rings. I often have a difficult time finding the right size due to my arthritic knuckles, so I wasn't surprised when I couldn't find one in this shop. However, I was drawn to a particular turquoise stone set in a pair of earrings.

When I asked the clerk about the stone, she explained that the local artist uses turquoise from Arizona where her father lives. My heart skipped a beat when I again thought about Sedona. The color of the stone had the familiar light blue tone but also a rusty patch, like the red rocks, separated by a black band. Thinking that, like our love, the stone was meant to be, I inquired about ordering a ring from the artist.

With the clerk's help, I made the connection and ordered the dramatic ring that would also represent my first impression of Joanne's paradise. Since the stone was from Arizona, I figured Mother Maui wouldn't mind either. My quest was complete.

We arrived on the smaller western end of Maui the next day. Our ground floor condo was nestled in a resort of several two-story buildings surrounded by lush tropical gardens and assorted palms. Even banana trees dotted the landscaped lawns and winding paths between buildings. A quiet peace rode on the breeze.

The resort sat on the edge of a small cove filled with underwater reefs where abundant tropical fish and green sea turtles congregated to feed. Two clear swimming pools completed the grounds while surfers rode foaming waves in the distance. On the far end of the buildings, a small dirt path led to a small private beach. I couldn't think of a more beautiful spot for a honeymoon getaway.

The inside of our condo was spacious and nicely decorated in brown, burnt orange, and sage green tones with images of sea turtles scattered throughout the rooms. Panama-style ceiling fans added an extra tropical flair. As we filled each space with our belongings, I felt so much gratitude that I said out loud, "Thank you, God." With that comment, Joanne stopped what she was doing and came over for a hug. As we held each other close, the familiar ring of her cellphone shattered the moment.

"Hi Joyce," Joanne greeted her sister. "What's up?" Her tone had a note of concern, as a phone call from the mainland, rather than a text message, would probably mean bad news. During the rest of the conversation, I had the sense that someone was in the hospital.

After she hung up, Joanne looked at me and there was no mistaking the seriousness of the call.

"Alex was rushed to the hospital," she explained, "with a really high fever and a red rash."

"Oh no," I said, worried that her three-year-old great nephew was in danger. "What's wrong?"

"They don't know yet so they have to do a bunch of tests." She was obviously upset about him. With this news, I felt a different kind of wave speeding toward us.

"They're going to keep us posted." Since Joanne's family was her priority, I knew this news would weigh on her for the remainder of our vacation. Then she added more bad news.

"Joyce also told me that Gloria is in the hospital too," she sighed. "She fell and broke her wrist and pelvis." Another of Joanne's cousins, Gloria was Carole Ann's much-loved older sister. The wave of concern was growing.

"Oh, I'm so sorry, Jo." The feeling of helplessness pervaded our hearts and minds. "Looks like all we can do is offer some Maui healing prayers." She nodded in agreement.

An hour later, my own cellphone rang.

"Hi Lin." The voice was my brother's. I couldn't imagine why he was calling since he usually preferred to text.

"Hi Ray." I tried to be calm. "What's going on?" I listened intently to his report.

"Just wanted to let you know that Ma's been having some weird episodes of shaking and even hallucinations," he said, trying to be reassuring about our ninety-year-old mother who lived near him. "Ann and I took her to the ER to get checked out and they finally decided she had an allergic reaction to that new medication for her diverticulitis." I quickly breathed a sigh of relief.

With my anxiety level returning to normal, I asked him to keep me posted and thanked him for being there. I had always been grateful for my thoughtful little brother but my hope for the evening was that bad news only came in threes.

Despite these concerns from home, Joanne and I continued to plan our week with as much gusto as we could muster. Since a rainbow appeared every morning on the patio while I wrote in my journal with my coffee, I interpreted the sign as hope for a new day of promise.

A day later, we learned that Alex had Kawasaki disease, a condition that causes inflammation in the walls of some blood vessels in the body. Evidently, it is most common in infants and young children. Thankfully, he could be treated and would recover gradually. We both sighed with relief and felt the weight lift.

While we wove relaxing on the beach, dining out, and souvenir shopping into our schedule, we focused on unique experiences for our main events. Attending a traditional luau, snorkeling with sea turtles, and visiting the ancient Iao (pronounced *eee ow*) Needle in the mountainous lush valley in central Maui were high on our list.

Since Joanne had already attended the oldest and most authentic luau on the island, she led the way in her sleeveless copper-colored sundress, complete with a flower in her hair. Even though I usually felt disdain for touristy stereotypes, my brightly colored Hawaiian shirt had been packed specifically for the luau. I was not immune to following the crowd.

With a perfect evening, a glorious sunset and Mai Tais in our hands, we joined five hundred guests on the tastefully decorated grounds by the water for a traditional buffet and night of entertainment. The native dances and music were dramatic and exciting as the performers related the history of the islands. I often stole glances at Joanne whose appetite and energy amazed me when I remembered the days of chemo and her struggle to even climb stairs. Thank you, God.

On the private condo beach with its steep grade and strong tide, Joanne loved to float for hours holding a Styrofoam noodle with her floppy sun hat and dark glasses. If I waved to her from my chair, she always returned the greeting with a cute queen wave while I laughed to myself. I wondered if she was thinking about cancer, about dying, or even about the next event. What I was sure about was her ability to use humor and love to enjoy the moment.

Snorkeling with the sea turtles had been one of Joanne's favorite topics ever since her first trip to Maui. With the cove only steps away from the condo, we eagerly donned our wet suits and facemasks as often as we could. The safest entry into the water that most people used was by some flat rocks where an official wildlife reserve agent monitored snorkelers' actions. Since the sea turtles are an endangered species, their protection is utmost in the minds of the authorities. Humans are not allowed to get too close or touch the animals.

On our second snorkel, we gingerly made our way from the flat rocks into the active waves. Thank goodness my knee didn't buckle. Joanne had an easier time and was quickly paddling out into the cove. Even though I had snorkeled successfully in the Caribbean and loved it, I was not a strong swimmer. But once past the choppy water, I relaxed with the colorful fish below.

Flashes of blues, yellows, and reds darted or poked along the coral. At times, larger schools of blimp-like fish slowly passed by without a thought to my presence. Then I spotted the prize. A huge green sea turtle was gracefully probing the rocks and reef and if I hadn't had a snorkel mouthpiece, my jaw would have dropped. We softly made eye contact and I sensed the animal's peaceful spirit. But I also had to admit I was a bit fearful that the turtle might not know about the rules and swim too close to me. She was enormous.

If Joanne had been nearby, I would have shared my excitement. But she was floating on the other side of the cove by this time. I could see her snorkel tube in the air while her face remained in the gentle waves. An occasional splash of her swim fins told me she was alive and engaged in the wildlife below.

After an hour in the water, we motioned to return to the rocks. With some maneuvering of our less than nimble bodies and help from fellow snorkelers, we emerged exhausted onto dry land and reported on our swim after catching our breath.

"Oh my god," Joanne exclaimed with wonder on her face. "I can't believe the experience I just had." She proceeded to describe an even more inspiring connection than my own.

"I spent so much time with this one turtle who stayed right with me." She was so excited. "Whatever motion I made, she repeated it." Images of nodding her head, raising an arm and even peeking out of the water were clear in my mind as she told me how much the turtle's spirit inspired her. It seemed that Joanne had been touched by something divine...perhaps Mother Maui. Her spirit glowed the rest of the day.

With our honeymoon winding down, we planned one more adventure to the Iao Valley State Park that would complete our exploration of the entire island. With an extensive history of Hawaiian kings, gods, battles and religious rites, the area is a thick rainforest with vegetation extending over many parts of the winding road. We set out on a cloudy day with hiking boots, maps, and binoculars ready on the front seat. Always prepared, I also grabbed my raincoat.

As we climbed another twisting road, the rain began to pelt the windshield. By the time we reached the empty parking lot, the rain came pouring down as heavy and loud as any soaking rain we had ever known. Since we were the only visitors, I was reminded of the special day at Beaver Tail when I had first asked Joanne to marry me. Remembering that day years before on our honeymoon seemed ironic and also meant to be. After fifteen minutes of steady rain, we were resigned to either exploring in the rain or turning back.

"So, what do you think?" I thought she might be tired and want to retreat.

"Well, let's get out and look around." She had that determined look again. "I'll use my beach hat and some plastic bags." Feeling carefree before we left, she hadn't bothered with a raincoat. "I'll put some around my shoulders too." I looked at the pelting fat rain and then at her meager protection with more than a little skepticism.

"Okay, if you want," I replied tentatively. I couldn't protect her from everything.

As a mother, I knew that other than wrapping a child in bubble wrap, total protection from harm and danger was impossible. I was also aware that children, and adults for that matter, learn how to defend themselves and become independent thinkers when faced with adversity. Protecting Joanne from cancer was another one of those impossibilities when I had to let go of my helplessness. And it appeared that it was up to my wife to protect herself from the torrential rain.

Still in the car, Joanne fashioned a couple plastic bags on her head with the plastic hanging down over her ears, covering her neck. Then she placed the wide-brim beach hat over the bags, creating as much head protection as she could. With the remaining bags around her shoulders, she held them together with one hand like a shawl while her free hand opened the door. Joanne loved to improvise.

We quickly exited the car and ran through inches of running water toward the covered billboard with visitor information. Even with my raincoat and ball cap, I could feel the rain seeping in. By this time we were laughing our heads off.

"That's like running into the water on the nude beach," I shouted above the rain. Then I took a look at her plastic bag outfit and laughed so hard I had to hold my stomach with my eyes closed. With her rain-drenched floppy hat and mismatched bag shawl held tight, she reminded me of an old Peruvian woman coming off the boat. I took her picture and waited until the ache in my sides faded before hiking part way up the flooded trail. Joanne had decided to wait, knowing I wouldn't be long. Once again, she was right as we soon returned to the car, thinking our kayaks would have been a better choice.

After two weeks in Maui paradise, we had mixed feelings about leaving. Certainly we felt sad to leave the natural beauty of the island and our friends. But with impending health concerns, we were ready to return to the routine and safety of our home paradise. Since I usually hated returning to the drudgery of chores and responsibilities, I was surprised at my transformation. My only explanation was that Joanne's strength and spirit had been lifted in Maui fortifying her to tackle whatever cancer threw her way. If she was ready, so was I.

As the plane lifted off the runway and I took my last look at Maui, I was struck by the shape of the island. The two connecting bulges reminded me of a pregnant woman. Maybe two weeks of Mother Maui's influence had affected my perspective or maybe my individual perception was as fleeting as identifying cloud shapes. Even so, I could almost hear her spirit say, *Be well, my child.* I also thought of Phoebe's feline mother and wondered if Mother Maui ever needed a break.

CHAPTER 20

A Time for Everything

With our hearts and minds full of Mother Maui, we returned to our home sanctuary where we were delighted to find that Little Miss Phoebe hadn't trashed the place. Since she had already presented multiple personalities before we left, we had been pleasantly surprised to find the good Phoebe greeting us at the door with her twitters and friendly rubs. Her cute innocent face said, *Oh good, you're back! Pick me up and love me,* as if she had never been naughty in her little life.

While we were away, the daily feeding and care from Joyce and Christine had kept the kitties happy and healthy. Their reliable help enabled us to relax and focus on the fun we had needed for healing our spirits. With renewed strength, we felt ready to return to the nitty-gritty of the next round of life.

The time had come to retrieve the imaginary cancer box off the shelf. Joanne had to resume the maintenance drug, Avastin, as well as a routine CT scan and blood work. With only a day to recover from jetlag, Joanne was back in the familiar lab. Since these brief visits had become an incidental part of her schedule, she usually drove herself to the infusion center and later waited at home for any significant lab results.

Three days after the CT scan, I walked through the back door of the house and plopped my briefcase and tote bag on the kitchen floor while announcing my arrival.

"Hi, honey, I'm home," I said in a singing voice, mocking the old TV sitcoms. I made my way to the couch where Joanne was lounging with her iPad. Even after a quick hello kiss, she remained intent on her work.

"Hi, I'm sorry," she apologized for not paying attention. "I'm checking in with the ladies on Inspire." She was referring to the online blog designed

217

for women with ovarian cancer. Joanne had relied on her new online friends for support and information since the early days of her diagnosis. Even with names like Rabbit Girl or High Hopes, women would write heartfelt entries about their various stages of treatment or answer questions as if they were gathered around a table for a coffee klatch. From the serious look on Joanne's face, I suspected that something was up.

"What's going on?" I sat down on my side of the couch facing her and waited a few seconds while she finished typing a comment.

"Well," she sighed as she put the iPad down on her lap. "I got a call from Dr. D. about the CT scan." Her whole body seemed to sag with the weight of the news.

"I have a new half inch tumor in my liver," she continued, "And more fluid in my lungs from the cancer." The fatigue on her face was more than from a tired body. Her expression told me she was getting tired of bad news.

"Oh shit," I said emphatically. Attempting to keep my anger and fear at bay, I focused on supporting my wife. "What did Dr. D. recommend?"

"I have to see him next week to talk about clinical trials and what to do next." Joanne was concentrating on the facts. "Since the Avastin isn't working, we have to look at other chemos instead." She paused for a few seconds and then looked at me squarely.

"I was so angry when I got off the phone, I felt like throwing this iPad across the room," she shouted at the world. "So many of these women online are in remission for years," she declared. "I don't understand it!" She slapped the pillow next to her. I waited silently with my hand on her shin as she quieted down like the aftermath of a thunderstorm passing through.

After a few minutes, I moved closer and simply held her in my arms. Sometimes there are no words. As much as we loved each other, I could only imagine her frustration and fear. Not being in her shoes, my words of understanding and comfort would be limited to those of an observer. With a few tears and sighs, Joanne finally looked at me and said, "Thanks, honey. Will you come with me next week?"

"Are you kidding? You wouldn't be able to stop me," I answered with conviction. I had never missed accompanying her on visits to the doctor and wouldn't want to be anywhere else.

"Are you going to be okay?" I asked her as we looked into each other's eyes. Concern for the moment as well as the future filtered into my heart and mind. Since I was determined to be strong for her, I wouldn't allow myself the luxury of expressing my fear of losing her. Those feelings went into their own box on the shelf. Since living in the moment had been my approach to life, my focus would continue in the same manner.

"I'm okay," Joanne reassured me. "Believe it or not, I'm in a good place right now after Hawaii." Having let go of her mini outburst, she smiled and spoke softly but with resolve. "I know that God is with me so I'm choosing to trust and not worry." After a few seconds, she added, "But I miss my turtle." She often mentioned the sea turtle she had snorkeled with in Maui.

Even though the news of another recurrence had rocked our boat, we somehow found enough determination and perspective to balance our attitudes. During the next few days, the arm of the pendulum came back to rest in the middle as we prepared to hear the doctor's recommendation. I often thought of ourselves as Weebles, a small toy with a round bottom whose advertisement had proclaimed, "Weebles wobble but they don't fall down." The toy company probably had no idea their toy would be used so often as a metaphor.

When we met with Dr. D., Joanne was ready with questions about various clinical trial drugs which they discussed as I took notes. Any new clinical trial chemotherapy that had shown promise was worth the extra paper work required to participate. The conclusion was that Doxil and Yondelis would be the combination of choice. Evidently, the Yondelis had been successful in Europe for extending remissions but the side effects would be different than her previous treatments.

"I believe this new combination will work for you, Joanne," the doctor reassured us. "The tumor is small and the amount of fluid is minimal." His positive attitude always calmed us down.

"What are the new side effects?" Joanne asked Dr. D. in a steady professional voice as if requesting the ingredients to a gourmet dish.

"Well, you won't lose your hair this time," he smiled with genuine warmth. "The Yondelis is known to affect the skin with itching and burning but most patients use icepacks on their hands and feet during the infusions which seems to help." When I heard icepacks, I gave a quick glance to her as I thought of her aversion to the cold and sympathized about the next endurance test. Joanne's eyes caught mine and she frowned with the same thought.

"Other side effects like mouth sores and extreme fatigue and nausea have also been reported," Dr. D. added with an apologetic face. "After you're cleared for the trial, chemo should start around mid-October every three weeks until you're stable." I noticed that the doctor did not mention *no evidence of disease.*

At least we still had a few weeks of camping and family parties before the grueling treatment resumed. My impending second knee replacement surgery was also scheduled for the end of October. As if we were paddling our kayaks toward the rapids, we braced ourselves for another demanding challenge.

As we left the doctor's office, Joanne remembered to request his signature on the renewal form for her disability parking placard. During her worst days of treatment, the red temporary card had been a godsend whenever we would have had to park at a distance. Not wanting to abuse the privilege, however, we had used the card only as a last resort. Dr. D. had taken the form to fill out and would send it in as requested.

Back in the recliner at the infusion center for the all-day round of treatment, Joanne had already received the steroids, Benadryl, and anti-nausea drugs while I sat in my usual chair beside her. The familiar warm blankets covered her from neck to toe while the hood of her sweatshirt draped over her head completed the outfit. The nurse was magically separating the entangled IV tubes as she prepared the first bag of strong chemo.

"Which one is that?" Joanne asked the nurse. Since she had brought special icepack sacks for her hands and feet, she anticipated pulling them out for the Yondelis.

"This is the Doxil," she replied. "The Yondelis will be the last one." The color of the bag she was hanging was a brilliant red.

"I have to say that looks like a hummingbird feeder," I chuckled as I looked at the red liquid. They both laughed at the comic relief.

"I *wish* it was just sugar water," Joanne said with emphasis. "Or even a cosmopolitan." Cosmopolitans were one of her favorite drinks, but she'd have to forego them during the treatment.

"That's even better," I agreed. I hated the thought of what that poison was doing to her body as we remembered happier times.

Years before when our relationship was new and we still felt like hormone-driven teenagers, a memorable night in P-town haunted us for years.

At the end of the summer, we were at yet another bed and breakfast for the weekend when we decided to watch the moon over the water. Since Joanne had had one too many cosmopolitans, I drove her dark purple Honda to the beach where we could sit in the car watching the waves.

"I don't think we're supposed to be here after sunset," I said cautiously as we drove through the open gate. I had noticed the sign at the entrance.

"Oh, they won't check," Joanne replied with bravado. With or without a few drinks, I knew very well that she enjoyed breaking some rules.

Since there were other cars in the parking lot also stretching the rules, I relaxed somewhat as I pulled into a space further down for everyone's privacy. As the sky darkened, early stars dotted the velvet backdrop and the crescent moon glowed over the ocean swells as if the show at the drive-in was about to begin. For a few minutes, we silently watched the peaceful scene unfold as we held hands in the car.

"This is so beautiful," I said softly. I turned and smiled at Joanne's loving face. With only the sound of the surf, we kissed each other lightly at first. As time seemed to stand still, our passion grew and we melted together. We hadn't noticed that the other cars had left the parking lot.

"Let's get in the backseat," she whispered. As we clumsily moved arms and legs over the console to reach the back, our giggles interrupted the mood. The thought crossed my mind that it hadn't been that long ago when Joanne had been reluctant to hold hands on the streets of P-town. She had definitely dropped her guard.

By this time, clothes were unbuttoned and zippers unzipped in the backseat when we heard a vehicle nearby come to a stop. We froze in place with hearts pounding in fear as well as passion.

As a light flashed through the driver's window, we clamored to redress as quickly as humanly possible considering the tight space. Through the glass, we heard a man's voice.

"What's going on here?" the voice called out with authority. He waited while we returned to the front seats. "I need to see your driver's license and registration." Then he added, "You know the beach is closed for the night."

After opening the window, I mumbled something about being sorry and handed the documents to the uniformed officer. Despite our own embarrassment, he made no comment about our escapade in the backseat. While he looked at the papers, I turned to Joanne who was attempting to stifle a smirk and probable laugh.

"Well, I won't fine you this time but consider this a warning," the officer kept a serious face. "And just to let you know, your name will be in the computer. So, be careful." He handed the documents back to me as I said my automatic thank you.

Naturally, he waited in his patrol car while we backed out and headed to the gate. I'm not sure if he could tell we were holding in our laughter, but we let it out as soon as he passed us and drove away.

"Oh jeez," I managed to say between laughs. "I knew we shouldn't have parked there," I added half-heartedly. Breaking the rules with Joanne was always an adventure that I seemed to enjoy as well.

"Can you believe that?" Joanne exclaimed with tears in her eyes from laughing so hard. "Now your name's in the computer." She laughed even harder.

"Well, it's your car," I reminded her. Suddenly, her laughter subsided.

"Oh, yeah."

We were both outlaws.

After the red Doxil had been drained from the bag, the nurse hooked up the bag with Yondelis. It was time to haul out the ice packs and wrap them around Joanne's feet and hands. As I helped her, my expression cringed along with her own. I really wanted to take her place, especially since her poor circulation from previous treatment would double the effect of the ice. This new phase seemed rather cruel since her body had already been through so much.

Six days after treatment, Joanne's stamina had surprisingly improved and she felt somewhat normal. With these new drugs, her exhaustion and nausea were more severe than previous chemos so she slept often and took extra medications for nausea during the recovery period. We also had to avoid infection once again since the Yondelis also lowers white blood cells. Thankfully, the masks that Joyce had provided in the past would be reinstated for use outside the house.

Whenever Joanne bounced back from the effects of the drugs, I often marveled at her resilience in mind as well as body. Her words, "I'm in God's hands," were not enough to convince me of her spirit. Her actions went beyond words when she gave to others despite her pain. As soon as the side effects wore off, she would call Jayden to check on him, give vegetables or garden tips away, or visit a friend down in the dumps and have tea. Her inner well for love was never dry.

Whenever Joanne and I had talked about our gratitude in spite of cancer, we thought about a metaphor found in one of our devotionals. The writing described people as a glass container. Whatever fills the glass is what spills out when it gets bumped. If there's lemonade, that's what comes out. Likewise, if we are filled with love and gratitude, that's what comes out when we get bumped with cancer or any adversity. Joanne had filled up with God and Maui spirit and that love was spilling out more than ever.

By the end of October in 2016 when Joanne was feeling better, it was time for my left knee surgery. Since I had experienced the procedure only seven months before, I was cocky about breezing through the hospital stay, recuperation, and physical therapy. I mistakenly thought I would maintain the same level of determination as last time in order to recover quickly. After all, Joanne would need my assistance through her difficult treatment.

As I lay in my hospital bed with my knee wrapped and pain killer flowing through my veins, I was only half aware of my surroundings in my sterile private room. I vaguely remembered walking with a physical therapist only hours after surgery the day before and I had just returned from another awkward therapy session after breakfast. Using the walker had been familiar but the pain felt new.

About to doze off, I heard a familiar voice.

"Hi Lin," Joanne called out to me in order to delay my nap. With her spiked purple hair, tasteful makeup, and stylish sweater coat, she breezed in like a refreshing wind. No one would have guessed she had cancer. She bent down to plant a kiss on my cheek.

Not wearing a mask for her protection, she apparently wanted to keep a low profile. Maintaining a normal chic appearance had always been one of her priorities.

"Hi, Jo, I'm so glad to see you," I smiled through sleepy eyes. Then I noticed she held something behind her back.

"Look who also came to see you," she said excitedly. With glee, she presented the furry object in front of her. It was the Love Bear with the fancy hat who sang "Love is all that I can give to you." It was the gift I had given Joanne after her major cancer surgery two years before.

"Oh, wow," I exclaimed. "I love it! Can she stay with me?" Feeling vulnerable in my weakened state, I wanted a cute friend around since Joanne couldn't stay.

"Sure," she replied. "That was my plan." She was so considerate and thoughtful. "Just make sure she comes back to me."

We only chatted for a short while before Joanne left for home where I would return in two days. Christine's visit after work was another bright light in my day, especially since she offered to look out for us at our home infirmary in the weeks to come. With Joyce and Carissa's help as well, we would have plenty of support. I needed to remember that there is a time to give and a time to accept help.

Since I had complied with hospital care and their instructions, my discharge happened as expected. As I rolled out of the hospital, I already felt weary about the recovery work ahead. When Joanne arrived to pick me up, however, I considered her struggle and thought, *You wimp! She's been through worse than you! Get on with it!* When I arrived home to the sunroom for peace and Phoebe for laughs, I had mustered a new resolve to buckle down as before.

"Can I get you anything?" Joanne asked me as I lounged on the living room couch that I had renamed my knee station. From the last time, I had discovered that the firm cushions provided the best location for rest and therapeutic exercises.

"No thanks, honey." I was concerned about her stamina since she had been waiting on me for everything for a week. "I'm about to do my next round of exercises." My determination had wavered somewhat since the ride home but I always returned to what I considered to be my new job.

The grueling sets and repetitions were required at least three times a day. They included stretches, bends, flexes and lifts on the couch, sitting on a chair and rising on stairs. Sometimes I winced and grunted but I usually pushed through the pain with the goal of regaining full range of motion and strength.

"I'm so proud of you honey," Joanne remarked as she entered the living room. "You're so good about doing those exercises." Other friends and family members had lately pulled me aside to tell me Joanne also commented about my fortitude to them as well.

"Thanks," I replied as Phoebe pounced on my stomach. "I can't say Phoebe's any help though, like Rosie was." I recalled Rosie's quiet support during my shoulder exercises.

"Are you having any balance problems in the bathroom anymore?" Joanne had insisted that she accompany me for butt alignment on the toilet seat during the first few days. Despite her recent good days, her general strength would not be enough to lift me from the floor. With her anxiety showing, she was aware that the new chemo was taking a greater toll on her body than months before.

When Joanne's second treatment in early November was postponed a week due to a low white blood cell count, the doctor recommended an addition to the procedure. From then on, she received an arm patch of Neulasta after chemo in order to combat the low count. Since the patch was timed to release the medication twenty-four hours after treatment, an extra visit during critical home recovery could be avoided. Our education about chemotherapy had advanced well beyond the 101 class.

One day during a chicken soup lunch and before my second round of exercises, Joanne came to the front door of the living room to collect the mail. The chilly air blasted into the room while she went out to the porch to the same spot where she had lost her hair over a year before. When she returned with a pack of mail in one hand, she also held up a small box addressed to her.

"Look what I got," she exclaimed. "It's from Pat in Maui." As she went into the kitchen to find the scissors to open it, I glanced at the mail on the coffee table and saw a large envelope also addressed to Joanne but couldn't identify it from my couch station.

"Oh, wow," she said from the kitchen. "This is perfect." She brought the present to me for show and tell. As she proudly held up a curved mauve-colored mug with a delicate handle, I could read the print that said, *Queen of Everything*. There was even a crown drawn above the lettering. Considering my wife, I agreed that it was indeed perfect.

After the excitement faded, I drew her attention to the large envelope. As she tore the envelope, we looked quizzically at each other not imagining what could be inside.

She silently held up the new disability parking placard that the doctor had signed for during our visit months before. This time, the color was blue, not red for temporary. Blue signified a permanent disability. The power of that card was crushing as we realized a new time was coming.

CHAPTER 21

Heart of a Warrior

After two hours of tossing and turning on the living room couch, I knew I had lost the battle. The nagging pain in my knee wouldn't let me sleep no matter what position I had created with multi-shaped pillows. A quick tap on my glow-in-the-dark wristwatch told me it was now 1:30 a.m. Earlier attempts in the recliner had been unsuccessful and strong pain meds only gave me nightmares. Reading was a possible solution but I chose the TV as the lazy way out.

With the chilly autumn air seeping into the house, I quickly grabbed my sweatshirt to stop the shivers. When I glanced outside, randomly falling snow-flakes on the front steps told me that New England winter wasn't far away.

Since my balance continued to be unreliable on stairs and I didn't want to wake Joanne, I had been sleeping at my knee station in the living room for the two weeks since surgery. While the couch was usually the best choice, there were occasional restless nights that had not been the case during my first recuperation. Despite recent improvement and the knowl-edge that my condition was temporary, I recognized my impatience and frustration as I quietly meandered into the TV room.

Keeping the volume as low as a whisper, I scrolled through the pro-gram guide on the screen hoping to find a sleepy science documentary or mindless sitcom. Not surprising, I gravitated to the movies that are as tempting to me as fast food popcorn chicken. Even viewing one good scene of a familiar movie is worth the search since I appreciate great lines and heartfelt acting. This time, I found an older film that I had never seen and was happy that it had just begun.

As I clicked into the movie, Phoebe sauntered into the room with her twitter as if to say, *What're doin'? Is it time to eat?* With sleepy eyes, she demanded some head rubs and quickly surmised this was not feeding time. As she glued her body next to my hip, I thought about Charlie who would, most likely, remain with his Joanne upstairs.

Twenty minutes later, I heard soft footsteps on the stairs and caught a glimpse of a sleepy Joanne making her way to the bathroom.

"Hi honey," I said from the darkness. A little startled, she looked up and came to the doorway.

"Hi, what's going on?" She glanced at the two night owls huddled around the TV. "Are you okay?"

"I'm okay but I just couldn't sleep with my knee." I wasn't surprised to see her since bathroom runs at night were the norm even before cancer.

"What the hell are you watching?" After she had absorbed a few seconds of the movie's content, a shocked look on her face told me she would not be joining our soiree.

"It's that movie, *300*, from a few years ago," I replied, guessing that she would not recognize the name. I also knew she would not appreciate the gory scenes.

"I don't know how you can watch that stuff late at night," she grimaced and quickly gave me a kiss before retreating to the bathroom and Charlie who was waiting devotedly for her return.

As I resumed watching the movie, I wondered at my choice as well until I became enthralled with the cinematography and the powerful message of strength, courage, honor and determination in the face of impossible odds. The unique chromatic lighting and effective slow motion created an artful impression despite the gore of battle with swords slicing heads and limbs at random. I concluded that the scenes were not for the faint of heart but the principles of fighting with honor were timeless.

The tenacious and clever Spartan king and his small band of three hundred muscular warriors stood their ground for days against the formidable monsters thrown at them by the Persian army of millions. The trained Spartans fought together by crouching and raising their shields, forming a turtle-like protection, and then organizing their spear attacks in unison. Despite inevitable defeat, their ferocious courage and undaunted spirit was beautiful. As I cheered them on, I thought they deserved a miracle. In the end, the miracle was the inspiration of their sacrifice that led other armies to eventually defeat the hideous Persian army later on.

Despite the excitement of the movie, I returned to the living room and found deep sleep shortly after my head connected with the pillow. While I was able to put the TV out of my head for the night, I would remember the parallels of the movie many times in the coming weeks as Joanne endured her new treatments.

A week after the movie, Joanne received her second round of Doxil and Yondelis that knocked her down for six days. Even with my knee pain and diminished stamina, I took my turn as caretaker since her condition was more debilitating than my own. Despite our overflowing gratitude to family and friends as they brought us covered casseroles and ran errands, we both couldn't wait to feel better.

"I sure hope this Biotene works," Joanne said to me when I passed the bathroom doorway one day. As she examined her mouth in the mirror, a bottle of the new rinse stood on the edge of the sink.

"Where's the sore?" I knew she had developed at least one painful spot the day before due to chemo.

"Well, I now have two of them," she answered as she pointed to a red swollen sore inside her lip and an even larger one inside her cheek. They looked nasty.

"Oh jeez, they look so painful," I commiserated and cringed with the memory of my own cold sores in the past. These fresh mouth sores from chemo were new to Joanne.

"You have no idea," she continued. "Think of ten times the pain of an ordinary cold sore." Joanne's face was pale and worn. "They throb all the time and it's so hard to eat." She poured a capful of the rinse and slowly swished the liquid in her mouth with her eyes closed. A few more rinses seemed to ease the pain.

"I'm so sorry you now have this to deal with," I felt helpless again. "As if your burning feet aren't enough, along with everything else." Despite the medications for side effects, her fatigue and nausea had escalated with the new chemo, causing her to remain at her couch station for hours each day.

"Yeah, what's one more thing, right?" Joanne sighed with resignation as she continued with another idea. "You know, I was thinking of using my medical marijuana license to get something for all of this." Even though her license had been approved the year before, she had been reluctant to use any cannabis products. Like her attitude about the disability parking pass, she did not want to abuse the privilege.

"I think that's a great idea," I replied remembering with fondness my pot-smoking days in the sixties. Of course, I realized that the medicinal products would be more sophisticated and specific for cancer but I endorsed her plan if marijuana could ease my wife's pain.

"I think I'll drive down there on one of my good days," she announced. Knowing that I still couldn't drive, she was determined to maintain her independence rather than ask Joyce. Fortunately, the Compassion Center for dispensing medical marijuana was only fifteen minutes from the house so the drive wouldn't wear her out.

No matter how lousy she felt, Joanne always left the house looking like a million bucks with her hair and makeup in place to complement her coordinated blouse, slacks, and quilted jacket. In contrast, my tailored look of turtlenecks, jeans, and sweater was probably worth fifty dollars. But more than her appearance was her positive and caring attitude toward others that took the spotlight off herself. Consequently, she rarely complained or elaborated on her pain and discomfort, even to me. On the day she left for the Compassion Center, I had to trust that she was feeling strong enough to make the trip.

While I was bending and lifting my knee during my second round of exercises, I heard Joanne open the back door and rustle her belongings in the kitchen.

"Hi, Lin," she called out to announce her arrival. "Glad to see you're doing your job." Since she didn't want to interrupt my concentration, she remained in the kitchen and opened the small paper bag at the counter.

"Hi, honey," I responded. "I'm just about done." Looking for any excuse to finish my drudgery, I ended the reps early. "How did it go?"

"Very good," she seemed excited. "I was really impressed with the intake. The technician was very professional." She made her way into the dining room where I was sitting in the straight-backed chair. In her hands were two items.

"What did you get?" I looked at the tube and black-foiled bag she held.

"You wouldn't believe how many choices there are, depending on your condition," she explained. "It's a real science but after the guy talked to me for a while, I decided to get this cream for itching and gummy bears for pain and helping me sleep." From her description, I thought a gummy bear would have helped me the night I watched the movie.

"Are you going to try them tonight?" I was hopeful that she had finally found some relief but I also wondered if she would share one with me.

LINDA L. SKIBSKI

"I'm going to use the cream right now," she exclaimed. "But I'll take a gummy bear tonight since I'm not sure how I'll react." Since cancer had already stolen some of her control, she wouldn't want to lose more. Then she added, "Even though they've taken out the THC that makes you high, I don't know if there's still some in there."

What fun is that? I thought as I decided I might ask for one later on.

"Oh, I have to tell you what happened when I stopped at the bank on the way home," she continued. "I saw someone I knew from work before I retired and she said, '*Joanne, you look so good!*'" As she related the story, her pride in her appearance shone on her face.

"Well, you do look good," I responded honestly. Of course, even bundled up at the infusion center, she always looked good to me.

"I don't know if she knew I was sick, but I didn't have the heart to tell her that I was so nauseous I could've vomited at her feet," she chuckled at the thought. "I might feel lousy, but at least I look good." To Joanne, her positive attitude was as powerful as any medication. Her outlook helped to lift me as well.

As it turned out, the marijuana gummy bear did help Joanne fall sleep but the effect lasted only a couple hours. While the cream also diminished her itching and burning, several applications were necessary for continued relief. The cancer monsters were relentless as our list of weapons grew.

Just before Thanksgiving, when we both struggled to find strength, faith, and relief, Joanne also struggled to find her breath. Of course, difficulty breathing only exacerbated her fatigue. Since this development reminded her of pneumonia, she immediately consulted with the doctor. Following a chest x-ray to determine the amount of fluid, he recommended a thoracentesis, or lung tap, at the hospital.

As an outpatient procedure, a lung tap could only be performed when the amount of fluid was significant. Otherwise, the lung could collapse. Our concern was that the technician be experienced enough to find the exact location for inserting the long needle into Joanne's back. Her research revealed that a lung tap was much more than a blood draw.

Sitting anxiously in yet another waiting room at the hospital, I looked lovingly at my wife whose slumped posture betrayed her exhaustion despite her stylish purple sweater outfit that matched her hair. We were both reading as we waited for her name to be called for the procedure.

"Are you nervous?" I asked the obvious. I wanted to let her know I would listen if she wanted to talk.

"A little," she admitted and then added, "But it can't be any worse than chemo and besides, I want to feel better." I admired her courage, especially in light of the past week's struggle.

After her name was called and she reassured me that she could manage on her own, I waited in the small lounge with my crosswords and novel. Time passed slowly as I tried to distract my thoughts from her ordeal.

Only a couple days before, we had been relaxing at home in the sun-room when I noticed her jotting some notes on loose notebook pages. After asking what she was doing, she showed me her diary entry.

> *Another day to give thanks to God for all my blessings, though I am down and out from chemo and Lin is hurting with her knee. There is so much to be grateful for. We have so much…a wonderful family, a great little house, two sweet kitties, and most of all each other. As we spend most of this week just resting, we look forward to next week's Thanksgiving celebration with our family. Today we rest and just be in the moment.*

By this time on the journey, I shouldn't have been surprised with her optimism but I noticed there were no words about her pain and discomfort. I had been grateful that she shared a piece of her hopeful heart.

Just like those three hundred warriors, Joanne was never going to give up. No matter what cancer threw at her, her plan was to defy the odds and continue fighting with ferocious courage and strength. The way she fought inspired me to lift my own shield against the enemy so that waiting in my chair while she endured this latest invasion was the least I could do. Now that my knee pain was only an ache and I was walking without a cane, I could rejoin her army both physically and emotionally.

After an hour, Joanne waved to me from the doorway indicating she was free to go.

"How did it go?" Even though I was eager to hear what she had to say, her pale and tired face gave away the answer.

"It was okay, I guess, but I hope I don't have to do that very often." She continued as we walked down the hallway. "Thank goodness they gave me a local because the needle was huge." Her eyes widened as she explained the required chair position with her arms draped over a table. "Even with the local, I could still feel the needle." I suddenly remembered fainting as a child whenever I stood in line at school waiting for a Polio needle vaccination.

"They took out a lot of fluid," she said in amazement. "But I can breathe better anyway." She seemed relieved and so was I while thinking that another battle was behind us. Without a crystal ball, I couldn't know that the brutality of the battles to come would exceed my imagination.

Now that we could count on one good week during each treatment round, we took advantage of the time for normal activities. Whenever we could, we welcomed the chance to attend the Congregational church service where we had our wedding ceremony. The peaceful sanctuary and inspiring music and message helped us to focus on our spirits rather than our ailing bodies. Whenever I sat with the large congregation, I often glanced at the smaller chapel off to the side and reminisced about our wedding day that, in some ways, seemed like eons before.

The Thanksgiving service during this difficult recovery included special choral music and greater pageantry than usual. For an hour, we absorbed the inspiring hymns and words of gratitude filling the air of the church from the pews to the high ceiling rafters. We seemed to breathe deep at the same time and exhale the weight of our physical and emotional pain together.

At the end of a heartfelt prayer led by our minister, we simultaneously noticed each other's tears streaming down our cheeks. As our shoulders shook briefly with silent sobs, I felt release from our ordeal and reached for Joanne's hand. We remained connected throughout the service by hands as well as hearts. At that moment, I concluded that even warriors had to break down during a lull in the fight.

As Christmas approached, my knee strength improved while Joanne's battle with chemo raged on. Dodging the icy sidewalks and bracing the cold wind contributed to my slower recovery but I had received clearance to drive and could walk much further than the corner. Since my full care-taking duties had resumed as well, Joanne could focus on the complexities of her chemo battle.

In light of our trials and Phoebe's penchant for glittery objects, our holiday decorations and activities were not as elaborate as in past years. Our smaller than usual Christmas spruce tree, now decorated from the waist up, had also been wired to the wall in order to prepare for our little beast. Additional lung taps and blood transfusions also interrupted the schedule despite our efforts to ignore them. Always hoping the treatments were destroying cancer, we anticipated every CT scan and CA 125 blood work result with bated breath.

By mid-January in 2017, the test results revealed only minimal effectiveness. Even though the tumor in Joanne's liver was smaller, fluid continued to build up in her lungs. Despite the doctor's reassurance that this chemo needed more time to work, Joanne admitted that her patience was waning. Waiting for results and worry about her body's endurance were often our topics of discussion, always with the undercurrent of wanting more years. Nonetheless, she soldiered on with fortitude to stay the course.

The time for the annual Senior Ski Trip in Vermont had arrived. Even though we had signed up the year before, our decision to attend wobbled on the proverbial fence. The only sure thing was that I would be snowshoeing, not skiing, if I went at all. My fragile knees dictated that much of the equation anyway.

Since the scheduled week for the trip coincided with her healthiest week in the chemo cycle, Joanne seriously considered throwing caution to the wind. While her heart tugged at her to go, however, she still couldn't imagine having the strength to even carry her skis, much less carve them down a hill. With a great deal of sadness, she decided to forego the ski adventure. My heart ached for her.

As we lounged in the cozy sunroom, also known as the snow globe in winter, we discussed the approaching trip to Vermont. With the cast iron gas stove in the corner flickering an inviting flame, Charlie zoned out on the floor in his favorite place of worship where heat pumped into the room. The good Phoebe slept soundly in her favorite rocker.

"I think you and Dave should still go," Joanne urged. "I'll be okay here and I know he'd really like to go." I considered what she was saying but I felt torn.

"I don't know, honey," I said softly and paused before continuing, "I hate leaving you here and I'd miss you so much in Vermont." I tried to imagine the scene but really didn't want to.

"Well, it's just for this year," she said with a hint of fading hope. It was the first time I detected any reservation in her voice. Then she added with resolve, "I'm still in this and I'm planning on skiing next year so don't count me out yet." Her determined spirit had returned as quickly as it had left.

"I would never count you out, Jo," I said honestly. "I'll call Dave to let him know you can't go this time and see what he says." If he volunteered to cancel, I would be fine with his decision. But thinking he would still want to go, I prepared to offer my services as chauffeur.

Dave and I did venture to Vermont, but the empty backseat in the car mirrored my empty heart. I missed Joanne terribly. The thought that this would be a permanent scenario plagued my spirit as I struggled to be in the moment. At least I could still call and text her to report our activities as well as send pictures to lift her spirit. I was grateful for any connection.

Like every year, the cozy inn, group of caring friends, and consistent schedule remained the same, which was a comfort once more. As I tested my new knees on snowshoes, I discovered the worth of the surgeries and regained my confidence for longer hikes. The week proceeded as usual until Wednesday afternoon when I felt a flu-like cold descending in my head. Hearing that others in the group had come down with terrible colds, I bought some medication from a local convenience store preparing for the worst.

By the next day, I was in agony with the flu. My head was pounding, my stomach was churning, and my body was burning with fever. Despite my annual flu shot, this nasty bug had found its way in to wreak havoc and the day was lost as I slept and moaned the hours away. Early in the morning as I was feeling half dead, my cellphone rang.

"Hi, Linda." I recognized Dave's friendly voice. "I missed you at breakfast. Are you all right?" He was genuinely concerned for one of his snow angels.

"Oh Dave," I couldn't help but moan. "I'm so sick." My eyes were like slits as if even opening my eyelids hurt. "I'm not going anywhere today."

"I'm so sorry to hear that," he replied sincerely. "Can I get you anything?"

"No thanks, not now anyway." I couldn't imagine living long enough to consider later.

"Okay, but call my cellphone if you need anything," he continued, "I'll check in with you when we get back from skiing." Then he added, "I'm not sure how much I'll ski anyway." Considering his eighty-eight years, the reality of a tired body was setting into his psyche. When we ended the call, I promptly fell asleep.

Later in the day, Dave was true to his word and delivered tea and toast when my stomach allowed. If it hadn't been for his tender concern, I would have succumbed to my misery. While I missed Joanne more than ever and looked forward to reuniting, I hated the thought of bringing this illness home to her weakened immune system.

By some miracle, I recovered enough the next day to pack my belongings, nibble on some breakfast, and drive us home as scheduled. Thankfully, Dave was spared from my illness and his moral support felt like a balm. Not only had he been a good neighbor, he was also a caring and dependable friend.

Having alerted Joanne to my plight, she prepared the house with separate hand towels, additional hand sanitizer, and even masks. With another round of chemo scheduled in a couple days, we always needed to remain vigilant about possible infection. Already battered from earlier treatments, her immune system could be even more compromised from these stronger chemicals.

Through our meticulous efforts, we were able to shield her from this unexpected threat and treatments continued. We often considered the irony of wanting this poison that seemed to be more hideous than the cancer itself. But we realized that fighting for Joanne's life required weapons of mass destruction.

In the next few weeks, she continued to use the small window of opportunity when she felt normal to attend her art classes, meet with her cousins, and run errands. Joanne's mantra to live with cancer never wavered. Her dream of a chemo-free summer also remained intact as the third anniversary of the cancer diagnosis loomed on the calendar.

As I drove to my next scheduled appointment for work, I contemplated the middle-aged, visually impaired man I had just left. When his progressive glaucoma had interfered with safety, he requested orientation and mobility instruction for greater self-sufficiency. For weeks, he had been learning outdoor travel techniques in order to negotiate his neighborhood for exercise as well as short trips to the nearby convenience store. With his tall frame, long stride, and newly developed cane technique, he had presented a confident picture of independence.

Unfortunately, he had had a recent heart attack that required a change in his mobility lesson plan until he regained his strength and stamina. Together we had altered his travel goals in order to protect his heart. Walking to the end of the driveway and then to the corner mailbox had to suffice temporarily.

While thinking of my client, I also remembered Valentine's Day and the season of the heart. Phrases like *take heart, follow your heart,* and *the heart of the matter,* popped into my head like the messages on pastel candy hearts. Not only is it a symbol of love but also courage and life itself. There is something true and central about the heart and I imagined that it must be an honor and awesome experience for a surgeon to hold a beating heart. Likewise, I thought of Joanne and me holding each other's hearts in love and connection as she displayed the heart of a warrior. That would be a perfect Valentine's Day card message.

After five months of nasty treatments, Joanne's body had taken a beating. While we waited for the results of the latest CT scan and blood work, we were planted in the TV room at dinnertime staring at the commercials during a break from the local news. With only tea and toast, Joanne was struggling to resist the temptation to retire for the night since she had had an exhausting day. Suddenly, her head perked up as an advertisement for St. Jude's Children Hospital came on the screen.

"I feel so bad for those kids," she said as adorable faces with bald heads smiled back at us. They were fighting cancer as well. "It's just not fair that they should have to suffer so much." Joanne was more concerned for them than for herself. I knew that she had donated to St. Jude's for years.

"I know," I said softly. Out of selfishness, however, my primary thought was for my wife. Like the Spartan's courageous battle, I thought Joanne also deserved a miracle for the way she fought.

A few minutes later, the house phone rang beside her.

"Hello, yes, this is Joanne," she said in a formal tone. "Oh hi, doctor." As she listened to his message, her smile faded and her eyes closed for a moment. After hanging up, she turned to give me the summary.

"Well, the chemo has made only a slight decrease in the tumor and nothing else." She sighed with frustration. "It's not worth it to me, so we're going to take a break from treatment," she said decisively. "In a few weeks, we'll meet with Dr. D. who said there's a new clinical trial that's had good results." She looked even more tired than before the call. "But he wants my kidney and blood levels to stabilize before starting something else." She paused with her thoughts.

"Well," I sighed, "at least you'll have time to recover." I knew that her fight wasn't finished. We sat and pondered this new turn of events as the TV noise continued.

"So, where do you want to go?" she finally asked me out of the blue, breaking the silence.

"What do you mean?" I couldn't imagine what she was thinking.

"I think we should go on a cruise," she replied.

Obviously, the strongest part of Joanne's body was her heart. My own heart loved the idea of a cruise but I wondered if this would be our last.

CHAPTER 22

❧

Just Cruisin'

With a break in chemotherapy, Joanne's appetite improved as if a switch had been pulled. Being a connoisseur of pancakes, her heart's desire one Saturday in early March 2017 was to visit the nearby Friendly's restaurant for breakfast. Always on a quest to find the best pancakes, Joanne had been surprised to discover that the New England restaurant chain offered the type of fluffy pancakes she loved. Not only did I enjoy going out for breakfast, but I was ecstatic to watch even a sliver of Joanne's recovery from chemo.

"Are you sure you're up for a cruise?" I asked, looking at my joyful wife across the booth's table as she savored the half portion of pancake on her plate. I knew if she didn't finish them off, she would ask the waitress to box her breakfast remains.

"Honey, I'm not always *up* for even getting up out of bed every morning," she said with conviction as she sipped her tea. "At least on a cruise, I'd have a change of scenery and feel kind of normal."

"That's true," I had to agree. As the waitress passed by with her coffee pot, I waved for a refill. My own breakfast of two eggs, two pancakes, and two bacon strips was long gone. Both my stomach and my heart were content.

"I guess no matter where we are, we'd be cutting back on our usual activities anyway," I continued with the thought that our aging bodies would keep our younger minds from running wild. On past cruises, we had enjoyed full days of physically demanding onshore excursions, hikes through rainforests and kayaking at the foot of glaciers. I imagined this next cruise would be less strenuous.

"I'll just have to do what I can do," Joanne said matter-of-factly. "Like at home, we can still have fun even if it means spending more time in our cabin." Then she added, "By the way, how are your knees and back?" I was reminded that she wasn't the only one with limitations.

"My knees are great but my back is killing me lately." I had to be honest as I considered another visit to my chiropractor for a tune-up. My chronic lower back pain had become more intense with the strain of knee recovery.

"See, if it isn't one thing it's another," Joanne continued as the waitress left our bill on the edge of the table. "If I didn't have cancer, I'd probably have something else by this time in my life." My silent wish was for the something else as she kept talking. Anything but cancer.

"I mean, I…or you…could have a heart attack tomorrow…or a stroke…or get hit by a bus," she said. Despite the silver lining inference, I decided this conversation was not exactly an uplifting way to start the day.

"I know," I conceded and then couldn't help myself with the overused line, "Like a box of chocolates, right?" Joanne raised her eyes to the ceiling and shook her head at the cliché.

"Yes, exactly," she said with a sigh and then paused, "I just wish I had gotten my uncles' long-life genes instead."

We both considered that thought as our eyes locked. Even though the aches and pains of aging were inevitable, my mind flashed back to the plaque in the sunroom, *Grow old along with me.* My next thought was a silent prayer to God for a miracle to make that happen. While we were indeed getting old, we weren't quite there yet. I wanted to believe that together we'd discover the second half of that quote: *The best is yet to be.*

As we rose from the booth to leave, Joanne, with her leftover pancake box in hand, turned to me with a different thought.

"I think you should finally try one of my gummy bears for your back," she said. I smiled but decided to wait once again until absolutely necessary. After all, Joanne needed them more than I did. "And then let's look at the cruise information," she added.

Until twelve years before, we had never considered taking a cruise. I never thought I would enjoy the experience that, in my mind, was reserved for elderly retired couples. Lounging on deck chairs, gorging on huge food buffets, and watching B-rated entertainment had not been my idea of a thrilling vacation, especially since we usually preferred more active get-aways like camping, hiking, kayaking, and renting jet skis. In some ways, cruising symbolized aging, which meant living with limitations. When the cruise industry expanded over the years, however, my perspective, thankfully, expanded as well.

A new world had opened up to us in 2005 when we booked an Olivia cruise to the Bahamas. Not surprising, our inspiration to sign up was that the lesbian-owned and operated travel company catered to our community. The entire ship would be filled with women who created a unique environment and energy that would surround us in spirit. Being on a cruise was incidental to the real draw of being in community. Other than annual lesbian festivals across the country, there were no opportunities at the time like the freedom of an Olivia cruise.

During that first cruise, any preconceived ideas about the aging population and sedate activities on board were shattered. Half of the passengers were younger, the excursions were adventurous, and the energetic dancing continued into the late night hours. The dining experience was exquisite with interesting women around our table, and the varied entertainers had been well-known celebrities, including Lily Tomlin and the country music star, Wynonna. With the delights we discovered on Olivia, no wonder we became hooked on cruise vacations. If cruising was equated with aging, then we were on board for both.

Unlike her first experience in Provincetown as a couple, where she'd been so worried about being seen in public being intimate with another woman, Joanne relaxed on our first cruise and had no hesitation about holding hands on deck, snuggling at the rail on a moonlit night, or extending a kiss during a show. The freedom to be ourselves always felt like heaven to me and was worth the extra fare. Even initial motion sickness could not dampen the spirit of our first cruise.

A year later in 2006, we were relaxing in the TV room after work with our devices in our laps when I received an email announcement from Olivia. Curled tight on the couch between us, little Buddy's feet twitched as if he were chasing a pigeon in his dream.

"Hey, Jo," I said as I started gathering more information online. "How would you like to go on another Olivia cruise?" Her head popped up from her screen as she turned to me with interest.

"What's that about?" she asked, always as curious as Oliver, our black and white who was curled up on his cat perch in another room undoubtedly guarding the house.

"Seems I've been selected to receive a two-for-one sale on their next cruise." I had started reading part of the email to her. "It says it's a for a week to the Western Caribbean, including stops in Guatemala and Belize." A longer cruise for half the price sounded good to me.

"Really?" She was enthused. "I like the idea of half price for sure." Always frugal, she rarely let a bargain pass by. Then she added, "And I loved Belize when I went there years ago." Her face lit up with the thought of a resort trip she had taken with a college friend. "The snorkeling was phenomenal."

"Should I book it?" I already knew the answer. "There's a deadline so we shouldn't wait." I loved the thought of all those women on board.

"Absolutely," she affirmed my idea then added, "You know, Lin, I really don't like the high cost of Olivia. They charge twice as much as a straight cruise."

With home improvement plans for adding a sunroom and a basement sump pump system in the near future, I understood her concern as a homeowner. Nonetheless, my whiney inner child prevailed, at least for the moment.

"But you can't find that kind of cruise experience anywhere else," I argued. "To me, it's worth the price." With the reality of house expenses, however, my inner adult sensed a need for compromise when planning future vacations.

"I know, but I think after this Olivia cruise we should think about cheaper cruises." Joanne had already taken charge with her common sense and I finally had to agree.

Following an amazing second trip with Olivia, we enjoyed two more cruises four years later in 2010. That January, we surprised Christine with a short cruise to the Bahamas as a college graduation gift and then, in late August, we sailed through the spectacular Inside Passage of Alaska with time to explore Vancouver as well. While we curtailed our public displays of affection on these straight cruises, we did enjoy the savings of lower fares. Unfortunately, saving money meant settling for romance behind the closed doors of the cabin and once again keeping our affection concealed.

As Joanne planned our impromptu cruise to the Eastern Caribbean during the chemo break, I continued jumping through the hoops of planning for retirement at the end of June. The decision to retire had not been an easy one for me. For thirty-seven years, I had been able to honestly tell those who would ask that I loved my job. While my profession as an orientation and mobility specialist had suited both my personality and strengths, the job had defined me as well. Until the year before, I hadn't formalized any plan to leave my identity and paycheck behind.

Once Joanne had retired following her diagnosis, however, she encouraged me to consider doing the same. After all, I was sixty-eight years old and she needed me more than ever. Even though her hints were gentle, I understood her need to share whatever retirement she had left. I also appreciated her patience with my decision.

Despite the lure of unscheduled retirement days, I couldn't deny my initial resentment that cancer would take one more thing from me. Working during the cancer fight had provided a space where I felt normal and confident. When teaching a lesson, I could focus on something totally removed from the stress of illness. Without my refuge, my ability to remain strong for the road ahead was uncertain. Fear and doubt were creeping into my psyche.

For months, I had gathered financial and health information in order to secure a safety net for the possibility of retirement. To my surprise and relief, those pieces to the puzzle fell into place as I continued my investigation.

Other deciding factors surfaced when I realized my walking pace had slowed and my attention to detail had become clouded. If I couldn't keep pace with some clients or neglected a turning vehicle during a street crossing, my effectiveness as an instructor was in question—and a client could land in the hospital. Since the safety of my clients was my priority, I concluded in January that retirement was indeed the right choice. Needless to say, Joanne had been ecstatic about my decision.

Our fifth cruise would set sail at the end of March and would include stops in Haiti, Puerto Rico, St. Maarten, and St. Kitts & Nevis. By this time in our cancer journey, we realized that we couldn't leave the total monster behind but we planned to ignore its effects as much as possible. Though she was still not feeling well and her energy was sapped, Joanne was steadily gaining strength for the voyage without chemo and had high hopes that she would enjoy our new travel destinations.

Despite the short notice, we secured a standard inside stateroom at a low cost and engaged our routine packing ritual a few days before departure. When I chose to leave my leather-bound journal at home, I acknowledged my own need to escape even from writing. On this trip, the adventure and challenge would be to apply one of our mantras, *Do what we can, when we can, because we can*. Everything else was up to God and the universe.

Feeling experienced with the long passenger lines that resembled huge boa constrictors at the port-of-call, we dragged our small, wheeled suitcases behind us as we crept through the boarding procedure. Even with Joanne's disability ID card qualifying her for the shorter line, the exhausting wait seemed to take longer than the cruise itself. My gratitude for pain free knees was overwhelming despite the extra scan through security, but my back continued to be a nuisance while standing.

"Are you sure you don't want me to get a wheelchair for you?" I asked Joanne as we waited. I had observed her drawn face and diminished conversation as we plodded along.

"No way, I'm fine," she said with a definitive reply. "I'll just sit on my suitcase when I need to." Even though the demands of air travel earlier in the day had already zapped her energy, Joanne did not want to appear weak.

"I can't wait to get to our cabin." She took the words out of my mouth. The only problem was that our room assignment was unknown due to our late reservation. The number would be provided when we checked in.

At the gate, with our cabin number finally in hand and our bags whisked away for later delivery by ship stewards, we once again entered the glitzy world of cruising. Surrounded by plush couches, etched glass stairways, polished wood rails, and glimmering tile floors, we oohed and aahed with the crowd as the indirect lighting accented every feature. Dramatic glass sculptures protruded from several walls as if the famous glass artist Chihuly had swept through the lobby on a rampage, creating enormous exotic flowers for our amazement. As I grabbed a complimentary glass of champagne, I felt my body relax on our temporary floating home.

Without much difficulty, we located our assigned cabin and opened the door.

"Oh my god," we exclaimed together.

Unlike other cramped staterooms from past cruises, this room was as spacious as a hotel suite. With cream-colored walls, forest green accents, and soft lighting, the ambiance was warm and inviting. A neatly made king-size bed called to Joanne from the far end of the room while a full couch and cozy chairs created a peaceful sitting area opposite the bed. A polished wood desk and counter lined most of the wall on the right where a prominent ice bucket cradled a chilled bottle of champagne complete with chocolate-covered strawberries and fancy shortbread cookies. The huge bathroom to the left of the front door could have housed a rock concert. We looked at each other with opened mouths.

"Are you sure this is our room?" Joanne managed to ask. "We certainly didn't pay for this."

"I don't know," I replied in total surprise. "They must've made a mistake." For an instant I thought Mother Maui might be taking care of us, but feared instead we'd soon be hustled off to a closet-sized cabin that would never be satisfactory now that we'd been tempted with this suite.

As I walked over to the champagne bucket to investigate further, I noticed an envelope on the desk. It had two passenger names written on the front. Unfortunately, they weren't ours.

"Look at this, Jo." With some disappointment, I showed the envelope to Joanne. "I'll call the front desk and find out what's going on."

"Okay, honey...thanks," she said with exhaustion dripping off each word. "I'm just going to rest a little." Curling into a ball on the huge bed, she lowered her head onto the sham-covered pillow and closed her heavy eyelids with relief.

After reaching the front desk clerk, I discovered that the original passengers assigned to our cabin had to cancel at the last minute and we'd been assigned the room at no extra cost. Evidently, one of the two women was a wheelchair user and frequent cruiser, hence the champagne, goodies, and large, handicapped suite. With the probability of needing the room for additional rest, Joanne could cruise in comfort. To our delight, the timing of our arrival and their cancellation had been a small miracle and we gratefully celebrated with another glass of champagne.

Our first day at sea was a time to relax by the pool, explore the ship, and secure our sea legs. Unlike me, Joanne experienced motion sickness during every cruise. Over time, she had discovered that wristbands positioned on specific pressure points had provided the most effective relief. On this vacation, they were a godsend for eliminating one more sickness that Joanne did not need on her list.

With so many choices for meals during the day, we usually opted for the expansive buffet for breakfast and lunch. However, at dinner, we always chose to relax at our assigned linen-covered table in the formal dining room with our clutch of new friends. Even with her unpredictable appetite, Joanne could usually find mild but tasty dishes on the menu.

"Hi there," a handsome gentleman in his sixties with wire-rimmed glasses greeted us as we sat down on the other side of the dinner table. "My name is Henry and this is my wife, Carla." He turned to face the attractive woman with salt and pepper hair seated beside him, as she smiled warmly in our direction.

"Hi, I'm Linda," I responded with a smile, "And this is my wife, Joanne." No one looked surprised, including Joanne. Either she didn't care anymore or she hadn't heard me.

In that moment, I marveled at how just a few words could say so much about who we were. To be able to greet strangers with the truth felt liberating, as if the spirit of the Olivia lesbian cruise had come along and resided within. To be sure, my bravery had depended on the receptiveness of our new friends, but the cancer struggle had also stripped away unimportant facades. Only truth and love mattered anymore.

Like varnish remover, both cancer and aging were stripping away a lifetime of layers, leaving bare wood. Whether we liked it or not, the once important layers of physical strength, intellect and emotional defenses were fading away. Inevitable aging was the slow process while Joanne's cancer worked with frightening speed. With both forces, the bare wood that remained was our hearts.

For the next hour, we chatted away with Henry and Carla as if we had known each other for years. After we said goodnight to our new old friends and returned to our cabin, I wondered at the ease of the conversation, and how much society had changed since Joanne and I had first met. Without the stress of hiding in the closet, we could look forward to relaxing dinners throughout the week.

The first port of call in Haiti was actually a brief few hours in a small tourist town called Labadie. For the most part, Joanne was able to walk along the beach and straw market but the humidity weakened our defenses. Sipping a tropical drink on the mediocre beach was sufficient for our first land stop. At least we saved our strength for the longer visit in Puerto Rico the next day.

As the ship crept to the dock at the bustling city of San Juan, our panoramic view of the multicolored buildings promised a different experience than the day before. Our plan was to use public transportation to explore some local history at a well-known fortress before locating a less known restaurant for lunch. Joanne already had the address of the local hangout.

With our map and information in hand, we left the shopping tourists behind and inhaled the sights and sounds of the city. While young and old hurried on foot, in cars, and on bicycles, aromas of Spanish food from street vendors filled the air along with Latin beats spilling from nearby shops around the common square. I wondered how the scene could be so vibrant when it was so damn humid.

Even waiting on a shady bench for the bus was tiring due to the heat. Thankfully, Joanne didn't seem to mind until an hour had passed without a sign of our bus. Rather than wasting more time pursuing our original plan, we consulted our guidebook and expertly conjured a Plan B.

"Oh, let's just walk," Joanne said with defiance. "I think we should go to this historic chapel a few blocks away and then walk up the side streets to our restaurant." In light of the hilly terrain and our aches and pains, her Plan B would be comparable to riding jet skis before snorkeling all afternoon. I loved her spirit and determination.

"Okay," I agreed without hesitation. Asking if she was up to it never crossed my mind.

At the historic chapel on a hill overlooking the harbor, we stopped briefly to read the plaque explaining the sight. Built in 1753, the name of the structure was Chapel of Christ the Savior.

"Lin, take a picture of this for your book." As she mentioned that improbable project again and pointed to the sign, I only complied, thinking it must the chemo making her crazy.

"All right, but you should be in it," I said as a compromise.

"No, I just want what it says." I reminded myself of her director expertise and agreed.

I took the picture of Joanne pointing to the sign and the line that read, "*Legend traces its origin to a miraculous happening at the site.*" Evidently, Joanne still prayed for a healing miracle. I had to admit that I did too.

The next day, as our bumpy bus wound its way to the expansive white sand beach on St. Maarten, my eyes bounced across the guidebook trying to focus on the beach names.

"What's the name of the beach we're going to, honey?" I asked Joanne sitting next to me as she looked out the window. "For the life of me I can't remember." With aging, I convinced myself that my brain had reached its capacity and would not accept any more extraneous material like names.

"I have no idea either," she replied. "Let me look, maybe it'll ring a bell." I handed her the page and she scanned the names for a few minutes.

"Oh, look at this," she said with a sly grin. "Maybe we're going to Orient Beach." Then she read part of the description, "*bathing au naturel is possible at Orient and other designated beaches.*" She started to laugh when I glanced sideways in her direction, remembering our nude beach day on the Cape.

"Very funny," I had to smile with the thought.

"I wonder if your name is still in the computer," she mused. Her face was wistful before her laughter resumed.

One aspect of cruising we had always appreciated was that the schedule could be as busy or as relaxing as we wanted. Between day trips onshore and events on board, Joanne's energy was exhausted so she often took cat-naps while I would wander the deck, read by the pool, or search for new birds with my binoculars at the rail. During these times alone, my feelings seemed to mimic the ocean swells. While I missed having Joanne by my side, I was grateful she was only a few steps away in our suite. I thought of all our energetic adventures in the past that had become too strenuous for her. But, in contrast, we had shared an offbeat walk on San Juan's hilly streets that brought us both such joy. Despite the ups, however, sadness would flow into my bones whenever I allowed myself to put my armor down by the pool.

By the time we arrived on peaceful St. Kitts and Nevis, our final land stop, Joanne's fatigue was catching up to her. Consequently, we opted for the bus tour excursion that would include gorgeous mountainous scenery, a short stop at a souvenir shop, and a quiet stay on one of their serene beaches. With buildings lower than palm trees, small artisan shops, and easygoing ambiance, the quiet island felt like natural medicine.

As promised, the mini-bus pulled onto a dirt and gravel parking area in front of the souvenir shop that stood alone overlooking the island's impressive mountains. Below us, we could see a narrow spit of land separating the dark Atlantic Ocean on the left from the turquoise Caribbean on the right. As we scanned the striking view, Joanne spotted a commercial photo op nearby complete with a dressed donkey, a monkey in a pink tutu, and their human hawker owner. Her eyes were glowing with delight at the sight of the small monkey in a tourist's arms.

"Oh, Lin, take my picture with this monkey," she begged. "Do it quick so the owner won't charge us." By our observation, he was charging five dollars per photo, a rate we felt was outlandish.

"Okay, hurry," I agreed. By now, we had become a team of outlaws. If Joanne had been daring in the backseat in Provincetown, facing cancer had only strengthened her innate outlaw nature, and I was thrilled to be her sidekick.

Joanne held and caressed her beloved monkey friend as if it were a baby. While I lifted my phone for the shots before the owner caught us, my thrill at the caper darkened as I remembered her immune system and the possibility of infection. But my thought was too late, and I decided, *What the hell.* The joy on her face would be worth the risk. I started snapping away, capturing forever that monkey joy.

Part of our relaxation regimen, especially on a cruise, was happy hour. Several lounging areas by ocean views were available and we chose a quiet area near the Chihuly-style glass sculptures for our last evening cocktail. As we chatted across the small round table, I took a picture of Joanne in my mind because she looked so wonderful. With her purplish hair, dangling earrings, and flowered blouse under a gray linen jacket, I was filled with love as our eyes met for a long gaze. Even the purple flower arrangement behind her head complemented her look.

"Honey, why don't you take a picture?" Joanne asked me as if she could read my mind. Once again, I snapped a shot and realized these pictures seemed to be creating a photo journal, stepping in for my leather journal back home. I couldn't explain it but her loving expression in this picture felt eternal or at least meant to be.

On most cruises, the last formal dinner is typically a big deal with extended menus and sparkling presentations by waitstaff and crew. In the past, we had enjoyed many gala dinners complete with glittering outfits. While we continued to enjoy a fine meal these days, formal wear had become less important over the years. Like other layers, the need to impress had also faded.

As dinnertime approached and we headed to our cabin to get ready, Joanne's stride had slowed considerably and her face looked exhausted. After we stepped through our cabin door, she seemed deep in thought.

"Honey, I just can't go to dinner tonight," she confessed as she plopped on the edge of the bed. "My stomach is a mess and I'm so tired." I could see she was ready to collapse and my heart sank at the reality of the cancer toll.

"That's okay," I said. " I can just order room service for my dinner while you sleep." I knew such moments were inevitable, so rather than try to persuade her to do more than she could, I had instinctively prepared to use Plan B at a moment's notice.

"No, no," she insisted. "You have to go to dinner. It's so special tonight... one of us should be there anyway." I knew she was serious but I dreaded the thought of going without her. On the other hand, I realized she would feel worse if I stayed in the cabin.

"Okay, but I'm not staying long," I reluctantly agreed.

Even though a sweatshirt and jeans would have been my preference considering my mood, I dressed to Joanne's approval and found my way to the dining room and our table.

"Hi Linda," Carla greeted me first. "Where's Joanne?" I could tell they both were concerned, especially since her cancer story had been revealed to them earlier in the week.

"Hi." I slumped into my seat. "Joanne's just not up to coming tonight. She's resting in the cabin." Despite their friendliness, I hated being there without my wife. Trying to be social was more difficult than coming out to our new friends.

Throughout the special dinner of filet mignon and lobster tail, I felt a deeper sadness than I had ever known. For the first time, I was attempting to live in the world without her and it gnawed at my heart. Needless to say, I left when I thought I could and extended goodbyes on Joanne's behalf. I almost ran back to our room.

By the time we returned home from the cruise, we were both exhausted and my back was killing me. Sleeping on a different mattress, hoisting baggage, and excessive standing had taken their toll. In contrast to my back, however, my new knees were my reward for all those dreaded exercises. Too bad there was no such thing as a back replacement.

"Lin, why don't you take one of my marijuana gummy bears for your back tonight?" We had just finished unpacking and were picking through the pile of mail in the kitchen.

"Okay, if you don't mind." Having resisted them so far, I was now ready to indulge and try anything for the pain until I could track down my chiropractor next week.

My expectations were uncertain as I chewed the soft little bear that reminded me of candy at a movie matinee as a kid. The taste was somewhat bitter, however, as I swallowed the last morsel. After finishing the mail, we made our way to the TV room for a look at the news. As the time passed, I thought I felt less back pain but wasn't sure.

"I'm going to be planting some seeds soon and hopefully working in the garden," Joanne announced after looking up from her iPad.

"Huh?" I had been totally engrossed in the weather report that seemed very cool.

After repeating herself, she stared at me for a few minutes before looking at her phone.

"I also have an appointment with Dr. D. next week about the next chemo," she informed me. "I hope you can come with me." Her voice finally reached my preoccupied brain.

"Oh, sure," I turned quickly to face her as she started to chuckle. "Is it time for bed?" I was surprised she hadn't proceeded upstairs already.

"Honey, it's only been fifteen minutes," she laughed then added, "I don't think you should have any more gummy bears."

"Guess I'm still cruisin'," I replied with a smile. Obviously, not all of the THC had been removed from the medicinal cannabis.

The gummy bears did help my back but their effectiveness soon wore off, just as they had for Joanne. Some weapons are like cheap firework duds while the more dangerous chemicals remained in the arsenal waiting for the next round of battle.

CHAPTER 23

❦

Planning and Planting

After the emotional high of our cruise and my gummy bear had worn off, our minds focused on the medical and house tasks at hand. First on our list was the visit with Dr. D. in order to plan the next chemo attack. Preliminary blood work had been completed prior to the appointment where we would hear the results of the routine tests.

"After the doctor, I want to go out to that organic nursery for some plants and vegetables," Joanne announced in the car that seemed to drive itself on the familiar ten-minute route to the hospital.

"Isn't it kind of early for planting?" After twenty years together, I had learned quite a bit about gardening just by osmosis, but Joanne was the resident expert in our house. Early April in New England still seemed too chilly in my opinion.

"Oh no, I could've planted lettuce before our cruise, but it didn't make sense while we were away." The excitement of promising new plants and vegetables was painted on her face. "There shouldn't be any more frosts, so we can get started." As a part-time procrastinator, I would have waited.

Breezing through the security procedure at the hospital lobby, we passed the familiar fish tanks, rubber tree plants, cozy couches and busy elevators to the fourth floor. I could feel the cancer cloud descending upon us just by walking through the hallways.

"Is it my imagination, or is this route longer than before?" Joanne was only half-joking in light of her weak stamina.

"It's the same, but your body's not," I replied as lightheartedly as I could. "We could have taken one of the wheelchairs at the lobby desk," I added. Surmising her rejection of the idea, I hadn't even mentioned it at the time, though the thought had crossed my mind as soon as I spotted one behind the desk. Planting the seed for next time, though, seemed to be the better approach.

"No, I don't need that," she confirmed my prediction as a silent sigh of relief filled my spirit. In my mind, if she didn't need a wheelchair, then there was more hope.

Tucked away in one of the exam rooms, we waited for the doctor, who swept into the room after the nurse had completed her preliminary vitals.

"Hi ladies," Dr. D. smiled as he greeted us with his warm handshake. "How was our cruise?" He loved to travel vicariously on our adventures.

After a brief description of our relaxing voyage and Joanne's symptoms, we got down to the business of new chemo.

"So, your blood work still shows low cell counts and kidney function, so we need to continue the break from chemo." No matter what news he presented, Dr. D. had a way of easing our fears and giving us hope.

"What do you recommend for the next chemo and when do you think I should start it?" Joanne had done some research but always wanted to know everything.

"I think we should go with Olaparib which is in the group of PARP inhibitors." He explained further, "It's sometimes used as a maintenance therapy for advanced ovarian patients." *Advanced.* Hearing that word made me cringe as if I had touched a hot burner.

"But it's in pill form and the side effects will be less than the last round you had." We glanced at each other with slight smiles at the thought of fewer side effects.

"But is it effective?" Joanne wanted to defeat cancer, not just reduce it. "You know me, I'm hoping for another remission."

"It has shown some good results so let's give this three months," the doctor said as he looked at Joanne with admiration. "If it doesn't do its job, then we'll consider another stronger mix." The sincere look on his face revealed his determination to keep Joanne alive.

Throughout treatment, I had appreciated our doctor's difficult job to shape the best plan of attack while maintaining quality of life. With the talent of a sculptor, he had to consider all aspects of Joanne's care in order to reduce and eliminate a formidable opponent. Balancing her physical endurance, response to different chemicals, and psychological toughness was an art form that I admired. Since we trusted his honesty and experience, the new plan for the chemo pill was set in place for June. As we left the office, our hearts and minds thankfully switched gears for the more pleasant task of finding plants.

Rolling along the country roads on the drive west of the city, we passed open grassy fields, stands of naked deciduous trees, and brown farmlands anticipating the bustle of spring planting. Splashes of yellow forsythia and daffodils dotted the landscape like the opening act for the more spectacular spring show in May and June. On a smaller scale, our own backyard presented the same promise with bunches of young purple, white, and yellow crocuses, delicate white snowdrops, and an array of daffodil and jonquil varieties revealing several shades of yellow. Every tiny green sprout in our yard or on the road brought a smile to Joanne's face.

"So, what are you planning to pick up today?" I asked my spunky partner as we approached the open-air property, complete with a greenhouse and tidy farmhouse.

The attractive oval sign between two sturdy posts came into view on the corner of the rural intersection. Bordered by a small purple vine, the forest green block letters read, "The Good Earth," with "organic gardening center" in smaller script underneath. Their slogan, "Where The Good Things Grow," made me think of our backyard.

"Well, I've made a list," she replied as she brought forth the garden notepad I had put in her Christmas stocking one year. "I want a few varieties of tomatoes, some bush beans, a couple cucumber plants, radishes, yellow squash, some herbs and a zuke." After taking a breath, she added, "And I need some soil and fertilizer to use with our compost."

"Are you going to get flowers yet?" Even though it was early in the season, I spotted some pansies on long tables as our tires crunched on the gravel parking lot.

"I'll look at what they have in the greenhouse but I really want to get a lot of perennials this year so maybe other places might be cheaper." She flipped through her notepad, and I caught a glimpse of the copious notes she had made as well as the layout drawings for the garden and raised vegetable beds. As she opened the car door and entered her world of living things, I knew she had forgotten all about cancer. She swept me away as well.

After grabbing one of the battered red wagons for toting plants, I fell into my place behind Joanne while she browsed between the rows of plants on wooden tables and in clusters on the ground. She found grape, beefsteak, cherry, and even purple tomatoes as well as the other vegetables on her list. When she came to the small cucumber plants, she grabbed two.

"Don't they kind of spread out?" I asked her, feeling proud that I at least knew enough to ask the question. "I mean, with the squash too in that raised bed, won't it be crowded?" She grinned before revealing another part of her plan.

"I know, but I was hoping you'd make a trellis against the house for the cukes," she answered nonchalantly. Even though making a trellis would be an easier project than the flowerbeds themselves, I don't remember seeing that assignment in her notepad.

"Oh, you were?" I responded with a side glance of affection for my schemer. "I don't know...the price might be one of your gummy bears." After we had a good laugh and before we finished paying for our purchases, I had already thought about a blueprint for the cucumber trellis... but I would leave the cannabis to her.

As an avid gardener, Joanne spent all year thinking about and planning for her yard. Even though only a few months were actually spent planting and growing, she immersed herself in organic knowledge and best practices during every season. Ever her enthusiastic wife, I had tagged along as her assistant digging holes, transferring overgrown patches, and accompanying her on backyard garden tours in P-town as well as visiting lavender and daylily farms wherever we vacationed. While I enjoyed sharing her avocation, I preferred the short-term planning required for flowerpots and boxes on the front porch that I would create later.

Over the past twenty years, our backyard garden had evolved into a glorious sanctuary for birds, butterflies, bees, and humans. Even though the spacious sunroom extended into the yard, eliminating the old patio and wisteria, there was plenty of lawn and abundant flowers on both sides of the property.

To the left of the sunroom stood a row of bridal veil bushes providing cascades of lacey white flowers in the spring and privacy from the driveway in the summer. A wooden arch covered with a deep purple clematis vine marked the end of the bushes and the start of the white garage sidewall.

Over time, a variety of enormous bushes had resided against the garage before Joanne's plan to switch them around, but the white Japanese dogwood tree in the back corner remained as the queen of the yard. Shades of blue, purple, pink, and lavender groundcover, ferns, and mountain laurel complemented each other, filling in the meditative area around the tree. As a bonus, the sweet aroma of lily of the valley always reminded me of my Nana's yard when I was a child.

Tall decorative grasses, high pink and white phlox, and multicolored irises the size of softballs lined the back natural wood fence as proud sentinels who seemed to forget about the line of twenty foot high cedars behind them. A small crabapple tree in the right back corner produced clutches of magenta blossoms in the spring and shade for any plants that preferred relief from the sun.

To the right of the sunroom, orange, yellow, and red daylilies danced with the breeze. Joanne's desire for unusual lilies, low sprawling pinks, sunflowers, and even tall, frilly gayfeather filled this sunny diverse bed where all varieties seemed to get along. Capping off the right side of the sunroom was a beautiful, but demanding, pink Rose of Sharon tree that reminded me of Hawaii with its hibiscus-looking blooms.

Just when I thought the abundant but small yard looked the best that it could be, Joanne would frequently announce a change to make it better than before. Consulting garden experts, testing soil samples, keeping track of drab areas needing color, and dividing large bunches of prolific plants were part of her ongoing improvement plan. We even had a compost bin, a rain barrel, an island mound of deep pink beach roses, and a mulched walkway leading to a small fire pit surrounded by two wooden Adirondack chairs. To me, the yard was complete, but to Joanne it would always be a work in progress.

"I'm going to post this hydrangea bush online to see if anyone wants it," she announced in late May as she stood like a flower herself in the middle of the cream and green-stripped hosta plants at her feet. "That way, whoever wants it can come and dig it out themselves." Our younger selves would have tackled the job with our own muscle but our older brains had wisely learned to seek alternative methods.

"Didn't we just plant that bush a couple years ago?" I asked with some exasperation. Sometimes Joanne's ideas to change things so often made my head spin.

"Yes, but it doesn't seem to like this shady spot next to the garage." She had already made up her mind as she continued her daily inspection of the yard. We made our way down the driveway to the raised beds along the sunny side of the house.

"Boy, these tomatoes look happy," I commented about the first bunch of plants that had already grown a few inches taller.

"They should with all the stuff I put in the holes before I planted them." She referred to the list of nutritious additives that included bone meal, eggshells, Epson salts, coffee grounds, baking soda, and even aspirin. "I also have to get the stakes out of the garage," she added, knowing I would assist with pounding the stakes and tying the plants.

"So, how do you like the trellis, honey?" I had sauntered to the cucumber vines in the second bed admiring my own work.

"I love it, Lin…it looks great," she said with a smile. "There's already something popping on them." We both examined the plant and looked at each other in amazement at the first sign of the vegetable.

"This reminds me of a pumpkin…like the one that grew out of the compost bin that year!" I exclaimed. I loved cucumbers but this did not resemble what I imagined would grow in our garden.

"Oh my god," she whispered, "I wonder what it is." Now we were both perplexed and already planning to research our little surprise.

As we returned to the backyard to continue our tour, I could almost hear her mind churning out more plans.

"Honey, I really want to fill up the garden with as many perennials as possible." Joanne had bent over to pluck some weeds near the daylilies as she continued. "I want to make it easy to take care of…especially for you." My heart caught for a second because I knew what she was talking about.

Not only was Joanne an excellent gardener and event planner, she was also a compassionate woman who I painfully realized was subtly preparing for her death. Without fanfare, she had been ticking off a to-do list in order to ease my burden as well as others in her family. Her loving heart had been thinking of me and planning to make my life easier in many ways just in case that miracle cure didn't happen. The topic of perennials in the garden represented the reality of losing my love, who was the only perennial I wanted.

Throughout our life together, Joanne never seemed to be satisfied with the house or even relationships, as if there was always room for improvement. When she looked at the patio, she imagined a sunroom. When she considered the deteriorating floorboards on the front porch, she made plans to reconstruct the whole porch. Rather than worrying about flooding in the basement with every downpour, we installed an elaborate sump pump system. If she became angry with a coworker, she tried to mend fences. For Joanne, improving her surroundings and preventing problems were the priorities that took center stage, especially when cancer threatened her time on earth.

While I loved to fix things and make improvements, I preferred to take my time, mull things over, and consider all possibilities. Not wanting to rock the boat and resisting change were parts of my personality that also seemed to affect my approach to everything. Like our different walking paces, my stride was slow but steady while Joanne moved quickly with purpose. We both arrived at the same corner but at different speeds.

Early in our relationship, our methods would clash while we drove each other crazy. While I wanted to read the instructions thoroughly before assembling the gas grill, she would simply look at the parts and jump in. Sometimes my methodical approach prevented disasters but other times, her expediency moved mountains. Over time, we took the best from each other and improved our tactics when accomplishing our goals. With cancer nipping at our heels, however, there was no time to waste.

By mid-June, tall orange daylilies, Shasta daisies, and salmon-colored astilbe took the place of the early spring flowers just as Joanne had planned. Added to the mix were the royal blue bee balm blossoms that, to my delight, always reminded me of exploding firecrackers. Despite the cucumber surprise, the parade of scheduled perennials felt reassuring in our world of unpredictable illness.

"Can you figure out what that plant is, Jo?" I was anxious to finally identify the mystery vegetable now that the small yellow orbs had developed. As we relaxed in the sunroom, Joanne waited to respond while she finished her iPad research.

"Well, I'll be damned," she replied. "Look at this, honey." I came over to her rocker to peer over her shoulder and plant a kiss on her head.

"It's a lemon cucumber," she announced. Up until now, I had imagined that the label, "cucumber," at the nursery had been incorrect.

"Never heard of it," I said with amazement. "I wonder how it tastes." Since there was no time to waste, I promptly left the sunroom to grab one off the vine.

After rinsing the new vegetable at the kitchen sink, I cut a piece for Joanne and returned to the breezy room. We bit into the cucumber at the same time and recorded the pleasant findings on our faces.

"This is delicious," I said between bites. Joanne nodded her head in agreement but did not ask for more.

"I think this might bother my stomach," she said reluctantly. Despite the pleasant surprise and the break from chemo, relentless cancer continued to steal even small moments of joy.

With my retirement date only a few weeks away, my work schedule was packed with final lessons, tedious paperwork, and retirement planning tasks. Like a scavenger hunt, the list was almost complete but my prize was only a vague promise of extra time, more fun, and less stress. For years I had sat at my desk, looking at a framed pen and ink drawing of a little boy and his dog walking down a country road with the caption, *I don't know where I'm going, but I'm on my way!* As retirement loomed ahead, the message seemed more appropriate than ever.

Despite my mixed emotions of excitement, anxiety, and sadness, I knew that God's hand was moving me into this new chapter at the right time. The same divine plan that had steered me to college in Pennsylvania, to my first mobility position in Michigan, and to my first lunch with Joanne was aligning the stars once again. Even though I had been a teacher for thirty-seven years, I would soon become what felt like the nervous college freshman preparing for new classes without a clue about my major. By deciding to take the leap, I was also following what I considered to be God's voice.

Leaving my job also meant leaving many clients that I respected and admired. Watching their confidence and independence grow as they responded to new mobility solutions was inspiring. With courage and determination, many had often expanded their possibilities beyond my expectations. My heart was sad to think I would be leaving some clients before they had completed their goals.

One vibrant woman in her late forties had initially described feeling like a prisoner in her spacious home due to her fear of travel as a blind person. Prior to losing her vision from diabetes, Lisa had been an adventurous wife and mother of three. Once gregarious and spontaneous, she had resigned herself to quiet days in her safe and familiar environment when her vision failed. She had lost hope, confidence, and joy.

"I can't believe I'm doing this," Lisa said to me as we started walking.

"You're doing a great job, Lisa," I responded as I dropped back behind her. For several months, she had been practicing new Orientation and Mobility techniques with grit and determination. As a result, her independence and spirit had blossomed.

With her colorful visor on her shoulder-length brown hair, a stylish flowered blouse with partial sleeves rolled up, and blue jean capris pants, she strode down the middle of the sidewalk of her small town. Except for the long white cane that she moved from side to side in rhythm with her pace, Lisa resembled Joanne enough to be sisters.

As Lisa came to a stop at a trashcan in her way, I silently observed her methodically search for a clear space with her cane as she had been taught. In seconds, she resumed her path with confidence and came to a stop at the curb of the first street crossing of the lesson. I took my place slightly behind her with a view of the entire intersection. Since Lisa had already learned how to align, listen, and use traffic sounds for a safe crossing, I was confident in her ability and remained silent. She completed the crossing and resumed the route as I dropped back once more.

While Lisa led the way past the row of small shops, I considered the irony of her growing independence while Joanne's freedom was diminishing due to cancer. If I could cure Joanne's illness with mobility lessons, I would have done so on the day of diagnosis, and I would have enjoyed writing that lesson plan. But the truth was she would need more than a white cane to navigate the road ahead.

Near the end of June, both Joanne and Christine were able to attend my fun-filled lunchtime retirement party at an informal restaurant near the downtown office one week before my last day. With heartfelt gifts, funny skits, and poignant speeches, I shared memories and laughs with my long-time friends and coworkers. Joy and sorrow about leaving my job mixed together like sweet and sour sauce when each flavor masks the other until the brain chooses to focus on one or the other. I couldn't decide which feeling filled me the most.

Before I knew it, the retirement party had come to an end. I gradually cleaned out my desk, and quietly drove home from the office to the next chapter that wouldn't be written until I walked through the back door of our house. As I entered the sunroom, Joanne greeted me with gorgeous flowers, festive balloons, and a silver ring with two curved hearts. Most of all, she hugged me tight with understanding and love like a mother sending her child to kindergarten. I thought the new chapter should be entitled *"Retirement 101."*

"I have a great idea," she said with a smile as we sipped our coffee on the first morning of my new retirement life. "Let's drive down to our favorite little beach in Westport and then have dinner at the Bayside to celebrate your first day." Her excitement was contagious.

"Okay, honey, I'd love that." I loved the quiet rocky beach she mentioned and the funky seafood restaurant overlooking the sea marsh. But more than celebrating my freedom, I wanted to celebrate the new chemo that allowed Joanne to enjoy these outings.

The Olaparib pill had begun as planned and the side effects, as Dr. D. had promised, were no worse than the other poisons she had endured. At least there were no more ice packs for her hands and feet, and no hair loss or extreme exhaustion this time. Despite the usual heartburn, limited endurance, and fatigue, Joanne soldiered on enjoying every day with her retired wife. Since the only new consideration with this chemo was avoiding sun exposure, heading to the beach would require bigger hats, longer sleeves, and her favorite umbrella attached to her beach chair. With all she had been through so far, she didn't mind the inconvenience.

"Before we go, I still want to move some of those tall phlox in the back to the side yard by the driveway." Joanne was always planning the garden. "Will you help me?"

"Of course I will," I said as I imagined her new *Honey do list*. "Just remember to put long sleeves on out there." I already knew she would wear her big floppy hat to protect her face from the sun.

"Oh, before I forget, look at this bookmark that Hospice sent me." Joanne still received mailings after her work with cancer support groups. She handed me the tastefully printed bookmark that read, *Something will grow from all you are going through, and it will be you.*

"Boy, that's appropriate for a gardener," I said with love. But the bookmark left me uneasy, as I silently hoped that the something growing wouldn't be another tumor.

CHAPTER 24

∽

Fish Out of Water

"I'm going for a Buddy Walk," I yelled to my half-awake wife who had already found her iPad on the couch.

At least I would begin my first retirement week with some exercise on the same twenty-minute walk in the neighborhood where Buddy and I had strolled years before. Even though he had been gone a decade, I still thought of him every time I took that route. After the walk, I didn't know what the hell I was going to do.

"Okay, honey," she answered with only partial focus as she checked her schedule, the news, and whatever else was on her sleepy mind.

With a cloudy humid day unfolding, I guided my new knees along the familiar sidewalk as I fell into a silent conversation with spirit. *Okay, God, I think I need some help here. If this is my new path, then you're going to have to help me figure this out because I don't know what to do next.* Even though I had uttered the same request for other situations throughout my life, this new uncertain phase called retirement lay before me like the cracked sidewalk ahead. The only difference was that retirement was not familiar at all.

Deep in thought, my mind tried to identify this strange phenomenon as the houses passed by. It dawned on me that all my life something or someone had dictated my schedule. Since birth, my parents, school, or work had determined my week. Daytime hours, homework, work deadlines, and even job searches had been governing most of my life. For the first time, I would be shaping my own schedule to whatever I desired. But *What exactly do I want?* kept gnawing at me as I rounded the corner to head home.

Halfway down the block coming toward me, a middle-aged woman held tightly onto a leash as she followed her small gray poodle who was clearly in charge, leading the way. For my occasional doggy fix, I loved greeting the neighborhood pets that cheerfully accepted my brief affection.

"Well, hello there, baby," I cooed as I bent slightly toward the poodle, raising my voice an octave to convey a non-threatening tone to the pooch. The smiling owner allowed her dog to inch closer.

"What's his name?" I asked her. It could have been *Happy* for all the joy he displayed.

"His name's Buddy," she said with pride and love.

"That's a great name," I said softly with a ping of sadness in my heart. As they left to continue their patrol, I considered the irony of the same name as my beloved pup and thought it might be a positive sign about retirement. Any little thing to ease into the journey wouldn't hurt.

When our house came back into view, I found Joanne in the driveway bending over a cluster of frilly yellow blooms as I ended my walk. She looked puzzled as I approached.

"Hi, Lin," she greeted me and then asked, "What's the name of this flower?" She seemed almost embarrassed.

"I'm pretty sure that's coreopsis," I guessed correctly but with surprise that Joanne had forgotten what should have been familiar to an avid gardener. Not too long before, I would have been the one to request that information from her.

"Oh, that's right," her voice lowered. "I should have known that." With exasperation she added, "I'm so frustrated with this chemo brain." She sighed and looked at me with fatigue as she shook her head. "A few minutes ago, I couldn't even remember those tall flowers by the back fence."

"You mean phlox?" I tried to be sympathetic but helpful at the same time.

"Yes," she sighed again. "Can you help me move some of these…coreopsis next to the phlox?" Her brain continued to struggle, especially with three years' worth of chemo side effects.

After the yard work, a banana smoothie for breakfast and coffee refills, I consulted my appointment book out of habit. As Joanne snoozed on the nap station before she would leave for her watercolor class, I flipped through the pages of earlier dates and times that reflected a busy schedule prior to my last day of work. Every line had been filled. Other than a few birthday reminders, doctor and car repair appointments, the pages after my retirement date were blank.

Even Joanne's calendar revealed more activity than my own. Despite the new chemo pill, her mild side effects allowed her to schedule lunches with friends, shopping trips with her sister, creative art classes, and even ukulele lessons. When I flipped back to my last day with my handwritten message, *Retired!*, I noticed that Joanne had secretly written underneath it in red, *Yippee, yippee!* But I wondered if she really needed me to be retired after all.

While Joanne attended her art class, and after puttering around the house and yard in my own brain fog, I carted my brand new journal out to the front porch. The journal with owls on the front had been a gift from my coworkers who explicitly wanted me to record whatever weird thoughts popped into my head. Thinking that retirement must be more than planning meals, collecting mail, and running errands, I agreed to examine my deeper perceptions like any long-time counselee in therapy would do.

My first thought was that I felt like a fish out of water. After being yanked from the lake and still hooked on the line, I was flapping around on foreign land. The retirement sensation wasn't exactly like vacation or recuperating from surgery, but a feeling like no other. Wandering in limbo or circling the airport for hours would better describe the sense that I didn't fit in. Someone I knew had advised me that the adjustment would take a year and I considered the possibility. Another elderly client had warned, "You won't like it…you won't find enough to do." Thinking about caretaking in the future, I doubted that I would be idle. But there was the possibility.

Despite my expectation that my retirement life would be linked to Joanne's and her cancer, I realized that I had to find my own way while Joanne flitted like a butterfly. Being retired for three years, her days and life had evolved separately from my working life. Looking at her schedule brought the realization that she was content with her independent activities. When she could, Joanne was out and about on her own leaving me to figure out my own purpose. Initially, I felt betrayed, but there was no one to blame. Like a new jigsaw puzzle, I decided to find the border pieces first and fill in the rest later.

A mental list of activities I enjoyed formed in my head. With the Fourth of July approaching, I thought of our past bike trips to the parade and remembered spending hours on my chunky bike as a child pretending

I was riding a horse. Holding onto the handlebar streamers like reins, I wove up and down the neighbors' driveways taking for granted my youthful strength, confidence, and balance. In retirement, riding my ten-speed more often was a possibility but the strength, confidence, and balance were rather questionable.

Reading books had always been one of my pleasures. Ever since elementary school, many carefree summer hours had been spent on a chaise lounge in the backyard reading my favorite titles chosen from the local bookmobile. Like a huge RV, the air-conditioned library on wheels had been an oasis where I had found *Nancy Drew Mysteries* and *The Black Stallion* book series that transported me to fantastic adventures. Having more time to read in retirement seemed to be a likely addition to my list but, considering cancer's insidious plan, I had doubts about finding carefree days.

As my activity list grew with playing golf, attending symphony concerts, playing hand bells, and camping with family and friends, it dawned on me that these were already ongoing activities that I loved. My retirement could be filled with new opportunities like becoming a Walmart greeter, fishing off a dock, or cleaning out closets but nothing on that list appealed to me. To my surprise, I even turned down an offer to work privately with a blind student. Despite the temptation, a voice within told me that retirement did not mean find a job. Now that the door of work had closed behind me, I felt it lock as I pondered the unopened door ahead. Despite my indecision about using free time, however, I realized that retirement could be an opportunity to do something different.

As the breeze moved through the front porch, the mellow wind chime resounded deep within as I admitted a truth: I was focusing on busy-ness because I was afraid. Not only afraid I would crumble if I lost Joanne, but also afraid of losing myself. Losing my confidence, my mind, and my talents in retirement would feel like my rusting Honda. My warped idea was to keep moving in order to avoid my fear and hold it together for Joanne who had enough on her mind.

While I wrapped up my journal entry for the moment, I felt peaceful after spilling my feelings onto the pages. Writing had always been an outlet for sorting things out, especially after years of stuffing my emotions into the bottom of a box. Whether to share my fears with Joanne, however, would require some thought. As I repeated the same prayer from my morning walk, the divine answer that whispered in my ear was *Love and Trust*.

I remained on the porch as Joanne's car pulled into the driveway. When I heard her car door slam, I entered the house to greet my budding artist in the kitchen.

"How was your class, honey?" I gave her a quick kiss and saw the excitement mixed with exhaustion on her face. "What did you work on today?" My genuine interest always seemed to buoy her spirit.

"Hi," she said as she plopped her art tote on the floor. "You'll like it." She snatched her folder and displayed a bright yellow and blue tropical angelfish amongst strands of kelp.

"I do like it...in fact, I love it," I had always been drawn to fish, even those in paintings. "It reminds me of snorkeling," I added. Thinking, *at least this fish is in water.*

"So, what exciting things have you been doing, my new retiree?" Joanne inquired as she reached for the Tums in the cupboard.

"Oh, not much...just writing on the front porch." I thought this might be a good chance to share my retirement ideas so I added, "Want to join me?"

"Not now, I'm so exhausted and I have such terrible heartburn," her face scrunched with a new wave of pain. "I have to lie down for a while."

Even though Joanne's coordinated appearance and moderate activity level sent a message of normalcy that she loved, I witnessed the toll cancer took on her body and spirit at times like these. The chemo side effects were relentless no matter what chemical combo she received. From experience, I suspected she would sleep for the next two hours when her appetite for dinner would, most likely, fizzle. Since my musings about retirement seemed inconsequential compared to her daily battle of ups and downs, I would table them for another time.

As I admired her fish painting while she slept, I remembered a metaphor that made sense to me when people would ask us how we coped with cancer. The image is a stormy ocean with monstrous waves roiling and white caps forming in the high winds. Thirty feet below the surface, the water is calm and unaffected by the storm, allowing unconcerned fish and other sea creatures to swim, hunt, and hide without a care for the world above. As long as Joanne and I kept our peace and focus at the thirty-foot level, we could manage to keep swimming.

On the other hand, by keeping my feelings below the surface of the storm where anger, fear, and resentment churned, I would never learn to navigate my ship. Occasionally, I needed to rise to the surface and experience the negative feelings that I had worked so hard to avoid. As painful as the struggle could be, talking and writing about the dark side was bitter medicine for the soul.

As the summer heat rolled in and our beach and camping excursions increased, my retirement sea legs wobbled less. With baby steps, I enjoyed more freedom when scheduling appointments, lunching with friends, and even doing laundry during the day rather than at night after work. I even learned to love Sunday nights and Monday mornings without the weight of homework or work stealing my time. Rather than a fish out of water, I was emerging from the water like a prehistoric aquatic creature evolving, adapting and transforming on land into something else. But I still hadn't shared my fears with Joanne whose rollercoaster days continued.

"Now that you're retired, honey, are you finally going to get a tattoo?" She turned to me in the car as we sped along the highway toward Maine in early August. On short notice, we had booked a week with our timeshare in Ogunquit that felt like a small miracle. Any reservation in the popular artsy town during August was exceptional.

Along with my sister and daughter, Joanne had been nudging me for years to take the plunge and get a *tatt*. Since all three of them had a range of tattoos, none of them understood my stubborn reluctance to get inked. Even though I admired others' tattoos, I never felt the need for one myself.

Every summer in July when Joanne and I stayed in P-town over her birthday, she religiously received a henna tattoo that eventually faded back home. One year after I had moved in, she vowed to get a *real* tattoo on her right ankle. After much deliberation about the design, she chose a small Mother Goddess image with arms raised overhead holding a purple orb. With Christine's help for enhancing the design, small curved pieces of ivy adorned each side of the purple-hued goddess. Reflecting her spiritual connection to the earth, the tattoo was perfect for Joanne.

"I have to admit, I am tempted to get a tattoo now that I'm a rebel retiree," I smiled back at her. But then I imagined subjecting myself to unnecessary pain and my smile faded as I chickened out in my head.

Like all our adventures, we savored every moment together in Maine while adapting our activities to the weather and Joanne's stamina. While she still collected brochures and I mapped out our routes, we also stayed close to our quiet unit at the Inn at the Falls resort so that she could rest when needed. Accessing the beach required the blue disability parking pass for less walking and discovering nature centers rather than mountain hiking became our Plan B. Browsing through a community garden brought a huge smile to her face and chatting with local gardeners equaled any balm.

"I can't believe we were able to get a reservation with our timeshare this late," Joanne commented as she picked at her piece of baked fish, looking across the rustic picnic table. The restaurant's dark blue umbrella overhead provided relief from the sun as we gazed over the peaceful salt marsh.

"I know," I said with emphasis. "I think it was meant to be...just for us." I looked into her loving eyes and continued cracking the lobster claw on my cardboard plate, wishing I could have ordered three more lobsters.

"Remember when we bought the timeshare?" Joanne had a mischievous grin that delighted me more than my lobster. There was a glimpse of my daring playmate. "I couldn't believe you said yes to it."

"Yes, I remember...guess it was a weak moment after all those times we pretended," I reminisced as we chuckled about our adventures.

During our first ten years together, I had learned that Joanne's quest for a bargain and free opportunities paid off for numerous weekend getaways attached to timeshare offers. If we agreed to spend a couple hours listening to a sales' pitch at a fancy resort, we could stay for free during that weekend. Without any intention of buying, we held firm to our preconceived agreement and expertly warded off even the manager's hard sell. We felt like the Thelma and Louise of the timeshare world.

In the spring of 2008, we finally met our match on Cape Cod with the point system of a "vacation club" that actually sounded like a good deal. In a weak moment, we signed the papers and popped the cork on the bottle they presented with the agreement. Without calling themselves a timeshare, their strategy worked and we ended our spree as bandits. Thinking about those shenanigans brought a nostalgic smile to my face as I felt gratitude and sadness entwine together while watching Joanne's spunk gradually diminish from the unrelenting cancer attack.

After reluctantly leaving our Maine escape and returning home, we faced another CT scan result to determine the chemo pill's effectiveness on her tumor. With anxious hope, we spent the late August morning at a small city park by the lazy Providence River not far from our initial walk during Waterfire so many years before. Waiting for a phone call from the doctor's office, we distracted ourselves with idle conversation and the placid view. Suddenly, her cellphone rang.

"Hello...this is Joanne," she looked down at the grass by our bench and listened intently. From her serious expression, I suspected bad news. "What's next then?" She listened again, shaking her head back and forth. Looking at her fallen face, I felt crushed as she finished the call.

"The Olaparib didn't work," she sighed and explained more. "There are two more tumors on my liver so they're going to start Doxil and Avastin together in two weeks." When the tears forming in her eyes abated, her anger rose from within like lava finding an exit.

"Fuck!" she yelled. "Fuck, fuck, fuck!" I could almost see steam spouting from the top of her head. "I can't believe I can't have just one more summer without this shit!" Joanne was fuming.

Despite my own angry reaction, her expressions were enough for both of us. I waited as she took a deep breath.

"I need to calm down," she said finally. "Let's go on one of those riverboat tours over there," she pointed to the metal dock where a commercial tour company conducted short cruises on the river.

"Sure thing," I agreed as we made our way down the slope. My own fears about cancer winning this battle were ballooning with every step.

Neither one of us had been on one of these boats in our city since we considered them to be tourist traps, but the relaxing ride served our purpose. Just floating on water was healing.

Forty-five minutes later, we were ready to splurge for a nice lunch at a fancy Italian restaurant nearby. The large brick patio entirely covered with thick grapevine overhead created an inviting and soothing space as if we were in a different country. Since the restaurant had just opened for the day, our wait in line was brief.

"This is nice," I commented as we settled into our seats at the table for two. After the waitress took our drink orders, we looked deep into each other's eyes with love and understanding.

"I'm so mad," Joanne said with controlled force. "I just don't know how much more I can do." Her moist eyes held onto mine as I reached for her hand on the tablecloth. She lightly squeezed my fingers as she continued.

"I'm having a hard time with God right now, you know?" Her tears welled up for a few minutes as I sensed her struggle that mirrored my own.

"I know," I whispered. "It doesn't seem like our prayers are being answered." The idea of that miracle cure kept moving away.

After a few sips of my wine and her iced tea, we continued sharing our thoughts and hearts about this new development. Considering the worst, we tenderly touched on the dreaded topic of death we so often avoided.

"Joanne, I don't know what I'll do without you." My eyes filled as I forced the words from my mouth. For years, we had expressed the same sentiment about each other but the reality now stood in front of us.

"I'm so afraid of losing you," I eked out. She held my hand tighter as a tear rolled down her cheek. A few minutes passed by while we ignored the growing lunch crowd.

"Well, you haven't lost me yet," she broke the silence. "And, really, you never will." Joanne had moved to a stronger mindset as she spoke.

When our lunch arrived, we fell into a lighter mood and made a decision to carry on with chemo and God. With resolve and determination, we left the restaurant fortified for the next battle. At that moment, my retirement felt like it was meant to be.

With the regimen of Doxil and Avastin chemotherapies every two weeks, life at the infusion center resumed in September 2017 and continued throughout the fall. Familiar side effects plagued Joanne with intensity. Mouth sores, diarrhea, nausea and shortness of breath increased as the weeks passed. As she attempted to balance illness with outings, Joanne inspired everyone. Not only did she continue camping, visiting cousins, and painting, but she also insisted that I follow my pursuits even when I hated to leave her alone. How she managed to minimize her symptoms remained a secret between her and her God.

"I'm so glad you retired, honey," Joanne said softly as I held her on the couch before bedtime. With her ongoing battle, I noticed that her demeanor had softened. Even she admitted that she relied on me more than ever for emotional support.

"You are?" I asked only because I already knew the answer. "I am too, but I wasn't so sure at first." As the months had passed and the hustle and bustle of Christmas had swept in, I could honestly say that my decision to retire was timed perfectly.

"I know it was difficult for you, but I love having you around," she looked up and gave me that beautiful smile. "Especially now..." she trailed off as we both thought about the most recent cancer development.

Following months of Doxil and Avastin, the routine CA 125 blood test in early December revealed a cancer cell count of over 3,300. With the count more than when she was first diagnosed, it was clear that the chemo was not working as planned. To make matters worse, the routine CT scan revealed additional fluid in her lung that would require more lung taps. The New Year would begin with a new combination of stronger infusions and like the Polar Express, the cancer train seemed to be ferociously out of control as it raced down the steepest hill.

"I think I'll head up to bed," Joanne announced as if the train had already slammed into her. "Can you help me up the stairs?" I knew she hated to ask but losing her balance would be worse.

"Sure, honey," I said. "Wish I could carry you up the stairs."

"I wish you could too but then I'd have to visit you in the hospital after you broke your back." We both had to chuckle with that thought.

After tucking Joanne into bed, I returned to my couch potato station and surfed the channels. I landed on an interesting PBS documentary about a ninety-six-year-old interior designer and fashion icon named Iris Apfel whose large, black round glasses seemed to be her signature. Initially, I didn't plan to watch the whole thing since my fashion sense is not my priority. However, I found her to be so interesting and creative that her pearls of wisdom reverberated through me.

While her fashion design and life could be described as big and bold, her recipe for staying alert and interested is to be on the move. Always do something, she advised, no matter what your age. As I considered what to do with my new retirement, I found myself asking, *What would Iris say?* With her inspiration about everything, I think she would say, *Whatever you do, that's terrific, keep it up!*

Knowing that my constant inspiration was already sleeping upstairs, I turned off the TV and climbed the stairs to snuggle with the love of my life no matter what lurked around the bend.

❦

CHAPTER 25

Crisis Number One

Two days after my introduction to the colorful Iris on PBS, Joanne rushed around the house shortly after sunrise as she prepared to pick up Joyce who was headed for foot surgery that day. Although the outpatient procedure for hammertoes would not be complicated, the recovery would keep her sister stationary as if her wings had been clipped. Since Joanne savored opportunities to defy her cancer symptoms, she planned to nurse her little sister back to health.

"I'm heading out, Lin," Joanne called to me as I trundled down the stairs with a yawn, looking forward to my first mug of coffee. With her lightweight overnight bag in hand, I caught my honey long enough for a hug squeeze and kiss before she scurried to her warm idling Honda, still running well after all these years.

"I'll miss you, my sweet," I said as I surveyed her face for signs of fatigue. "If you need me for anything, let me know." Knowing that helping others buoyed her spirit, I hadn't tried to stop her. Joanne needed to give to others as much as she needed chemo to live.

"I'll see how it goes…don't worry," she tried to reassure me. "I don't know how many nights I'll stay since Carissa will be helping too, but I'll keep you posted." She was anxious to be on her way but stopped herself as she reached for the doorknob.

"Oh, I almost forgot," she blurted out. "Could you get that little silver bell from the hutch?" She explained further, "Joyce asked me to bring it along so she can ring it when she needs me." Despite the sweet sound that I could never hear when Joanne used it, the bell held sentimental value in their family ever since Annie had used it years before. Its presence would be moral support.

Even before coffee, I rushed to retrieve the bell before Joanne sailed out the door on her mission of mercy. With gratitude, I smiled to think she could still sail anywhere.

As I sipped my hot coffee and pondered my day's mundane schedule, I couldn't help but renew my astonishment at Joanne's ability to recover from days of exhaustion and malaise. Just when her body seemed fully drained of strength, her activity resumed as if she had signed another contract for more life. Whether the stronger chemotherapies after the New Year would upset the balance remained to be seen. For now, the only constant was her determination to continue as planned and spend a traditional warm-weather week in Kissimmee near Orlando in mid-January.

My morning thoughts also lingered on the blur of Christmas preparations and favorite activities with our families and friends. Plans were in place for gatherings at Carissa's as well as my brother's prior to the actual holiday. Every year, however, the faint possibility that this could be our last Christmas together hung in the air like flimsy smoke from an extinguished candle. The thought always pricked my heart like an ice pick. Thankfully, the hope and light from the holiday usually squashed the morbid idea and restored my optimism as we entered the New Year.

By the time the ball dropped on Times Square 2018, Joyce's foot was healing nicely and Joanne prepped for a new chemo combination. Starting right after the holiday, infusions of Gemzar and Cisplatin were the new weapons recommended by Dr. D. Since one of her fears had always been the possibility of becoming platin resistant, we were encouraged that one of the platins had even been considered at this time. With fear and trepidation about these strong poisons entering an already battered body, the new battle commenced.

Sadly, Joanne's cousin Joe, whose health had been deteriorating, had died at home close to the start of chemo. On that sad day, Joanne needed a lung tap and on the day of his funeral, she hurried off to the infusion center for another round of Gemzar. The juxtaposition of Joe's death and her treatment chilled my bones with foreboding. Nonetheless, she endured the physical chemo side effects and heartbreak about her cousin as we started packing for Orlando while considering another lung tap for good measure.

Joanne's lung taps had evolved from a dreaded procedure to a welcomed relief that improved her breathing. She always felt better afterward and left the hospital with a bounce in her step. Consequently, having a lung tap the day before our flight to Florida appeared to be as essential as toothpaste. And traveling out of town had always been an essential boost to her spirit, as if we could leave cancer behind in Rhode Island.

As the direct three-hour flight soared above the clouds and New England snow, Joanne rested her head on her neck pillow propped against the window. Wrapped in her thick polar fleece jacket, she had closed her eyes early into the flight. After consulting my maps, car rental information, and guidebooks, I attempted to lose myself in my current murder mystery. But gazing out the window into the wild blue yonder while my love slept pulled my attention away from my book.

For once, I could not contemplate the big picture thousands of feet above the earth as I worried about Joanne. Compared to our past flights to exotic places, she seemed especially frail as the new chemo had already begun to sap her strength. Even though I initially questioned the wisdom of taking this trip, I remembered that other adventures during chemo had actually soothed our souls. With continued trust in those precedents, I tried to relax.

Despite her earplugs, the descending plane's change in pressure woke Joanne as excruciating pain shot through both her ears. Even though she had experienced this dilemma during past flights, it seemed especially cruel this time when she already felt lousy. To make matters worse, she couldn't hear well even after we had landed and deplaned which meant I would be her interpreter as well as loving wife.

Without a hitch, we meandered through the airport maze, secured our economy rental car, and located the sprawling Star Island Resort in time for a light supper in the closest eatery we could find. Even a chain restaurant would have to do considering our fatigue. Since we hadn't been satisfied with our tiny first floor room overlooking the parking lot, the cooperative desk clerk switched our accommodations by the time we returned from dinner. We had been through way too much in four years to settle for a room the size of a postage stamp, especially after our last cruise experience had spoiled us.

Leaving our exploration of the resort until morning light, we fell into bed for a much-needed rest. Despite her restlessness throughout the night, Joanne slept well enough to stroll the tropical landscaped grounds the next day as we searched for basic groceries and croissants for breakfast. With plenty of inviting benches and lounge chairs around the massive kidney-shaped pools and hot tubs, we made a note to use them later.

Overlooking the stands of palm trees and colorful flowers on the courtyard below, our third floor, two-bedroom suite greatly improved our mood compared to the first unit. With a full kitchen, long couch, spacious bedrooms and two baths, we felt gratitude to spirit for helping us out once again. Despite the beauty of the resort, however, I had a sense of foreboding while noticing Joanne's slow pace and weakness as we enjoyed the warm sun and peaceful setting. Resting on a lounge chair, wrapped in her black sweat suit due to her chills, was the most activity she could handle on that first Sunday.

By Sunday night, the coughing started. As a possible side effect from both chemotherapies, we anticipated the possibility along with a slight fever. To combat these maladies, I ran an errand to the nearby Walgreens for cough medicine, a fever thermometer, and Tylenol. What I really wanted was a magic wand from a Disney fairy godmother.

Despite the relaxing sunny weather on Monday, our moods were clouded with worry as Joanne's coughing intensified. The medicine allowed her to walk around the grounds in the morning and even complete a round of mini-golf in the courtyard, but our adventures came to a halt in the afternoon when her tired body demanded bed rest. As the hours ticked away, her fever began to climb.

"Honey, why don't you take a walk while I take a nap?" Joanne knew what she needed but she also realized that a walk outdoors would be a break for her caretaker. "The Tylenol will help with my fever, so I'll be okay."

Nice try, Joanne, I thought to myself. I knew she didn't want me to worry but my anxiety would follow me no matter what space I occupied. Nonetheless, I decided to check out the nature trail that followed a marshy waterway and some magnificent live oak trees. Maybe some unusual birds would distract me from my concern.

"Okay," I agreed, "but I'll have my phone with me in case you need me to come back."

Since taking time for myself had not been a luxury I would usually allow, I approached the nature trail with half a heart. As I passed the peaceful marsh grasses, expansive views, water lilies, and wooded trails, my mind filled with Joanne back in the room. While missing her curiosity, laughter, and stolen kisses on this mini-hike, I decided to take some pictures so that she could at least share the sights later. Whether we would enjoy any of our favorite Orlando adventures on this trip remained a crapshoot.

"Hi sweetie, I'm back," I announced softly when I heard her rustle in the bedroom. I tiptoed into the bedroom doorway as her hacking cough forced her to sit up. With an immediate glance on her flushed face, I suspected her fever had returned. "Let me take your temp." I went into action and felt her forehead that was as hot as a burner.

Her fever was 103 degrees. With more medication and some hot tea and toast, Joanne managed to perch on the couch for thirty minutes before returning to her reclined position in the bedroom. As her coughing resumed, however, her body shook with each episode as if her insides were erupting.

"Honey, do you want me to call a rescue?" I couldn't imagine her body surviving much more assault.

"No, I think we should call Dr. D.'s office to let them know what's going on," she said sensibly. After all, we were in another state, not a different country. Consulting familiar medical staff who knew her case would be reassuring.

After making the hurried call, the plan was to manage awhile longer with over-the-counter meds and a prescription for her cough since the chemo side effects usually abate. However, if her fever continued to climb and symptoms worsened, a trip to the emergency room would be in order. As I swung into full caretaker mode like a mother lion, I braced for the worst.

Throughout the night, Joanne's coughing never stopped. Every hour felt like ten years as she moaned after each exhausting episode. As her fever rose past 104 degrees despite the Tylenol, I knew we had to take action.

"Jo, I think you should go to the hospital," I whispered before daylight as I lay beside her. "Do you want me to drive or call a rescue?" Since I had already mapped the route, I felt confident I could find the Orlando hospital that had an oncology department. The rescue would be obliged to bring her to the less equipped hospital nearby.

"Let's drive," Joanne managed to say between coughing spells.

After preparing to bring the essentials for a possible overnight, I helped Joanne get dressed and loaded her into the rental while it was still dark. As we sped along the highway, the first red light of day cracked on the horizon amid the gathering morning rush of traffic. Forty-five minutes later, we rolled into the driveway of the emergency room.

Somehow I remained focused until the attendant aligned a wheelchair next to the passenger door and assisted Joanne into the chair. As she struggled to rise from the car and turn toward the technician, for the first time her frailty caused me to think she might die. *Oh God, not like this...this can't be the end*, I pleaded. The image of her skiing perfectly down the black diamond slope flashed in my mind in disbelief.

Even though we moved through the emergency process in what seemed like slow motion, I felt relieved that we were surrounded by medical personnel who could help more than I could back at the resort. As expected, an array of tests were performed before she was admitted to a private room on the oncology floor. With IV tubes, stronger medications, and attentive nurses, Joanne settled into the hospital atmosphere. Luckily, I was allowed to bunk on a guest cot in her room.

The revolving door of doctors, nurses, specialists and aides continued to spin throughout the day while Joanne's cough and fever quieted, allowing her to rest between their visits. While the medical staff investigated her condition and consulted the oncology team in Rhode Island, my confidence that she would live gained momentum.

"How are you feeling, honey?" I asked her later in the day as she surfaced from a well-deserved nap. I had already explored the bustling hallways and nearby spacious waiting room with comfortable seating, TV, and wide windows overlooking the palm trees of downtown Orlando. I had also used the time to text our families with the latest crisis news.

"I'm better but I feel so weak," she replied. At that moment, a cheery nurse bustled in and introduced herself in light of the personnel shift change.

"Hi there, I'm Jane, your night nurse." In her thirties, tall with shoulder-length brown hair, Jane moved with professional aptitude and compassion. I felt that we were in good hands.

"What?" Joanne strained to hear. Since her temporary hearing loss continued to plague her, I stepped closer to interpret and inform Jane about the side effect from our flight. *Another reason for my presence in the room.* I thought, with gratitude that I could still be useful.

As Joanne's fluctuating condition kept one step ahead of the doctors, we realized that our vacation would be spent in the Orlando hospital.

When her platelets, potassium, and white blood cell counts would drop, the nurses administered trials of medications in order to stabilize her body. Much of the time, gowns, masks, gloves, and plastic face shields were required for all who entered the room, including me, in order to prevent infection. With viral pneumonia as a possible diagnosis, additional complications would be disastrous.

Returning to the resort never entered my mind. My joy was being with Joanne, not walking into an empty suite alone. As the new routine evolved into consulting with doctors, sharing meals by her bedside, relaxing in the lounge, and watching TV, we rejoiced when Joanne's strength gradually increased over the next several days. Improving enough to return to Rhode Island became the medical goal and we prayed for that to happen. The hopeful plan was for discharge on Friday, pack suitcases at the resort, and switch to an earlier flight on Saturday.

One day toward the end of the week, I agreed to leave our temporary hospital home for a walk around the grounds, which included a peaceful garden complete with bubbling fountains and a labyrinth for meditation. I prayed to my God for Joanne's continued strength, gratitude for her life, and restoration of my faith in that miracle cure. Contemplating our circumstances, I also decided I had had enough of Orlando.

As I rose from the stone bench next to a small gurgling fountain, I noticed two stray cats peeking out from under some low palm fronds. Two curious faces, one orange tabby and one gray and white, observed me with caution. Not wanting to carry any infection back to Joanne, I refrained from petting the two cuties but I knew she would love to share the story of this feline encounter.

As I entered the room with my gown and mask, my eyes smiled at her miniature body sitting in the giant recliner as if she were the little girl character Edith Ann, portrayed by Lily Tomlin, who swung her legs in the oversized rocker. Despite her disheveled purple hair and unstylish hospital robe, she looked as cute as those kitties in the garden.

"Well, you're looking better," I bubbled. "Have you been walking in the hallway again?" The nurses had been getting her up on a regular basis once her legs could hold her.

"Yes, they have," she replied with pride. "I think I'm actually going to make it back home." Even though she wouldn't be skiing any time soon, we knew she could travel without a debilitating cough and high fever.

"I have to tell you about the kitties I saw in the hospital garden." I described the scene by the bench as she listened with delight.

"Wish I could've seen them," she said wistfully.

"Well, it's probably a good thing you didn't because you would have wanted to feed them like all the others." I referred to other Florida trips when Joanne would patiently befriend and then feed groups of stray cats that hung out along woodsy parking lots bordering shopping malls.

"You're right I suppose." She waited a few minutes before adding, "I always loved helping Mr. Stray...I wonder whatever happened to him."

Shortly after Cara Mia had died in 2002, a small black stray cat with brilliant yellow eyes wandered into our backyard looking for a handout. From his scrawny frame, we surmised that free meals were hard to find in our suburban neighborhood. Thinking that Cara's spirit might have sent him our way, Joanne promptly adopted him. Whenever he waited quietly by the back patio, she provided the high-class meal he learned to expect. Always skittish but apparently grateful, we simply called him Stray and later, Mr. Stray, out of respect.

For ten years, we provided food and scrap-wood shelters in the cold blast of winter for Mr. Stray. When building makeshift houses finally became a burden, however, we upgraded his home to an expensive, well-built outdoor cathouse that looked like a miniature red barn complete with a small weathervane on top. We even rigged an electric heating pad specially designed for felines. When Mr. Stray no longer visited, our hearts were broken to think he had used up his nine lives. With even greater magnitude and helplessness, my heart ached to think Joanne's nine lives were being snatched away by a ninja in the night.

In our hospital vacation spot, we reminisced about our favorite homeless kitty as we prepared to tackle the trip home. Despite the wonderful care of the oncology staff, we fled Orlando Hospital with relief on Friday afternoon as if we had only a small window of opportunity to return to New England before something else happened. In a hurried rush, we scooped up our belongings, rearranged our flight for Saturday morning rather than the original night flight, and almost kissed the ground in Rhode Island once we had landed.

Three days after our return, a doctor's visit and blood work revealed unbelievable results. What seemed to be a crisis in Orlando to us only meant a week's delay with the chemo schedule at home. Considering the extreme side effects, we had expected chemo to stop. But to our surprise, Joanne's CA 125 had been reduced from 5,000 to 1,576 indicating that the chemo had been effective in less than a month's time. With greater monitoring of the side effects, however, we didn't dare plan any additional trips to faraway places.

As the snow drifted from the sky surrounding our sunroom snow globe, we finished our morning meditation in front of the cozy gas stove. Joanne had completed another round of chemo the day before as we contemplated another Valentine's Day and the fourth anniversary of diagnosis day.

"So, do you think I'm going to make it this time?" Joanne asked me in heartfelt honesty. "I mean, Orlando was scary but then my numbers improved." The crazy rollercoaster cancer ride baffled our expectations.

"I really don't know, Jo." My head wanted to shout optimism but my heart knew better. Joanne's ability to bounce back during these past four years couldn't last forever I feared…or could it? "It could happen," I proposed.

"I'm beginning to wonder," she said thoughtfully. "I'm getting tired of feeling so awful most of the time…but if this works, then I'll keep fighting as long as I can." Her resolve contradicted her weak physique.

Then she added, "Just in case, I need to go over some funeral changes I've made." My heart sank with the practical reality of her words. As if in a daze and thinking this was premature, we discussed her plans as if it was just another vacation we were planning, while holding our breaking hearts together.

Later that day as I paid some bills while glued to my retirement station chair, Joanne approached with an envelope in her hand,

"Don't forget to send in a donation to Tree House," she directed as she handed the contribution request to me. One of her favorite charities, the Tree House Humane Society in Chicago, provided sanctuary, health care, and adoption services for all homeless cats no matter what their circumstances. Since the early seventies in a three-story house, their services had grown to state-of-the-art facilities beyond the Chicago area.

"I won't forget," I reassured her. "Too bad we couldn't have brought those two Orlando strays to Tree House." The image of their tiny faces pulled at my heartstrings.

"I know...remember when we went there, honey?" Joanne brought to mind a memorable trip to Tree House in 2008 that cemented our bond with the charity.

While attending one of the international conferences for my professional organization, Joanne had tagged along to see the sights of Chicago together during my down time. Along with deep-dish pizza, the former Sears Tower sky deck, and the iconic Cloud Gate bean sculpture, we planned an adventure using the "L" train to visit Tree House. Since I loved to plan public transportation routes, Joanne contentedly followed my lead.

The address looked exactly like the Victorian style house pictured on the old brochures. Even without an appointment, the receptionist greeted us warmly as did their regal white and gray longhair who kept his position on the nearby cat tree. As he opened one eye, he granted us an audience for a few pets and head scratches. After the young lady at the desk asked if we'd like a tour, she summoned another volunteer to cover her station.

In every bold-colored room on every floor, we met cats of every size, shape, color, and demeanor. Some roamed in confined spaces, others romped and rolled in larger play areas while some older skeptical cats peered through safe spaces on shelves above our heads. Cat toys, window perches, dangling feathers, and well-planned havens filled the inviting house. If I had been a stray cat, I would have moved into this feline heaven in a heartbeat.

Nonetheless, these resident cats had once been in crisis. Our guide reiterated some of the horror stories we had read about in previous newsletters about their dire circumstances on the streets of Chicago. Often found injured, defenseless, or near death, these kitties had used up much of their nine lives prior to finding sanctuary at Tree House, where some remained forever if not adopted. Since we were impressed with their compassionate services, we left a check at the desk as a donation on our way out. And our contributions had continued without question every year since.

Weeks rolled by in a blur of chemo infusions every two weeks, lung taps, blood transfusions, ultrasounds, blood work, and CT scans. Even though staying home, avoiding germs and renting movies occupied most hours, the idea of a short cruise to Bermuda in June skipped across our minds like flat stones on a smooth lake. We just couldn't help ourselves.

By early March 2018, Joanne's CA 125 number was down to 407. We would have celebrated if Joanne hadn't felt like a semi-truck had smashed into her most days. Despite the effectiveness of the Gemzar and Cisplatin, we questioned the price she had to pay and, like Rocky the fighter, we wondered how long her tired body could endure the onslaught of weapons.

As we braced our imaginary boats for more rapids, would we steer clear like the *African Queen* or sink like the *Titanic?* Whether we were ready or not, the next crisis was bound to meet us head on.

CHAPTER 26

❦

Crisis Number Two

"I want to get a statue of Mary for the garden," Joanne announced one cool Saturday morning in mid-March 2018 as I gathered my belongings to leave the house. Almost out the door for my golf league's seasonal kick-off brunch, I turned my head in her direction as I considered her statement.

"Sure, as long as there's no bathtub behind her," I added my two cents and smiled while realizing that she wasn't asking for permission. Cancer may have weakened her body and memory, but nothing seemed to stop her chutzpah.

"No bathtub, I promise," she referred to the often-used white backdrop for the serene statue that I swore was a real tub. "But I want one in good condition for free." She had definitely given some thought to this quest.

"Where are you going to get that?" I asked. Considering her outlaw streak, I thought she might snatch one from someone's yard. I also wondered why she was so intent about Mary all of a sudden.

"I'm going to put it out there online and see what happens," she said matter-of-factly. I sensed that she fully expected success.

"Okay, go for it." I couldn't argue as I bent down for a quick kiss good-bye. "I'll be back around one." Further discussion about her reasons would have to wait.

During the forty-minute drive to the brunch at a fancy country club, I thought about Mother Mary. Unlike Joanne's Catholic upbringing, my Protestant roots had not elevated her to Mother of God status when I was a child. As an adult, however, I learned to connect with the comforting idea of a divine mother. Praying to a feminine spirit for my daughter's protection, health for my pregnant niece, or healing from ovarian cancer seemed appropriate. In my heart's imagination, Mary would understand because she had empathy.

While I occasionally prayed to Mary over the years and said hello to her statue along the highway, she became elevated to me in spirit. However, I did not imagine her to be a quiet, milquetoast personality. To me, she was a strong Jewish mother whose love was ferocious and her resolve as tough as granite. Contrary to the sweet smile of the familiar image, my statue of Mary would reveal a determined face, focused eyes, and tenacious spirit. Nonetheless, I would accept whatever statue Joanne found, even if it came with a bathtub.

As my dependable Civic sped along on the highway, it dawned on me that I had once played Mary in a church Christmas pageant when I was eleven or so. My part was simply to sit quietly on stage, gaze at the baby doll in the wooden manger and, ironically, look serene amid the usual manger scene players. With the traditional blue and white cloths covering my head, I probably looked like the notable statue.

Even at that young age, I had felt honored to be chosen for the coveted role. When one of the church women commented to me afterward that I had looked like an angel, I figured I had portrayed Mary justly. Contrary to my inflated ego, however, my sister and brother did not agree with the angel assessment since they knew me better as a fallen angel.

In the car, as my thoughts strung together like a spider web, I remembered my elderly third grade Sunday school teacher, Miss Ethel Matthews, whose loving words and thoughtful actions had influenced my life. Not only did she send homemade birthday cards to every student throughout their lives, but she had also assigned a Bible verse to each child. The first letter of the chosen verse corresponded to the first letter of the student's name.

With the letter *L* for Linda, she bestowed upon me the familiar verse from Matthew that begins "*Let your light so shine…*" Even though I have often fallen short of the message, I never forgot Miss Matthews's kindness and foresight as if she had always expected the verses to follow us forever. Thinking about Joanne and despite the different letter, I could have assigned the same verse to her as Mother Mary's divine light seemed to fill her spirit while her body declined.

As I entered the sunroom that afternoon after a scrumptious brunch, Joanne greeted me with a broad grin and exciting news.

"Honey, guess what?" she exclaimed proudly. "I found a statue."

Explaining that someone in the neighborhood had responded within a couple hours of her online request, Joanne's face beamed. With reassurance that their free statue was in excellent condition, she had made arrangements for me to retrieve Mary and deliver her to our backyard.

"You don't mind, do you?" she said, not really expecting a refusal. "I think it's big and heavy so I'll call Rory if it's too much to unload." As usual, she had thought of everything, including the enlisted help of Carissa's muscled boyfriend and partner.

"I don't mind, honey, but I have to ask." I was curious and added, "Why are you so driven to get Mary's statue in our yard?" Until now, religious statues other than angels and St. Francis had not been important additions to the garden.

"I don't know really," she stared into the yard, "I guess I'd just feel more comfort having her here." An ominous feeling hung in the air as I suspected she harbored frequent thoughts about dying, especially after the Orlando crisis. Despite our closeness, she kept her innermost thoughts to herself, her God, and apparently Mother Mary.

The pristine two-and-a-half-foot statue was indeed heavy. Even the young husband who loaded Mary into my trunk strained to move the solid cement form that I could hardly adjust once it was in my car. Luckily, the short ride home would spare the Civic's shock absorbers from damage.

As promised, Rory arrived in our driveway fully expecting to simply lift her from the car and gallantly place her in the back corner of the garden. To his surprise and chagrin, however, he had to agree that our hand truck would be necessary to move our new addition. Together, we secured Mary for transport and slowly rolled her through the grass to her new home under the small crabapple tree. Unless lightning struck or the Incredible Hulk invaded our yard, Mother Mary with her open arms was here to stay. In record time, Joanne had gotten her wish.

As the Gemzar and Cisplatin pounded the tumors into submission each week, Joanne's body struggled to fortify low blood cells with the help of occasional transfusions and eliminate accumulating fluid in her lungs with taps every ten days. As long as the CA 125 cancer count decreased, however, we longed for a stable summer. Without the prospect of *No Evidence of Disease* anymore, we would settle for good days when her strength returned.

Two weeks after Mary showed up in mid-March, we returned to the house in time for lunch following another lung tap on Friday morning. Our afternoon schedule also included a routine visit to our tax preparer ten minutes away.

"Lin, I'm not up to going this afternoon," Joanne announced after lunch. "I really need to rest...can you go for both of us?" Reclining on her familiar couch station, she had already curled up with her initialized polar fleece blanket that had been a gift from her mother years before. With her glass of water and phone handy, she looked ready for a stress free nap, wrapped in her mother's love.

"Sure, honey," I replied as I gathered our tax papers and notebook. "It shouldn't take long." After tucking her in, I headed out wondering how much we would have to pay in taxes.

After ten minutes in the waiting area, a neatly dressed woman in her sixties called my name and escorted me to her tiny office. I had just taken my seat across from her computer table when I felt my silenced phone vibrate with a voicemail message. Since the caller ID revealed Joanne's name, I excused myself and listened to the call. Her whispered voice was so weak, I could hardly hear what she was saying.

"....Linda....I passed out....I'm on the floor....I need help." A long pause made me think she had ended the call. Then I heard, "Come home please...I think I have to go to the hospital."

My heart started racing when I noticed a second voicemail that turned out to be a shortened repeat of the first message. Joanne had called within two minutes of her first attempt when I hadn't answered. In a frenzy, I scooped up my papers, apologized to the tax lady and flew out to my car. Angry with myself for silencing my phone and abandoning my wife in the first place, I tried to call her as I drove. But she didn't answer. My next call was to 911.

Crumpled on the hardwood floor and area rug next to her couch, Joanne whimpered my name when I ran to her. The glass of water, still intact but on its side, had been knocked over next to her head where her cellphone lay halfway in her hand. *Oh my God*, I thought as I tried to lift her to a seated position.

"No...No...." she struggled to talk, "I can't sit up...I can't breathe... and I feel so dizzy." With her face devoid of color and her strength draining from her limbs, I was petrified that she would die on the TV room floor if the 911 rescue didn't arrive soon.

"What happened, Jo?" I tried to keep her conscious.

"I…was…getting up…to go….to the…bathroom," she managed to eke out the words. "I don't…know…how long…I was out." In my head, I calculated fifteen or twenty minutes but couldn't be sure. Just then, the front doorbell rang.

As I directed two burly emergency workers into the house, my emotions switched to autopilot. The experienced men who filled the tiny TV room went into action with their blood pressure cuff, miniature flashlights, and medical bags. Still unable to sit up without pain, Joanne's weak body flopped as if her bones had been removed. Since one of the technicians announced that her blood pressure had dangerously dropped, a rush to the hospital was next.

In minutes, the able men had lifted Joanne onto a skinny transport chair in order to weave through the narrow doorways of our house. Strapped in the chair, her face contorted with pain as she was wheeled through the living room and front door, coming to a stop on the sidewalk where a padded stretcher waited. Whether she would ever return to her beloved home stung my heart and mind while I snatched my bag in order to follow the rescue.

With lights flashing and the siren screaming, the bright red rescue truck led the way on its hurried mission to save my wife. For two blocks, my Honda seemed to huff and puff to keep up before I realized the effort was fruitless. As a common vehicle, I could never dash through red lights and weave around stopped motorists, some of whom had obeyed the law and pulled over.

In my frantic state, I summoned divine help to breathe, slow down, and reach the emergency room in one piece. Even the country song, "Jesus, Take the Wheel," popped into my head. For the rest of the fifteen-minute drive, with spirit in the passenger seat, I managed to replace some of my fear with a temporary peace.

Unlike Orlando, where I had been close to Joanne throughout her ordeal, here in our own hometown Joanne and I had become separated without my knowing if she was dead or alive. Luckily, I found a parking space near the entrance of the Women and Infants' Hospital ER, scrambled through the security process, and explained who I was to the receptionist.

At that moment, I was so grateful that we were legally married. As Joanne's wife, there was no question about my right to even be there and receive any information about her status. Years before gay rights laws, I would have been denied access like so many loving couples had been in the past. The added heartbreak must have been overwhelming.

With minutes ticking by as I waited for information, I couldn't imagine what had happened at home. Other than needing a nap when I had left the house, Joanne hadn't been in distress. Now, here she was in what seemed like critical condition. Before I could think any more about the reason, however, a young female technician called me into the cubicle area.

Weaving through the bustling hallways, we finally stopped at Joanne's curtained room. Propped up in the mechanical bed with a cloth hospital gown and blanket draped over her, Joanne was alive but weak. Familiar IV tubes and now oxygen flowing through the nosepiece were providing some relief for her breathing but she struggled to keep her eyes open.

As I softly kissed her forehead and whispered my hello, a friendly strawberry blonde nurse who had been adjusting the oxygen introduced herself.

"Hi, my name is Angela," she said with compassion. "I'll be your primary nurse while you're here." I thought her name was appropriate for her caring, professional demeanor. "Joanne, do you need anything right now?"

"No thanks, I'm feeling better," she replied. My thought was that she certainly looked better than earlier when I had found her on the floor.

"After we get some tests done, the doctor will be back to talk with you," Angela reassured her. "Just use the call button if you need me." *Wish we had had one of those in the TV room back home* I thought as Angela swept the curtain back to leave.

After a long, deep look with our eyes, Joanne and I smiled at each other and shook our heads in amazement at this unexpected scare.

"I can't believe it," she broke the silence. "All I did was stand up from the couch and then I woke up on the floor," she continued her tale. "There was water near my face and Phoebe was sniffing my cheek." With her feline talents, I secretly wondered if Phoebe could be trained to be like Lassie, the always successful rescue dog on TV.

"Well, it was pretty scary when I found you," I confessed. "I'm just glad I wasn't far away." *It could've been so much worse,* I thought as we waited for the tests to begin.

While Joanne was whisked away for a chest x-ray, CT scan, and whatever else the medical staff needed, I kept vigil in her cubicle texting and calling our families about the latest crisis. Feeling like a professional hospital family member after four years on this exhausting ride, I confidently assured our loved ones that all was well. Once again, I felt grateful that she was in capable hands and prayed we would return home soon, not knowing that the worst was yet to come.

After what seemed like hours of waiting, reading, and watching the monitors, Joanne's breathing did not improve as expected. Each time the nurse increased the amount of oxygen flowing into her airways, she shook her head with disbelief. As we reacted to the nurse with anxious glances, the tension in the room ballooned and my pulse quickened.

Finally, the middle-aged doctor and his young resident entered the cubicle with serious faces.

"Hi, Joanne, I'm Dr. Pasquale and this is Dr. Hamilton," he greeted us as he gestured to the young woman by his side. "From all the tests and information, it appears that the lung tap you had this morning caused bleeding into your left lung. Along with your low platelet count, this also caused your blood pressure to drop so that you passed out." His direct eye contact silently told us the crisis was not over.

"Unless we can get a chest tube into your lung as soon as possible, your condition is critical." As the doctor spoke, other medical staff entered the space and swiftly prepared monitors, poles, and switches for transport.

Then, he really scared us when he said, "Before we can move you to Rhode Island Hospital where they perform this procedure, we need to have verbal confirmation about your wishes for resuscitation." He looked at both of us with respect but urgency as well. "I'll give you a couple minutes alone."

When all the medical staff had stepped out of the space, I looked at Joanne's pale face and tried to read her eyes. Whenever we had discussed this topic before, the conclusion seemed clear: resuscitate if there's hope for survival but not if it means sustaining an unconscious life with machines. Now faced with the real possibility, I felt my heart changing my mind. Intense fear of losing Joanne clouded my decision.

"I can't agree with a *Do Not Resuscitate* order, Jo," I said quietly. "I just can't." I couldn't believe how quickly I had turned to jelly.

"Lin, we had talked about this," Joanne said calmly. "You know I don't want to be a vegetable." Then she added, "And you wouldn't want to see me like that either." Despite her difficult breathing, she said the right words to pull me back to earth. I had to let go and trust in divine order.

"Okay, but you better not leave me yet," I warned with a smile and glistening eyes. She returned my look of love just as the doctors returned.

The next fifteen minutes could only be described as a frantic chariot race through basement corridors to reach the other hospital. The doctors had explained that the underground route would be faster than trying to secure a rescue or helicopter transport. Ironically, we had been waiting for hours in the cubicle and now we were rushing like refugees fleeing a dangerous country.

As we passed stored equipment, unpainted walls, and signs for maintenance services, I felt gratitude for my new knees that enabled me to keep up with the team of doctors, nurses, and technicians. With expertise, they guided Joanne's bed without hesitation to the elevator that would bring us to the Trauma ICU.

As we approached our destination in the sterile trauma center, I glanced into the room where another team of medical staff stood ready for the emergency chest tube procedure. Expecting to follow Joanne, I took only two steps into the doorway when a nurse deftly guided me out to the waiting room.

"I'm afraid you'll have to wait out here until they're finished," she said with sincere sympathy. "I'll let you know when you can go in." She smiled and touched my shoulder.

"Thank you," I replied then thought to ask, "Will I be able to stay with her tonight?" Since it was nine o'clock and I remembered my stay in the Orlando Hospital, I expected to bunk with my wife once again.

"You can stay here in the waiting room but not in the ICU room... there's another patient in there as well," she explained, and then scurried on to other tasks.

While I scanned yet another large waiting room, I let out an exhausted sigh as I took a seat near an electrical outlet where I could charge my phone. Even though no one else was around, pillows and blankets on nearby seats were evidence that someone had slept in the uncomfortable chairs and might return. Alone and feeling completely drained, I considered our new circumstances as I gazed out the wide windows into the ebony night.

With my sad reflection looking back at me, I realized how close we had come to the end and how quickly my fear about losing her had surfaced... again. In comparison, however, the crisis in Orlando two months before had been merely a dress rehearsal for this intensified event. Now, with the reality of cancer's outcome sinking in, my once confident battle cry weakened while I waited in the stillness of the waiting room. My brain was too tired to imagine the next challenge.

After another hour, I approached Joanne's hospital bed where she slept in peace. When I touched her arm, her eyes opened slightly and a smile crossed her face.

"Hi, honey," I said. "How are you feeling?" Compared to the afternoon, she had already improved one hundred percent. With pain meds and the chest tube, I felt relieved to think her recovery would allow us to slow dance in the kitchen once again.

"I feel much better but I'm so weak," she whispered. "Are you going home now?" Even though I had considered sleeping in the waiting room, I realized my back would never recover from those chairs no matter how many pillows I procured from the nurses.

"I don't know…do you want me to stay?" I asked, knowing I would manage if need be.

"No, no, honey," she said before closing her eyes for the third time. "You need to take care of the kitties…but you could come back in the morning though, right?"

"Of course, my sweet, and I'll stay all day." I would do anything for my wife.

Joanne stayed in the trauma unit for the next six days. As she continued to gather strength amid the ups and downs of hospital recovery, our routine droned on with my all-day visits, her round-the-clock specialized medical care, and occasional visits from family and friends. Despite unexpected complications like an air leak in her lung that delayed removal of the chest tube, her strength gradually improved, enabling her to transfer to a regular room the day before discharge. As if breaking out of prison, Joanne fled the hospital as soon as she received the word. As no surprise, the status of chemotherapy would be determined at the next visit with Dr. D. in mid-April. Crisis number two seemed to be over.

On Easter, three days after discharge from the hospital, twenty family members and friends chattered around a long restaurant table laden with brunch. Sunny egg dishes, pancakes dripping with syrup, crispy bacon, veggie omelets, hot coffee, and warm blueberry muffins had been delivered by our waitress only moments before we all bowed our heads for a prayer.

With her purplish spiked hair and pink flowered blouse under a long purple sweater coat, no one would have guessed how sick Joanne had been only days before. Her vibrant colors portrayed wellness and life, not the pale draining of life in the hospital. Around the table, she now spoke in her normal voice while silence fell on every head.

"Oh God, thank you for this joyful day, the love around this table and the food we are about to eat. May your light fill our hearts and minds forever and ever. Amen."

As the dishes clattered and voices rose in conversation and laughter, I marveled that Joanne was sitting next to me at all. Not only was I convinced of her nine lives, but she always seemed to land on her feet as well. In the Easter season of new life, her recovery from this crisis was my inspirational example and I could almost detect a broader smile on Mother Mary's serene face. Only she seemed to know what adventure came next.

CHAPTER 27

Cracks in the Dam

While ominous media news during the spring of 2018 told us the world could be falling apart, other positive stories provided hope that the human race could unite. Suicide bombings, train crashes, terrorist attacks and even an Ebola flare-up contrasted with Prince Harry and Megan's wedding, a double amputee's summit of Mt. Everest, and an eventual triple-crown winner at the Kentucky Derby. Choosing to focus on the good or bad always influenced our attitude…even in the smaller world of our cozy house.

Despite her healthy appearance at Easter, over the following two weeks Joanne's recovery from the chest-tube crisis was a slow process. Under my care at home, she needed help getting dressed, preparing meals, taking a shower and keeping doctors' appointments. Slow motion could have described all daily tasks. Even our collection of surgical supplies, like bath seats, wedge pillows, and canes, was growing. When her appetite eventually improved from Jell-O to chicken, Joanne's energy for poking around in the garden also returned…just in time for more chemo. Some outings, however, were priorities.

"Do you want me to drive, Jo?" I asked as we bustled out of the house in April on our way to pick up Jayden. As dusk settled on Friday the thirteenth, we considered ourselves lucky to escape our home confines for some fun before her upcoming treatment on Monday.

With tickets to a children's stage production of *The Lion King*, Joanne's plan had always been to provide Jayden with diverse experiences, no matter what cancer had to say about it. Eating out at a Chinese restaurant near the theater was another part of her ambitious plan as well.

"No, I can drive," she insisted as we climbed into her steadfast Accord. Despite her increasing stamina, I worried that she would use up her energy quota on the drive to the show. Knowing my wife, however, I also realized that appearing strong and healthy to Jayden was important to her so that he wouldn't worry about his Auntie Jo.

Encouraging news from the doctor two days before had also bolstered our spirits. Despite our concern that the CA 125 count now had risen from 407 to 733, we had hope that the reason for the rise could be recent inflammation. With improved red blood cell and platelet counts, reduced tumor size and Joanne's returning strength, four rounds of only Cisplatin were recommended. The nasty Gemzar that wreaked havoc on her body in March would be eliminated. Grasping for a lifeline, we held onto any ray of hope the doctor presented.

"Hi, Auntie," Jayden bubbled as he threw himself into the passenger seat. Retreating to the backseat, I had relinquished the front so they could connect on the twenty-minute drive. After demanding cursory kisses from him, we settled into easy conversation on the drive. His excitement with the night out as well as our attention filled the car as we sped along the highway, leaving cancer in the dust.

Finding available parking near the restaurant and theater on the busy one-way streets was never easy. Circling past already-filled lots reminded me of planes waiting to land. As Jayden and I scanned for any empty space, I suddenly had a brilliant idea.

"Jo, let's use your blue parking pass," I offered. "I think this would be a great time to use it." Any chance to save her strength sounded good to me.

"Okay," she replied without hesitation. "Jayden, can you get it from the glove compartment, please?" In the past, she had used the parking privilege only when necessary. Tonight, with her unusually quick decision, I suspected she was already tired.

As if Mother Mary was looking out for us, we spotted one empty handicapped space in a small lot directly behind the theater. With only a short walk to our Chinese dinner and then the show, the fun evening with Jayden enfolded.

After eggrolls, pork fried rice, sweet and sour chicken, and just egg drop soup for Joanne, we waddled over to the bustling vintage theater where we located our red velvet seats three rows from the stage. Not surprising that Auntie Jo would choose the best tickets for her great nephew.

As we settled into our seats and perused our programs amid the crowd's noisy anticipation, I noticed Joanne's pale face and sagging shoulders. Not wanting to draw attention to her fatigue, I caught her eye and smiled.

"How about if I drive home?" I suggested in a low voice.

"Okay," she said, again without hesitation. I knew that whatever exhaustion I could detect was, most likely, only the tip of the iceberg.

With creative images of elephants, giraffes, and lions lumbering through the aisles toward the stage filled with illusions of rock ledges and savannah, the young peoples' production of *The Lion King* was impressive. Strains of the music, "Circle of Life" and "Can You Feel the Love Tonight?" brought tears to my eyes as the lyrics amplified a deeper meaning with the possibility of losing Joanne. As we immersed ourselves in the show, I often touched her hand to share an unspoken thought. And also for reassurance that she was still sitting beside me.

After the show as I drove home with two sleepy passengers, I considered the upcoming chemotherapy scheduled in two days. Until now, I hadn't remembered that Cisplatin was one of the early treatments Joanne had received following her major surgery four years before. With that realization, I sensed that we had come full circle in some way...the circle of life. I also prayed, *God, if you're going to hand her a miracle cure, now would be a good time.*

By the second week in May, Joanne had received two infusions of Cisplatin. But her CA 125 count had risen again from 733 to 1,002. Compared to the passing-out crisis in March, her strength and activity had improved immensely. But compared to a year before, her life was limited to fewer outings and more naps. Even another nerve-wracking lung tap was performed successfully this time to alleviate difficulty breathing so she could resume her art classes and social events. Every time the cancer cell count rose, however, I sensed another crack in the imaginary dam that had been holding the cancer floodwaters back. We had experienced a similar feeling years before with Joanne's house.

With every heavy rainstorm since we had first met, a sense of doom invaded our psyche as we braced for flooding in the basement. Prior to the eventual costly installation of an underground sump pump system, we tended our basement stations like the family in *Mary Poppins* when their neighbor fired his rooftop cannon, rattling precious vases and wall hangings. We always thought we were ready for anything.

During a heavy storm, like clockwork, water would seep into the finished basement from at least four corners, requiring wet vac machines and enough chamois cloths to wallpaper the entire house. God forbid if we were away on vacation. One year, we returned from P-town to three inches of water covering the entire floor.

A few years later, water found its way through cracks in the wall near a major pipe that we had neglected to paint with sealer. With the saturated ground and intensifying rain, water actually gushed from the wall around the pipe like a woodland waterfall. All night long, round-the-clock, we vacuumed, mopped, and wrung chamois cloths until the rain abated and our temporary fixes held. Shortly after that exhausting night, the sump pump system idea was born. With the underground drains and pump finally installed, water was redirected outside along with our stress.

In a different sense, we were running out of fixes for the cracks in the dam that held cancer at bay—we could almost hear the gushing water on the other side. Like caulking, Cisplatin seemed to be our only hope but so far it didn't look promising. Since I wasn't ready to let cancer take over, I tried to ignore the insidious rise in cell count.

Throughout May, our routine life now included additional health concerns. Just to complicate her symptoms, Joanne's hernia pain increased, her coughing resumed, and recurring nausea plagued many nights. Even though her general strength returned for simple tasks like preparing meals and monitoring backyard wildlife, climbing the long flight of stairs to our attic bedroom was limited to once a day. Whenever her red blood cells dipped, blood transfusions pumped her up with liquid energy for a couple weeks. But even with the help of myriad medications, long naps, and reduced activities, I watched Joanne's body slowing down like a car approaching a red light. By the end of May, when the CA 125 count rose to 1,852 and the doctor cancelled chemo altogether because it was no longer working, I could almost hear a huge crack form in the dam that was about to burst.

"Do you want to use one of these today?" I asked Joanne as I pointed to the folded wheelchair behind the hospital security desk. The long walk to the fourth floor oncology department seemed much more challenging than even a few months before.

"You know, I think I will use it this time...until we get to the waiting room upstairs anyway." By this time, Joanne's willingness to accept some help had mushroomed out of necessity.

Despite the familiar location in the building, our appointment with a new specialist for a major change in Joanne's treatment plan made us feel like newcomers. We were about to enter the new world of Palliative Care with Dr. L., who would explain her approach and options. Knowing that the focus would be on relieving pain, not curing the cause, Joanne forged ahead with anticipation of feeling better while living in the moment. Even though I shared her search for relief, I feared that the monster had been set free and we had no weapons to stop it.

"Joanne?" The young nurse's aide stood smiling in the doorway of the peaceful waiting room as we rose from our cushioned seats amid the tropical-like plants, water fountains, and sunlight streaming from the wall of windows. Although we let her lead, we certainly knew the way.

The aide escorted us to an unfamiliar conference room that resembled a cozy living room with a view, reminding me of diagnosis day more than four years before. Expecting to meet with only the new doctor, an ominous feeling filled the room when other medical staff slowly entered the room one by one. With some familiar faces, however, I felt reassured that this apparent summit meeting would be beneficial.

In her mid-forties with soft brown hair to her shoulders, the palliative care specialist, Dr. L., led the meeting with compassion and expertise. One of her residents, an intern and our favorite physician assistant, Mia, rounded out the group.

After summarizing Joanne's medical journey and confirming her present symptoms, Dr. L. began a litany of suggestions for treating her uncomfortable ailments. Steroids for exhaustion, medical marijuana for hernia pain, and Tessalon Perles for her hacking cough sounded great. Up until that point, the atmosphere in the room was nonchalant as if we were discussing pain relief with a pharmacist or a string of pearls as a chic accessory. Suddenly, with an uncharacteristic assertiveness, Mia interrupted and spoke directly to Joanne.

"Joanne, you realize that chemotherapy is no longer an option, right?" Mia said with conviction. My impression was that she wanted to be honest with us and convey the hidden message about the nature of these new treatments.

"I know, Mia, " Joanne returned with equal assertiveness. "I realize these things are for my comfort...no more cure." Then she added, "I know that Dr. D. said the chemo would probably shorten my life now sooner than the cancer." Despite her words, however, I secretly knew she held out for a miracle cure, even now.

"Okay, I just wanted to make sure you understood the meaning of palliative care," Mia softened her words as my heart felt another crack along with the dam.

Ending on a positive note, the meeting held promise that Joanne's body could at least feel better for as much fun as possible for whatever time remained. With this new phase, we were determined to make the most of every moment and find adventure in the garden, the beach, and the eyes of people we loved. My heart had to focus on the positive no matter how much it felt like breaking.

With the new palliative care treatments, Joanne returned to pulling weeds in the garden, sleeping without pain, and lunching with friends and family. Her relief from chronic pain filled her brilliant smile and bolstered her spirit with hope. The pattern of bouncing back from dire circumstances reminded me of her nine lives and distracted me from the reality of cancer. We enjoyed every good day and dismissed the bad while we could. Without a verbal decision, we also tabled any further heartbreaking discussions about her death until later.

During the second week of June, we gathered at a local diner for brunch with our *Church of the Little Women* group. With her cornflower blue knit top, two-tone blue lightweight jacket for cold air conditioning, and spiked purplish hair, Joanne looked great according to everyone around the table. Before she had a chance to ask again, I took her picture for my archives.

After evaluating the pancakes and exhausting every subject from cousin updates to house projects, Joanne asked the group for some information.

"Does anyone know which DMV office would be less crowded right about now?" She scanned our inquisitive faces as we marveled at her resilience. Referring to the Department of Motor Vehicles, her plan was to renew her driver's license as soon as we departed the diner. A hopeful idea, I thought, considering her health prognosis, but very Joanne-like considering her determination to defy cancer.

"The one on Route 44 near Apple Valley Mall is small and usually empty," Carole Ann offered. Others in the group nodded their heads in

LINDA L. SKIBSKI

agreement. Everyone seemed amazed that she would consider another errand after our two-hour brunch, but no one would ever try to stop her.

Locating the small office nestled in the strip of stores was the easiest part of our day, other than savoring our tasty eggs and pancakes. We knew we were in trouble when the line of customers already extended the full length of the spacious room.

"Honey, why don't you sit along the wall while I stand in line?" I suggested. With her slow pace and weary face, I wondered if going there was such a great idea as she started to fade before my eyes.

"I don't mind if I do," she replied as she sank into a molded plastic chair with arms. At least the chair would hold her in place.

As the time crept by and the variety of people in line inched their way to the counter, I often glanced at Joanne who tried to prop her head up with her palm cradling her chin. Thinking of her healthy image at the diner only an hour earlier, I was astounded at the contrast of her now exhausted body slumped in the chair.

Forty-five minutes later, I was next in line and could hear the DMV clerk instruct the customer to submit the application and paperwork before posing in a chair for the picture. With new state rules, drivers were not allowed to smile and hairdos had to be pushed back from foreheads for a clear view of the face. Needless to say, the resulting pictures looked austere and not very complimentary. I motioned to Joanne to approach the counter as the woman in front of me finished her business.

With some effort, Joanne ambled to the clerk and presented her papers. In muffled tones, I assumed she heard the same instructions about the photo as she plopped into the photo chair, looking utterly exhausted.

Then, just as the camera snapped, she quickly pulled the right strap of her top down her arm, coyly revealing a bare shoulder. While I cracked up at her defiance of the rules, the two middle-aged women behind us also noticed her action. As they exploded with laughter too, Joanne simply rose from her chair with the slightest smile as if she was proud to still be a rebel. At that moment, I loved her more than ever.

On the twenty-first anniversary of the day we had met in June, a series of torrential rains and wind had swept through the area while my sister was visiting for two nights. Even the power had flickered off during the night, wreaking havoc with our answering machine. At least we never had to worry about a flooded basement any longer.

For years, Joanne's job was to record the greeting on the answering machine, primarily due to her technical know-how. Since she was willing and able, I never refused her offer to fix the greeting after a storm had knocked out our electronics.

"...we are not able to take your call at this time. Please leave a message and we'll get back to you as soon as possible. Thank you." Joanne's voice drifted through the house as Chris and I poured our coffee in the kitchen. Just as she entered the kitchen to join us, the front doorbell rang.

When I opened the living room door, our friendly neighbor across the street greeted me with an anxious look.

"Hi Linda, I just wanted to let you know your tree out front is ripped up by the roots and is ready to fall on your porch," he said nervously. "Come and look." I wasn't about to hesitate.

Sure enough, the thirty-foot nondescript tree on the curbside strip of grass was precariously lying against the second tree nearby. Since it pointed in the direction of the front porch roof, there was no question where it would land next.

"Oh my god," I exclaimed as I rushed back to the house to report the news.

"I'm going to call 911," Joanne announced as she flew into action. As Chris and I continued to be aghast, the cancer patient took charge and brought an emergency arbor team to our door within minutes.

For the next three hours, we provided an audience for the workers who impressively reduced the tree without damage to our house or each other. As I watched the sad event, I was reminded of countless beloved trees that had been felled intentionally or by the power of nature's fury. No matter what the circumstance, I had always mourned the loss of the tree's spirit and missed its beauty, shade, and greenery.

As the old tree by the curb came down, I couldn't help but think it was an omen. The cancer storm seemed to be on our doorstep and the floodwaters had swallowed the dam. Now even Joanne's strong spirit was in jeopardy.

⤬

CHAPTER 28

Everybody Loves Clean Sheets

"**O**kay, you two…here we go," I whispered as I turned from the kitchen counter holding two small stainless steel bowls filled with the morning portion of wet cat food. After tiptoeing down the attic stairs to find Joanne sleeping on the couch, I tried to move quietly and quell Phoebe's hungry vocals. Always the gentleman, Charlie's meows were already muted.

As Little Miss Piggy wound her body around my feet, delaying the food delivery she craved, I inched my way to her placemat. After placing her precious bowl on the floor, Charlie and I entered the sunroom where he could graze in peace with the glass door closed. Without the separation, she would have gobbled both breakfasts in record time if allowed.

While the kitties munched, I grabbed my fresh coffee and stood at the kitchen counter mindlessly flipping through one of the thousand mail order catalogs I received every day. Without paying much attention to the must-have doodads like microwave plate covers and frog-shaped wind chimes, I wondered why Joanne had left our bed during the night to remain downstairs on the couch.

Ever since the second follow-up visit with the palliative care doctor two weeks before, Joanne's aggravating symptoms had been controlled with the medications Dr. L. had recommended. Despite the soaring rise in CA 125 count from 1,852 to 4,550 in less than three weeks, she had experienced only moderate chronic pain. With interrupted sleep the previous night, however, a possible new problem lurked. But I would have to wait until she woke up to find out what had happened.

Flipping over the next catalog page, I spotted a plaque entitled *What Cancer Cannot Do*. The fancy script underneath revealed that cancer cannot cripple love, shatter hope, corrode faith, destroy peace, kill friendship, suppress memories, silence courage, invade the soul, steal eternal life, or conquer the spirit. Despite the noble words, my reaction was mixed.

While I agreed that our faith, hope, love, and spirit generally remained intact during our fight with cancer, there were times when our peace was destroyed and our courage ebbed. If we had allowed cancer to take over completely, everything on the plaque's list would have suffered because cancer wanted it all. Despite the unknown author's attempt to make us feel better, I wondered if they had ever personally understood what cancer could really do.

Like a fierce game of tug-of-war, we had wrestled often to hold onto the spiritual foundation of our existence. The struggle wasn't easy and sometimes, we staggered under the weight of sadness and despair. In the end, with divine guidance, we accepted that cancer could destroy Joanne's body, but we would not allow the monster to take the things that really mattered.

Amazed that I could find such deep thoughts in a mail order catalog, I heard Joanne stir in the TV room. After a few minutes, she silently approached me from behind and hugged my body close in a good morning hello. In that moment, I treasured the simple things that cancer could not touch.

"Hi, honey," I said as I turned around for a quick kiss. "What happened to you last night?" I knew the problem was more than a bathroom break.

"It's this itching," she sounded annoyed. "I couldn't stand it so I came down to get that marijuana cream," she continued. "I didn't want to wake you up so I stayed down here."

For the last few days and for no apparent reason, her entire body had begun to itch. The cream provided some relief but, like the gummy bears, the effectiveness was only temporary, requiring several applications.

"Maybe you should call the doctor and find out what's going on," I suggested before adding, "Maybe there's some other treatment." After so many years of weird chemo symptoms, we assumed the intense itching was just another ailment to add to the list.

"I think I will," she said with determination. "Can't hurt anyway." After a couple minutes, she added, "And besides, I want to take care of this before we go to that resort in Connecticut next week." A few weeks before, Joanne had made reservations for a five-day stay at a fancy beach resort. Out of habit, she couldn't resist planning a getaway.

"And don't forget our reservation in Little Compton," I added, thinking about our plan to camp with the RV for a relaxing overnight on the beach at the end of the week. After four years of making impromptu plans, procrastinating was no longer part of my vocabulary.

Four days later, before the July 4th holiday, Joanne proceeded to the hospital for blood work in order to investigate the new itching problem. While we waited there for the lab results, she was unexpectedly redirected to the ER for an emergency CT scan and ultrasound. Since the blood work revealed high liver and kidney functions, which meant the organs weren't processing correctly, additional testing had been ordered as well. Here was another emergency room, another ultrasound, and another batch of bad news.

The bottom line was that her kidney and gall bladder were involved as well as the liver that caused yellowing of her skin and eyes along with the nasty itching. In order to monitor the new development and complete more testing, an overnight stay in the hospital was recommended. Cancer was definitely attempting to steal our faith, hope, and spirit.

The next day while we anticipated discharge from the hospital, we heard a slight rap on the door.

"Hi there," Dr. D. greeted us as he stepped into Joanne's room. With a subdued cheeriness, he relaxed on the foot of her bed like an old friend and asked how she was feeling.

"I'm tired but okay." Joanne looked him in the eye, expecting his honesty as always. "What's the scoop, doctor?"

"Well, even though the tumors in your liver seem to be the same size as before, the cancer has affected its function along with the gall bladder and kidneys." His voice was steady but filled with compassion. "Since chemo is not an option, I'm afraid there's nothing more I can recommend." No one made a sound for what seemed like hours.

"How much time do you think?" Joanne eked out the words that she had never wanted to say. Right then, I remembered the discussion years before with Carissa, Dr. D., and me after her surgery when we had heard him say four and a half to five years. Now it was almost four and a half years since that day.

"My guess is weeks, but you can surprise me with months if you'd like," Dr. D. said with admiration and a slight smile, knowing how much Joanne liked to fight this insidious disease. "I wish I could offer more, Joanne." The doctor's face looked tired from having to say these words too many times to more cancer patients than he could probably count.

"I know," Joanne replied with equal admiration. "You did all you could do." In our heads, we always knew this day would come, but our hearts needed time to catch up. To me, the scene felt bizarre.

"I would recommend that you sign up for hospice care soon so it will be in place when you need it," Dr. D. offered as we chatted for a few minutes longer before the visit ended. With glistening eyes and words of thanks, we all shook hands as the doctor rose from the bed, departing the room and our lives.

Staying the course with our usual modus operandi, which was to enjoy every moment and be still, we tried to absorb this new phase of the cancer journey with God's grace and peace. The only other choice we had was to squander Joanne's remaining time with sobbing and grief. But there would be time enough for that. While she had breath, we would love and cherish every simple pleasure.

Since one of those joys had always been camping on Little Compton beach with our camper van, Minnie, we decided to keep the reservation for the overnight if Joanne could tolerate the travel. With new medication for the intense itching, she had an eyedropper full of extra energy once again, all for conquering the world. Nonetheless, we could always abort our mission if needed.

Being a Thursday night, only one other RV unit was parked on the opposite end of the lot, providing the quiet privacy Joanne craved. With Minnie's awning cranked out, the picnic table set, and our chairs facing the water, we had settled in during the afternoon. We were definitely enjoying every moment and thanking God for our peace.

After a simple dinner of roast chicken leftovers and fresh corn, only occasional beach walkers, the sound of crashing waves, and the gentle ocean breeze added to our peaceful scene. Looking forward to an early campfire, I rearranged the chairs and prepared the fire pit as early stars poked out from the dusky sky. Sharing this setting with my love felt like heaven to me. As Joanne ambled to her chair with weary steps, however, I knew the campfire would be a short one.

"Oh, what a nice fire," she smiled as she sank into her folding chair while the flames crackled into the night air. By now, scads of blinking stars had revealed themselves as I slid my chair closer to hers.

"How are you doing, honey?" I asked as I gently placed my hand on hers. Her pensive face told me she knew my question was meant to cover mind and spirit as well as body.

"I guess I'm not going to bounce back this time," she sighed with resignation. She waited a few minutes before continuing. "I'm really tired of feeling so awful, Lin…so, I'm ready to go because of that." I could only imagine the grind of chronic pain day after day, but I didn't want to imagine not touching her hand or even sitting next to her as she slept.

"Are you afraid?" I had to ask again. Over the years, our discussions about death included the fear factor but now that the prospect was closer than ever, I wondered if her perception had changed.

"No, I'm not afraid to die…I'm in God's hands and I'm okay," she murmured. "My prayer is that I don't suffer." Memories of her mother's death flooded back to me when Annie was lucid enough to say I love you and reveal a window into the realm of spirit. I already knew that Joanne pictured the same experience for herself. The innate teacher in her wanted to report to us what was happening for future reference.

As the quintessential event planner, Joanne had even researched groups of musicians and singers who provided quiet music around a deathbed. Wanting privacy even at the end of her life was a priority as well. Contrary to wanting lots of angels around her bed during surgery, she did not want a big group of people gathered around her bed staring down at her when she died. These logistical details about her transition had been discussed long before without the emotion that was now gushing like lava. I still couldn't picture the reality of her death.

As the steady fire warmed our faces like our love, we held hands and stared into the flames while the breeze strengthened, blowing sparks into the air like fireworks. A mixture of deep sadness and gratitude filled my heart.

"I don't know what I'm going to do without you, Jo," I whispered and squeezed her hand as hot tears filled my eyes. As if we had been two sturdy oak trees growing side by side with roots entangled, I felt as if those roots were being ripped apart.

"I know," she said softly as her eyes glistened in the firelight. "I really hate leaving you but I promise I'll always be around in spirit." In that moment, all of our quests for spirit led to this focused connection to our God and each other. "Remember, we always said we're together for a reason...forever." She turned to me with a tender, but tired, smile and love-filled eyes. The constant sound of the waves kept a steady and reassuring cadence as we held each other's gaze.

"Forever," I repeated and added, "Remember your bear... *You know it's love when forever's not enough?*" She nodded as we both thought of the little bear with the fancy hat I had given to her after her cancer surgery.

As the wind whipped off the ocean and ominous dark clouds covered the stars, we retreated to the camper as the rain splattered the awning. In our rush, I neglected to crank it back into the casing, thinking the storm would pass.

An hour later as we melded together like spoons in bed and drifted into dreams, the storm intensified outside. Waking with worry about the rattling awning, I decided to battle the fury and finally close it before the storm ripped it off the van. Angry with myself for ignoring the task earlier, I crawled out of the camper, murmured my intent to a sleepy Joanne, and attempted the procedure.

Like a scene in the movie, *The Perfect Storm*, with the wind and rain slashing my entire body as well as the awning, I struggled to collapse the braces and fit them into the storage space. Just then, Joanne appeared like a stalwart crewmember ready to hold the awning while I worked. Despite my efforts to send her back, she insisted she could help.

For twenty minutes, we braced the storm and finally saved the awning from being shredded. Joanne's strength and effort amazed me. Sheer tenacity, grit, and perhaps adrenaline stood next to me in my struggle that night as she always had for years. And maybe, forever.

By Monday, I had doubts about Joanne's ability to travel to the resort in Connecticut. Her functioning to perform even simple tasks had dropped to a new level. Taking a shower was exhausting, climbing stairs was comparable to Mount Everest, and visiting with loved ones who came to the house required a long nap afterward. Not only itching but bloating gas, severe heartburn, vomiting, and fatigue intensified within days of the RV overnight trip. Even though I had helped her pack the night before, I reassured her that we could abandon the resort trip at the last minute if needed.

"Oh no," she said with defiance. "I really want to go no matter what… and I'm paying for everything." With her insistence, I loaded the car by noon and prepared for the hour and a half drive. For the first time, Joanne did not argue about packing a support cane to aid her walking.

As expected, I had surprised her with a bright bouquet of travel flowers and an early musical birthday card in the shape of a bottle that featured a beach scene. When the fake cork was lifted, lights flashed on the scene and a happy tune played. "I got my toes in the water, ass in the sand, not a worry in the world, a cold beer in my hand…life is good today." Even though she loved the gifts, a heavy sadness descended on our hearts with the unspoken knowledge that this would be our last birthday vacation together. I also realized that the getaway was her gift to me.

Water's Edge was a well-established premium resort and spa on the Connecticut coast. Set on acres of sloping landscaped lawns and gardens, the long, white, three-storied buildings faced spectacular views of Long Island Sound. Wide-paved walkways wound through the grounds leading to shaded sitting areas, a private white-sand beach, and a large, clear swimming pool surrounded by cushioned chaise lounges, round tables, and sturdy umbrellas. Every detail was pristine and extravagant like a luxurious paradise.

After checking in and securing the room keycard, an efficient staff person transported our bags to our first floor home away from home. Unfortunately, our room was as tiny as an ordinary cruise ship cabin and with a view of yet another parking lot. *This will never do*, I thought. So, while Joanne immediately plopped down on the bed for a snooze, I revisited the main desk for an upgrade.

Convincing the poised clerk that we needed their best room no matter the cost, I reserved the Royal Suite that would be available the next day for the remainder of our stay. Tolerating the mini room for one night was the least of our worries anyway. After roaming the luxurious lobby and scouting the fine dining restaurants within the resort, I returned to the room to find Joanne awake but still resting.

"Hi, honey…what did you find out?" Joanne asked in a weak voice. Despite the convenient location of the tiny tot room, she had definitely agreed to the upgrade idea.

"Well, we're moving on up to the Royal Suite tomorrow," I said with pride. "It's on the top floor in an older section but it's much larger they said." Even though the room would require a longer walk from the elevator, I thought my queen deserved some royal treatment.

"I'm sorry we have to stay here tonight," I added. "At least it's still a quality room…and bigger than the camper."

"It's okay, honey," she answered as she closed her eyes again. "And at least we'll have clean sheets, not a sleeping bag." One of Joanne's simple pleasures was slipping into bed with clean sheets. She never failed to giggle with delight when relishing the feel of crisp linens at bedtime.

With cancer changing our focus and stripping away the extraneous layers of our lives, we relished the small joys within reach of each day. Along with the sudden visit of a hummingbird in the garden, Phoebe's weird antics or an unexpected hello-how-are-you call from Jayden, clean sheets remained on Joanne's list of treasured pleasures. Sometimes looking at the big picture meant tuning into the smallest detail.

To my surprise, Joanne found the energy to direct us to dinner after her rest. On the deck with lobster dinners before us, bibs around our necks, a gorgeous sunny view of the trimmed grounds and sparkling ocean on the horizon, I marveled at her resilience. Not expecting her to tolerate the delicious fare, I often glanced at her plate with wonder as she kept pace with me. While her yellowish skin reminded me of the enemy taking over, however, I struggled to keep my tears at bay.

One of the resort's conveniences that became one of Joanne's simple pleasures and lifesavers was their shuttle service from the main building down to their beach and pool. With frequent service, the chauffeured golf carts enabled us to enjoy the activities that we used to drive miles to discover during past adventures.

Following a continental breakfast and leisurely morning the next day, we ventured via shuttle to the private beach. As Joanne cautiously plodded with her cane down the carpeted hallway to the lobby where we would meet the golf cart, I suspected our beach visit would be brief.

By the time we settled into our chaise lounge chairs lined up at the small beach, the hot humid air was already oppressive. Even the numerous umbrellas for shade kept the air from circulating for all the guests sitting nearby. For the next hour, whenever I looked over at Joanne's pale face, I knew she was having a bad day.

"Jo, we don't have to stay here if you're not feeling well," I offered with deep concern.

"I know…just a while longer," she pushed her words out.

Without warning and without caring, she leaned over her lounge chair and vomited in the sand. As I put my hand on her head, she vomited again and moaned. Whether the strangers nearby recognized her condition as cancer or a hangover didn't matter to me. I simply covered the remains with sand and offered her some water.

"I'm so sick, Lin," she whispered between low moans. "Let my stomach settle a little and then we'll go back." I had already planned that move in my head when I realized how grave her symptoms had become. In the recent past, she would have cared about appearing strong despite her pain. With this event, cancer now seemed to be stripping everything, including pride, from my wife.

After a long nap and more meds, Joanne recovered enough to make the move to the Royal Suite in the late afternoon. Once again, a friendly staff person whisked our belongings to the massive room on the top floor. With its angled ceiling eaves, tawny Romanesque pillars, full kitchenette, enormous bathroom and Jacuzzi, and crow's nest balcony, our upgrade was everything a queen would need. Even a double-sided fireplace in the middle of the suite helped to create a peaceful ambience. With a swell of gratitude, we thanked spirit for our good fortune.

As we gazed out of our balcony early the next morning with our hot coffee mugs waiting on the round glass table between us, Joanne put her iPad down long enough to take a sip and enjoy the view. Tempted to ask what messages she might be sending, I decided to respect the privacy she prized and kept silent. The only words I had glimpsed from the iPad screen were "Love, Joanne."

"This is probably one of the best views from a room we've ever had," I thought out loud. Reminiscing about our adventures had always been one of our favorite pastimes.

"Oh, I don't know," she mused. "Hawaii was pretty gorgeous." I nodded in agreement. "I do love this cozy, private balcony though," she added.

"Of course, we've had lots of spectacular views outside of our rooms," I continued to remember. "Like the Grand Canyon, Alaska, the hot air balloon ride in Sedona, even the beach in Little Compton, right?"

"Hmmm," she nodded in agreement. As she stared at the ocean, however, I sensed that part of her was looking forward, not backward. Her spirit seemed to be transitioning somewhere else while we pondered our past adventures. She waited before continuing.

"No matter where we've been, my best view is looking at you, Lin." She turned and smiled with love. "I love you so much and I'm so grateful to God for you," she locked onto my tear-filled eyes. I reached for her hand as tears spilled down my cheeks. Before I could speak, she went on.

"The hardest thing for me is leaving Jayden, Alex, and Christine." Her tears interrupted her next words, "Not seeing them grow up or being there when Christine has babies...it breaks my heart." She paused a few minutes, letting her tears subside.

"Even though I'm sad to leave you, Joyce, Carissa and everyone, I'm more than seventy percent ready to leave." Like the familiar pain scale of one to ten, Joanne had been using percentages as a measure of her readiness to die. In contrast, I would never be ready for her death. We remained silent for the next few minutes.

"I can't believe you're going somewhere without me," I finally said, thinking of the big picture. "You'll have to scout it out for me...get some brochures...maybe even plan our itinerary." We chuckled with the thought.

"I'll save you a seat," she promised with a smile. If we couldn't have everything we wanted, like twenty-one more years, at least we could hope for our spirits to connect forever. Like portion control when a taste of something good can be sufficient, I felt that God was saying that twenty-one years of love together on earth had to be enough.

On Thursday, the day before our departure from the resort, we relaxed around the pool under the umbrella's shade. With her chic wide-brimmed straw hat, white gauzy blouse covering her black and white print bathing suit, and smiling face behind her dark sunglasses, Joanne did not look sick. Gratefully, her symptoms had taken a vacation for the day so that she could manage some lunch, read her book with the breeze ruffling the pages, and look forward to soaking in the Jacuzzi after dinner.

"On days like these, I hate to leave," she announced as she looked up from her book. Looking relaxed, she could have meant leaving the pool or the resort. But I thought she probably meant leaving this life on earth. I decided not to ask in order to preserve the moment.

When we drove away from the calm of Water's Edge heading into cancer's storm, I gripped the wheel hoping to find the strength we would need for whatever rapids lay ahead. Once again, it was Friday the thirteenth, but I felt our luck was running out.

"Jo, thank you so much for this trip," I said to her just before she settled for a doze while the car droned on the highway. "I know how hard it was for you and I appreciate it more than I can say." While she had pushed herself to remain with me on our last bittersweet adventure, I thought of the mail order plaque listing cancer's limitations and agreed that cancer could not destroy us completely.

"You're welcome, honey," she replied before closing her sleepy eyes.

With Joanne's upcoming birthday two days later on Sunday, the fifteenth, I had planned some simple pleasures to celebrate her birth. Since her appetite had waned even since our return from the resort, I decided to make the fancy two-layered Jell-O mold she could still tolerate for her birthday cake. With careful planning for Sunday, Christine and I also wanted to take her on a mystery ride to an enormous sunflower field next to a scrumptious creamery for ice cream. The last surprise would be clean sheets on our bed.

After putting the sheets on that Saturday night, I stood next to the bed wondering how many more times we would curl up next to each other like magnets. With a deep sigh, I came down the stairs to find Joanne wrapped in her mother's blanket as she dozed on the couch.

"Are you coming to bed, sweetie?" I whispered as I bent down to kiss her head. Even with her eyes open, her body continued to sleep.

"Honey, I just can't climb the stairs anymore," she replied. From that moment on, I knew we would never sleep together again and my heart ached.

On Joanne's birthday, she loved the Jell-O birthday cake that gratefully didn't melt from the lit candle but she was too exhausted to take the mystery ride. Instead, cut sunflowers graced the room with their cheery yellow faces. As she smiled for the picture with her cake, I remained in awe of her relatively healthy appearance while she blew out the candle. With a slight grin, she kept her birthday wish to herself.

Sadly, the celebration of Joanne's birthday on Sunday came to an end. Later that day, we made arrangements for hospice to arrive on Monday with the delivery of a hospital bed. The devastating phase we had fought so hard to avoid for four and a half years was now on our doorstep.

CHAPTER 29

❧

Last Breath

We had always referred to the pint-sized room leading upstairs as the computer room. When we had met twenty years before, it was Joanne's bedroom. At that time, there actually was a computer on the desk, as well as a dresser and Joanne's twin bed. After the attic had been transformed into our spacious master bedroom, however, the computer room was converted to the dresser room where only the desk and three white wicker sets of drawers filled the space. Even though the bulky computer eventually vanished when laptops joined our upgraded family, we continued to call it the computer room.

With Joanne's typical artistic flare, one wall had been painted a light blue with the other walls painted a muted sage green. Light filtered into the room through sheer floral curtains surrounding one small bedroom window, framing a cat perch braced to the sill and a single antique chair with arms. The deep closet that she had sacrificed for me when I had moved in was located opposite the window and now held my functional wardrobe. Along with tasteful wall photographs and drawings by artists she knew, her pride and joy was the two-by-two foot jewelry case I had installed on the wall behind the attic stairway door that housed her enviable collection of earrings, bracelets, and other accessories. Over the years, we had dubbed the case *Joanne's boutique*.

On Monday, the day after her sixty-eighth birthday, the computer room would change again as we rearranged the furniture for the arrival of the hospital bed in the late afternoon. Ironically, that room would become her bedroom once more.

With each passing day after our return from the resort, Joanne's

311

energy was visibly draining from her body. She never had energy to leave the house and accepted help with everything, especially since she couldn't trust her balance. After cancelling all previous appointments for the week, we slipped into a new realm of functioning with hospice staff. New plans were in place for an intake nurse, social worker, primary nurse, and powerful drugs like morphine for whatever time remained. While I shifted into autopilot, the whirlwind of preparations kept a lid on my feelings as I answered the front door on Monday afternoon.

"Hi, my name is Jennifer," the tall professional woman greeted me as I opened the door. I sensed her compassion immediately. "I'm the intake nurse for Hope Hospice."

"Hi, I'm Linda, Joanne's wife," I said as I extended my hand for a shake and added, "C'mon in." After lifting her equipment case from the porch floor, she stepped through the doorway into the living room.

"Oh, what a cute house," Jennifer exclaimed as she glanced around the always tidy first floor. Reminded of the years I had spent visiting clients' homes for work, I felt strangely out of place on the receiving end of this professional visit.

"Thank you," I replied, anxious to proceed and get the help we needed. "Joanne's this way in the TV room," I offered as I pointed to the narrow hallway around the corner from the dining room. As I led the way, I announced our approach to Joanne and found her sitting up on the couch with her legs extended on the cushions, alert and cute as ever.

After pleasantries and introductions, Jennifer settled onto the edge of the recliner while I drew the footstool under me to create a circle of conversation. Like the ghost of Christmas past, she gathered a medical history from Joanne, who answered all questions without hesitation. Jennifer's warm smile and easy manner melted our anxiety as she eventually finished her paperwork and rested her notebook on her lap.

"You know, Joanne, you really look like you're forty-eight, not sixty-eight," she said as she looked Joanne in the eye with sincerity. "In fact, I can't believe how good you look considering what you're going through." Since we had often heard this comment during the past four years, we weren't surprised. With an experienced nurse saying the words, however, a glimmer of hope rose in my heart that perhaps she really did have weeks left.

After Jennifer continued with an overview of hospice, what to expect and the reassurance that we could call anytime with questions, she confirmed that two more professionals would be visiting during the week. The primary nurse, like the ghost of Christmas present, would be meeting us the next day for the practical do's and don'ts of everyday care like administering medications, keeping a written log, and watching for changing symptoms. Later in the week, the third visitor would be a social worker who would support us emotionally and psychologically if needed. Everything seemed to be in place even though I would never be ready for the ominous event.

In a strange way, I compared the preparations to that of pregnancy and childbirth. We were also anticipating a major life event, researching what to expect, and even rearranging a room like a nursery. To complete the metaphor, we had even contacted Carissa to borrow a baby monitor so that I could respond to Joanne's needs in the middle of the night. Like giving birth, we thought we were prepared for death since we had heard countless stories about what to expect. But we really wouldn't know what death would be like or when it would happen until the unknown mystery was revealed. All we could count on was divine love and trust.

With a quick visit by the equipment technician late Monday, the computer room was suddenly filled with an adjustable hospital bed, an over-the-bed table on wheels, and a commode. Since the mattress was as hard as a slab of cement, however, the next day Rory muscled Joanne's own mattress from her side of our king bed to replace the hard hospital slab. Not only was Joanne missing from our bedroom, but her mattress was now removed as well, adding another heartache for me. For four and a half years, I had been gradually losing small parts of Joanne, but now the changes were racing forward like a tropical storm. My entire body felt heavy with grief.

"Did you sleep better last night, honey?" I asked Joanne as I caressed her forehead on Wednesday morning while she remained in the hospital bed.

"Yes, I did," she replied with a sleepy whisper. "Can you help me into the bathroom and then onto the couch?" Despite the nearby commode, Joanne preferred the normal routine whenever possible, especially if she thought it meant less work for me.

In addition to the intense itching, which the doctors had been unable to control, her symptoms now included shortness of breath, upset stomach, severe heartburn, abdominal and back pain, as well as difficulty eating and drinking. Even the famous Jell-O mold was no longer an option, leaving watermelon and tea as her priorities. Although the array of medications alleviated some of her distress, she vowed to delay morphine that would fog her mind. Every day seemed like a year as cancer grabbed her from all directions.

With the expert help from hospice, my focus was to relieve her pain as much as possible and keep it together in order to support my love. Even upstairs alone at night when I could have fallen apart, I watched Joanne tossing and turning on the baby monitor screen until I fell asleep. If I had allowed myself to cry, I'd be useless.

By early Thursday morning, Joanne was exhausted from frequent vomiting, lack of sleep, and coping with so much pain. The blur of making phone calls, consulting with medical staff, informing family, and making decisions felt like a tornado ripping through the house. Even the kitties found refuge in their secret hiding places somewhere in the house. When the primary nurse arrived at noon, I sighed with relief to have another guiding hand in the house.

"Hi Vicky," I greeted the middle-aged nurse at the front door. With her auburn hair pulled back, she smiled and checked in with me about Joanne's condition. Now that she was familiar with the layout of the house, she quickly found Joanne half asleep on the couch and completed the vitals scan. Returning to the kitchen, we discussed the next steps in the plan.

"How much time do you think she has?" I asked softly. Vicky locked eyes with me but waited a few seconds before answering.

"Well," she started, "a good rule of thumb is that if changes occur monthly, then it's months…if changes happen weekly, then it's weeks… and if changes occur daily, then it's days." She stopped as her words sank into my heart and mind. What she meant was that Joanne had days to live and all I could do was stand there in disbelief. Gratefully, Vicky continued.

"I've consulted with her doctor and it looks like there's a large tumor pressing on her abdomen," she said with honesty and added, "She may not be able to eat again." I think I nodded but found it hard to focus on her words. Only a week earlier, we had shared a lobster dinner at the resort.

"When should we think about transferring her to the hospice center?" I managed to eke out. During one of the initial hospice interviews, the topic of transferring to the skilled nursing facility had been discussed with reluctance. While Joanne had agreed to the idea in order to spare me, I knew that she secretly wanted to die in her beloved home.

"I can put in the order at any time she wants," Vicky replied. "Even then, the transfer can wait if you want." Since Joanne had no control over her deteriorating body, she could at least have a say about her spirit.

"I'll also be filling up the syringes for morphine and Lorazepam for anxiety," she added. Also known as Ativan, the drug would alleviate Joanne's shortness of breath as well. "That way, you'll have them ready when she needs them."

I wondered if or when Joanne would accept these potent drugs and hoped I could make that decision for her. From what I had heard, morphine hastens the dying process and I worried that I would be causing my wife's death, not alleviating her suffering.

After Vicky left the house, Joanne slept and I stared out at the garden from the sunroom, thinking about forever. Even though I wanted Joanne with me forever, I did not want her pain to go on. I was helpless to stop her suffering and could only think about medications, possibly rubbing her feet, and doing her bidding for the least little thing. More than anything, I felt numb. So numb that I couldn't even say a prayer, as if talking to God, Jesus, or even Mother Mary would dangerously open my heart beyond repair.

As the beauty of Joanne's colorful garden filled my view, I considered her words about our connection forever in spirit. Maybe the miracle cure was never meant to be a physical healing of her body, but rather a healing for her spirit instead. Just then, a brilliant yellow goldfinch with black wings landed on the back railing of the steps and peered into the glass sliding door as if confirming my idea. Hearing Joanne stir in the other room, I interrupted my spirit quest and hurried to her side. There was little time for reflection when each moment demanded action.

"Hi, sweetie," I said as she rose onto her elbow. "Can I get you anything?" I brushed her hair with my hand and kissed her cheek.

"Just some water...and maybe one of those fruit juice popsicles," she added. At this stage, I never knew what, if anything, would appeal to her.

"Okay," I replied, happy to help in any possible way. "I also have those morphine and Ativan syringes filled whenever you need them." Out of mutual respect, Joanne was still in charge.

"Honey, I'd like to talk with Carissa first about those meds," she referred to her niece who by now was an experienced nurse. For years growing up, her young niece had asked her for advice, but now Joanne sought her opinion at this critical time.

After a restless night with intense abdominal pain, I encouraged Joanne to accept her first dose of morphine early Friday morning. With my reminder that Carissa had given permission, she accepted the liquid as her body calmed. Only a couple hours later, I suggested the Ativan for her increasing anxiety and difficulty breathing. Still in charge, she requested verification by Vicky before accepting yet another strong drug. By noon, the second dose of morphine was needed as Joanne slipped further away. Into Friday night, her only request was for ice chips and cannabis cream for the itching.

As Saturday inched forward, neither one of us slept more than half an hour at a time. With severe acid reflux, frequent vomiting that now included blood, and sheer exhaustion, Joanne struggled to get comfortable. In the early morning, she even asked for morphine without prompting. After taking the dose and scrunching her face in pain, she looked long into my eyes.

"I don't understand why I have to suffer so much," she uttered and continued, "I thought Jesus already suffered for us." I really didn't have an answer for that one as I thought we were experiencing our own Good Friday.

"I don't know, honey," I whispered as I rubbed her back, "I don't know."

Later in the morning, as I stood by the bed gazing at the love of my life who was finally sleeping, I closed my eyes and rested my hand on her purplish hair. Silently, I opened my heart to my God and prayed for light to flow from her head to the tips of her toes. *God, she deserves your peace and light. Hold her close and carry her in your loving arms. Amen.* With tears in my eyes, I knew our little team of three was about to change forever. I just didn't know when.

Without knowing how long the cycle of meds, restless sleep, sitting up, vomiting, and pain would continue, calls to hospice provided reassurance while Christine and Joyce spent the afternoon at the house in support and relief. While we briefly considered transferring her to the hospice center, I couldn't imagine she would make the trip. Throughout the day, Joanne remained in the hospital bed in the computer room.

Even though I was allowed to give morphine and Ativan every hour if needed, I worried that giving her too much would hasten her death. Since she appeared in a foggy state by noon on Saturday, however, I realized that her wish for lucidity at the end, like her mother, would not happen. Wanting to relieve her suffering instead, I reluctantly administered the morphine and promptly felt responsible for denying her wish. Guilt would stalk me for that decision, yet I knew that guilt would stalk me if I withheld the morphine as well.

With no change in Joanne's condition, I encouraged Joyce and Christine to take a break and return home for dinner. Promising to keep them posted, I settled on the couch in front of the TV after reluctantly administering another round of meds to help Joanne sleep. In my mindless state, I fixed my stare on the screen and sat motionless with my numb heart. Just as I thought of finding some soothing music on a music channel, I heard a moan from the computer room. After sprinting to the doorway, I saw Joanne sitting up and pointing furiously to the commode.

Really? I thought as I considered the next move. "Do you need the commode?" I asked Joanne who only nodded her head in agreement. She was still in charge.

"Okay," I sighed as I helped her stand. With only a lift and turn, I managed to maneuver her body to the seat. However, I immediately discovered she did not need the commode but rather she needed a bucket for the unnatural gush of blood from her mouth that signaled the end to me. With shaking hands, I used the nearby wastebasket and held her head in my arms.

"Oh, God, *NO!*" I yelled. "Don't leave me!" I couldn't believe it was happening as my salty tears slid to the corners of my mouth. In complete surprise, I kept repeating the same selfish words over and over: *"Don't leave me! Don't leave me!"* Why couldn't I say, *"It's okay, Joanne, you can let go,"* like I was supposed to do? My self-centered reaction was a total shock to me. While I felt weak and useless once again, tremendous guilt crept deeper into my bones.

Scrambling for my cellphone, I managed to call hospice and Joyce who phoned Christine, Carole Ann, and Carissa who was out of town. While the hospice nurse was forty-five minutes away, Joyce and Christine reached the house in ten minutes. Carole Ann followed while Carissa raced home a couple hours later. Throughout the blur of visitors, I continued to hold Joanne's head, waiting for the nurse.

Before Joyce had arrived, while we were still alone, Joanne lifted her head to look at me. Since she couldn't speak, I could only imagine the words she wanted to say. With an expression unlike any other I had ever seen, she conveyed love, surprise, confusion, and shock rolled into that one look.

"I love you too," I whispered, "forever." Even as she lowered her head and gulped for air, she wouldn't let go.

Joyce was the one who was strong enough to tell Joanne she could leave when she wanted. No doubt, she had waited for her sister to arrive before leaving this world. Minutes later, while Joyce and Christine had retreated to the kitchen, I held her head as Joanne breathed her last breath at 7:15 p.m. When I noticed the time, I immediately thought of her birthday, July 15, as I continued to hold her head while I sobbed.

Later on, I would notice the small ceramic plaque on the doorknob next to Joanne's final breath. Ironically, the familiar quote read, *Life is not measured by the breaths we take but by the moments that take our breath away.* Despite the cliché, the message seemed appropriate for Joanne's life that had been filled with spectacular moments.

In my muddled state after her last breath, only snapshots of the next few hours remain in my memory. Family entered the room, tears flowed, and voices of love could be heard while we waited for the hospice nurse.

When she finally arrived, I reluctantly released Joanne's head so that the nurse and Joyce could move her to the hospital bed. As they gently maneuvered her torso and limbs, I noticed her crossed legs and bare feet lying at the foot of the bed. Strangely, her legs and feet reminded me of Christ on the cross, which then drifted to another thought acknowledging the divine spark in Joanne.

Thinking of the day we had met when I first shook her hand and melted into her smile, our journey of love flashed before me. We had learned so much from each other as our lives and hearts entwined. By example, she had taught me that expressing anger with love was okay, that honest communication built a foundation, that being proactive led the way to accomplishment, and that we are instruments of God's love to others. With Joanne by my side, my confidence had grown, my heart had expanded, and my divine light had matured. While she had left her tired body behind, her spirit had already burst into every corner of my heart and, most likely, reached everyone she knew. I felt blessed and honored to call her my wife.

My disjointed notions continued to be distractions while the family dressed Joanne. Joyce, Christine, and Carole Ann lovingly slipped on her favorite cornflower blue peasant blouse, denim capris, and slim sandals before Joyce meticulously coiffed her purplish spiked hair, reminding me of her wig experience years before. I secretly hoped she was floating above us, nodding with approval at how cute she looked. Even Charlie jumped on the bed as if she were only sleeping.

Feeling numb and broken at the same time, I answered questions, signed paperwork, and called the funeral home director who would send a transport whenever we were ready. While we waited for Carissa and Jayden to arrive, I lingered in the computer room either sitting or lying on the bed next to Joanne. Suddenly feeling anxious about her departure from her house, I wanted to delay calling the funeral home. I was already holding my heart together like an old broken overcoat in a fierce wind. Escorting her out into the night would blow it wide open.

When Carissa and Jayden finally stepped into the computer room, new tears flowed like a raging river. After hugs and kisses, I departed to the living room so they could say goodbye to their loving auntie. Hearts were breaking.

Late that night, the funeral director and her transport crew proceeded quietly through the house with their familiar task. Respectfully, they moved Joanne to their wheeled stretcher with dignity and used a white blanket to cover her from the neck down.

As she rolled through the living room for the last time, I thought of the day she had passed out in March when she was in agony on her way to the rescue van. Even though her agony was now over, my heart was in pain to think she would never return. How I would live in this house alone without her was beyond my imagination. As I stood on the sidewalk with tears flooding my eyes, I could hardly see the funeral vehicle pull away from the curb.

One by one, people left the house exhausted. Without my asking, Christine had already planned to stay the night to ease her pain as well. Since the funeral technicians had moved Joanne's mattress upstairs, my daughter could keep me company and monitor my fragile state.

With the stress and fatigue of the entire week slamming into me like the proverbial ton of bricks, I fell into bed, glad to have Christine for company. After just a few words before drifting off, I turned away from her and onto my side while my tears flowed and my shoulders shook.

Suddenly, I felt a hand brush my hair off my forehead. The soothing touch seemed unmistakable. My eyes popped open in the darkness, but no one was there. I could hear Christine's even breathing as she slept. *Joanne, is that you?* I thought, but dared not say. Lying perfectly still, I waited for the touch again.

CHAPTER 30

❦

After the Storm

On Monday, two days after Joanne died, the hospice technician entered the computer room to retrieve the bed, table, and commode. Unbelievably, it had only been one week earlier when he had delivered them. Like cleaning up tree limbs and rubble after a tornado, he deftly collapsed and wheeled the pieces out of the house, following the same path Joanne had taken on her final trip. As he worked, I wondered if he had found any pieces of my heart along the way.

My world had turned to gray as if I was wandering in my own twilight zone with half a mind, body, and spirit. Despite my desire to sit like a piece of granite in a catatonic state, I marveled that I could push myself to complete simple tasks like feeding the cats, sipping coffee, and making phone calls. Speaking words, moving my feet, and looking at my list of things to do took all of my energy. It was as if I had cancer too. At times, my heart physically ached.

Planning her funeral while the world crumbled around me initially seemed to be a daunting task. But like a drowning victim who needs to focus on the eyes of the rescue swimmer, I kept my focus on my God, my family, and my friends as they carried me along. As the service fell into place, I considered writing a eulogy. Since she had given her best to me and countless others, speaking at the funeral would be the least I could do to honor my wife.

With an awareness of Joanne's calming spirit as I stood at the podium on that day, I referred to the email updates I had sent for years to inform loved ones of her progress, hoping the writing would reveal her personality and how she had lived with ovarian cancer. As tear-filled eyes looked back at me while I read, I mentioned her love, faith, generosity, tenacity, and sense of fun, along with her desire that we celebrate, not mourn, her life. With a surprisingly steady voice, I enumerated many things she had loved, like her house, garden, cats, ice cream, traveling, and monkeys, before reading the last thought.

> *"Sometimes Joanne and I would talk about what we might be able to do to signal our loved ones from the spirit world. We talked about butterflies, hummingbirds or visits in dreams. However, I will look for her in the wind that is a blessing on a hot day or calming as it blows the autumn leaves around my feet. Wind can also be strong, powerful and as thrilling as the ocean waves crashing on the rocks. Wind signals change and motion, and Joanne was all of these. She was my love…now and forever."*

Even though I had been satisfied with my reading, I had no idea of the spirit connections that would come next, reminding me that Joanne was still in charge.

In the following days, while I struggled with uncharacteristic anxiety, indecision, and grief, I initiated my duties as executor of Joanne's will with a sense of purpose. Thank goodness my organizational skills remained intact in order to gather information, set timelines, and contact the growing list of agencies and companies who needed copies of everything. Whenever sadness overwhelmed me, however, I dropped the paperwork and went to the beach.

On the hot, humid Sunday one week after the funeral, I pushed myself out the door to drive alone to Horseneck Beach. Naturally, everyone and their cousin had the same idea so the parking lots were loaded, forcing me to land in the furthest lot with a long walk to a quiet area on the expansive rocky beach. Even though I could have recruited someone to join me on this impromptu trek, I needed to feed my spirit alone with Joanne's memory. In my heart, she was with me.

Settling into my low adjustable beach chair with my book, a snack, and a beach towel from Hawaii, I surveyed the blue and green ocean peppered with people of all ages wading, diving, or jumping the crashing waves. With the sun beating down, I didn't wait long to don my old-lady water shoes and head to the water. I could almost hear Joanne's familiar words: *Don't go out too far, Lin.*

The relatively warm New England water was glorious. As the strong but refreshing waves splattered my body from all directions, I tried to enjoy the moment and let nature distract me from my sadness for the next half hour. As the undertow pulled my legs further away from the shore, however, I suddenly realized I was indeed out too far. Joanne's words echoed in my head just as a monarch butterfly flew past my face. *How odd to see a butterfly flying out here on the ocean,* I mused. Without another thought, I turned around and headed back to my chair on the sand.

Less than twenty minutes later, two lifeguards in their mini Jeep raced past me and jolted to a stop fifty yards to my left. Leaping from the vehicle with orange rescue floats, they raced to the pounding surf and swam out to a struggling swimmer who was caught in a rip current close to where I had seen the butterfly. The woman seemed exhausted as they all paddled to shore. *Wow, that could've been me,* I thought as I silently thanked Joanne.

Needless to say, I was grateful an hour later for a second time when a middle-aged couple caught in the relentless rip current was rescued from the same spot by the same team of lifeguards. Even though I did return to the waves for a second dip later on, I did not venture past my waist. Just like Joanne wanted. Whether the message was coincidence, my own voice, or Joanne's influence did not matter to me because the connection I felt with her was comforting.

"Hi, Auntie Loop," Carissa called out to me at the backdoor a couple weeks after my beach day. Her mission in our driveway would be bittersweet since she had arrived to transport Joanne's eggplant purple Honda Accord to her house as her auntie had always wished. As part of her will, the paperwork for transferring the car had been completed and Carissa, despite her heartache, appreciated the dependable vehicle.

"Hi, Carissa," I called out as I met her in the sunroom with a brief hug. "Did Rory drive you over?"

"Yeah, he's waiting in the car because Alex's in the backseat," she said in a hurried rush. As a young family, they rarely stayed put. But I sensed Carissa's fragile emotional state when we turned our heads to look at Joanne's car in the driveway.

After cleaning it out, springing for a topnotch car wash, and checking the oil, I was satisfied that the Honda was ready. Like Joanne, the car looked younger than its 197,000 miles.

"Do you remember that you were her first passenger when she bought it?" I asked as we continued to admire the shiny chrome.

"Of course, I felt so important," Carissa replied with tears in her eyes. "She always said I'd have it someday."

"And now you will," I whispered as I put my arm around her shoulder. After a few minutes of silence, I added with a smile, "Guess you didn't think it would take so long, right?" We both chuckled about the car's endurance and moved toward the driver's door.

"I'll take good care of it," Carissa promised as she climbed into the front seat. I knew she would as my heart ached. Watching the purple Honda back out of the driveway, I wondered if releasing pieces of Joanne would ever get easier.

Every day, whenever I passed the spot in the computer room where Joanne had died, I would pause, place my hand on the wall, and say, *I'm sorry, I'm so sorry*, thinking about my guilt and selfishness. Despite vivid dreams and a strong feeling that she was still beside me, I continued to punish myself for my inability to give her permission to leave when she took her last breath. One day, it dawned on me that she really hadn't left.

As I browsed through the mail by the kitchen counter, I flipped through yet another free calendar, thinking I could use the ones I had saved to wallpaper a room. With a weakness for beautiful photographs of nature, I already had collected a pile just in case I had an emergency for a stunning picture. When I spotted a sea turtle swimming amongst a colorful reef full of tropical fish, I paused and thought of Joanne's breath-taking experience snorkeling in Hawaii. In a moment of brilliance, I decided the picture should be posted in the room where she had died. At least I would have a positive thought whenever I passed the sad spot. With a warm inner glow, I even considered the idea that Joanne could now swim with her favorite sea turtle whenever she wanted.

"So, where do you want your ashes, honey?" I had asked Joanne during one of our more practical discussions about death long before the end.

"Oh, I don't know," she had paused to consider the question with nonchalance. By that time in her cancer journey, her priority was her spirit rather than the final destination of her remains.

"Just scatter me in the garden," she finally decided, but added, "Maybe a little left over for the cemetery where my mother and father are buried." True to her personality, she wanted to minimize the fanfare and skirt the rules. Essentially, she gave me permission to do whatever felt right…a lesson I should have remembered to use for my guilt at her death later on.

With the coordinated efforts of both families, an intimate ceremony in the backyard garden was planned on a Tuesday night in early September. Until that time, Joanne's ashes had been held in a square, rose-colored tin on the kitchen counter. As the heartbeat of our home, the kitchen was a place of honor, but I could almost feel her laughter with the absurd thought that it was the same spot where she used to make homemade pizza or where we used to dance to the Christmas music box. No matter where her ashes rested, however, I could never fathom that she was really in that box.

Details about the ashes ceremony emerged as everyone played a part in the planning process. Carissa called the dove release company that Joanne had recommended for her funeral, Christine set up music, Joyce helped with a light supper afterward, and Jayden offered to help with the burial. In addition to preparing the ground, I also wrote a few thoughts to read.

Prior to the day, I had pondered Joanne's previous words about scattering her ashes but decided to find one spot where she could reside uncontained underground. As I scanned the garden, my eyes came to rest on Mother Mary's statue. *Aha!* I thought, *At Mary's feet would be perfect.* Since Joanne had found comfort in her image during illness, Mary could be an unexpected comfort to me in grief. Most likely, the statue had known her true purpose all along.

Digging the hole in the morning felt bizarre, as if I was preparing to bury one of our cats. While I contemplated the sanity of Joanne's wishes, I realized that this event sealed the deal with her physical world. She was free while I was stuck like a fly on sticky paper. As I stood up from my task, I thought, *Well, honey, you have to help me take care of this garden, you know.* With a large stone ready to secure the spot later on, I completed my dig and returned to the house for the gathering later that night.

While the setting sun peeked through the tall cedars in the backyard, an informal softness fell upon our property as ten close family members filtered into the house. Unlike the funeral, there was no receiving line, no fixed displays of pictures and flowers, and no clergy. With fewer distractions, however, my tears gathered just behind my eyeballs from the start of the hour. Since everyone seemed to be in the same condition, I didn't feel alone.

"I think the dove guy is here," Jayden called out as we all turned in his direction at the driveway. With everything in place, we had been milling on the lawn waiting for the older man who would release three pure white homing doves at the conclusion of our mini-service.

"Hi, Joe," Carissa said as she approached the gentle man with salt and pepper hair. After placing the small bird carriers on the grass, he extended his hand to her and nodded a general greeting to the group.

"Hi everybody," he said with respect. "Will it be okay if I just stay off to the side here and wait for your signal?" We all reassured him that his presence was welcomed.

With some of us on either side of Mary's statue, the song, "Somewhere Out There," began to play as I carried the surprisingly heavy rose-colored tin of ashes to the back of the yard. A lump formed in my throat as I remembered how important the song had been to Joanne when we first met. Long before, she had gazed at the stars praying for her meant-to-be love and here I was laying her to rest. Disbelief and shock overwhelmed me.

As the song ended, everyone stood quietly to listen to my short reading:

> As you all know, Joanne loved this garden. It was her sanctuary. A quiet place of peace where she could connect with the earth, watch her flowers sprout and be free to get her hands dirty.
>
> While she usually had a general plan for the garden, she never liked a strict, overly tidy look to it. She preferred the free-flow of wildflowers and occasional surprise of an unknown plant. In fact, all of the tomato plants this year popped up on their own.
>
> I guess I wasn't really surprised that Joanne wanted to leave some of herself here in this garden where she was so connected. Although she's here in spirit every day, now she's connected even more. I think she would be pleased.
>
> Love you forever, Jo.

By the time I had finished, my tears were over the rim and I could hardly see the words on the page. We stood in silence for a few moments followed by a simple prayer. As Jayden and I turned to pour the ashes into the hole and gently shovel the soil on top, verses from a familiar song drifted into the air, "Perhaps love is like a resting place, a shelter from the storm. It exists to give you comfort, it is there to keep you warm..." When we had walked down the aisle to that song years before at our wedding, the lyrics had been perfect, just as they were now.

When Carissa signaled to Joe and his doves, he approached carefully and explained that anyone who wanted to release the doves by hand could do so. As he taught us how to handle the birds, I thought, *Joanne would have loved this!*

Within minutes, we were ready and it seemed the doves were too. One, two, three! We raised our cupped hands into the air, and the birds exploded into the golden sky in a flurry of white feathers lifting higher and higher toward the heavens. Excited gasps and cheers followed behind the three symbols of peace and hope. Lost feathers floated to the ground and were scooped up as mementos as we retreated to the house and life without Joanne.

There was no escaping grief. Like cancer, I could only be distracted for a short time before overwhelming sorrow toppled me like an unexpected linebacker grabbing for my knees. Wandering alone from room to room, idle chitchat with others, or taking a Buddy walk in the neighborhood did little to stomp out grief. Even the more enjoyable trips to Seattle and South Carolina with my sister and daughter could not eliminate my sadness for very long. I felt ripped apart in a way I had never experienced and realized I would never be the same person again.

Soothing relief only occurred when I reminisced about Joanne, wrote in my journal, expressed my feelings to a willing listener, or noticed signs of her presence. I certainly paid attention to butterflies, hummingbirds, and even a praying mantis that lingered on the sunroom for a day. Since the insect had never appeared in our yard for twenty-one years, my interest was piqued as I remembered that Joanne had seen one on her mother's car the day Annie had died. I chose to believe my praying mantis was a sign of comfort from my wife.

Another beach experience added to my growing list of connections just before Ashes Day. Once again, I had dropped my responsibilities for the day and headed to the Audubon Sanctuary Beach alone where we had often spent quiet time in our beach chairs, reading, birding, and usually eating out at our favorite beach restaurant nearby. The rocky beach is great for finding heart stones and watching waves without a crowd.

On this day, I had already found two heart stones lying side-by-side along with two monarch butterflies continuing to flit around the spot where Joanne usually sat. But then, I heard a small truck approach the right-angle bend in the road and come to a stop. After a couple minutes, I heard music. *It must be an ice cream truck*, I thought. Since it was a Wednesday, I considered the truck's presence an oddity, even in summer, for the typically sparse area.

When I suddenly recognized the song, I had to smile. Strains of "It's a Small World" drifted in the breeze. It had been one of Joanne's favorite songs because her mother had loved it, along with the Disney World ride by the same name. She knew I hated the song with its never-ending, much too sweet jingle. What were the chances of an ice cream truck in the middle of nowhere showing up just then in order to deliver that particular tune? I was so shocked that I even forgot to buy an ice cream.

I was no stranger to living alone, but I had no idea how I would live without Joanne. Throughout my life, I had thrived with an independent single lifestyle in Pennsylvania as well as Michigan for years. Living alone seems to be one of those basic lessons everyone faces at some point. But after two decades of sharing my love and life, I suddenly felt like a stranger to myself. Feeling so empty, I couldn't see who was now inside. I sensed that surviving this change would require abundant time and honesty.

Strangely enough, I found solace in the garden. By Joanne's side, I had always assisted with the weeding, deadheading, and transplanting clusters of overgrown flowers. By myself, I discovered that weeding is mindless enough to be soothing and deadheading is satisfying while requiring little effort. Joanne's spirit voice would pull me out into the garden for these mundane tasks despite my cranky reaction. But after a few minutes digging in the dirt, I would thank her for the therapy.

One Saturday in mid-September, I had just finished a round of yard work and had decided to fix some lunch. Tuna salad with cheese on toast made my mouth water as I also reached for a Honey Crisp apple. With a wooden folding tray already set up, I balanced my plate, water and apple on my arms as I entered the TV room where I planned to watch the PGA golf tournament.

Halfway through my lunch, without any warning, Joanne's recorded voice filled the air, "*Hi, you have reached…..we're not able to take your call at this time. Please leave a message, we'll be back to you as soon as possible. Thank you.*" It was the same message she had recorded months before after a power outage. This time, there had been no phone call or ring of any kind and the message played all the way through. As I turned my head toward the phone, my eyes popped open along with my mouth. I couldn't imagine what had caused the machine to play the message without a prompt, other than Joanne of course.

"Wow," I said out loud. "How'd you do that?" In my mind, she must have been thanking me for all the yard work I had accomplished.

The answering machine had never operated like that before or since. All I know is that I loved it. Like most humans, I've often wondered what experiences lay beyond this physical world. Who knows what spirit can accomplish in an unknown dimension? Now, my spirit quest included Joanne and the comfort I feel when unexpected spirit connections surprise and delight me.

With the holidays lurking ahead, however, I braced for the dreaded firsts...First Thanksgiving, First Christmas, First New Year's, not knowing what to expect as I steered my kayak into more rapids.

CHAPTER 31

✑

Still the One

If I had fractured an arm, the healing process would have been predictable, temporary, and bearable. Even recovery from my knee replacement and shoulder surgeries had improved with time and physical therapy. Healing a broken heart, however, was a different kettle of fish.

By itself, time did nothing to heal my broken heart. If I had anchored myself to a chair, waiting for time to heal, only sores and stiff bones would have been the result. The wound to my emotional state was blood raw and there was no bandage or ointment to protect it. No scar formed because my vulnerable heart was bumped every time I touched our empty bed, heard a love song, or looked at displays of greeting cards I would never receive or send. All I could do was to use time for whatever eased my pain each day.

Even though I was still breathing, my joy was gone and, like a symptom of the common cold, my taste for everything was bland. I went through the motions of handing out Halloween candy but sat staring in the dark, remembering Joanne's kitty costume at our first party as a couple. I ate Thanksgiving dinner at Carissa's bustling house, but had to leave early as my heart ached too much. A few days later, as I checked the half-lit Christmas lights in the basement, I realized that I was like those lights with only some of mine on. Navigating this darkness was an unfamiliar existence.

The first holidays raced by while I shielded my heart with numbing emotional Novocain. At least I kept pushing myself to try on events and activities, knowing that I could change my mind if the fit wasn't right for my spirit. Thank goodness, my loving family and friends seemed to understand my indecision and sadness. Joanne seemed to understand as well while her spirit connections continued to enfold me.

One particularly sad day in early December while I was cleaning out Joanne's small antique desk in the dining room, I found a folded paper with a printed quote by Henry Scott Holland from1910 sandwiched among some tax forms. Earlier in the day, I had been wondering whether her spirit was still with me. As I started to read the quote, I knew the answer.

"Death is nothing at all. It does not count. I have only slipped away into the next room. Nothing has happened. Everything remains exactly as it was. I am I, and you are you, and the old life that we lived so fondly together is untouched, unchanged. Whatever we were to each other, that we are still..."

I wasn't so sure about the message at first but toward the end, tears filled my eyes when I read, *"Why should I be out of mind because I am out of sight? I am but waiting for you, for an interval, somewhere very near, just round the corner. All is well. Nothing is hurt; nothing is lost. One brief moment and all will be as it was before. How we shall laugh at the trouble of parting when we meet again."*

Finding the quote that Joanne had saved was another *Wow* moment for me and it cheered me up to think she could be in the other room. I also remembered her words months before when she had said, "I'll save you a seat." Thinking about my own death someday, I was reminded that we are only a breath away.

After returning the paper, it dawned on me that the date was December 10, also the anniversary of her mother's death. Coincidence or not, I wouldn't have been surprised if that had been part of the discovery as well.

"Is that the last batch, Mama?" Christine called out to me from the dining room as she removed the warm chocolate chip cookies from the cookie sheet held in her gloved hand. It was Christmas Eve Day and Cookie Central was in full swing.

"Yes, this is finally the last one," I replied as I closed the oven door with an exhausted sigh.

For years, Christine and I had designated an entire day before Christmas for baking our traditional molasses cookies, thumb prints, chocolate chip, and occasionally sugar cookies. Usually, Joanne had been happy to leave us alone, but she always loved to appoint herself as an official taste tester, especially for the chocolate chip delights. I missed her thievery.

"It's a good thing there aren't more because there's no more room," she exclaimed as I joined her at the table laden with rows of cookies lined up like toy soldiers. I reached up to give my tall daughter a warm hug.

"I'm so glad you still want to do this with me, honey," I murmured into her shoulder. Despite our love for the traditional recipes, I suspected she would have chosen more exotic bakes á la Martha Stewart.

"Of course, Mama," she smiled down at me, "I love this every year… and especially this year." I gave her an extra squeeze.

Since cookie day had been scheduled later than usual, our traditional Christmas Eve festivities were affected this year as well. Usually, we would attend our favorite five o'clock candlelight church service before returning home for shrimp, scrumptious snacks and drinks while transporting ourselves into my favorite Christmas movie, *It's a Wonderful Life*. By the time we finished cleaning up this year, however, it was too late to rush out the door for church.

"Maybe we should just make up our own service," Christine suggested. "I can go online for some readings and music." As soon as I heard her words, I thought of Joanne and the services she had constructed for our *Church of the Little Women* group during past holiday seasons.

"Okay, I'll look for some candles in the box Joanne had downstairs for the group," I offered, and hurried down the basement steps.

I quickly spotted the labeled cardboard box on a high shelf at the back of the basement and lifted the lid only enough to reach inside the box for the candles I wanted. As I tilted the box forward to grab the candles, a wad of small notepapers that were clipped together fell out of the box onto the basement floor. After taking the candles, I examined the papers.

Oh, my god, I thought. In Joanne's handwriting was the last Christmas service she had composed for our little group several years before. Everything was there. Readings, music, poems, Bible references, and even an order of service had been provided. Nothing else had fallen out of the box, only what we needed.

Needless to say, Christine and I were excited to think Joanne had joined us around the candle and twinkling lights in the sunroom while we read, sang, and meditated in peace. We also agreed that, for years, she had probably wished for a Christmas Eve service at home like this rather than enduring a trek to church in the cold. At least now the cold didn't matter and she wouldn't have to watch the same movie for the hundredth time unless she wanted to. With her heavenly intervention, my first Christmas without her was surprisingly special.

Shortly after Joanne's Honda had left our driveway for Carissa's, my eighteen-year-old Civic developed major mechanical issues signaling its demise. As if in sympathy, my car had become undependable at a time when my own coping skills were frayed enough. In an uncharacteristic move from someone who balks at change, I decided to buy a new, larger Honda with all the extras. Part of the audio package included Sirius XM, a streaming music feature that hooked me from the start.

Listening to music in my car had always been a pleasure and now my options seemed endless. In my state of grief, however, everything seemed to make me cry, except for hard rock and classical music. Other than my usual symphony station, my new favorite setting on Sirius became Classic Vinyl that reintroduced me to sixties rock.

Spawned from anger, frustration, injustice and general angst, rock music reflected, more than ever, the feelings I now felt next to grief. Like a teenager, I could relate to the pounding lyrics and insane beat. And one doesn't cry when cranking up Led Zeppelin, ZZ Top, the Who, and Pink Floyd. I found an emotional outlet and relief from sad songs in my new car, as I gradually became a rocker retiree.

My need for constant proof that Joanne's spirit remained with me must have been annoying to her if I used my imagination about her new world. Like a Doubting Thomas, I often questioned her presence if weeks passed by without a sign. Even spending time together in realistic, vivid dreams couldn't match the treasured physical incidents that blew my mind.

One Saturday morning in early February while my sister was staying at the B&B, as she still liked to call our house, I plodded down the stairs to begin the day. Since I didn't hear any stirring sounds from the basement guestroom, I planned to complete my kitty chores and brew some fresh coffee before Chris awoke.

Just as I turned the corner into the kitchen, I stopped dead in my tracks. On the floor to my right was one of the heavy burner grates from the gas stovetop on the opposite side of the room. I just stared at it and wondered, *How in the world did that happen?* Since Phoebe is a feline nut, I initially blamed her. Just as quickly, however, I thought of Joanne who could be saying emphatically, *Do you believe me now?*

"Did you hear any loud sound coming from the kitchen last night?" I asked Chris as she entered the kitchen for some hot coffee. Since the guestroom is directly below the kitchen, I thought she would have heard a heavy grate falling or sliding across the floor.

"No, I didn't hear a thing," she answered incredulously when I explained the story to her. Since the cats had never managed to fling the grates before or since, we concluded that Joanne must have been busy once again. I smiled to myself and added the incident to the list.

My first Valentine's Day without my love could have been a disaster. We had celebrated the holiday in so many beautiful ways over the years but now only memories filled my hollow heart. After a depressing three-day *Twilight Zone* marathon over New Year's, I had learned that staying at home like a recluse and turning inward did not help my mood. This holiday of the heart had to be different for my own survival.

I decided to drive to Connecticut and take my ninety-two-year-old mother out for a Valentine's Day lunch at her favorite fancy restaurant. Still sharp and living independently in a second-floor apartment without an elevator, she loved to go out to eat, especially with any of her children. Before leaving for the two-hour trip, I purchased some colorful flowers just as I would have done for Joanne and looked forward to the day. Little did I know that my mother would be dead in less than two weeks after our lunch.

On February 26, just when I had told God I wouldn't be able to cope with any more major losses for a while, I was racing in my car to Connecticut again to take care of my mother, who had been complaining of severe stomach flu symptoms for two days. Since she never got sick, I was gripping the steering wheel with anxiety like a post-traumatic-stress-disorder victim. Despite the early morning traffic and her worsening condition, I made good time.

With an overnight bag in the backseat and intermittent phone messages from my sister-in-law, Ann, along the way, I finally found the hospital emergency room where the ambulance had transported Dottie. Since Ann lived near my mother and most of our family members were working, the two of us formed the onsite team that would consult with doctors and keep everyone informed. The scene felt all too familiar to me as I kicked into autopilot once again.

At every hour, Dottie's painful condition worsened since atherosclerosis had blocked blood to her abdomen and nothing could be done. When the outcome looked grim, she said to us, "Don't worry about me...I'm ready."

As some family members gathered and phone calls were made to others out of town, she was transferred to a private room by suppertime when additional morphine was administered. Before she slipped into unconsciousness, she joked with the nurses and enjoyed her family encircling her bed. As the hours crept by, everyone eventually filtered out of the room, leaving me to stay overnight with her as I had planned.

Good grief, God, I thought as I sat beside the bed, holding my mother's hand and brushing her hair from her forehead. *Is this my lot in life now?* Once again, I was at a deathbed by myself. But this felt different than my last hour with Joanne.

While I was certainly sad and in shock that my mother was dying, I knew she was ready. Whether she could hear me or not, I talked to her and even gave her permission to leave whenever she was ready. By rectifying something I hadn't been able to do for Joanne at her last breath, I felt peace. Without knowing it, Dottie had helped me in her final moments. Maybe God knew what He was doing after all.

By chilly April, I was still wearing our house uniform of a hooded gray sweatshirt, sweatpants, and an oversized T-shirt. Looking like twins, we had always felt cozy and comfortable with the outfits we plopped on the floor at bedtime. Surprisingly, the kitties preferred to curl up on the football-field sized bed or cat perch by the window rather than the pile of sweat clothes on the floor by the bed.

On April first as I rolled out of bed, my sleepy eyes wandered to the spot where I had left my uniform. Both the hooded sweatshirt and sweatpants were gone. *What the hell?* I thought.

After scanning the entire bedroom, including under the bed, I tried to imagine what or who had moved my outfit as I made my way downstairs. No sign of them anywhere. Of course, I considered blaming nighttime kitty antics, but remained perplexed since Phoebe and Charlie had never bothered with my clothes prior to this.

For the next ten minutes, I wandered through the house searching for my missing uniform. The scene was a mystery, as if I was reliving an episode from CSI or participating in an Easter egg hunt. Where could they be?

While I stood bewildered between the living room and dining room, a piece of cloth caught my eye. As my mouth dropped open, I found my hooded sweatshirt and pants on the floor behind the couch in the living room. I couldn't believe it. While I retrieved them, I had to chuckle when I remembered it was April Fools' Day. I could almost hear Joanne laughing as I shook my head in disbelief. Once again, I had no explanation and the caper was never repeated.

Despite the new life of spring crocuses and daffodils in the garden, my wintry mood often prevailed as I tried to find my way through each day. Feeling like the caretaker of Joanne's house, I busied myself with chores and executor duties while maintaining my interests in the hand bell choir, golf league, and symphony concerts. While I could have easily glued myself to a chair, a force within pushed me to move out of the house even when I didn't want to.

As my seventieth birthday loomed ahead and I lamented not receiving a card from Joanne, a strange and vivid dream the night before revealed a floating container of icing overhead slowly piping the words, *Happy Birthday*, onto a table in front of me. A few days later, my alarm clock radio upstairs unexpectedly started playing the song, "Marry Me," by the group Train, and, in the camper van, I discovered the lost harmonica Joanne loved to play after it had been missing for years. To my amazement and delight, the entire month seemed to be one birthday gift after another.

Considering how our lives had influenced each other, I shouldn't have been surprised with these spirit connections. By the time we had met, we were both confident individuals, well established in our careers, and able to cope with adversity. But our love, respect, and faith helped us to stretch mind, body, and spirit to new heights. Together, we learned that there was something attractive about challenges and that we were stronger than we could imagine. By the time of her death, we had also learned not to become too attached to this world. Focusing on spirit was the everlasting lesson our love had taught me and as I reflected on that lesson, Joanne's spirit felt alive and well.

In retirement and after a death, cleaning out closets seems to be on everyone's to-do list. As the one-year anniversary of Joanne's death crept closer, I reluctantly directed my self-pity into my closet for sorting and discarding all unnecessary relics. Since my tendency toward sentimentality and hoarding practical doodads filled more than a few boxes, I knew the job might take more than one day.

As I ploughed through a shoebox filled with old greeting cards, my sadness grew with the thought of our wedding anniversary looming in the next few days. Coinciding with the day we had met in June twenty-two years before, my memory of Joanne's smile washed over me as I relived our lunch at the deli. As I thought of that day again, and how we had both very nearly missed finding each other, I realized that the powerful force that had brought us together seemed to be just as strong as ever. In time, maybe that love and power could stitch me back together as well.

Flipping through the cards, I found a music anniversary card that Joanne had given to me in 2008. Against a muted mauve background, the message in beautiful script read, "*There's a certain comfort only you can provide, a special feeling of happiness only you can give me.*" My eyes started flooding as I opened the card to read, "*That's how I know you're the only one for me.*"

The only problem with the card was that the song didn't play. Only clicks sounded as I read Joanne's handwriting, "*Happy Anniversary, my sweet! I love you with all my heart—forever. You're the only one and always will be. Love, Jo.*" Of course, she had drawn a tiny cat as her trademark along with the year.

With determination, I repeatedly opened and closed the card, hoping to restore the song. Very gradually, bits and pieces of "You're Still the One" by Shania Twain could be heard until the entire clip played as good as new. In my mind's eye, I could picture Joanne and me dancing to the tune that touched my heart. As an anniversary gift for my sad heart, the card continues to play.

Thinking that Joanne had rewarded me for cleaning out my closet, I kept rooting through my boxes. An hour later when I reached the bottom of a pile of mementos, I pulled out a beige envelope addressed to *Lin*. On the back, was the date, Feb.'03. I couldn't imagine what it was as I removed the notecard from the envelope.

As I started to read her note, my heart caught in my throat while the faded memory of the unopened letter returned to my mind.

Dear Lin,

If you are reading this, it means I have gone over to the other side to be with my Mom, Dad, Nonie, Cara Mia and Joy. Know that I am happy and safe.

Now I remembered this was the letter she had given to me when we had struggled to make our relationship work and had undergone counseling. At that time, she had instructed me to open the letter only after she had died. Tucking it away at the bottom of the box, I had forgotten about it for sixteen years.

> *I want you to know that you truly have been the love of my life. You always made me feel loved no matter what was going on between us. I tried my best to be a good partner to you. I know sometimes it was hard for you to put up with me. We were together to help each other grow—and that happened. I will always love you and watch over you from the other side. Think of me when you see the birds. I'm as free as they are now. Remember I'm only on the other side of the veil and just a breath away. We will always be connected.*
>
> *I love you very much, Jo.*

Needless to say, I was speechless and filled with awe. The timing for finding the letter was perfect. With gratitude, I accepted the gift as a sign and continued to share these connections with others who had also experienced her spirit. At times, I wondered if she missed us as much as we missed her.

By September 2019, just over a year after Joanne's death, Hurricane Dorian had been pounding the Bahamas and was cruising northward along the Atlantic coastline. Luckily, only strong winds and minimal rain affected Rhode Island before the storm drifted out to sea.

On the morning after the wind, I grabbed the kitties' dishes for their breakfast and glanced out of the backdoor from the sunroom. Curiously, the empty watering can I stored by the rail flowerbox had been moved to the middle of the doorway. Immediately thinking of the wind, I placed the still upright can back in its place. With a steaming mug of coffee in hand twenty minutes later, I opened the front door to the porch for daily inspection. My gaze lowered to the middle of the doorway where a gorgeous red begonia flower lay on the porch floor.

Well, good morning, Joanne, I thought at first, before admitting that the wind probably had something to do with its placement. *Although, I did say I would look for her in the wind,* I added to my musings. Without another thought, however, I tended to my day and neglected the findings for two weeks.

A few days before the annual tent camping trip with Christine and Chris, I sauntered down the stairs early one morning anxious to prepare my camp list. As I entered the short hallway leading to the dining room, I noticed the cats' two-foot-high scratching post in the middle of the doorway. Normally, the post stays to the left of the doorway against the dining room wall. *Boy, those kitties sure had a party last night,* I thought as I slid the scratching post back to its spot before visiting the bathroom.

Thirty seconds later, I exited the bathroom and dropped my jaw. The scratching post was back in the middle of the doorway. "*Oh…my…god,*" I said out loud.

There had been no sound and both Phoebe and Charlie were in other parts of the house crying for their precious food. Scenes from poltergeist movies flashed through my mind initially, but then I remembered the watering can and begonia flower also found in the middle of doorways. Other than letting me know she is with me, however, any additional message remained unclear. Since I had decided to tackle the book writing project she had always expected, I wondered if she was cheering me on… or not.

Surprisingly, the second year of holidays after Joanne died were more difficult than the first, as if the Novocain had worn off. Even with soothing family and friend connections, the realization of life without her settled further into my psyche. Thankfully, her spirit contacts also continued to settle into the holes of my heart.

Following a hospice memorial service in early December with gentle snow falling outside the chapel windows, the classical guitarist played "Somewhere Over the Rainbow" as his last number while Christine and I sobbed, remembering the funeral. Another time, after setting up the Christmas village in our dining room, I decided to include the broken miniature ski hill that Joanne loved even though the tiny skiers on conveyor belts hadn't moved since last year. One day later as I puttered at the kitchen counter thinking about our Vermont ski trip, I lifted my head when the sound of the ski hill motor finally reached my consciousness. To my delight, the little skiers were on the move and continued like new for months. Each time a coincidence occurred, I felt a layer of peace wrap around me like Joanne's initialed blanket from her mother.

With the world coming to a screeching halt due to Covid-19, in order to cope I tried to think of quarantine as a cocoon rather than a prison. Choosing to embrace the psychological darkness for something positive reminded me of nighttime's peace, crescent moon, distant stars, and unexpected beauty like the flower that blooms for only one night each year before it dies. In my cocoon, however, I gratefully had no anxiety about losing a job or income so I could easily focus on my book project that I had committed to months before. Even though writing without distractions felt therapeutic and productive, my emotions continued to wobble as I relived my journey with Joanne.

One day in late March as I was changing the sheets on our bed, the memory of Joanne's last birthday when I had put clean sheets on the bed for a surprise surfaced in my heart. As sadness engulfed me, I opened her nightstand cabinet door and reached for the sticky roller for removing the ever-present cat hair from the comforter. When returning the roller, I glanced inside at the contents that I had already examined months before.

To my surprise, I discovered an unfamiliar paperback book entitled, *Here If You Need Me* resting on top of other books I recognized. From the blurb on the back, the story was a memoir by a wife and mother whose husband had died in a tragic car accident. Her journey from grief to faith to happiness looked intriguing, but I did not remember the book from my previous cleaning expedition. As I flipped through the pages, I found the title page and once again dropped my jaw.

The author had signed it...*for Linda, Vaya con Dios!* In other words, Go with God. Since I had no recollection of the book, much less the personal message, I was overwhelmed that I would find it at that low point in my day.

For days afterward, I racked my brain unsuccessfully for any memory of the book, the author, or any book signing we may have attended in our travels. I even considered that Joanne had intended to gift it to me but never had the chance. Not only was the title and story appropriate for my soul, but the song "Vaya con Dios" has beautiful lyrics about love, parting, and memories as if it could be our new theme song. When I found the astonishing book, I felt blessed and grateful for Joanne who had always been God's gift to me.

Joanne DiBello was a gardener who loved to help living things grow. With great love, she cultivated and nurtured wildflowers, abundant vegetables, timid creatures, fearful children, and despairing adults. Never satisfied with the status quo, her constant goal was to improve everything, including herself.

With great faith in her God, she had nurtured the divine spark within and set the example for others, including me, to keep growing no matter what the obstacle. Her personal message is that death is not the end, so the spirit quest continues. In my grief, when I bemoaned having had only twenty-one years with Joanne, I hadn't realized that we really do have forever. While I miss my love every day, I know that eventually I will find my joy as I live and travel down the road with God. Like the message on the drawing of the country boy with his dog, *I don't know where I'm going, but I'm on my way.*

One day in late May 2020 toward the end of tulip season, I noticed one unusual dark tulip growing proud and alone in the garden not far from Cara Mia's kitty grave. I had never seen one like it before in the backyard. Showing a gorgeous deep red-purple color with wild feathery petals, the flower bloomed for weeks. Christine later confirmed my suspicions when she exclaimed, "That looks just like Joanne's hair!"

Happily, I could see that Joanne was still in charge.

About the Author

Linda Skibski is a retired Orientation and Mobility Specialist for the blind and visually impaired, having taught in Michigan and Rhode Island for thirty-seven years. Born and raised in Springfield, MA, she has a B.A. degree from Eastern University near the Philadelphia area and a specialized M.Ed. degree in Peripatology from Boston College, MA. While this is her first book, writing has always been a persistent avocation that now demands her time. She lives in Providence, Rhode Island, with two kitties who have trained her well.

Made in the USA
Middletown, DE
11 February 2021